The *Essential*
William James

The *Essential*
William James

Edited by **John R. Shook**

Prometheus Books

59 John Glenn Drive
Amherst, New York 14228–2119

Published 2011 by Prometheus Books

Cover image © 1967 by Dover Publications, Inc.
Cover design by Liz Scinta

Inquiries should be addressed to
Prometheus Books
59 John Glenn Drive
Amherst, New York 14228–2119
VOICE: 716–691–0133
FAX: 716–691–0137
WWW.PROMETHEUSBOOKS.COM

15 14 13 12 11   5 4 3 2 1

Library of Congress Cataloging-in-Publication Data

James, William, 1842–1910.
    [Selections. 2011]
    The essential William James / edited by John R. Shook.
       p. cm.
    ISBN 978–1–61614–439–5 (alk. paper)
    ISBN 978–1–61614–440–1 (e-book)
    1. Pragmatism. 2. Psychology—Philosophy. 3. Religion—Philosophy. 4. Ethics, Modern. I. Shook, John R. II. Title.

B945.J21 2011
191—dc22

                                      2010051997

Printed in the United States of America on acid-free paper

Contents

Introduction, by John R. Shook   7

PART ONE: EXPERIENCE AND MIND

 1. What is an Emotion? (1884) 47
 2. The Stream of Consciousness (1892) 67
 3. The Self (1892) 89
 4. Does 'Consciousness' Exist? (1904) 105
 5. A World of Pure Experience (1904) 123
 6. How Two Minds Can Know One Thing (1905) 147

PART TWO: KNOWLEDGE AND ACTION

 7. The Will to Believe (1897) 157
 8. The Function of Cognition (1909) 179
 9. What Pragmatism Means (1907) 197
10. Pragmatism's Conception of Truth (1907) 215
11. The Pragmatist Account of Truth
  and Its Misunderstanders (1909) 233
12. The Meaning of the Word Truth (1909) 251

PART THREE: ETHICS AND RELIGION

13. The Dilemma of Determinism (1897)   255
14. The Moral Philosopher and the Moral Life (1897)   283
15. The Energies of Men (1907)   307
16. *The Varieties of Religious Experience*: Philosophy (1902)   325
17. *The Varieties of Religious Experience*: Conclusions (1902)   345
18. Pragmatism and Religion (1907)   365

Notes   381

Sources and Editing Methods   411

INTRODUCTION

John R. Shook

William James was born in New York City on January 11, 1842. His father, Henry James Sr., was a wealthy and religious intellectual who had close relationships to prominent literary figures, including the transcendentalist Ralph Waldo Emerson. James's father provided his children with an unusual education while the family lived in a variety of cities across America and Europe. His younger brother, Henry James, became a significant novelist whose writings display a deep affection for European culture. William's own preference was for America and its people's love of adventure and invention.

After abandoning painting, James studied biology, quickly accepting Darwin's theory of evolution. He pursued a medical degree at Harvard University and graduated with an MD in 1869. In 1872 James began teaching physiology at Harvard, but his primary interest was psychology, especially the physiological and experimental psychology that he had seen during earlier travels to Europe. James was permitted to teach this new psychology at Harvard starting in 1875, and he founded the first psychological laboratory in America. Since psychology theorized about the mind's operations, it was then considered as a part of philosophy, and James soon became a professor of both psychology and philosophy. Through the 1880s he wrote about consciousness and the functions of the mind, and he published *The Principles of Psychology* in 1890.

The Principles of Psychology is still the most important and provocative psychological text ever written by an American, deeply influencing John Dewey's philosophy. Some of the writings of his friend Charles

Peirce closely supported James's views on belief and truth. James announced his allegiance to pragmatism in 1898, and he defended his version of pragmatic empiricism against the other two dominant philosophies of that time, *deterministic materialism* and *absolute idealism*. His entire career was devoted to teaching at Harvard University. James gave the Gifford Lectures in Scotland, resulting in his path-breaking work *The Varieties of Religious Experience* in 1902. His most famous book, *Pragmatism*, was published in 1907. A series of journal articles published during 1904–1909 presented his theories about radical empiricism, knowledge, and truth; they were collected together for *The Meaning of Truth* (1909) and *Essays in Radical Empiricism* (1911). Two more books presenting his explorations of experience and reality, developing his vision of a pluralistic metaphysics, were completed before he died: *A Pluralistic Universe* (1909) and *Some Problems of Philosophy* (1911). James died in Chocorua, New Hampshire, on August 26, 1910, and the intellectual world hailed the passing of one its most provocative and original thinkers.

EXPERIENCE AND MIND

James's pragmatism developed from his investigations into the mind's capacities. Philosophy in the 1880s and 1890s was energized by controversies that would now be called issues in "philosophy of mind" or "philosophical psychology." Responsibility for such an explosion of intense creativity and debate rests primarily on two profound developments: the rising acceptance of Darwinian evolution and the expanding interest in psychological experimentation. These developments encouraged the revolutionary notion that humans must be studied as natural organisms applying intelligence for survival in varied environments. William James and John Dewey were leading psychological philosophers during this period who explored the emerging frontiers of philosophy of mind. They established a novel approach to the understanding of human cognition and behavior, known as *functionalism*. Not to be confused with a later "functionalist" philosophy of mind inspired by electronic computing, this original functionalism dealt directly with the biological nervous system.

Functionalism was primarily defined by its thesis that psychology is the study of mental life as an adaptive organic process. This study of the mind as a natural ability is an attempt to replace Cartesian dualism with a nonreductive naturalism. Functionalism is a kind of voluntarism that replaces the notion of an unnatural free will with voluntary control: a natural capacity for humans to make deliberate decisions and regulate their habitual behavior. Functionalists such as James and Dewey were unusual naturalists, because most naturalists are strict materialists who suppose that the universe is composed solely of basic matter/energy obeying fundamental natural laws. Psychological functionalism did not try to reduce mental operations to physical events, but it did note many essential correlations between mental events and brain events. Some specific examples were already startling to late-nineteenth-century investigators. The brain's neurons themselves do not store memories, because only the connections between neurons are changed by experience. Experience itself causes the brain's neural connections to change and grow, so that the brain becomes better prepared to process and react to repetitive stimuli. Also, there is no part of the brain that appears to be executively controlling all the other brain activities. One of the most surprising discoveries was that the reactions of the nervous system require time to happen. This should not be surprising, since the nervous system works by sending electrical charges through the long connections of thousands of nerve cells. This physiological fact implies that all thinking consists of processes occurring through durations of time.

Events in phenomenal consciousness and events in neural activity share many essential features. Both have durations in time, have continuities with prior and prospective events, become more firmly linked by repetition, have triggering causes (especially sensory causes), release further impulses toward motor action, are focused on responding to environmental conditions, and are sustained by proving useful for achieving organic ends such as acquiring food or evading danger. Thus, many similarities of essential features and functions suggested far more than just close correlation between mind and brain. Functionalists like James were tempted toward metaphysical speculations that would resolve the mind-body problem. Perhaps conscious experience is a real aspect of physical nature; or perhaps the correlations between mind and body indicate a deeper underlying reality of which both mind and matter are manifestations. James grew convinced that human experience is just as naturally real as anything else known by science, and he had little patience with scientists or philosophers who left consciousness out of their account of ultimate reality.

In the nineteenth century, materialistic philosophers reduced the mind to just the mechanical workings of the brain, or they declared that consciousness is an entirely epiphenomenal and useless by-product of the brain's activity. The largest contribution of materialism to a modern philosophy of mind rested on its mechanistic theory of the origin of ideas. Materialism supported sensationalistic empiricism by locating the source of information about the world exclusively in the mechanical activities of the sense organs, stimulated by the transmission of motion from forceful contact with physical bodies in nature. Information about the surrounding environment is generated by the correct kind of interaction between the natural world and the natural workings of the brain. Aside from possessing a properly working nervous system, the perceptive observer is treated as a passive receptacle of this representational information, for which the observer deserves no responsibility or credit. Sensationalistic empiricism permits the rational manipulation of information into more complex combinations of association. But aside from the use of standard logical tools, any deviant manipulation or creation of ideas can only distort accurate representations of the external world, risking deception, illusion, and error.

Materialism and sensationalism prevailed over German idealisms and lingering dualisms, standing victorious across Europe from Scotland to Austria during the middle decades of the nineteenth century. But despite the obvious affinities between materialism, evolution, and psychological experimentation, their combination in the 1870s slowly eroded sensationalism's dominance. This erosion was assisted by suddenly reborn post-Kantian idealisms, which exposed the many inconsistencies and paradoxes of any empiricism that claims that knowledge of the natural world of physical objects and their lawful behavior is "built up" solely out of raw sensory materials possessing neither coherence nor meaning. Sensationalism's denial that the mind's knowing faculties help to construct the basic experiential information was opposed by idealism's counterclaim that without such constructive assistance, no genuine experience of the world could occur. Evolution's perspective on the physiological role of the nervous system, and psychological experimentation on actual mental processes, decisively tipped the scales against sensationalism and representationalism. Together they established that the human observer selected, filtered, and shaped experiences of the world.

This revolution replaced the passivism required by sensationalism with the activism taught by *voluntarism*, which was a major inspiration for functional psychology. Voluntarism emphasized the role of the will in directing all human experience and activity. Voluntary actions should even encompass the acquisition of information about the environment. This goes well beyond the fact that organisms must orient themselves to sources of sensations by claiming that the very content and meaning of any experience is partially informed by the goal-directed activity pursued by an organism. Voluntarism was compatible with idealism to the extent that they agreed that the ongoing mental activities of a human being were largely responsible for the significance and meaning of one's experience. Voluntarism and idealism were unified by many philosophers in *organicism*. Organicism, inspired by the German Romantic idealisms of Schelling and Hegel, rejected the materialistic and deterministic philosophy with the metaphor of the living organism. Its staunch defense of teleological explanations of both human behavior and the natural world enjoyed a renaissance in the late nineteenth century.

Philosophers at the forefront of physiological and experimental psychology in Germany were typically aligned toward idealism, voluntarism, and organicism. Primary examples include Gustav Fechner, Hermann Helmholtz, Hermann Lotze, and Wilhelm Wundt. The

Americans most completely aligned with voluntaristic organicism were William James and John Dewey. However, they replaced the idealistic foundation for voluntarism with a liberal and nonreductive naturalism. They explicitly applied biological and physiological terms and principles, along with teleological explanations about functions and ends, to their experimental study of the mind's processes. Their philosophy of mind was developed and defended by a combination of three methods used by the science of psychology in the nineteenth century: introspection (describing the ideas of one's conscious thought), experimental psychology (correlating the reports of subjective introspection with sensory stimulations), and physiological psychology (examining the physiological working of the nervous system). These methods were also used in the twentieth century and are still used today, together with the newer methods of behaviorism. James used all three methods to develop his theory of psychology.

Physiological psychology deeply impressed James, and his functional psychology soon challenged dominant theories of knowledge. For example, the vast connectivity and continuity of nervous tissues and their electrochemical exchanges was quite unlike the static and discrete character of ideas according to empiricist philosophies. Empiricism required drastic revisions to accommodate the voluntarism and functionalism demanded by brain research. Rationalism was in trouble, too. No Cartesian theater of the mind could be particularly located in the brain, nor could any a priori Kantian categories. Dualistic philosophers were not pleased by such discoveries of psychology, because they could not accept that mind had much in common with matter. In his first book, *The Principles of Psychology* (1890), James refused to deal with the metaphysical question of whether materialism or idealism was correct. As far as scientific psychology can go, James rested with psychophysical parallelism: if any mental process is happening in a person's mind, then there must also be a parallel physical process also happening in that person's brain at the same time. However, as he trusted what psychology was discovering about the centrality of voluntary consciousness, he grew convinced that experience is a central feature of reality.

James was deeply frustrated by reductionism, epiphenomenalism, and determinism. Some materialistic philosophers claimed that the mental process is reducibly identical to its parallel physical process. This identity, if real, would mean that if all physical processes are predetermined to happen by exact natural laws, then all mental processes are also predetermined, and therefore free will cannot exist. Epiphenomenalist philosophers denied mind-brain identity, instead suggesting that a mental process is generated by a brain process as an accidental by-product. Epiphenomenalism claims that nothing that happens in the mind could ever cause anything to happen in the physical processes of the brain, so there is no free will, since no mental idea or desire or wish could ever be responsible for anything that the nervous system does. When I reach for a cup of water, the processes of my nervous system are responsible for two things: my arm muscles moving my hand toward the cup, and my experience of feeling my hand reaching for the cup. But nothing in my mind causes my hand to reach for the cup. My consciousness is only a useless by-product of my brain that can never really control anything I do.

James decided that human consciousness cannot be reductively identified with any sort of physical material. Our thoughts are not really material things, and they are not caused by material things. This denial has led many philosophers toward accepting dualism. James does not reject dualism in the *Principles of Psychology*, but he does reject dualism in his later writings about experience and knowledge. James decided to reject a core metaphysical view that treated mind and matter as substances having qualities. He therefore turned away from regarding consciousness as any sort of physical material, and he denied that consciousness is any sort of mental material either.

At the start of the 1900s, James was ready to publicly announce his novel metaphysical theory. Consciousness, according to James, was not a substantial thing but instead a continuous process or stream of qualitative experiences of things, displaying all the relational and functional features discerned by psychology. Experience or consciousness or mind as such does not exist, as if it had a reality all its own apart from natural things.

What exists are the innumerable things with which we are acquainted. We do not experience experience itself, but real existing things that happen to be experienceable. When James speaks of *consciousness* or *experience*, he is referring to available experienced things around us in the natural world, not any kind of reality apart from those things.

James's rejection of the existence of the mind as a spiritual substance or an inner mental theater was a rejection of Descartes's theory of the mind, and it was also a rejection of Christianity's idea of the soul. Most philosophers and psychologists before James's time and also during James's life were Christians who believed in the existence of the immaterial soul, and they developed their philosophies of mind in harmony with Christian doctrines about the soul. The soul was needed to explain individual personality and why our experiences were always our own and not someone else's. The soul was also needed to explain human immortality and to explain how God passes moral judgment upon each of us after our deaths. James believed that philosophy and psychology should be more scientific by freeing themselves from religious conformity. James also believed that his new theory of consciousness could explain personal individuality.

Some philosophers, especially David Hume, had also rejected the idea that the mind was a substance having qualities. But when Hume described consciousness, he talked about impressions (perceptions) and ideas that had their own independent and self-sufficient reality. A substance, by definition, is not dependent on the existence of anything else. Hume replaced Descartes's picture of the mind as a whole substance that contained thoughts with his own picture of consciousness as a collection of substantive thoughts. Hume helped to inspire the "associationist" theory of mind that James had to repudiate; James later derided associationism as the "mind-dust" theory. James did not believe that ideas or thoughts were atomistically self-sufficient and independent, because our consciousness does not appear to be a collection of independent perceptions and thoughts. Kant agreed, but he attempted to explain how consciousness appears to us by postulating a hidden "transcendental ego" that links the "sensations" together into coherently connected experience always infused by the "I think" thread. James pointed out that if no substantial sensations really exist, then there is no need to postulate any transcendental ego. Psychology should simply study actual, lived human experience, the "streams" of consciousness, and postulate hidden processes only if absolutely necessary. James's *Principles of Psychology* provides many studies of actual, living human experience. He criticizes associationism by giving examples of how consciousness cannot be made of independent parts only externally related. He then criticizes Kantian transcendentalism by showing how living human consciousness contains all the relations and connections needed to explain the important features of human experience.

Experience cannot be a series of disconnected ideas succeeding each other through time. James agreed with Kant and other idealists that if experience was only a chain of ideas, then we would never have any sense of personal identity through time. Every idea would completely occupy our attention, and then the next would completely occupy our attention, and the first idea would be completely forgotten. And then a third idea would come along to erase the second idea. The ability to remember ideas does not help to give us personal identity, because a remembered idea would simply be a fourth idea that completely erases the third idea. A person would never be able to understand that all these ideas were hers. Kantian idealism postulates that a hidden mental process links all these ideas together so that a person can understand that all these ideas are hers. James instead argues that consciousness itself contains the needed links, because experiences partly interfuse at their margins, flowing into each other, and some experiences are hence experiences of relations between other experiences. There is no need for a hidden mind to know its thoughts, because a thought could know other thoughts using the thoughts of the relations between experiences.

James's examination of experience in *The Principles of Psychology* found the five basic features of any thought:

1. A thought is always a part of just one personal stream of consciousness. No thought can be part of two streams of consciousness, and no thought can exist separately from a stream of consciousness.

2. A thought exists only for a short time. A similar thought may reappear, but it cannot be the same thought twice. There is no place in the mind where thoughts are stored.
3. A thought always has a feeling of belonging with the other thoughts in the same stream of consciousness. A thought contains a feeling of being related and connected with other thoughts in its stream.
4. A thought always seems to be about something else that is independent of the thought. No thought is simply about itself. A thought is always pointed at something that exists beyond the immediate stream of consciousness.
5. A thought can influence the next thoughts in the stream. Thoughts are attentively focused and selective. A thought always has the feeling of effort to control what sort of thought will follow it.

The requirement that every thought can belong to only one stream of consciousness is a claim that admits that dualism is basically correct. In his later writings, James eliminated this requirement and rejected dualism, suggesting instead that some kinds of experiences can exist in two or more streams of consciousness at the same time.

James realized that too many philosophers uncritically held on to unscientific notions that consciousness is quite atomistic, static, and representational. Some philosophers used the results of experimental psychology to claim that all human experiences are basically composed of simple colors, sounds, and other sensations. This claim helped to support the philosophy of *associationism*. James did agree that experimental psychology should show how two or more simple sensations could combine to make a complex experience. For example, hearing three tones of sound at the same time can cause a person to hear a musical chord. But when a person hears a chord, that person cannot hear the three tones distinctly. Instead, the tones combine through brain processing to make a new fourth kind of tone, which is called the chord. The heard chord cannot represent anything in external reality but instead is a creation for consciousness. Another example is lemonade, which can be made with lemon juice, sugar, and water. When a person tastes lemonade, the person does not taste water and sugar and lemon juice. The three ingredients blend together to produce a new fourth taste of lemonade. People do not experience the sensational parts of an experience because they can only experience the unified combination. James argues that the psychologist's ability to discriminate the sensational parts that cause a complex thought by using the methods of experimental psychology is not an ability of the person actually having the complex thought. A philosopher who claims that all thoughts are made of simple sensations commits a logical fallacy that James calls the *psychologist's fallacy*. Experience is always of unified wholes, not parts. Hume's argument that we cannot experience the relations between ideas commits the psychologist's fallacy.

The Principles of Psychology, *Psychology: Briefer Course*, and his writings on experience and belief from 1890 to 1903 developed James's pragmatic philosophy that was closely related to his theory of the stream of consciousness. After 1903 James explicitly separated these two theories. The most important writings are "Does 'Consciousness' Exist?" and "A World of Pure Experience," both published in 1904. He declared that his theory of experience, which he called *radical empiricism*, does not depend on the truth of pragmatism. James understood that there could be many kinds of pragmatism, including the pragmatisms developed by his friends Charles Peirce, John Dewey, and F. C. S. Schiller. James did develop his own kind of pragmatism that continued to be closely related to and dependent on his radical empiricism. James understood that there is a problem for his pragmatism, as pragmatism could be interpreted to be saying that each person has his own truth, because each person has only his own experience. The idea that each person has his own truth is called *subjectivism*. Personal idealism also suffers from this problem of subjectivism. James wanted to treat truth as objective, because truth is about the relationship between a mental idea and something independently existing beyond the mental idea.

Dualism solves this problem by proposing a physical world beyond experience, but James rejected dualism. A dualistic theory of knowledge claims that true mental ideas are those that accurately represent the real features of physical reality. Dualism leads toward skepticism, because dualism cannot identify which of our ideas are accurate representations. Dualism proposes that when a person knows that she sees the moon, she only sees a mental copy of the moon. No one can directly see a physical object, if dualism is correct, because everything that we see is only an idea in our own mind. However, when we see an object, we do not notice any ideas and we (rightly) believe that we see only the physical object.

Absolute idealism, such as the philosophy of James's friend and Harvard colleague Josiah Royce, proposed to solve the subjectivism problem by describing everything real as mental and all human experience as a dependent part of the absolute (God) mind. The existence of God guarantees the objectivity of truth. James rejected absolute idealism because the dependence of human experience on God reduces human freedom and moral responsibility. Royce's absolute idealism is a kind of theism, and James could not accept any theism. Although there are many pragmatic themes in Royce's understanding of the human mind, his absolute idealism argues that there must be a transcendental self that guarantees the existence of one independent and objective world that is the same for all people.

All three philosophies, personal idealism, dualism, and absolute idealism, assume that consciousness is a particular kind of thing and that knowledge is a relation between consciousness and some other kind of thing. James instead believes that when the object is perceived, there is no relation between two things, because the knower and the known are the same experience. James refers to perception as *knowledge by acquaintance* and states that this kind of knowledge does not happen because something in consciousness has correctly represented something that is not in consciousness. Knowledge by acquaintance happens because the thing perceived is a part of the stream of consciousness. In "Does 'Consciousness' Exist?" James claims that if "consciousness" refers to a substantial mind that contains representations of objects, this kind of consciousness does not exist. The only kind of consciousness is the stream of consciousness that contains perceived objects. James emphasizes the fact that experience is not contained within a substantial mind by stating that all experience is "pure" experience because it is essentially neither mental nor physical. There is no need for a substantial mind to hold together the experiences because experiences are connected by relations within experience itself.

James's philosophy of radical empiricism claims that all of reality is made of various kinds of experience. This philosophy is pluralistic, because James does not claim that reality is made of one single kind of material called "experience" that can have many forms and varieties. Instead, James claims that an uncountable number of very different kinds of things exist, and they all have only one thing in common: they can be part of a stream of consciousness.

Critics of radical empiricism complained that James was designing a kind of solipsism. If philosophy can only debate experience, and if the only experience that anyone has is the experience within one's own stream of consciousness, then the world can only consist of the contents of that stream of consciousness. Is there really any world beyond one's own stream of consciousness? Critics wanted James to answer this question: Does a perceived object continue to exist after a person has turned his vision in a different direction and when it is no longer any person's stream of experience? Personal idealism's answer is negative. Dualism's answer is negative, if by "perceived object" one means the idea of the object, while if "perceived object" means the physical object, then the answer is instead affirmative. Absolute idealism's answer is affirmative, since the perceived object would still be perceived by God. James wanted to answer this question affirmatively. But he also wanted to argue that when a person perceives an object, the object itself is perceived and not merely a mental copy of the object. He also wanted to believe that it is possible for two people to perceive the same object at the same time.

The only way to satisfy all these affirmative answers is to declare that it is possible for a perceived object to join one or more streams of experience without becoming dependent on any of those streams of experience for its existence. The relations between a perceived object and the rest of a stream of experience are within the stream of experience, so that the relationship itself is experienced. But the relation between a perceived object and a stream of experience is not a necessary relation but instead a contingent relation. The perceived object does not always have to be a part of a stream of experience, but it is possible for it to occasionally join a stream of experience. Furthermore, we can only conceive of the perceived object as experienceable, because we do not know how to conceive of the object in any other way. If we remove from our conception of an object all of its features that it has in experience, there would be nothing left of the object to think about. Therefore, we must conceive the object as continuing to be a set of related experiences even when it is not part of any other stream of experience.

This statement of the contingent relationship between the perceived object and a stream of consciousness is the conclusion of James's radical empiricism. It permits James to redefine the meanings of "mental" and "physical" by using revised ideas of the "objective" and "subjective." The physical object is a pattern of experiences considered as having its own existence independent of its relations with my own stream of consciousness, even though these two series of experiences can merge during my perception of the physical object. During the merging of perception, I can call the object mental also if I consider how the object is a part of my stream of consciousness. An experience can be both physical and mental at the same time, depending on which set of the experience's relations are selected for consideration. Dualists believe that a perception always has two parts: the experience of the object, and the object that is perceived. James denies that experience has such an "inner duplicity."

In perception, or what James calls knowledge by acquaintance, the object perceived is identical with the perception of the object. If we ignore the perception's relations with other surrounding experiences, we have only "pure" experience. Usually we do not ignore the surrounding relations, and we classify experiences as mental and physical automatically. In his writings from 1904 to 1905, James attempted to explain the difference between physical and mental objects by postulating his principle of *pure experience*. All things in experience are neither essentially physical nor mental, because they are "pure" experience when they are considered in themselves. It is a mistake to see in "pure experience" anything pure in two other senses, which James did not intend. James did not regard experience as pure in the sense of having no mixture or involvement with concepts. Pure experience can be replete with concepts, as an experience's organization is an indication of the ways that it is interrelated with proximate experiences in streams. Nor did James intend to treat the "purity" of an experience as any infallible sign of its epistemic truth. While there is a kind of full reality presented by the immediacy of experience, since there is no "veil" of consciousness between a thought and its object, James reserved "truth" for the demonstrated capacity of a thought to lead toward its intended object. The objects in immediate experience are valid enough, but we normally intend more, as we do not need what we already have.

While all real things are pure experience, real things can at one time function as mental things, and at other times they can function as physical things. A "physical" object must have two abilities. It has the ability to join in relations with the other ideas of a stream of consciousness. It also has the ability to continue to exist as experience even while it is not a part of any person's stream of consciousness. James declares that such physical objects really exist. A "mental" object can only exist while it is part of a stream of consciousness. The principle of radical empiricism states that thoughts have only contingent relations to other thoughts. Therefore, there is no thought that must always belong to a stream of consciousness. There are no thoughts that must always be mental. We can distinguish between physical and mental experiences only by observing the series of contingent relations that experiences have with other experiences.

If I stand in the center of a room that has a picture hanging on each wall and slowly turn around so that I see each wall in succession, everything that I see is an experience. All four pictures will be in my stream of consciousness. If I consider only the relations that the four pictures have with each other as following each other in my stream of experience, then the pictures are mental. I can say, "I saw the first picture, then the second picture, then the third picture, and then the fourth picture." If I consider only the relations that one of pictures has with the other objects in the room, then that picture is physical. I can say, "The picture was hanging on the east wall of the room for the entire time that I was looking around at the walls, and for a brief time the picture was also in my experience." The brief experience of the picture is a pure experience, because by itself it is neither mental nor physical. Its nature is defined by the sequence of events in which it participates. In my example, it participated in two different sequences of events at the same time, and these sequences briefly merged at the moment that I was looking at the picture.

James was not entirely satisfied with this principle of pure experience. From 1906 to his death in 1910, James's doctrine of radical empiricism sometimes supported a different view called *panpsychism*. Panpsychism holds that every existing thing has its own inner experience or sentience. The primary reasons for his dissatisfaction with the theory of pure experience had to do with its capacity to effectively handle two serious metaphysical questions: (1) what is the nature of the physical object while it is not being experienced, and (2) how can two people experience the same object at the same time? The first question must be answered by radical empiricism by saying that the object is not a physical object, and it is not a mental object either, when it is not in any stream of experience. But the object must still be capable of being an experience, since everything must be conceived as a possible experience according to James. But who experiences the object? James was often tempted to say that the object can experience itself. James did argue in his *Principles of Psychology* and later writings that there is no need to postulate a mind that knows its own experiences, because each experience in the stream of thought simply experiences itself, all by itself. Therefore, if our own experiences can be experiences for themselves, then any object can be an experience for itself. James was willing, in his later writings, to suggest the philosophy of panpsychism: that all existing things are experiences for themselves as well as possible experiences for others.

James was also attracted to panpsychism because it could solve his problem of explaining how two people could experience the same object at the same time. His doctrine of the stream of consciousness, as presented in his *Psychology*, emphasized that a thought had to be a completely unified thing without parts or internal relations. A thought could have external relations with other thoughts, and it is possible for an experience to be externally related to two different streams of consciousness. But no thought could have "perspectives" that present one quality when observed from one direction, and from another perspective appear to have a different quality. Let this doctrine be called the *unique quality* doctrine. Between 1904 and 1908, James realized that an experience, if conceived according to this unique quality doctrine, could not be the same for two different people. Suppose that an object O is experienced by a stream of consciousness for person A, and O is also experienced by a stream of consciousness for person B. If O is in A's stream of consciousness, that means that the experience of O must be O in its relation to the next thoughts in A's stream. The same is true for B. If O is in B's stream of consciousness, that means that the experience of O must be O in its relation to the next thoughts in B's stream. The object O must have two different qualities: its relations to A's stream, and its relations to B's stream. However, according to the unique quality doctrine of thoughts presented in James's *Psychology*, no object in experience can have two different qualities depending on its relations to other things.

James realized that the "unique quality" doctrine was a false doctrine because it requires that an object be conceived as static, unchanging, and timeless. It is true that you cannot look at an object and see two of its perspectives at the same time. If you are standing in front of a building, you cannot see both the front of the building and the back of the building at the same time. But we know that a building has both a front and a back side. Perhaps thoughts and experiences have perspectives too. James rejected associationism because it portrayed thoughts as unchanging, unrelated, and made of simple parts. James corrected associationism when he declared that thoughts can be related by other thoughts, but he argued that thoughts must have some unique and static quality. By 1907 James realized that this was a mistake. He realized that only "intellectualist logic" requires that any object that can be identified must have a unique and static quality. When James had attempted to identify individual thoughts in *Psychology*, he still relied on some intellectualist logic to specify particular thoughts. That is why he described the stream of consciousness as a chain of a series of consecutive thoughts. The only difference between his view and associationism is that James found that some of the thoughts in the stream were relations, while associationism declared that it was impossible to experience relations.

By 1907 James was ready to entirely stop using intellectualist logic to describe consciousness. Instead of requiring that each thought be a separate, static existence, James fulfilled a view sketched in his *Psychology* by describing thoughts as having overlapping and merging parts. Only after 1907 did James portray consciousness as a genuine stream of flowing and merging thoughts. While the intellectual discrimination of specific thoughts can be made, James argued that this discrimination does not accurately capture the actual flow of lived experience. When we use concepts to identify thoughts as this specific thought or that other specific thought, we are breaking up and stopping the stream of thought to create something that was not really there in pure experience. If consciousness is truly a stream, then any part of the stream is always merged with any next part. We might notice the waves of the stream, but the waves have no fixed, unchanging boundaries and are always connected to other waves near them. Experiences are just like waves of water in the stream, and all experiences are continually merging with other experiences.

This new conception of experiences as always changing and having merged parts with other experiences solves James's problem of explaining how one object can be observed by two different people at the same time. The object must be a complex experience for itself, capable of merging with multiple streams of consciousness at the same time. Any real thing must be an object of experience that could merge with other experiences, including the experiences of people. James did not explain thoroughly this theory of panpsychism, although later philosophers such as Alfred North Whitehead extended the radical ideas in James's late writings.

KNOWLEDGE AND ACTION

Scientific psychology demonstrates how lived experience is actively goal directed. Our thoughts are aimed at controlling our behavior, and so all thoughts are directly or indirectly involved in deciding how to act. Human experience is not only a process; it is also creative. The ability of thoughts to control actions, and the ability of thoughts to incorporate aspects of previous thoughts without being completely predetermined by them, provide human beings with free will. James's psychology supports his pragmatism. Even though James did not announce that he was a pragmatist alongside his friend Charles Peirce until 1898, *Principles of Psychology* clearly states that thoughts must directly or indirectly serve the practical activities of the human being. His essays on "The Will to Believe" and "The Function of Cognition" expand on his voluntaristic theory of knowledge.

Experience as a whole, according to James, is only partially unified. Because we do not have only one thought at a time but many thoughts happening together, our thoughts can lead us toward many actions at the same time. We can control our actions, so that we can accomplish one action before trying to accomplish another, but this is an ability of self-control that must be learned. Children do not have much control of their thoughts, causing them to be unable to complete complex tasks. Adults sometimes have difficulty organizing their thoughts so that organized actions happen in the correct way. James's theory of the stream of consciousness can explain why we have conflicting thoughts and competing motivations for different actions. Human rationality, for James, is essentially the struggle for practical control over these diverse and divergent currents in thought.

James is a voluntarist, and therefore he cannot not agree that "evidence" consists of all the perceptions that are passively received by the senses from the natural world. Evidence for a hypothesis must be relevant to the hypothesis, which means that evidence must be selectively chosen from all the things in experience. Also, the evidence needed to support hypotheses must be created under experimentally controlled conditions.

A hypothesis must predict what would happen under specified experimental conditions. Because evidence, both scientific and religious, must be predicted and selectively created, philosophers cannot claim that evidence has nothing to do with human activity. In "The Will to Believe" James points out that only human activity establishes evidence, and people would not try to establish evidence for a hypothesis unless they believed that the hypothesis might be true. Other philosophers have argued that a scientist must never believe a hypothesis at all until sufficient evidence is collected to support it. But James argues that this skeptical attitude would prevent many kinds of hypotheses from ever being tested and found to be correct. Both science and religion require that some small amount of belief is necessary so that truths can be learned by investigators. This is a shared foundation for both science and religion.

James argues that for both science and religion, the origins of a hypothesis must be ignored when the hypothesis is tested by the evidence. Hypotheses may come in sleeping dreams or arrive in day-dreams of imagination, but what matters to rationality is how hypotheses are empirically testable. Along with Peirce, James was one of the first philosophers to sharply distinguish what later twentieth-century philosophers have called the *logic of discovery* from the *logic of justification*. Pragmatism is a transformed empiricism that focuses on the logic of justification. The accumulation of past experience causes inquirers to postulate hypotheses, but what justifies acceptance of a hypothesis is its ability to correctly predict future experiences. One of the primary problems with representationalist theories of experience and knowledge is that they treat accomplished knowledge as quite static, so that conformity with past experience is the top priority and criterion of epistemic success. But psychology shows that genuine experience does not work this way. Only anticipated future experiences really matter, as consciousness is trying to adequately anticipate contingent future events. Representations of how the world has been are only meaningful insofar as they are tools for doing what needs to be done next. The validity of a representation of the world lies in its demonstrated capacity to help shape the consequences of conduct, and not in any static mirroring of what the world might be like independent from human engagement. In short, good representations dynamically change the world, they do not statically "mirror" the world.

The philosophy of radical empiricism is compatible with, and supports, James's version of pragmatism. Two basic principles animate James's pragmatism, grounded on the science of functional psychology. First, a thought or idea always leads toward some further and future thoughts in experience. Thoughts are not passive and disconnected from each other. Thoughts are active and creative, because they stimulate additional experiences that grow from them. Second, thoughts are meaningful only because they are always about some other experience and can help bring about that other experience by motivating us to act. James recognizes that many thoughts never directly result in any active exploration of the world. Some thoughts are merely imaginative speculations that no one would claim are true. These speculations are pragmatically meaningless because they have nothing to do with human action. Meaningful thoughts do produce novel experiences through human activity.

When we have an opportunity to learn from other people and compare our thoughts about the world, we can together experiment with thoughts to see whether they do produce their intended consequences. James's theory of truth tries to explain how we can evaluate ideas by testing their intended consequences. Ideas can only be evaluated for truth if they do have practical consequences, and two different ideas can be compared if their practical consequences are different. James agrees with Peirce that the pragmatic method of evaluating ideas by their practical consequences is the essence of the scientific method.

James sometimes describes his approach to truth as a much-needed clarification of the classical *correspondence theory of truth*. The correspondence theory of truth has two meanings, an ordinary meaning and a philosophical meaning. In ordinary language, a person knows the truth when that person can describe an event exactly as it really happened. If a person has knowledge by acquaintance with an event, then that person could know the truth. A person does not know the truth if he cannot describe an event exactly as it really happened. Many events take place even though no one observed them. If an unobserved event takes place, there is no truth to be told about that event because no one can describe exactly what happened. We might guess what actually happened later, and some people are very good at determining what probably happened (such as police detectives). But unless someone could prove that he actually witnessed the event, such as a crime, no one could have the truth. James's theory of truth is designed to agree with this ordinary understanding of "truth." James speaks of a person's meaningful idea as capable of "leading" one toward its object. A witness in possession of some true ideas about the witnessed event ought to be able to return to the scene of the crime and recognize its main features.

The correspondence theory of truth according to philosophers is more complex. According to the philosophical theory of truth, any event, whether or not it is actually observed, could be known as a truth. Suppose the unobserved event is a tree falling down after being struck by lightning. If I observe the lightning bolt from a mile away, I can see that the lightning bolt has struck somewhere in a forest. But I am too far away to see individual trees, and I did not see any tree fall down. Now suppose I then think the thought "A tree fell down after being hit by that lightning bolt." According to the ordinary meaning of "truth," I do not know a truth about any tree—I have only made a guess. But a tree really did fall down. According to the philosophical theory of truth, my thought is a truth. My thought is a truth because it does state the real events. My thought is "A tree fell down after being hit by that lightning bolt," and the actual event in the forest a mile away was a tree falling down after being hit by that lightning bolt. There is a correspondence between my thought and the actual event far away, and that is enough to make my thought true.

According to the ordinary meaning of truth, I cannot have a true thought if I cannot prove that my thought is actually correct. But according to the philosophical correspondence theory of truth, my thought is true regardless of whether I ever do prove it to be correct. If I never walk out into the forest, never find a fallen tree, and never observe the fire burns on the tree, I still have a true thought. James rejects this philosophical theory of correspondence. According to James's pragmatic theory of truth, I cannot have a true belief unless I could successfully prove my belief to be correct. Only that verifying capacity establishes any connection of reference between an idea and its object. For the philosophical correspondence theory of truth, somehow a person's idea could "really" successfully refer to some external object, even if the person had no understanding that this object exists, and had no grasp that his idea was referring to it. James, like other pragmatists, found this notion of reference completely mysterious and contrary to a scientific understanding of the mind.

The modern philosophical theory of correspondence truth was developed primarily by metaphysical dualists who believed that all of our ideas were inside our minds. Since we could never compare our ideas with the physical world, because the physical world could never be experienced in any way, metaphysical dualists decided that truth did not require proof in actual experience. According to dualism, if an idea does copy reality, then that idea is true, and it does not matter if I can never prove that my idea actually does copy reality. Metaphysical dualism always inspires a revolt by skepticism. Skepticism about truth is the view that we can never discover whether any of our ideas are true knowledge. James's pragmatism is designed to prevent skepticism, which is a familiar task for empiricisms.

Preventing skepticism could be assisted by noticing how modern science no longer attempts to establish static "pictures" of the world. Simple pictures of objects in perception can be captured and remembered by images in the imagination, which Locke and Hume called "ideas." But complex scientific theories do not try to form copying images of the world. Modern science primarily attempts to discover the laws of natural processes, like gravity. Natural processes are not "facts" that can be stated as relations between observed qualities. We cannot see most natural processes, and we do not know how to picture them. Any models or pictures of such things as atoms are not taken too seriously by scientists themselves. Nor is the notion that science aims at perfect truth. There are so many natural processes, and so many different ways to describe their operations, that there can no longer be any expectation that we will soon make our theories consistent with each other and perfectly true.

The criteria for knowledge of natural processes must be something other than correspondence. James offered the criteria of *satisfactory working*. The true idea is what satisfactorily works. Since there are varying degrees of working, there can be many degrees of truth. There are also many different kinds of working, depending on the sort of idea or theory involved. All satisfactory workings of ideas requires some sort of active human experience to follow out the consequences of those ideas.

James, unlike Peirce, does not have a sophisticated philosophy of science to offer. His examples in his writings that illustrate his definition of truth are typically simple examples of ordinary life and not laboratory experiments. The advantage of using James's definition of truth, however general, is that it covers both ordinary life and laboratory experiments. Because pragmatically meaningful ideas, thoughts, and theories must lead toward some practical consequences, the testing of their truth is just the testing of their value for actually leading toward their intended goals. For the highly abstract conceptions of scientific theorizing, James proposed that a scientific theory about some hidden or obscure aspect of nature, remote from ordinary experience, must still direct experimental inquiry toward predicted observable consequences. Even if instruments cannot lead us to a direct experience of a theorized entity, it must lead us to the expected "vicinity" of that entity's behavior and that behavior's effects that can be experimentally observed. James's account of the method of scientific prediction, while primitive, meshes with the sophisticated philosophy of science offered by Charles Peirce and later theories of science.

James was most concerned to deal with the ordinary intelligence we use in daily life. Knowledge by acquaintance is the most fundamental kind of knowledge, but it is also, by itself, not very useful. People cannot always be focused on the immediate present. In order to achieve our future goals, we must have ideas that suggest how to get from where we are now to where we want to be. These ideas must instruct us how to perform a series of actions that will result in a practical experience. These ideas attempt to represent the final stage of the process where the practical consequences are.

James describes this second kind of knowledge as *knowledge by representation*. Unlike the static picturing ideas postulated by former empiricisms, James proposed that mental representations must be dynamic. Representational knowledge requires that an idea directs the stream of consciousness through a series of connected experiences of the natural world that arrive at a perception (a knowing by acquaintance) of the intended thing. If all knowledge were knowledge by acquaintance, then the problem of solipsism could arise. But our ability to have knowledge by representation requires that a natural world of experienceable things must always surround us. James constantly stated that a thought must point beyond itself to something that exists independently of it. He also points out that early in life, babies discover that objects continue to exist even while they are not observed. For the rest of our lives, we believe that "reality" is what is permanent and not within our control while our perceptions are changing under our control.

James sometimes called his theory of truth an *epistemological dualism*. Epistemological dualism states that an idea is true only because it is about some other independent existence. All metaphysical dualists are also epistemological dualists, but some epistemological dualists could instead be empiricists, such as James. When we have knowledge by acquaintance, we have something in our experience that does not depend on that experience for its existence. When we have knowledge by representation, we are led toward something that exists independently of our experience even though it can come into experience. The metaphysical dualist claims that we can never experience nature. James claims that we can experience nature, and that is the only way for us to ever have any knowledge and truth. Furthermore, because nature is present in our experiences, and experienced nature is objective and available for other experiences of it as well, there is nothing to prevent two streams of experiences, two minds, from perceiving the same thing at the same time. The independent physical object can simultaneously be a part of two experiences of it. There is no need to postulate two different experienced things, one for each mind.

Many critics attacked James's theory of truth by accusing his theory of declaring that the truth is only whatever anyone wants to believe. These critics instead say that the truth does not depend on what we believe. This accusation is false, because when we test some idea that we want to believe, the test may not succeed and then we must admit that the belief is false. James does say that a true idea is one that is believed and survives testing.

Other critics attacked James's theory of truth by accusing his theory of declaring that truth is only what each individual person believes is true. These critics instead say that the truth is what all people must together believe is true. This accusation is false, because most of our beliefs are shared by others. We should test our shared beliefs together, and agree that the true beliefs are those that successfully work as intended. James does say that some true ideas are only believed by single individuals. Each person has many beliefs that other people do not care about at all.

Some philosophers have attacked James's theory of truth because it would not allow truths about things too small to be observed or things completely hidden from observation, such as forces of nature. James does not say that theories about hidden things are meaningless. Theories must have practical consequences for human experience. A theoretical model of the parts of an atom can never lead a scientist through nature toward an individual atom so that she can have knowledge by acquaintance of an electron. However, the model of the atom can lead a scientist to a design of an experiment to test whether the observable effects of electrons actually do happen as predicted by the theory. A pragmatically meaningful theory must make predictions about what would be observed under controlled conditions.

Many of the philosophers who criticized James's theory of truth did not believe that James really had a theory of truth, because truth must be absolute. These philosophers declared that if a belief could possibly be revised by future discoveries, then it could not be true. A truth must be absolutely true, which means that it would never be revised. Peirce did define scientific truth in this way, and was annoyed by James's use of the word *truth* in a wider and diluted sense. James did agree with Peirce that an absolutely true belief is a belief that could never be revised by further investigation and experiment. James also wanted to talk about kinds of truths that were less than perfect. Nearly all of human knowledge is less than perfect. Our knowledge is not completely false, either. James's epistemological position, like that of all pragmatists, is instead the position of *fallibilism*. Knowledge is always potentially revisable. While knowledge settles doubt, reaching a resolution of doubt is not the same psychological state as achieving an enduring certainty. Pragmatism has no place in its epistemology for permanent and irreplaceable a priori certainties. We should understand that there are degrees of knowledge and truth, and that any knowledge we now possess could fail to work in the future.

The pragmatic theory of truth also portrays knowledge as relative to a context of purposes. For example, a surveyor of land knows how to measure the dimensions of a section of land and determine how much area is enclosed by the property lines of that piece of land. Surveying knowledge allows people to make very accurate maps of neighborhoods and towns and cities. However, surveying knowledge only works for small areas of land, because the methods of surveying assume that the land is mostly flat. The mathematics used by surveying is Euclidean geometry, which works only for flat areas of space. If a mapmaker wants to measure the land area of an entire country, he cannot use only surveying knowledge. Because the earth is a sphere, the land does not obey Euclidean geometry but instead spherical geometry. There is a different kind of knowledge of mapping large areas of land, and today we can use satellite surveying. Surveying knowledge is not shown to be false because it cannot be used to accurately measure large areas of land. Surveying knowledge does not attempt to make large measurements, and satellite surveying does not attempt to make small measurements. Both methods of knowledge are valid for their own separate purposes because they work for their separate purposes.

Methods of knowing owe their validity to the human purposes that those methods are designed to serve. James denied that there is any generic or universal "method of knowing" that aims at some unitary "truth." There are many purposes, many methods, many knowings, and many truths. However, James was not an extreme relativist about knowledge, as if he were happy to take all kinds of knowledge as equally valid. Quite the opposite: as a pragmatist, he asserted that we must maintain a consistent harmony among all forms of verified knowledge. Severe inconsistencies among kinds of knowledge would not only generate purely cognitive contradictions but also instigate clashing behavioral motivations. We cannot easily get through a day if we are driven to conduct ourselves one way for a while, and then pursue contrary and destructive conduct next. No doubt people can sustain contradictory beliefs so long as they are held in suspension in the contemplative imagination, but contradictory beliefs engaged in control of action only result in contradictory action, which is disabling and dysfunctional. One of the critical functions of philosophizing is to design comprehensive worldviews capable of supplying the intellectual harmonies necessary for consistent conduct. One way to accomplish consistency, the monistic or reductionist way, is to elevate one method to supremacy and to demote all other methods as invalid or inferior. Another way, James's way of pragmatism and pluralism, is to credit each validated method of knowing for its unique and irreplaceable contribution to human success.

We have discussed how James expected that the basic methods of ordinary intelligence must be consistent and continuous with the refined methods of experimental science. Likewise, James expected that the methods of moral conduct should be consistent with the methods of religious conduct. The next section discusses James's proposal for meshing morality and religion, and then concludes with James's suggestions for reconciling religion with science.

ETHICS AND RELIGION

James discerned much continuity between morality and religion. Both are concerned with the maintenance of relationships; morality is about social relationships among people, and religion is about one's relationship with the ultimate reality. Both morality and religion urge us to become certain kinds of persons, different than we are now. Unlike science's fixation on what positively exists and what is predictably going to happen, both morality and religion are focused on how we decide what we ought to become into the future. This significant difference is a basis for an "is-ought" dichotomy, and James does agree that there is no simple logical path from what is to what ought to be. James would not reduce or ground "oughts" to what does exist. Instead, James insists that any choice over what we shall become always goes well beyond any knowledge of what currently is the case.

Morality and religion essentially involve deliberate control over the formation of mental habits. This is also an essential feature of logical and scientific reasoning, since control over belief formation and acceptance is foundational there as well. However, logic and science tend to support determinism rather than freedom. James insisted that where decisions over the sort of person we shall strive to become are involved, people must be able to freely choose their futures. James enthusiastically endorsed and defended the concept of free will in many of his writings. He did not define free will as an ability to disobey or suspend natural laws, and he did not regard free will as an unnatural power that could interfere with the operations of physical energies. James did not ignore science in his defense of free will, and he repeatedly appealed to scientific knowledge for support.

James argued for the existence of free will in *The Principles of Psychology* by explaining that we can introspect into our experience and notice that we do feel our control over our bodies. We feel that we are in control and that we decide what we will do. But feeling our control does not prove that we really are in control, because our feeling could give us only the illusion of being in control. James then asks the question of why we do have such feelings of decision and control. James, along with materialists and epiphenomenalists, accepted the theory of evolution. According to evolution, our abilities have evolved into existence only because they have proven useful for human survival. Why did our mental experiences of decision and control evolve into existence? James's preferred answer is that our mental control must actually exist so that it can be useful for human survival. Human consciousness and all our feelings, including our feeling of being in control of our actions, actually cause our behavior. James's essay on "The Energies of Men" pursues this idea that our feelings of dynamic control over our bodies are not illusions but rather are true signs of our metabolic energies in our nervous system. Mind and body are so tightly connected that rigorous mental control over thoughts and habits produces genuine physiological changes to the brain and permits remarkable control over much of the rest of the body. No theory of the mind that treats consciousness as accidental or epiphenomenal could easily explain these phenomena.

In "The Dilemma of Determinism," James treats determinism as a scientific postulate, and he does not deny that a core principle of scientific method is the deterministic quest for rigid laws of nature. However, James also was a pluralist about methodology—a principle from one methodological field has validity for only that field. Science cannot empirically prove that determinism is actually valid for all reality, as there is no experiment that could confirm the perfect mathematical rigidity of any natural law. As a postulate, the notion of determinism works well in science, but it does not work at all in morality. If people believe that there is no free will, then people cannot believe that they are controlling the future course of their conduct, and hence morality cannot exist. James rejected any "soft determinism" or "compatibilism" that proposes that morality can exist even if we live in an entirely deterministic world. James constantly took the first-person perspective: what is it like to choose? Morality exists only if people are convinced that they are controlling the future course of the world by steering between genuine optional futures. Only when a person believes that at least two outcomes are possible, and that her personal free choice of one over the other actually steers the course of the future, would that person believe that she is determining what shall come to be, and that she is responsible for that outcome. We cannot rationally believe both in determinism and personal control over optional futures.

By setting up a forced choice between believing in determinism and believing in free will, James then offers the pragmatist compromise: no field of inquiry is forced to adopt a methodological postulate from some other field. Morality is not forced to accept determinism, especially when science itself cannot empirically prove determinism to be universally valid. For all we know, James frequently hints, we may live in a partially open universe where a bit of chancy wavering is a feature of all habits of nature (strict mathematical laws are only approximations of nature's behavior), leaving open genuinely optional futures. Because morality demands a postulate that we live in, and take advantage of, a partially open universe of genuine options, then we moral beings have every right to firmly believe this postulate.

This pragmatic compromise between scientific determinism and free will does not easily fit onto the typical map of choices among determinism and indeterminism, or hard determinism and soft compatibilism. Because James is a pragmatist, he is not taking the position that we may enjoy the illusion of freedom even while we know we have none. No field of knowledge knows that there is no degree of freedom in the world. Some fields of knowledge (such as the physical sciences) postulate that there many strict regularities holding between events, and other fields of knowledge (such as morality) postulate that there are slight contingencies that open up between events. For James, both presumptions may be correct, and freedom is real: human beings are dynamic energies that take advantage of regular patterns of forces in order to partially direct the course of the future. Although the future is not perfectly predictable, this does not mean that chance is in control rather than law. People do not make choices by chance, nor is chance responsible for our free will. For James, chance does not do anything; only positive forces of nature do anything, and we are organic powers of nature alongside all the other natural powers.

As moral beings, we are not just confronted with daily choices among options, but we are also forced to think about how we make our choices. What shall be our habitual responsibilities to each other? Answering this question is undertaken by ethics, and philosophers have perennially attempted to determine a rational basis for our moral habits. In "The Moral Philosopher and the Moral Life," James expresses his discontent with any rationalistic philosophy offering an abstract principle of the good or the right. James cannot fault philosophers for wanting to design a supreme order of moral values; we all seek better harmonies among the many goods that tragically cannot all be satisfied in this world. James simply denies that reason could locate a single supreme harmonization useful for the real world. Instead, we must undertake selective and partial reorderings of moral values as we go through life. As a pragmatist, James suggests that ethics should be experimental, taking inherited moral values from culture as they come and trying out modified value orderings to see if human satisfactions can be generally increased. To the extent that ethics applies this spirit of experimental inquiry and takes social facts seriously, ethics can be scientific, and philosophers doing ethics would become architects of social reform. However, James warns against any notion that this experimental social ethics should aim at designing some single best culture for all humanity. This would be a futile effort, because people are always creating new values and new forms of human associations. Future cultures will modify and supplement the supreme moral values we now prize, and novel tragic compromises between old values and new values cannot be prevented.

In the concluding section to "The Moral Philosopher and the Moral Life," James proposes that religion has an essential role to play for successful ethical theorizing. This proposal also has a central role in the philosophical chapters of *The Varieties of Religious Experience* and his essay "Pragmatism and Religion." James suggests that the ethical quest for a satisfactory harmonization of moral values, and the ethical motivation to pursue this harmonization, are dramatically enhanced if a person adopts the religious attitude toward life. James nowhere suggests that nonreligious people cannot be moral; a moral culture may encompass a wide range of religious belief from fervor to indifference, and may contain peoples of many religions. James's philosophical claim is that religion enhances the moral life to such a great degree that the ethical philosopher should respect the religious perspective. James himself is convinced that ethics can only be completed by religion.

In "The Will to Believe" James cleared the way for the religious life against rationalistic objections. Some philosophers, especially atheists, think that people should refrain from any belief in God until sufficient evidence for God has been collected. These philosophers use the scientific method as their model for rationality, and according to the scientific method, it is rational to withhold belief in a hypothesis until sufficient evidence is gathered. James argues that science cannot show that God does not exist, and if we wait for scientific evidence to prove that God does exist, we will wait forever. Scientific evidence is really not relevant to the religious choice to believe in God. Science deals with events within nature, while religion deals with ultimate reality and destiny. Unlike the scientific method, which deals with only trivial choices, the religious method deals with momentous choices. If we do not decide to become religious, we are irrational, because we would lose a unique opportunity to improve the value of our lives. James reminds us that the validity of a belief lies in its capacity to lead to human successes. The nature of religious evidence, those consequences for our lives that flow from belief in God, must be quite different from the nature of scientific evidence.

In *The Varieties of Religious Experience*, James explores many ways in which belief in God produces dramatic consequences for the lives of believers. For James's philosophical project, four effects of religious belief are most important. First, religion offers a relationship with the supreme reality that answers fundamental questions about our origins and our destinies. Second, religion opens up a realm of religious consciousness where experiences of bliss and salvation can console us through tragedies. Third, religion is capable of inspiring us to take part in a grand cosmic drama led by a powerful divinity who calls for our most strenuous efforts against evils and tragedies. Fourth, religion suggests a supreme moral order of divine values that, though ideal and unattainable from our small human place, can supply a model for our own efforts to harmonize the moral values of our lives.

These four major effects of religious belief are the foundations for James's overall project of philosophically defending the religious life. To live the moral life, a person must be able to undertake hopeful moral projects, and must be able to survive failures as well as enjoy successes. When a

person believes that God is real and that one must be in the proper relationship with God, then God's plan for the world supplies a model of
supreme harmonization of moral values toward which we can strive to
imperfectly realize in this life. However, tragedy looms everywhere: our best
efforts may not be enough; great success in one area means something else
has been neglected; nowhere can anyone be confident that any improvements will last very long. Most significantly, each person knows that in the
long run, bodies and minds only decay and die. Religion supplies both the
motivation sufficient to undertake the most strenuous and sacrificial efforts
on behalf of moral ideals and the consolation sufficient to emotionally
handle the terrible tragedies that we know are inevitably coming.

To summarize, James holds that the religious life makes the moral life
far more achievable, which supplies the pragmatic justification for religion. The moral life also provides the experimental check on the
religious imagination. Only those divinities that best fulfill the needs of
the moral life should be accepted by humanity. Here, too, James is a pluralist who has no single God to recommend, although he does endorse
some vague central features that do pass ethical review. God should be
able to overlap and interpenetrate with human awareness, should have
plans for the world that are both potentially achievable and need human
assistance for fruition, and should provide some eternal destiny for what
is best in us after we have exhausted ourselves in the moral struggle.
James therefore endorses a vague anthropomorphic deity with great
powers who is thoroughly interfused with nature and the human spirit.
No coldly impersonal God, all-powerful dictatorial God, or remotely
deistic God could satisfy James's ethical philosophy.

Throughout his career, James defended a personalistic philosophy.
Personalism tries to understand all reality primarily through concepts
significant in personal experience. Personalism is opposed to imperson-
alist philosophies that try to conceive of reality using only abstract concepts that are remote or detached from personal experience. Some
impersonalisms are "logicist" philosophies that use pure logic or mathematics to define reality. Other impersonalisms are "materialist" philosophies that use only abstract scientific terms, such as *energy* or *mass*, to

define reality. James's personalism refuses to permit the categories of logicism and materialism to dictate all fields of human endeavor. His doctrine of radical empiricism demands that reality be conceived in terms of the contents of human experience. Logic and science are not inhuman; they both acquire their categories by refining concepts originating in ordinary experience (as there is no transpersonal origin of human concepts), but those specialized categories can never acquire exclusive validity over all human experience and knowledge. Everything personal is equally valid and real.

James's capacity to embrace all the variety of human experience tested the limits of his pluralism. His efforts to clarify his metaphysical pluralism resulted in two later books, *A Pluralistic Universe* and *Some Problems of Philosophy*. Pluralism declares that the universe is not fundamentally one thing, but is instead a plurality of an infinite number of different kinds of things that can contingently interact and merge and separate again. James sometimes referred to reality as an "unfinished universe" of open possibilities, and his pragmatism reflects the sort of intelligence required for dealing with such a universe.

A BIBLIOGRAPHY OF JAMES'S BOOKS

The Principles of Psychology. New York: Henry Holt, 1890.
Psychology: Briefer Course. New York: Henry Holt, 1892.
Is Life Worth Living? Philadelphia: S. B. Weston, 1896.
The Will to Believe, and Other Essays in Popular Psychology. New York: Longmans, Green, 1897.
Human Immortality: Two Supposed Objections to the Doctrine. Boston: Houghton Mifflin, 1898.
Talks to Teachers on Psychology, and to Students on Some of Life's Ideals. New York: Henry Holt, 1899.
The Varieties of Religious Experience: A Study in Human Nature. New York: Longmans, Green, 1902.
The Sentiment of Rationality. New York: Longmans, Green, 1905.
Pragmatism: A New Name for Some Old Ways of Thinking. New York: Longmans, Green, 1907.

The Energies of Men. New York: Moffat, Yard, 1908.
The Meaning of Truth: A Sequel to "Pragmatism." New York: Longmans, Green, 1909.
A Pluralistic Universe. Hibbert Lectures at Manchester College on the Present Situation in Philosophy. New York: Longmans, Green, 1909.
The Moral Equivalent of War. New York: American Association for International Conciliation, 1910.

Posthumous Books

Memories and Studies. Edited by Henry James Jr. New York: Longmans, Green, 1911.
Some Problems of Philosophy: A Beginning of an Introduction to Philosophy. New York: Longmans, Green, 1911.
Essays in Radical Empiricism. New York: Longmans, Green, 1912.
Collected Essays and Reviews. New York: Longmans, 1920.
William James on Psychical Research. Edited by Gardner Murphy and Robert O. Ballou. New York: Viking, 1973.
William James on Exceptional Mental States: The 1898 Lowell Lectures. Edited by Eugene Taylor. Amherst: University of Massachusetts Press, 1990.

Critical Editions

The Works of William James. 18 volumes. Frederick Burkhardt, General Editor; Fredson Bowers, Textual Editor; Ignas K. Skrupskelis, Associate Editor. Cambridge, MA: Harvard University Press, 1975–1984.
The Correspondence of William James. 12 volumes. Edited by Ignas K. Skrupskelis, Elizabeth M. Berkeley, and John J. McDermott. Charlottesville: University Press of Virginia, 1992–2004.

FURTHER READING

Bordogna, Francesca. *William James at the Boundaries: Philosophy, Science, and the Geography of Knowledge.* Chicago: University of Chicago Press, 2008.
Carrette, James, ed. *William James and the Varieties of Religious Experience: A Centenary Celebration.* London: Routledge, 2005.

Cormier, Harvey. *Truth Is What Works: William James, Pragmatism, and the Seed of Death*. Lanham, MD: Rowman and Littlefield, 2000.

Cotkin, George. *William James: Public Philosopher*. Baltimore: Johns Hopkins University Press, 1990.

Goodman, Russell B. *Wittgenstein and William James*. Cambridge: Cambridge University Press, 2002.

Heft, Harry. *Ecological Psychology in Context: James Gibson, Roger Barker, and the Legacy of William James's Radical Empiricism*. Hillsdale, NJ: Erlbaum, 2001.

Lamberth, David C. *William James and the Metaphysics of Experience*. Cambridge: Cambridge University Press, 1999.

Lapoujade, David. *William James, empiricism et pragmaticisme*. Paris: Presses Universitaires de France, 1997.

Levinson, Henry Samuel. *The Religious Investigations of William James*. Chapel Hill: University of North Carolina Press, 1981.

Myers, Gerald. *William James: His Life and Thought*. New Haven, CT: Yale University Press, 1986.

Oliver, Phil. *William James's Springs of Delight: The Return to Life*. Nashville, TN: Vanderbilt University Press, 2000.

Pawelski, James. *The Dynamic Individualism of William James*. Albany: State University of New York Press, 2007.

Putnam, Ruth Anna, ed. *The Cambridge Companion to William James*. Cambridge: Cambridge University Press, 1997.

Richardson, Robert D. *William James: In the Maelstrom of American Modernism, a Biography*. Boston: Houghton Mifflin, 2006.

Seigfried, Charlene Haddock. *William James's Radical Reconstruction of Philosophy*. Albany: State University of New York Press, 1990.

Simon, Linda. *Genuine Reality: A Life of William James*. New York: Harcourt Brace, 1998.

Slater, Michael R. *William James on Ethics and Faith*. Cambridge: Cambridge University Press, 2009.

Suckiel, Ellen Kappy. *Heaven's Champion: William James's Philosophy of Religion*. Notre Dame, IN: University of Notre Dame Press, 1996.

Part One

Experience and Mind

1

What is an Emotion?

The physiologists who, during the past few years, have been so industriously exploring the functions of the brain, have limited their attempts at explanation to its cognitive and volitional performances. Dividing the brain into sensorial and motor centers, they have found their division to be exactly paralleled by the analysis made by empirical psychology, of the perceptive and volitional parts of the mind into their simplest elements. But the *aesthetic* sphere of the mind, its longings, its pleasures and pains, and its emotions, have been so ignored in all these researches that one is tempted to suppose that if either Dr. Ferrier or Dr. Munk were asked for a theory in brain-terms of the latter mental facts, they might both reply, either that they had as yet bestowed no thought upon the subject, or that they had found it so difficult to make distinct hypotheses, that the matter lay for them among the problems of the future, only to be taken up after the simpler ones of the present should have been definitively solved.

And yet it is even now certain that of two things concerning the emotions, one must be true. Either separate and special centers, affected to them alone, are their brain-seat, or else they correspond to processes occurring in the motor and sensory centers, already assigned, or in others like them, not yet mapped out. If the former be the case we must deny the current view, and hold the cortex to be something more than the surface of "projection" for every sensitive spot and every muscle in the body. If the latter be the case, we must ask whether the emotional "process" in the sensory or motor centre be an altogether peculiar one,

47

or whether it resembles the ordinary perceptive processes of which those centers are already recognized to be the seat. The purpose of the following pages is to show that the last alternative comes nearest to the truth, and that the emotional brain-processes not only resemble the ordinary sensorial brain-processes, but in very truth *are* nothing but such processes variously combined. The main result of this will be to simplify our notions of the possible complications of brain-physiology, and to make us see that we have already a brain-scheme in our hands whose applications are much wider than its authors dreamed. But although this seems to be the chief result of the arguments I am to urge, I should say that they were not originally framed for the sake of any such result. They grew out of fragmentary introspective observations, and it was only when these had already combined into a theory that the thought of the simplification the theory might bring to cerebral physiology occurred to me, and made it seem more important than before.

I should say first of all that the only emotions I propose expressly to consider here are those that have a distinct bodily expression. That there are feelings of pleasure and displeasure, of interest and excitement, bound up with mental operations, but having no obvious bodily expression for their consequence, would, I suppose, be held true by most readers. Certain arrangements of sounds, of lines, of colors, are agreeable, and others the reverse, without the degree of the feeling being sufficient to quicken the pulse or breathing, or to prompt to movements of either the body or the face. Certain sequences of ideas charm us as much as others tire us. It is a real intellectual delight to get a problem solved, and a real intellectual torment to have to leave it unfinished. The first set of examples, the sounds, lines, and colors, are either bodily sensations, or the images of such. The second set seem to depend on processes in the ideational centers exclusively. Taken together, they appear to prove that there are pleasures and pains inherent in certain forms of nerve-action as such, wherever that action occur. The case of these feelings we will at present leave entirely aside, and confine our attention to the more complicated cases in which a wave of bodily disturbance of some kind accompanies the perception of the interesting sights or sounds, or the passage of the exciting train of ideas. Surprise, curiosity, rapture, fear, anger, lust, greed, and the like, become then the names of the mental states with which the person is possessed. The bodily disturbances are said to be the "manifestation" of these several emotions, their "expression" or "natural language"; and these emotions themselves, being so strongly characterized both from within and without, may be called the *standard* emotions.

Our natural way of thinking about these standard emotions is that the mental perception of some fact excites the mental affection called the emotion, and that this latter state of mind gives rise to the bodily expression. My thesis on the contrary is that *the bodily changes follow directly the* PERCEPTION *of the exciting fact, and that our feeling of the same changes as they occur* IS *the emotion.* Common sense says, we lose our fortune, are sorry and weep; we meet a bear, are frightened and run; we are insulted by a rival, are angry and strike. The hypothesis here to be defended says that this order of sequence is incorrect, that the one mental state is not immediately induced by the other, that the bodily manifestations must first be interposed between, and that the more rational statement is that we feel sorry because we cry, angry because we strike, afraid because we tremble, and not that we cry, strike, or tremble, because we are sorry, angry, or fearful, as the case may be. Without the bodily states following on the perception, the latter would be purely cognitive in form, pale, colorless, destitute of emotional warmth. We might then see the bear, and judge it best to run, receive the insult and deem it right to strike, but we could not actually *feel* afraid or angry.

Stated in this crude way, the hypothesis is pretty sure to meet with immediate disbelief. And yet neither many nor far-fetched considerations are required to mitigate its paradoxical character, and possibly to produce conviction of its truth.

To begin with, readers of the Journal do not need to be reminded that the nervous system of every living thing is but a bundle of predispositions to react in particular ways upon the contact of particular features of the environment. As surely as the hermit-crab's abdomen presupposes the existence of empty whelk-shells somewhere to be found, so surely do the hound's olfactories imply the existence, on the one hand, of deer's or foxes' feet, and on the other, the tendency to follow up their tracks. The neural machinery is but a hyphen between determinate arrangements of matter outside the body and determinate impulses to inhibition or discharge within its organs. When the hen sees a white oval object on the ground, she cannot leave it; she must keep upon it and return to it, until at last its transformation into a little mass of moving chirping down elicits from her machinery an entirely new set of performances. The love of man for woman, or of the human mother for her babe, our wrath at snakes and our fear of precipices, may all be described similarly, as instances of the way in which peculiarly conformed pieces of the world's furniture will fatally call forth most particular mental and bodily reactions, in advance of, and often in direct opposition to, the verdict of our deliberate reason concerning them. The labors of Darwin and his successors are only just beginning to reveal the universal parasitism of each creature upon other special things, and the way in which each creature brings the signature of its special relations stamped on its nervous system with it upon the scene.

Every living creature is in fact a sort of lock, whose wards and springs presuppose special forms of keys,—which keys however are not born attached to the locks, but are sure to be found in the world near by as life goes on. And the locks are indifferent to any but their own keys. The egg fails to fascinate the hound, the bird does not fear the precipice, the snake waxes not wroth at his kind, the deer cares nothing for the woman or the human babe. Those who wish for a full development of this point of view, should read Schneider's *Der thierische Wille,*—no other book shows how accurately anticipatory are the actions of animals, of the specific features of the environment in which they are to live.

Now among these nervous anticipations are of course to be reckoned the emotions, so far as these may be called forth directly by the perception of certain facts. In advance of all experience of elephants, no child can but be frightened if he suddenly finds one trumpeting and charging upon him. No woman can see a handsome little naked baby without delight, no man in the wilderness see a human form in the distance without excitement and curiosity. I said I should consider these emotions only so far as they have bodily movements of some sort for their accompaniments. But my first point is to show that their bodily accompaniments are much more far-reaching and complicated than we ordinarily suppose.

In the earlier books on Expression, written mostly from the artistic point of view, the signs of emotion visible from without were the only ones taken account of. Sir Charles Bell's celebrated *Anatomy of Expression* noticed the respiratory changes; and Bain's and Darwin's treatises went more thoroughly still into the study of the visceral factors involved,—changes in the functioning of glands and muscles, and in that of the circulatory apparatus. But not even a Darwin has exhaustively enumerated *all* the bodily affections characteristic of any one of the standard emotions. More and more, as physiology advances, we begin to discern how almost infinitely numerous and subtle they must be. The researches of Mosso with the plethysmograph have shown that not only the heart, but the entire circulatory system, forms a sort of sounding-board, which every change of our consciousness, however slight, may make reverberate. Hardly a sensation comes to us without sending waves of alternate constriction and dilatation down the arteries of our arms. The blood vessels of the abdomen act reciprocally with those of the more outward parts. The bladder and bowels; the glands of the mouth, throat, and skin; and the liver are known to be affected gravely in certain severe emotions, and are unquestionably affected transiently when the emotions are of a lighter sort. That the heart-beats and the rhythm of breathing play a leading part in all emotions whatsoever, is a matter too notorious for proof. And what is really equally prominent, but less likely to be admitted until special attention is drawn to the fact, is the continuous co-operation of the voluntary muscles in our emotional states. Even when no change of outward attitude is produced, their inward tension alters to suit each varying mood, and is felt as a difference of tone or of strain. In depression the flexors tend to prevail; in elation or belligerent excitement the extensors take the lead. And the various permutations and combinations of which these organic activities are susceptible, make it abstractly possible that no shade of emotion, however slight, should be without a bodily reverberation as unique, when taken in its totality, as is the mental mood itself.

The immense number of parts modified in each emotion is what makes it so difficult for us to reproduce in cold blood the total and integral expression of any one of them. We may catch the trick with the voluntary muscles, but fail with the skin, glands, heart, and other viscera. Just as an artificially imitated sneeze lacks something of the reality, so the attempt to imitate an emotion in the absence of its normal instigating cause is apt to be rather "hollow."

The next thing to be noticed is this, that every one of the bodily changes, whatsoever it be, is *felt*, acutely or obscurely, the moment it occurs. If the reader has never paid attention to this matter, he will be both interested and astonished to learn how many different local bodily feelings he can detect in himself as characteristic of his various emotional moods. It would be perhaps too much to expect him to arrest the tide of any strong gust of passion for the sake of any such curious analysis as this; but he can observe more tranquil states, and that may be assumed here to be true of the greater which is shown to be true of the less. Our whole cubic capacity is sensibly alive; and each morsel of it contributes its pulsations of feeling, dim or sharp, pleasant, painful, or dubious, to that sense of personality that every one of us unfailingly carries with him. It is surprising what little items give accent to these complexes of sensibility. When worried by any slight trouble, one may find that the focus of one's bodily consciousness is the contraction, often quite inconsiderable, of the eyes and brows. When momentarily embarrassed, it is something in the pharynx that compels either a swallow, a clearing of the throat, or a slight cough; and so on for as many more instances as might be named. Our concern here being with the general view rather than with the details, I will not linger to discuss these but, assuming the point admitted that every change that occurs must be felt, I will pass on.[1]

I now proceed to urge the vital point of my whole theory, which is this. If we fancy some strong emotion, and then try to abstract from our consciousness of it all the feelings of its characteristic bodily symptoms, we find we have nothing left behind, no "mind-stuff" out of which the emotion can be constituted, and that a cold and neutral state of intellectual perception is all that remains. It is true, that although most people, when asked, say that their introspection verifies this statement, some persist in saying theirs does not. Many cannot be made to understand the question. When you beg them to imagine away every feeling of laughter and of tendency to laugh from their consciousness of the ludicrousness of an object, and then to tell you what the feeling of its ludicrousness would be like, whether it be anything more than the perception that the object belongs to the class "funny," they persist in replying that the thing proposed is a physical impossibility, and that they always *must* laugh, if they see a funny object. Of course the task proposed is not the practical one of seeing a ludicrous object and annihilating one's tendency to laugh. It is the purely speculative one of subtracting certain elements of feeling from an emotional state supposed to exist in its fullness, and saying what the residual elements are. I cannot help thinking that all who rightly apprehend this problem will agree with the proposition above laid down. What kind of an emotion of fear would be left, if the feelings neither of quickened heart-beats nor of shallow breathing, neither of trembling lips nor of weakened limbs, neither of goose-flesh nor of visceral stirrings, were present, it is quite impossible to think. Can one fancy the state of rage and picture no ebullition of it in the chest, no flushing of the face, no dilatation of the nostrils, no clenching of the teeth, no impulse to vigorous action, but in their stead limp muscles, calm breathing, and a placid face? The present writer, for one, certainly cannot. The rage is as completely evaporated as the sensation of its so-called manifestations, and the only thing that can possibly be supposed to take its place is some cold-blooded and dispassionate judicial sentence, confined entirely to the intellectual realm, to the effect that a certain person or persons merit chastisement for their sins. In like manner of grief: what would it be without its tears, its sobs, its suffocation of the heart, its pang in the breast-bone? A feelingless cognition that certain circumstances are deplorable, and nothing more. Every passion in turn tells the same story. A purely disembodied human emotion is a nonentity. I do not say that it is a contradiction in the nature of things, or that pure spirits are necessarily condemned to cold intellectual lives; but I say that for *us*, emotion dissociated from all bodily feeling is inconceivable. The more closely I scrutinize my states, the more persuaded I become, that whatever moods, affections, and passions I have, are in very truth constituted by, and made up of, those bodily changes we ordinarily call their expression or consequence; and the more it seems to me that if I were to become corporeally anesthetic, I should be excluded from the life of the affections, harsh and tender alike, and drag out an existence of merely cognitive or intellectual form. Such an existence, although it seems to have been the ideal of ancient sages, is too apathetic to be keenly sought after by those born after the revival of the worship of sensibility, a few generations ago.

But if the emotion is nothing but the feeling of the reflex bodily effects of what we call its "objects," effects due to the connate adaptation of the nervous system to that object, we seem immediately faced by this objection: most of the objects of civilized men's emotions are things to which it would be preposterous to suppose their nervous systems connately adapted. Most occasions of shame and many insults are purely conventional, and vary with the social environment. The same is true of many matters of dread and of desire, and of many occasions of melancholy and regret. In these cases, at least, it would seem that the ideas of shame, desire, regret, &c., must first have been attached by education and association to these conventional objects before the bodily changes could possibly be awakened. And if in *these* cases the bodily changes follow the ideas, instead of giving rise to them, why not then in all cases?

To discuss thoroughly this objection would carry us deep into the study of purely intellectual Aesthetics. A few words must here suffice. We will say nothing of the argument's failure to distinguish between the idea of an emotion and the emotion itself. We will only recall the well-known evolutionary principle that when a certain power has once been fixed in an animal by virtue of its utility in presence of certain features of the environment, it may turn out to be useful in the presence of other features of the environment that had originally nothing to do with either producing or preserving it. A nervous tendency to discharge being once there, all sorts of unforeseen things may pull the trigger and let loose the effects. That among these things should be conventionalities of man's contriving is a matter of no psychological consequence whatever. The most important part of my environment is my fellow-man. The consciousness of his attitude toward me is the perception that normally unlocks most of my shames and indignations and fears. The extraordinary sensitiveness of this consciousness is shown by the bodily modifications wrought in us by the awareness that our fellow-man is noticing us *at all*. No one can walk across the platform at a public meeting with just the same muscular innervation he uses to walk across his room at home. No one can give a message to such a meeting without organic excitement. "Stage-fright" is only the extreme degree of that wholly irrational personal self-consciousness which every one gets in some measure, as soon as he feels the eyes of a number of strangers fixed upon him, even though he be inwardly convinced that their feeling towards him is of no practical account.[2] This being so, it is not surprising that the additional persuasion that my fellow-man's attitude means either well or ill for me, should awaken stronger emotions still. In primitive societies "Well" may mean handing me a piece of beef, and "Ill" may mean aiming a blow at my skull. In our "cultured age," "Ill" may mean cutting me in the street, and "Well," giving me an honorary degree. What the action itself may be is quite insignificant, so long as I can perceive in it intent or *animus*. *That* is the emotion-arousing perception; and may give rise to as strong bodily convulsions in me, a civilized man experiencing the treatment of an artificial society, as in any savage prisoner of war, learning whether his captors are about to eat him or to make him a member of their tribe.

But now, this objection disposed of, there arises a more general doubt. Is there any evidence, it may be asked, for the assumption that particular perceptions *do* produce widespread bodily effects by a sort of immediate physical influence, antecedent to the arousal of an emotion or emotional idea?

The only possible reply is, that there is most assuredly such evidence. In listening to poetry, drama, or heroic narrative, we are often surprised at the cutaneous shiver which like a sudden wave flows over us, and at the heart-swelling and the lachrymal effusion that unexpectedly catch us at intervals. In listening to music, the same is even more strikingly true. If we abruptly see a dark moving form in the woods, our heart stops beating, and we catch our breath instantly and before any articulate idea of danger can arise. If our friend goes near to the edge of a precipice, we get the well-known feeling of "all-overishness," and we shrink back, although we positively *know* him to be safe, and have no distinct imagination of his fall. The writer well remembers his astonishment, when a boy of seven or eight, at fainting when he saw a horse bled. The blood was in a bucket, with a stick in it, and, if memory does not deceive him, he stirred it round and saw it drip from the stick with no feeling save that of childish curiosity. Suddenly the world grew black before his eyes, his ears began to buzz, and he knew no more. He had never heard of the sight of blood producing faintness or sickness, and he had so little repugnance to it, and so little apprehension of any other sort of danger from it, that even at that tender age, as he well remembers, he could not help wondering how the mere physical presence of a pailful of crimson fluid could occasion in him such formidable bodily effects.

Imagine two steel knife-blades with their keen edges crossing each other at right-angles, and moving to and fro. Our whole nervous organization is "on-edge" at the thought; and yet what emotion can be there except the unpleasant nervous feeling itself, or the dread that more of it may come? The entire fund and capital of the emotion here is the senseless bodily effect the blades immediately arouse. This case is typical of a class: where an ideal emotion seems to precede the bodily symptoms, it is often nothing but a representation of the symptoms themselves. One who has already fainted at the sight of blood may witness the preparations for a surgical operation with uncontrollable heart-sinking and anxiety. He anticipates certain feelings, and the anticipation precipitates their arrival. I am told of a case of morbid terror, of which the subject confessed that what possessed her seemed, more than anything, to be the fear of fear itself. In the various forms of what Professor Bain calls "tender emotion," although the appropriate object must usually be directly contemplated before the emotion can be aroused, yet sometimes thinking of the symptoms of the emotion itself may have the same effect.

In sentimental natures, the thought of "yearning" will produce real "yearning." And, not to speak of coarser examples, a mother's imagination of the caresses she bestows on her child may arouse a spasm of parental longing.

In such cases as these, we see plainly how the emotion both begins and ends with what we call its effects or manifestations. It has no mental *status* except as either the presented feeling, or the idea, of the manifestations; which latter thus constitute its entire material, its sum and substance, and its stock-in-trade. And these cases ought to make us see how in all cases the feeling of the manifestations may play a much deeper part in the constitution of the emotion than we are wont to suppose.

If our theory be true, a necessary corollary of it ought to be that any voluntary arousal of the so-called manifestations of a special emotion ought to give us the emotion itself. Of course in the majority of emotions, this test is inapplicable; for many of the manifestations are in organs over which we have no volitional control. Still, within the limits in which it can be verified, experience fully corroborates this test. Everyone knows how panic is increased by flight, and how the giving way to the symptoms of grief or anger increases those passions themselves. Each fit of sobbing makes the sorrow more acute, and calls forth another fit stronger still, until at last repose only ensues with lassitude and with the apparent exhaustion of the machinery. In rage, it is notorious how we "work ourselves up" to a climax by repeated outbreaks of expression. Refuse to express a passion, and it dies. Count ten before venting your anger, and its occasion seems ridiculous. Whistling to keep up courage is no mere figure of speech. On the other hand, sit all day in a moping posture, sigh, and reply to everything with a dismal voice, and your melancholy lingers. There is no more valuable precept in moral education than this, as all who have experience know: if we wish to conquer undesirable emotional tendencies in ourselves, we must assiduously, and in the first instance cold-bloodedly, go through the *outward motions* of those contrary dispositions we prefer to cultivate. The reward of persistency will infallibly come, in the fading out of the sullenness or depression, and the advent of real cheerfulness and kindliness in their stead. Smooth the brow, brighten the eye, contract the dorsal rather than the ventral aspect of the frame, and speak in a major key, pass the genial compliment, and your heart must be frigid indeed if it do not gradually thaw!

The only exceptions to this are apparent, not real. The great emotional expressiveness and mobility of certain persons often lead us to say, "They would feel more if they talked less." And in another class of persons, the explosive energy with which passion manifests itself on critical occasions, seems correlated with the way in which they bottle it up during the intervals. But these are only eccentric types of character, and within each type the law of the last paragraph prevails. The sentimentalist is so constructed that "gushing" is his or her normal mode of expression. Putting a stopper on the "gush" will only to a limited extent cause more "real" activities to take its place; in the main it will simply produce listlessness. On the other hand, the ponderous and bilious "slumbering volcano," let him repress the expression of his passions as he will, will find they expire if they get no vent at all; whilst if the rare occasions multiply which he deems worthy of their outbreak, he will find them grow in intensity as life proceeds.

I feel persuaded there is no real exception to the law. The formidable effects of suppressed tears might be mentioned, and the calming results of speaking out your mind when angry and having done with it. But these are also but specious wanderings from the rule. Every perception must lead to *some* nervous result. If this be the normal emotional expression, it soon expends itself, and in the natural course of things a calm succeeds. But if the normal issue be blocked from any cause, the currents may under certain circumstances invade other tracts, and there work different and worse effects. Thus vengeful brooding may replace a burst of indignation; a dry heat may consume the frame of one who fain would weep, or he may, as Dante says, turn to stone within; and then tears or a storming-fit may bring a grateful relief. When we teach children to repress their emotions, it is not that they may *feel* more, quite the reverse. It is that they may *think* more; for to a certain extent whatever nerve-currents are diverted from the regions below, must swell the activity of the thought-tracts of the brain.[3]

The last great argument in favor of the priority of the bodily symptoms to the felt emotion, is the ease with which we formulate by its means pathological cases and normal cases under a common scheme. In every asylum we find examples of absolutely unmotived fear, anger, melancholy, or conceit; and others of an equally unmotived apathy which persists in spite of the best of outward reasons why it should give way. In the former cases we must suppose the nervous machinery to be so "labile" in some one emotional direction, that almost every stimulus, however inappropriate, will cause it to upset in that way, and as a consequence to engender the particular complex of feelings of which the psychic body of the emotion consists. Thus, to take one special instance, if inability to draw deep breath, fluttering of the heart, and that peculiar epigastric change felt as "precordial anxiety," with an irresistible tendency to take a somewhat crouching attitude and to sit still, and with perhaps other visceral processes not now known, all spontaneously occur together in a certain person; his feeling of their combination *is* the emotion of dread, and he is the victim of what is known as morbid fear. A friend who has had occasional attacks of this most distressing of all maladies, tells me that in his case the whole drama seems to centre about the region of the heart and respiratory apparatus, that his main effort during the attacks is to get control of his inspirations and to slow his heart, and that the moment he attains to breathing deeply and to holding himself erect, the dread, *ipso facto*, seems to depart.[4]

The account given to Brachet by one of his own patients of her opposite condition, that of emotional insensibility, has been often quoted, and deserves to be quoted again:—

"I still continue (she says) to suffer constantly; I have not a moment of comfort, and no human sensations. Surrounded by all that can render life happy and agreeable, still to me the faculty of enjoyment and of feeling is wanting—both have become physical impossibilities. In everything, even in the most tender caresses of my children, I find only bitterness. I cover them with kisses, but there is something between their lips and mine; and this horrid something is between me and all the enjoyments of life. My existence is incomplete. The functions and acts of ordinary life, it is true, still remain to me; but in every one of them there is something wanting—to wit, the feeling which is proper to them, and the pleasure which follows them. . . . *Each of my senses, each part of my proper self, is as it were separated from me and can no longer afford me any feeling; this impossibility seems to depend upon a void which I feel in the front of my head, and to be due to the diminution of the sensibility over the whole surface of my body, for it seems to me that I never actually reach the objects which I touch. . . . I feel well enough the changes of temperature on my skin, but I no longer experience the internal feeling of the air when I breathe. . . .* All this would be a small matter enough, but for its frightful result, which is that of the impossibility of any other kind of feeling and of any sort of enjoyment, although I experience a need and desire of them that render my life an incomprehensible torture. Every function, every action of my life remains, but deprived of the feeling that belongs to it, of the enjoyment that should follow it. My feet are cold, I warm them, but gain no pleasure from the warmth. I recognize the taste of all I eat, without getting any pleasure from it. . . . My children are growing handsome and healthy, everyone tells me so, I see it myself, but the delight, the inward comfort I ought to feel, I fail to get. Music has lost all charm for me, I used to love it dearly. My daughter plays very well, but for me it is mere noise. That lively interest which a year ago made me hear a delicious concert in the smallest air their fingers played,—that thrill, that general vibration which made me shed such tender tears,—all that exists no more."[5]

Other victims describe themselves as closed in walls of ice or covered with an India-rubber integument, through which no impression penetrates to the sealed-up sensibility.

If our hypothesis is true, it makes us realize more deeply than ever how much our mental life is knit up with our corporeal frame, in the strictest sense of the term. Rapture, love, ambition, indignation, and pride, considered as feelings, are fruits of the same soil with the grossest bodily sensations of pleasure and of pain. But it was said at the outset that this would be affirmed only of what we then agreed to call the "standard" emotions; and that those inward sensibilities that appeared devoid at first sight of bodily results should be left out of our account. We had better, before closing, say a word or two about these latter feelings.

They are, the reader will remember, the moral, intellectual, and aesthetic feelings. Concords of sounds, of colors, of lines, logical consistencies, teleological fitnesses, affect us with a pleasure that seems ingrained in the very form of the representation itself, and to borrow nothing from any reverberation surging up from the parts below the brain. The Herbartian psychologists have tried to distinguish feelings due to the *form* in which ideas may be arranged. A geometrical demonstration may be as "pretty," and an act of justice as "neat" as a drawing or a tune, although the prettiness and neatness seem here to be a pure matter of sensation, and there to have nothing to do with sensation. We have then, or some of us seem to have, genuinely *cerebral* forms of pleasure and displeasure, apparently not agreeing in their mode of production with the so-called "standard" emotions we have been analysing. And it is certain that readers whom our reasons have hitherto failed to convince, will now start up at this admission, and consider that by it we give up our whole case. Since musical perceptions, since logical ideas, can immediately arouse a form of emotional feeling, they will say, is it not more natural to suppose that in the case of the so-called "standard" emotions, prompted by the presence of objects or the experience of events, the emotional feeling is equally immediate, and the bodily expression something that comes later and is added on?

But a sober scrutiny of the cases of pure cerebral emotion gives little force to this assimilation. Unless in them there actually be coupled with the intellectual feeling a bodily reverberation of some kind, unless we actually laugh at the neatness of the mechanical device, thrill at the justice of the act, or tingle at the perfection of the musical form, our mental condition is more allied to a judgment of *right* than to anything else. And such a judgment is rather to be classed among awarenesses of truth: it is a *cognitive* act. But as a matter of fact the intellectual feeling hardly ever does exist thus unaccompanied. The bodily sounding-board is at work, as careful introspection will show, far more than we usually suppose. Still, where long familiarity with a certain class of effects has blunted emotional sensibility thereto as much as it has sharpened the taste and judgment, we do get the intellectual emotion, if such it can be called, pure and undefiled. And the dryness of it, the paleness, the absence of all glow, as it may exist in a thoroughly expert critic's mind, not only shows us what an altogether different thing it is from the "standard" emotions we considered first, but makes us suspect that almost the entire difference lies in the fact that the bodily sounding-board, vibrating in the one case, is in the other mute. "Not so very bad" is, in a person of consummate taste, apt to be the highest limit of approving expression. "*Rien ne me choque*" is said to have been Chopin's superlative of praise of new music. A sentimental layman would feel, and ought to feel, horrified, on being admitted into such a critic's mind, to see how cold, how thin, how void of human significance, are the motives for favor or disfavor that there prevail. The capacity to make a nice spot on the wall will outweigh a picture's whole content; a foolish trick of words will preserve a poem; an utterly meaningless fitness of sequence in one musical composition set at naught any amount of "expressiveness" in another.

I remember seeing an English couple sit for more than an hour on a piercing February day in the Academy at Venice before the celebrated "Assumption" by Titian; and when I, after being chased from room to room by the cold, concluded to get into the sunshine as fast as possible and let the pictures go, but before leaving drew reverently near to them to learn with what superior forms of susceptibility they might be endowed, all I overheard was the woman's voice murmuring: "What a *deprecatory* expression her face wears! What a self-abnegation! How *unworthy* she feels of the honor she is receiving!" Their honest hearts had been kept warm all the time by a glow of spurious sentiment that would have fairly made old Titian sick. Mr. Ruskin somewhere makes the (for him) terrible admission that religious people as a rule care little for pictures, and that when they do care for them they generally prefer the worst ones to the best. Yes! in every art, in every science, there is the keen perception of certain relations being *right* or not, and there is the emotional flush and thrill consequent thereupon. And these are two things, not one. In the former of them it is that experts and masters are at home. The latter accompaniments are bodily commotions that they may hardly feel, but that may be experienced in their fullness by *Crétins* and Philistines in whom the critical judgment is at its lowest ebb. The "marvels" of Science, about which so much edifying popular literature is written, are apt to be "caviare" to the men in the laboratories. Cognition and emotion are parted even in this last retreat,—who shall say that their antagonism may not just be one phase of the world-old struggle known as that between the spirit and the flesh?—a struggle in which it seems pretty certain that neither party will definitively drive the other off the field.

To return to our starting point, the physiology of the brain. If we suppose its cortex contains centers for the perception of changes in each special sense-organ, in each portion of the skin, in each muscle, each joint, and each viscus, and to contain absolutely nothing else, we still have a scheme perfectly capable of representing the process of the emotions. An object falls on a sense-organ and is apperceived by the appropriate cortical centre; or else the latter, excited in some other way, gives rise to an idea of the same object. Quick as a flash, the reflex currents pass down through their pre-ordained channels, alter the condition of muscle, skin, and viscus; and these alterations, apperceived like the original object, in as many specific portions of the cortex, combine with it in consciousness and transform it from an object-simply-apprehended into an object-emotionally-felt. No new principles have to be invoked, nothing is postulated beyond the ordinary reflex circuit, and the topical centers admitted in one shape or another by all to exist.

It must be confessed that a crucial test of the truth of the hypothesis is quite as hard to obtain as its decisive refutation. A case of complete internal and external corporeal anesthesia, without motor alteration or alteration of intelligence except emotional apathy, would afford, if not a crucial test, at least a strong presumption, in favor of the truth of the view we have set forth; whilst the persistence of strong emotional feeling in such a case would completely overthrow our case. Hysterical anesthesias seem never to be complete enough to cover the ground. Complete anesthesias from organic disease, on the other hand, are excessively rare. In the famous case of Remigius Leims, no mention is made by the reporters of his emotional condition, a circumstance which by itself affords no presumption that it was normal, since as a rule nothing ever *is* noticed without a pre-existing question in the mind. Dr. Georg Winter has recently described a case somewhat similar,[6] and in reply to a question, kindly writes to me as follows:—"The case has been for a year and a half entirely removed from my observation. But so far as I am able to state, the man was characterized by a certain mental inertia and indolence. He was tranquil, and had on the whole the temperament of a phlegmatic. He was not irritable, not quarrelsome, went quietly about his farm-work, and left the care of his business and house-keeping to other people. In short, he gave one the impression of a placid countryman, who has no interests beyond his work." Dr. Winter adds that in studying the case he paid no particular attention to the man's psychic condition, as this seemed "*nebensächlich*" to his main purpose. I should add that the form of my question to Dr. Winter could give him no clue as to the kind of answer I expected.

Of course, this case proves nothing, but it is to be hoped that asylum-physicians and nervous specialists may begin methodically to study the relation between anesthesia and emotional apathy. If the hypothesis here suggested is ever to be definitively confirmed or disproved, it seems as if it must be by them, for they alone have the data in their hands.

P.S.—By an unpardonable forgetfulness at the time of dispatching my MS. to the Editor, I ignored the existence of the extraordinary case of total anesthesia published by Professor Strümpell in *Ziemssen's Deutsches Archiv für klinische Medicin* xxii., 321, of which I had nevertheless read reports at the time of its publication. [*Cf.* first report of the case in *Mind* X., 263, translated from *Pflüger's Archiv.* Ed.] I believe that it constitutes the only remaining case of the sort in medical literature, so that with it our survey is complete. On referring to the original, which is important in many connections, I found that the patient, a shoemaker's apprentice of 15, entirely anesthetic, inside and out, with the exception of one eye and one ear, had shown *shame* on the occasion of soiling his bed, and *grief*, when a formerly favorite dish was set before him, at the thought that he could no longer taste its flavor. As Dr. Strümpell seemed, however, to have paid no special attention to his psychic states, so far as these are matter for our theory, I wrote to him in a few words what the essence of the theory was, and asked him to say whether he felt sure the grief and shame mentioned were real feelings in the boy's mind, or only the reflex manifestations provoked by certain perceptions, manifestations that an outside observer might note, but to which the boy himself might be insensible.

Dr. Strümpell has sent me a very obliging reply, of which I translate the most important passage. "I must indeed confess that I naturally failed to institute with my *Anaesthetiker* observations as special as the sense of your theory would require. Nevertheless I think I can decidedly make the statement, that he was by no means completely lacking in emotional affections. In addition to the feelings of *grief* and *shame* mentioned in my paper, I recall distinctly that he showed *e.g., anger*, and frequently quarrelled with the hospital attendants. He also manifested *fear* lest I should punish him. In short, I do not think that my case speaks exactly in favor of your theory. On the other hand, I will not affirm that it positively refutes your theory. For my case was certainly one of a very centrally conditioned anesthesia (perception-anesthesia, like that of hysterics) and therefore the conduction of outward impressions may in him have been undisturbed."

I confess that I do not see the relevancy of the last consideration, and this makes me suspect that my own letter was too briefly or obscurely expressed to put my correspondent fully in possession of my own thought. For his reply still makes no explicit reference to anything but the outward manifestations of emotion in the boy. Is it not at least conceivable that, just as a stranger, brought into the boy's presence for the first time, and seeing him eat and drink and satisfy other natural necessities, would suppose him to have the feelings of hunger, thirst, &c., until informed by the boy himself that he did all these things with no feeling at all but that of sight and sound—is it not, I say, at least possible, that Dr. Strümpell, addressing no direct introspective questions to his patient, and the patient not being of a class from which one could expect voluntary revelations of that sort, should have similarly omitted to discriminate between a feeling and its habitual motor accompaniment, and erroneously taken the latter as proof that the former was there? Such a mistake is of course possible, and I must therefore repeat Dr. Strümpell's own words, that his case does not yet refute my theory. Should a similar case recur, it ought to be interrogated as to the inward emotional state that co-existed with the outward expressions of shame, anger, &c. And if it then turned out that the patient recognized explicitly the same mood of feeling known under those names in his former normal state, my theory would of course fall. It is, however, to me incredible that the patient should have an *identical* feeling, for the dropping out of the organic sounding-board would necessarily diminish its volume in some way. The teacher of Dr. Strümpell's patient found a mental deficiency in him during his anesthesia, that may possibly have been due to the consequences resulting to his general intellectual vivacity from the subtraction of so important a mass of feelings, even though they were not the whole of his emotional life. Whoever wishes to extract from the next case of total anesthesia the maximum of knowledge about the emotions, will have to interrogate the patient with some such notion as that of my article in his mind. We can define the pure psychic emotions far better by starting from such an hypothesis and modifying it in the way of restriction and subtraction, than by having no definite hypothesis at all. Thus will the publication of my article have been justified, even though the theory it advocates, rigorously taken, be erroneous. The best thing I can say for it is, that in writing it, I have almost persuaded *myself* it may be true.

2

The Stream of Consciousness

The order of our study must be analytic. We are now prepared to begin the introspective study of the adult consciousness itself. Most books adopt the so-called synthetic method. Starting with 'simple ideas of sensation,' and regarding these as so many atoms, they proceed to build up the higher states of mind out of their 'association,' 'integration,' or 'fusion,' as houses are built by the agglutination of bricks. This has the didactic advantages which the synthetic method usually has. But it commits one beforehand to the very questionable theory that our higher states of consciousness are compounds of units; and instead of starting with what the reader directly knows, namely his total concrete states of mind, it starts with a set of supposed 'simple ideas' with which he has no immediate acquaintance at all, and concerning whose alleged interactions he is much at the mercy of any plausible phrase. On every ground, then, the method of advancing from the simple to the compound exposes us to illusion. All pedants and abstractionists will naturally hate to abandon it. But a student who loves the fullness of human nature will prefer to follow the 'analytic' method, and to begin with the most concrete facts, those with which he has a daily acquaintance in his own inner life. The analytic method will discover in due time the elementary parts, if such exist, without danger of precipitate assumption. The reader will bear in mind that our own chapters on sensation have dealt mainly with the physiological conditions thereof. They were put first as a mere matter of convenience, because incoming currents come first. *Psychologically* they might better have come last. Pure sensations were described on page 12 as processes which in adult life are well-nigh unknown, and nothing was said which could for a moment lead the reader to suppose that they were the *elements of composition* of the higher states of mind.

The Fundamental Fact. The first and foremost concrete fact which every one will affirm to belong to his inner experience is the fact that *consciousness of some sort goes on*. *'States of mind'* succeed each other in him. If we could say in English 'it thinks' as we say 'it rains' or 'it blows,' we should be stating the fact most simply and with the minimum of assumption. As we cannot, we must simply say that *thought goes on*.

Four Characters in Consciousness. How does it go on? We notice immediately four important characters in the process, of which it shall be the duty of the present chapter to treat in a general way:

1) Every state tends to be part of a personal consciousness.
2) Within each personal consciousness states are always changing.
3) Each personal consciousness is sensibly continuous.
4) It is interested in some parts of its object to the exclusion of others, and welcomes or rejects—*chooses* from among them, in a word—all the while.

In considering these four points successively, we shall have to plunge *in medias res* as regards our nomenclature and use psychological terms which can only be adequately defined in later chapters of the book. But every one knows what the terms mean in a rough way; and it is only in a rough way that we are now to take them. This chapter is like a painter's first charcoal sketch upon his canvas, in which no niceties appear.

When I say *every 'state' or 'thought' is part of a personal consciousness*, 'personal consciousness' is one of the terms in question. Its meaning we know so long as no one asks us to define it, but to give an accurate account of it is the most difficult of philosophic tasks. This task we must confront in the next chapter; here a preliminary word will suffice.

In this room—this lecture-room, say—there are a multitude of thoughts, yours and mine, some of which cohere mutually, and some not.

They are as little each-for-itself and reciprocally independent as they are all-belonging-together. They are neither: no one of them is separate, but each belongs with certain others and with none beside. My thought belongs with *my* other thoughts, and your thought with *your* other thoughts. Whether anywhere in the room there be a *mere* thought, which is nobody's thought, we have no means of ascertaining, for we have no experience of its like. The only states of consciousness that we naturally deal with are found in personal consciousnesses, minds, selves, concrete particular I's and you's.

Each of these minds keeps its own thoughts to itself. There is no giving or bartering between them. No thought even comes into direct *sight* of a thought in another personal consciousness than its own. Absolute insulation, irreducible pluralism, is the law. It seems as if the elementary psychic fact were not *thought* or *this thought* or *that thought*, but *my thought*, every thought being *owned*. Neither contemporaneity, nor proximity in space, nor similarity of quality and content are able to fuse thoughts together which are sundered by this barrier of belonging to different personal minds. The breaches between such thoughts are the most absolute breaches in nature. Everyone will recognize this to be true, so long as the existence of *something* corresponding to the term 'personal mind' is all that is insisted on, without any particular view of its nature being implied. On these terms the personal self rather than the thought might be treated as the immediate datum in psychology. The universal conscious fact is not 'feelings and thoughts exist,' but 'I think' and 'I feel.' No psychology, at any rate, can question the *existence* of personal selves. Thoughts connected as we feel them to be connected are *what we mean* by personal selves. The worst a psychology can do is so to interpret the nature of these selves as to rob them of their *worth*.

Consciousness is in constant change. I do not mean by this to say that no one state of mind has any duration—even if true, that would be hard to establish. What I wish to lay stress on is this, that *no state once gone can recur and be identical with what it was before*. Now we are seeing, now hearing; now reasoning, now willing; now recollecting, now expecting; now loving, now hating; and in a hundred other ways we know our minds to be alternately engaged. But all these are complex states, it may be said, produced by combination of simpler ones; do not the simpler ones follow a different law? Are not the *sensations* which we get from the same object, for example, always the same? Does not the same piano-key, struck with the same force, make us hear in the same way? Does not the same grass give us the same feeling of green, the same sky the same feeling of blue, and do we not get the same olfactory sensation no matter how many times we put our nose to the same flask of cologne? It seems a piece of metaphysical sophistry to suggest that we do not; and yet a close attention to the matter shows that *there is no proof that an incoming current ever gives us just the same bodily sensation twice.*

What is got twice is the same OBJECT. We hear the same *note* over and over again; we see the same *quality* of green, or smell the same objective perfume, or experience the same *species* of pain. The realities, concrete and abstract, physical and ideal, whose permanent existence we believe in, seem to be constantly coming up again before our thought, and lead us, in our carelessness, to suppose that our 'ideas' of them are the same ideas. When we come, some time later, to the chapter on Perception, we shall see how inveterate is our habit of simply using our sensible impressions as stepping-stones to pass over to the recognition of the realities whose presence they reveal. The grass out of the window now looks to me of the same green in the sun as in the shade, and yet a painter would have to paint one part of it dark brown, another part bright yellow, to give its real sensational effect. We take no heed, as a rule, of the different way in which the same things look and sound and smell at different distances and under different circumstances. The sameness of the *things* is what we are concerned to ascertain; and any sensations that assure us of that will probably be considered in a rough way to be the same with each other. This is what makes off-hand testimony about the subjective identity of different sensations well-nigh worthless as a proof of the fact. The entire history of what is called Sensation is a commentary on our inability to tell whether two sensible qualities received apart are exactly alike. What appeals to our attention far more than the absolute quality of an impression is its *ratio* to whatever other impressions we may have at the same time. When everything is dark a some-what less dark sensation makes us see an object as white. Helmholtz calculates that the white marble painted in a picture representing an architectural view by moonlight is, when seen by daylight, from ten to twenty thousand times brighter than the real moonlit marble would be.

Such a difference as this could never have been *sensibly* learned; it had to be inferred from a series of indirect considerations. These make us believe that our sensibility is altering all the time, so that the same object cannot easily give us the same sensation over again. We feel things differently accordingly as we are sleepy or awake, hungry or full, fresh or tired; differently at night and in the morning, differently in summer and in winter; and above all, differently in childhood, manhood, and old age. And yet we never doubt that our feelings reveal the same world, with the same sensible qualities and the same sensible things occupying it. The difference of the sensibility is shown best by the difference of our emotion about the things from one age to another, or when we are in different organic moods. What was bright and exciting becomes weary, flat, and unprofitable. The bird's song is tedious, the breeze is mournful, the sky is sad.

To these indirect presumptions that our sensations, following the mutations of our capacity for feeling, are always undergoing an essential change, must be added another presumption, based on what must happen in the brain. Every sensation corresponds to some cerebral action. For an identical sensation to recur it would have to occur the second time *in an unmodified brain*. But as this, strictly speaking, is a physiological impossibility, so is an unmodified feeling an impossibility; for to every brain-modification, however small, we suppose that there must correspond a change of equal amount in the consciousness which the brain subserves.

But if the assumption of 'simple sensations' recurring in immutable shape is so easily shown to be baseless, how much more baseless is the assumption of immutability in the larger masses of our thought!

For there it is obvious and palpable that our state of mind is never precisely the same. Every thought we have of a given fact is, strictly speaking, unique, and only bears a resemblance of kind with our other thoughts of the same fact. When the identical fact recurs, we *must* think of it in a fresh manner, see it under a somewhat different angle, apprehend it in different relations from those in which it last appeared. And the thought by which we cognize it is the thought of it-in-those-relations, a thought suffused with the consciousness of all that dim context. Often we are ourselves struck at the strange differences in our successive views of the same thing. We wonder how we ever could have opined as we did last month about a certain matter. We have outgrown the possibility of that state of mind, we know not how. From one year to another we see things in new lights. What was unreal has grown real, and what was exciting is insipid. The friends we used to care the world for are shrunken to shadows; the women once so divine, the stars, the woods, and the waters, how now so dull and common!—the young girls that brought an aura of infinity, at present hardly distinguishable existences; the pictures so empty; and as for the books, what was there to find so mysteriously significant in Goethe, or in John Mill so full of weight? Instead of all this, more zestful than ever is the work, the work; and fuller and deeper the import of common duties and of common goods.

I am sure that this concrete and total manner of regarding the mind's changes is the only true manner, difficult as it may be to carry it out in detail. If anything seems obscure about it, it will grow clearer as we advance. Meanwhile, if it be true, it is certainly also true that no two 'ideas' are ever exactly the same, which is the proposition we started to prove. The proposition is more important theoretically than it at first sight seems. For it makes it already impossible for us to follow obediently in the footprints of either the Lockian or the Herbartian school, schools which have had almost unlimited influence in Germany and among ourselves. No doubt it is often *convenient* to formulate the mental facts in an atomistic sort of way, and to treat the higher states of consciousness as if they were all built out of unchanging simple ideas which 'pass and turn again.' It is convenient often to treat curves as if they were composed of small straight lines, and electricity and nerve-force as if they were fluids. But in the one case as in the other we must never forget that we are talking symbolically, and that there is nothing in nature to answer to our words. *A permanently existing 'Idea' which makes its appearance before the footlights of consciousness at periodical intervals is as mythological an entity as the Jack of Spades.*

Within each personal consciousness, thought is sensibly continuous. I can only define 'continuous' as that which is without breach, crack, or division. The only breaches that can well be conceived to occur within the limits of a single mind would either be *interruptions, time*-gaps during which the consciousness went out; or they would be breaks in the content of the thought, so abrupt that what followed had no connection whatever with what went before. The proposition that consciousness feels continuous, means two things:

    a.   That even where there is a time-gap the consciousness after it feels as if it belonged together with the consciousness before it, as another part of the same self;

    b.   That the changes from one moment to another in the quality of the consciousness are never absolutely abrupt.

The case of the time-gaps, as the simplest, shall be taken first.

a. When Paul and Peter wake up in the same bed, and recognize that they have been asleep, each one of them mentally reaches back and makes connection with but *one* of the two streams of thought which were broken by the sleeping hours. As the current of an electrode buried in the ground unerringly finds its way to its own similarly buried mate, across no matter how much intervening earth; so Peter's present instantly finds out Peter's past, and never by mistake knits itself on to that of Paul. Paul's thought in turn is as little liable to go astray. The past thought of Peter is appropriated by the present Peter alone. He may have a *knowledge*, and a correct one too, of what Paul's last drowsy states of mind were as he sank into sleep, but it is an entirely different sort of knowledge from that which he has of his own last states. He *remembers* his own states, whilst he only *conceives* Paul's. Remembrance is like direct feeling; its object is suffused with a warmth and intimacy to which no object of mere conception ever attains. This quality of warmth and intimacy and immediacy is what Peter's *present* thought also possesses for itself. So sure as this present is me, is mine, it says, so sure is anything else that comes with the same warmth and intimacy and immediacy, me and mine. What the qualities called warmth and intimacy may in themselves be will have to be matter for future consideration. But whatever past states appear with those qualities must be admitted to receive the greeting of the present mental state, to be owned by it, and accepted as belonging together with it in a common self. This community of self is what the time-gap cannot break in twain, and is why a present thought, although not ignorant of the time-gap, can still regard itself as continuous with certain chosen portions of the past.

Consciousness, then, does not appear to itself chopped up in bits. Such words as 'chain' or 'train' do not describe it fitly as it presents itself in the first instance. It is nothing jointed; it flows. A 'river' or a 'stream' are the metaphors by which it is most naturally described. *In talking of it hereafter, let us call it the stream of thought, of consciousness, or of subjective life.*

b. But now there appears, even within the limits of the same self, and between thoughts all of which alike have this same sense of belonging together, a kind of jointing and separateness among the parts, of which this statement seems to take no account. I refer to the breaks that are produced by sudden *contrasts in the quality* of the successive segments of the stream of thought. If the words "chain" and "train" had no natural fitness in them, how came such words to be used at all? Does not a loud explosion rend the consciousness upon which it abruptly breaks, in twain? No; for even into our awareness of the thunder the awareness of the previous silence creeps and continues; for what we hear when the thunder crashes is not thunder *pure*, but thunder-breaking-upon-silence-and-contrasting-with-it. Our feeling of the same objective thunder, coming in this way, is quite different from what it would be were the thunder a continuation of previous thunder. The thunder itself we believe to abolish and exclude the silence; but the *feeling* of the thunder is also a feeling of the silence as just gone; and it would be difficult to find in the actual concrete consciousness of man a feeling so limited to the present as not to have an inkling of anything that went before.

'Substantive' and 'Transitive' States of Mind. When we take a general view of the wonderful stream of our consciousness, what strikes us first is the different pace of its parts. Like a bird's life, it seems to be an alternation of flights and perchings. The rhythm of language expresses this, where every thought is expressed in a sentence, and every sentence closed by a period. The resting-places are usually occupied by sensorial imaginations of some sort, whose peculiarity is that they can be held before the mind for an indefinite time, and contemplated without changing; the places of flight are filled with thoughts of relations, static or dynamic, that for the most part obtain between the matters contemplated in the periods of comparative rest.

Let us call the resting-places the 'substantive parts,' and the places of flight the 'transitive parts,' of the stream of thought. It then appears that our thinking tends at all times towards some other substantive part than the one from which it has just been dislodged. And we may say that the main use of the transitive parts is to lead us from one substantive conclusion to another.

Now it is very difficult, introspectively, to see the transitive parts for what they really are. If they are but flights to a conclusion, stopping them to look at them before the conclusion is reached is really annihilating them. Whilst if we wait till the conclusion *be* reached, it so exceeds them in vigor and stability that it quite eclipses and swallows them up in its glare. Let anyone try to cut a thought across in the middle and get a look at its section, and he will see how difficult the introspective observation of the transitive tracts is. The rush of the thought is so headlong that it almost always brings us up at the conclusion before we can arrest it. Or if our purpose is nimble enough and we do arrest it, it ceases forthwith to be itself. As a snowflake crystal caught in the warm hand is no longer a crystal but a drop, so, instead of catching the feeling of relation moving to its term, we find we have caught some substantive thing, usually the last word we were pronouncing, statically taken, and with its function, tendency, and particular meaning in the sentence quite evaporated. The attempt at introspective analysis in these cases is in fact like seizing a spinning top to catch its motion, or trying to turn up the gas quickly enough to see how the darkness looks. And the challenge to *produce* these transitive states of consciousness, which is sure to be thrown by doubting psychologists at anyone who contends for their existence, is as unfair as Zeno's treatment of the advocates of motion, when, asking them to point out in what place an arrow *is* when it moves, he argues the falsity of their thesis from their inability to make to so preposterous a question an immediate reply.

The results of this introspective difficulty are baleful. If to hold fast and observe the transitive parts of thought's stream be so hard, then the great blunder to which all schools are liable must be the failure to register them, and the undue emphasizing of the more substantive parts of the stream. Now the blunder has historically worked in two ways. One set of thinkers have been led by it to *Sensationalism*. Unable to lay their hands on any substantive feelings corresponding to the innumerable relations and forms of connection between the sensible things of the world, finding no *named* mental states mirroring such relations, they have for the most part denied that any such states exist; and many of them, like Hume, have gone on to deny the reality of most relations *out* of the mind as well as in it. Simple substantive 'ideas,' sensations and their copies, juxtaposed like dominoes in a game, but really separate, everything else verbal illusion,—such is the upshot of this view. The *Intellectualists*, on the other hand, unable to give up the reality of relations *extra mentem*, but equally unable to point to any distinct substantive feelings in which they were known, have made the same admission that such feelings do not exist. But they have drawn an opposite conclusion. The relations must be known, they say, in something that is no feeling, no mental 'state,' continuous and consubstantial with the subjective tissue out of which sensations and other substantive conditions of consciousness are made. They must be known by something that lies on an entirely different plane, by an *actus purus* of Thought, Intellect, or Reason, all written with capitals and considered to mean something unutterably superior to any passing perishing fact of sensibility whatever.

But from our point of view both Intellectualists and Sensationalists are wrong. If there be such things as feelings at all, *then so surely as rela-*

tions between objects exist in rerum natura, *so surely, and more surely, do feelings exist to which these relations are known.* There is not a conjunction or a preposition, and hardly an adverbial phrase, syntactic form, or inflection of voice, in human speech, that does not express some shading or other of relation which we at some moment actually feel to exist between the larger objects of our thought. If we speak objectively, it is the real relations that appear revealed; if we speak subjectively, it is the stream of consciousness that matches each of them by an inward coloring of its own. In either case the relations are numberless, and no existing language is capable of doing justice to all their shades.

We ought to say a feeling of *and*, a feeling of *if*, a feeling of *but*, and a feeling of *by*, quite as readily as we say a feeling of *blue* or a feeling of *cold*. Yet we do not: so inveterate has our habit become of recognizing the existence of the substantive parts alone, that language almost refuses to lend itself to any other use. Consider once again the analogy of the brain. We believe the brain to be an organ whose internal equilibrium is always in a state of change—the change affecting every part. The pulses of change are doubtless more violent in one place than in another, their rhythm more rapid at this time than at that. As in a kaleidoscope revolving at a uniform rate, although the figures are always rearranging themselves, there are instants during which the transformation seems minute and interstitial and almost absent, followed by others when it shoots with magical rapidity, relatively stable forms thus alternating with forms we should not distinguish if seen again; so in the brain the perpetual rearrangement must result in some forms of tension lingering relatively long, whilst others simply come and pass. But if consciousness corresponds to the fact of rearrangement itself, why, if the rearrangement stop not, should the consciousness ever cease? And if a lingering rearrangement brings with it one kind of consciousness, why should not a swift rearrangement bring another kind of consciousness as peculiar as the rearrangement itself?

The object before the mind always has a 'Fringe.' There are other unnamed modifications of consciousness just as important as the transitive states, and just as cognitive as they. Examples will show what I mean.

Suppose three successive persons say to us: 'Wait!' 'Hark!' 'Look!' Our consciousness is thrown into three quite different attitudes of expectancy, although no definite object is before it in any one of the three cases. Probably no one will deny here the existence of a real conscious affection, a sense of the direction from which an impression is about to come, although no positive impression is yet there. Meanwhile we have no names for the psychoses in question but the names hark, look, and wait.

Suppose we try to recall a forgotten name. The state of our consciousness is peculiar. There is a gap therein; but no mere gap. It is a gap that is intensely active. A sort of wraith of the name is in it, beckoning us in a given direction, making us at moments tingle with the sense of our closeness, and then letting us sink back without the longed-for term. If wrong names are proposed to us, this singularly definite gap acts immediately so as to negate them. They do not fit into its mould. And the gap of one word does not feel like the gap of another, all empty of content as both might seem necessarily to be when described as gaps. When I vainly try to recall the name of Spalding, my consciousness is far removed from what it is when I vainly try to recall the name of Bowles. There are innumerable consciousnesses of *want*, no one of which taken in itself has a name, but all different from each other. Such feeling of want is *toto coelo* other than a want of feeling: it is an intense feeling. The rhythm of a lost word may be there without a sound to clothe it; or the evanescent sense of something which is the initial vowel or consonant may mock us fitfully, without growing more distinct. Every one must know the tantalizing effect of the blank rhythm of some forgotten verse, restlessly dancing in one's mind, striving to be filled out with words.

What is that first instantaneous glimpse of someone's meaning which we have, when in vulgar phrase we say we 'twig' it? Surely an altogether specific affection of our mind. And has the reader never asked himself what kind of a mental fact is his *intention of saying a thing* before he has said it? It is an entirely definite intention, distinct from all other intentions, an absolutely distinct state of consciousness, therefore; and yet how much of it consists of definite sensorial images, either of words or of things? Hardly anything! Linger, and the words and things come into the mind; the anticipatory intention, the divination is there no more. But as the words that replace it arrive, it welcomes them successively and calls them right if they agree with it, it rejects them and calls them wrong if they do not. The intention *to-say-so-and-so* is the only name it can receive. One may admit that a good third of our psychic life consists in these rapid premonitory perspective views of schemes of thought not yet articulate. How comes it about that a man reading something aloud for the first time is able immediately to emphasize all his words aright, unless from the very first he have a sense of at least the form of the sentence yet to come, which sense is fused with his consciousness of the present word, and modifies its emphasis in his mind so as to make him give it the proper accent as he utters it? Emphasis of this kind almost altogether depends on grammatical construction. If we read 'no more,' we expect presently a 'than'; if we read 'however' it is a 'yet,' a 'still,' or a 'nevertheless' that we expect. And this foreboding of the coming verbal and grammatical scheme is so practically accurate that a reader incapable of understanding four ideas of the book he is reading aloud can nevertheless read it with the most delicately modulated expression of intelligence.

It is, the reader will see, the reinstatement of the vague and inarticulate to its proper place in our mental life which I am so anxious to press on the attention. Mr. Galton and Prof. Huxley have, as we shall see in the chapter on Imagination, made one step in advance in exploding the ridiculous theory of Hume and Berkeley that we can have no images but of perfectly definite things. Another is made if we overthrow the equally ridiculous notion that, whilst simple objective qualities are revealed to our knowledge in 'states of consciousness,' relations are not. But these reforms are not half sweeping and radical enough. What must be admitted is that the definite images of traditional psychology form but the very smallest part of our minds as they actually live. The traditional psychology talks like one who should say a river consists of nothing but pailsful, spoonsful, quartpotsful, barrelsful, and other moulded forms of water. Even were the pails and the pots all actually standing in the stream, still between them the free water would continue to flow. It is just this free water of consciousness that psychologists resolutely overlook. Every definite image in the mind is steeped and dyed in the free water that flows round it. With it goes the sense of its relations, near and remote, the dying echo of whence it came to us, the dawning sense of whither it is to lead. The significance, the value, of the image is all in this halo or penumbra that surrounds and escorts it, or rather that is fused into one with it and has become bone of its bone and flesh of its flesh; leaving it, it is true, an image of the same *thing* it was before, but making it an image of that thing newly taken and freshly understood.

Let us call the consciousness of this halo of relations around the image by the name of 'psychic overtone' or 'fringe.'

Cerebral Conditions of the 'Fringe.' Nothing is easier than to symbolize these facts in terms of brain-action. Just as the echo of the *whence*, the sense of the starting point of our thought, is probably due to the dying excitement of processes but a moment since vividly aroused; so the sense of the whither, the foretaste of the terminus, must be due to the waxing excitement of tracts or processes whose psychical correlative will a moment hence be the vividly present feature of our thought. Represented by a curve, the neurosis underlying consciousness must at any moment be like this:

Let the horizontal in Fig. 52 be the line of time, and

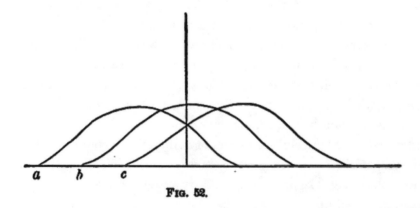

FIG. 52.

let the three curves beginning at *a*, *b*, and *c* respectively stand for the neural processes correlated with the thoughts of those three letters. Each process occupies a certain time during which its intensity waxes, culminates, and wanes. The process for *a* has not yet died out, the process for *c* has already begun, when that for *b* is culminating. At the time-instant represented by the vertical line all three processes are *present*, in the intensities shown by the curve. Those before *c*'s apex *were* more intense a moment ago; those after it *will be* more intense a moment hence. If I recite *a*, *b*, *c*, then, at the moment of uttering *b*, neither *a* nor *c* is out of my consciousness altogether, but both, after their respective fashions, 'mix their dim lights' with the stronger *b*, because their processes are both awake in some degree.

It is just like 'overtones' in music: they are not separately heard by the ear; they blend with the fundamental note, and suffuse it, and alter it; and even so do the waxing and waning brain-processes at every moment blend with and suffuse and alter the psychic effect of the processes which are at their culminating point.

The 'Topic' of the Thought. If we then consider the *cognitive function* of different states of mind, we may feel assured that the difference between those that are mere 'acquaintance' and those that are 'knowledges-*about*' is reducible almost entirely to the absence or presence of psychic fringes or overtones. Knowledge *about* a thing is knowledge of its relations. Acquaintance with it is limitation to the bare impression which it makes. Of most of its relations we are only aware in the penumbral nascent way of a 'fringe' of unarticulated affinities about it. And, before passing to the next topic in order, I must say a little of this sense of affinity, as itself one of the most interesting features of the subjective stream.

Thought may be equally rational in any sort of terms. *In all our voluntary thinking there is some* TOPIC *or* SUBJECT *about which all the* members of the thought revolve. Relation to this topic or interest is constantly felt in the fringe, and particularly the relation of harmony and discord, of furtherance or hindrance of the topic. Any thought the quality of whose fringe lets us feel ourselves 'all right,' may be considered a thought that furthers the topic. Provided we only feel its object to have a place in the scheme of relations in which the topic also lies, that is sufficient to make of it a relevant and appropriate portion of our train of ideas.

Now we may think about our topic mainly in words, or we may think about it mainly in visual or other images, but this need make no difference as regards the furtherance of our knowledge of the topic. If we only feel in the terms, whatever they be, a fringe of affinity with each other and with the topic, and if we are conscious of approaching a conclusion, we feel that our thought is rational and right. The words in every language have contracted by long association fringes of mutual repugnance or affinity with each other and with the conclusion, which run exactly parallel with like fringes in the visual, tactile, and other ideas. The most important element of these fringes is, I repeat, the mere feeling of harmony or discord, of a right or wrong direction in the thought.

If we know English and French and begin a sentence in French, all the later words that come are French; we hardly ever drop into English. And this affinity of the French words for each other is not something merely operating mechanically as a brain-law, it is something we feel at the time. Our understanding of a French sentence heard never falls to so low an ebb that we are not aware that the words linguistically belong together. Our attention can hardly so wander that if an English word be suddenly introduced we shall not start at the change. Such a vague sense as this of the words belonging together is the very minimum of fringe that can accompany them, if 'thought' at all. Usually the vague perception that all the words we hear belong to the same language and to the same special vocabulary in that language, and that the grammatical sequence is familiar, is practically equivalent to an admission that what we hear is sense. But if an unusual foreign word be introduced, if the grammar trip, or if a term from an incongruous vocabulary suddenly appear, such as 'rat-trap' or 'plumber's bill' in a philosophical discourse, the sentence detonates as it were, we receive a shock from the incongruity, and the drowsy assent is gone. The feeling of rationality in these cases seems rather a negative than a positive thing, being the mere absence of shock, or sense of discord, between the terms of thought.

Conversely, if words do belong to the same vocabulary, and if the grammatical structure is correct, sentences with absolutely no meaning may be uttered in good faith and pass unchallenged. Discourses at prayer-meetings, re-shuffling the same collection of cant phrases, and the whole genus of penny-a-line-isms and newspaper-reporter's flourishes give illustrations of this. "The birds filled the tree-tops with their morning song, making the air moist, cool, and pleasant," is a sentence I remember reading once in a report of some athletic exercises in Jerome Park. It was probably written unconsciously by the hurried reporter, and read uncritically by many readers.

We see, then, that it makes little or no difference in what sort of mind-stuff, in what quality of imagery, our thinking goes on. The only images *intrinsically* important are the halting-places, the substantive conclusions, provisional or final, of the thought. Throughout all the rest of the stream, the feelings of relation are everything, and the terms related almost naught. These feelings of relation, these psychic overtones, halos, suffusions, or fringes about the terms, may be the same in very different systems of imagery. A diagram may help to accentuate this in difference of the mental means where the end is the same.

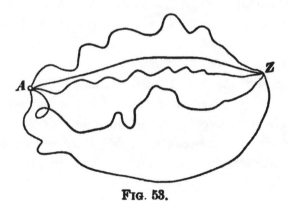

Fig. 53.

Let *A* be some experience from which a number of thinkers start. Let *Z* be the practical conclusion rationally inferrible from it. One gets to this conclusion by one line, another by another; one follows a course of

English, another of German, verbal imagery. With one, visual images predominate; with another, tactile. Some trains are tinged with emotions, others not; some are very abridged, synthetic and rapid; others, hesitating and broken into many steps. But when the penultimate terms of all the trains, however differing *inter se*, finally shoot into the same conclusion, we say, and rightly say, that all the thinkers have had substantially the same thought. It would probably astound each of them beyond measure to be let into his neighbor's mind and to find how different the scenery there was from that in his own.

The last peculiarity to which attention is to be drawn in this first rough description of thought's stream is that—

Consciousness is always interested more in one part of its object than in another, and welcomes and rejects, or chooses, all the while it thinks. The phenomena of selective attention and of deliberative will are of course patent examples of this choosing activity. But few of us are aware how incessantly it is at work in operations not ordinarily called by these names. Accentuation and Emphasis are present in every perception we have. We find it quite impossible to disperse our attention impartially over a number of impressions. A monotonous succession of sonorous strokes is broken up into rhythms, now of one sort, now of another, by the different accent which we place on different strokes. The simplest of these rhythms is the double one, tick-tock, tick-tock, tick-tock. Dots dispersed on a surface are perceived in rows and groups. Lines separate into diverse figures. The ubiquity of the distinctions, *this* and *that*, *here* and *there*, *now* and *then*, in our minds is the result of our laying the same selective emphasis on parts of place and time.

But we do far more than emphasize things, and unite some, and keep others apart. We actually *ignore* most of the things before us. Let me briefly show how this goes on.

To begin at the bottom, what are our very senses themselves, as we saw on pp. 10–12 [of original edition—Ed.], but organs of selection? Out of the infinite chaos of movements, of which physics teaches us that the outer world consists, each sense-organ picks out those which fall within certain limits of velocity. To these it responds, but ignores the rest as completely as if they did not exist. Out of what is in itself an undistinguishable, swarming *continuum*, devoid of distinction or emphasis, our senses make for us, by attending to this motion and ignoring that, a world full of contrasts, of sharp accents, of abrupt changes, of picturesque light and shade.

If the sensations we receive from a given organ have their causes thus picked out for us by the conformation of the organ's termination, Attention, on the other hand, out of all the sensations yielded, picks out certain ones as worthy of notice and suppresses all the rest. We notice only those sensations which are signs to us of *things* which happen practically or aesthetically to interest us, to which we therefore give substantive names, and which we exalt to this exclusive status of independence and dignity. But in itself, apart from my interest, a particular dust-wreath on a windy day is just as much of an individual *thing*, and just as much or as little deserves an individual name, as my own body does.

And then, among the sensations we get from each separate thing, what happens? The mind selects again. It chooses certain of the sensations to represent the thing most *truly*, and considers the rest as its appearances, modified by the conditions of the moment. Thus my table-top is named *square*, after but one of an infinite number of retinal sensations which it yields, the rest of them being sensations of two acute and two obtuse angles; but I call the latter *perspective* views, and the four right angles the *true* form of the table, and erect the attribute squareness into the table's essence, for aesthetic reasons of my own. In like manner, the real form of the circle is deemed to be the sensation it gives when the line of vision is perpendicular to its center—all its other sensations are *signs* of this sensation. The real sound of the cannon is the sensation it makes when the ear is close by. The real color of the brick is the sensation it gives when the eye looks squarely at it from a near point, out of the sunshine and yet not in the gloom; under other circumstances it gives us other color-sensations which are but signs of this—we then see it looks pinker or bluer than it really is. The reader knows no object which he does not represent to himself by preference as in some typical attitude, of some normal size, at some characteristic distance, of some standard tint, etc., etc. But all these essential characteristics, which together form for us the genuine objectivity of the thing and are contrasted with what we call the subjective sensations it may yield us at a given moment, are mere sensations like the latter. The mind chooses to suit itself, and decides what particular sensation shall be held more real and valid than all the rest.

Next, in a world of objects thus individualized by our mind's selective industry, what is called our 'experience' is almost entirely determined by our habits of attention. A thing may be present to a man a hundred times, but if he persistently fails to notice it, it cannot be said to enter into his experience. We are all seeing flies, moths, and beetles by the thousand, but to whom, save an entomologist, do they say anything distinct? On the other hand, a thing met only once in a lifetime may leave an indelible experience in the memory. Let four men make a tour in Europe. One will bring home only picturesque impressions—costumes and colors, parks and views and works of architecture, pictures and statues. To another all this will be non-existent; and distances and prices, populations and drainage-arrangements, door- and window-fastenings, and other useful statistics will take their place. A third will give a rich account of the theatres, restaurants, and public halls, and naught besides; whilst the fourth will perhaps have been so wrapped in his own subjective broodings as to be able to tell little more than a few names of places through which he passed. Each has selected, out of the same mass of presented objects, those which suited his private interest and has made his experience thereby.

If now, leaving the empirical combination of objects, we ask how the mind proceeds *rationally* to connect them, we find selection again to be omnipotent. In a future chapter we shall see that all Reasoning depends on the ability of the mind to break up the totality of the phenomenon reasoned about, into parts, and to pick out from among these the particular one which, in the given emergency, may lead to the proper conclusion. The man of genius is he who will always stick in his bill at the right point, and bring it out with the right element—'reason' if the emergency be theoretical, 'means' if it be practical—transfixed upon it.

If now we pass to the aesthetic department, our law is still more obvious. The artist notoriously selects his items, rejecting all tones, colors, shapes, which do not harmonize with each other and with the main purpose of his work. That unity, harmony, 'convergence of characters' as M. Taine calls it, which gives to works of art their superiority over works of nature, is wholly due to *elimination*. Any natural subject will do, if the artist has wit enough to pounce upon some one feature of it as characteristic, and suppress all merely accidental items which do not harmonize with this.

Ascending still higher, we reach the plane of Ethics, where choice reigns notoriously supreme. An act has no ethical quality whatever unless it be chosen out of several all equally possible. To sustain the arguments for the good course and keep them ever before us, to stifle our longing for more flowery ways, to keep the foot unflinchingly on the arduous path, these are characteristic ethical energies. But more than these; for these but deal with the means of compassing interests already felt by the man to be supreme. The ethical energy *par excellence* has to go farther and choose which *interest* out of several, equally coercive, shall become supreme. The issue here is of the utmost pregnancy, for it decides a man's entire career. When he debates, Shall I commit this crime? choose that profession? accept that office, or marry this fortune?—his choice really lies between one of several equally possible future Characters. What he shall *become* is fixed by the conduct of this moment. Schopenhauer, who enforces his determinism by the argument that with a given fixed character only one reaction is possible under given circumstances, forgets that, in these critical ethical moments, what consciously *seems* to be in question is the complexion of the character itself. The problem with the man is less what act he shall now resolve to do than what being he shall now choose to become.

Taking human experience in a general way, the choosings of different men are to a great extent the same. The race as a whole largely agrees as to what it shall notice and name; and among the noticed parts we select in much the same way for accentuation and preference, or subordination and dislike. There is, however, one entirely extraordinary case in which no two men ever are known to choose alike. One great splitting of the whole universe into two halves is made by each of us; and for each of us almost all of the interest attaches to one of the halves; but we all draw the line of division between them in a different place. When I say that we all call the two halves by the same names, and that those names are 'me' and 'not-me' respectively, it will at once be seen what I mean. The altogether unique kind of interest which each human mind feels in those parts of creation which it can call me or mine may be a moral riddle, but it is a fundamental psychological fact. No mind can take the same interest in his neighbor's me as in his own. The neighbor's me falls together with all the rest of things in one foreign mass against which his own me stands out in startling relief. Even the trodden worm, as Lotze somewhere says, contrasts his own suffering self with the whole remaining universe, though he have no clear conception either of himself or of what the universe may be. He is for me a mere part of the world; for him it is I who am the mere part. Each of us dichotomizes the Kosmos in a different place.

Descending now to finer work than this first general sketch, let us in the next chapter try to trace the psychology of this fact of self-consciousness to which we have thus once more been led.

3

The Self

The Me and the I. Whatever I may be thinking of, I am always at the same time more or less aware of *myself*, of my *personal existence*. At the same time it is *I* who am aware; so that the total self of me, being as it were duplex, partly known and partly knower, partly object and partly subject, must have two aspects discriminated in it, of which for shortness we may call one the Me and the other the *I*. I call these 'discriminated aspects' and not separate things, because the identity of *I* with *me*, even in the very act of their discrimination, is perhaps the most ineradicable dictum of common-sense, and must not be undermined by our terminology here at the outset, whatever we may come to think of its validity at our inquiry's end.

I shall therefore treat successively of A) the self as known, or the *me*, the 'empirical ego' as it is sometimes called; and of B) the self as knower, or the *I*, the pure ego of certain authors.

A) THE SELF AS KNOWN

The Empirical Self or Me. Between what a man calls *me* and what he simply calls *mine* the line is difficult to draw. We feel and act about certain things that are ours very much as we feel and act about ourselves. Our fame, our children, the work of our hands, may be as dear to us as our bodies are, and arouse the same feelings and the same acts of reprisal if attacked. And our bodies themselves are they simply ours, or are they *us?* Certainly men have been ready to disown their very bodies and to regard them as mere vestures, or even as prisons of clay from which they should some day be glad to escape.

We see then that we are dealing with a fluctuating material; the same object being sometimes treated as a part of me, at other times as simply mine, and then again as if I had nothing to do with it at all. *In its widest possible sense*, however, *a man's Me is the sum total of all that he CAN call his*, not only his body and his psychic powers, but his clothes and his house, his wife and children, his ancestors and friends, his reputation and works, his lands and horses, and yacht and bank-account. All these things give him the same emotions. If they wax and prosper, he feels triumphant; if they dwindle and die away, he feels cast down,—not necessarily in the same degree for each thing, but in much the same way for all. Understanding the Me in this widest sense, we may begin by dividing the history of it into three parts, relating respectively to—

a.   Its constituents;
b.   The feelings and emotions they arouse,—*self-appreciation*;
c.   The acts to which they prompt,—*self-seeking and self-preservation.*

a. The constituents of the Me may be divided into two classes, those which make up respectively—

The material me;
The social me; and
The spiritual me.

The Material Me. The *body* is the innermost part of the material me in each of us; and certain parts of the body seem more intimately ours than the rest. The clothes come next. The old saying that the human person is composed of three parts—soul, body and clothes—is more than a joke. We so appropriate our clothes and identify ourselves with them that there are few of us who, if asked to choose between having a beautiful body clad in raiment perpetually shabby and unclean, and having an ugly and blemished form always spotlessly attired, would not hesitate a moment before making a decisive reply. Next, our immediate family is a part of ourselves. Our father and mother, our wife and babes, are bone of our bone and flesh of our flesh. When they die, a part of our very selves is gone. If they do anything wrong, it is our shame. If they are insulted, our anger flashes forth as readily as if we stood in their place. Our home comes next. Its scenes are part of our life; its aspects awaken the tenderest feelings of affection; and we do not easily forgive the stranger who, in visiting it, finds fault with its arrangements or treats it with contempt. All these different things are the objects of instinctive preferences coupled with the most important practical interests of life. We all have a blind impulse to watch over our body, to deck it with clothing of an ornamental sort, to cherish parents, wife, and babes, and to find for ourselves a house of our own which we may live in and 'improve.'

An equally instinctive impulse drives us to collect property; and the collections thus made become, with different degrees of intimacy, parts of our empirical selves. The parts of our wealth most intimately ours are those which are saturated with our labor. There are few men who would not feel personally annihilated if a life-long construction of their hands or brains—say an entomological collection or an extensive work in manuscript—were suddenly swept away. The miser feels similarly towards his gold; and although it is true that a part of our depression at the loss of possessions is due to our feeling that we must now go without certain goods that we expected the possessions to bring in their train, yet in every case there remains, over and above this, a sense of the shrinkage of our personality, a partial conversion of ourselves to nothingness, which is a psychological phenomenon by itself. We are all at once assimilated to the tramps and poor devils whom we so despise, and at the same time removed farther than ever away from the happy sons of earth who lord it over land and sea and men in the full-blown lustihood that wealth and power can give, and before whom, stiffen ourselves as we will by appealing to anti-snobbish first principles, we cannot escape an emotion, open or sneaking, of respect and dread.

The Social Me. A man's social me is the recognition which he gets from his mates. We are not only gregarious animals, liking to be in sight of our fellows, but we have an innate propensity to get ourselves noticed, and noticed favorably, by our kind. No more fiendish punishment could be devised, were such a thing physically possible, than that one should be turned loose in society and remain absolutely unnoticed by all the members thereof. If no one turned round when we entered, answered when we spoke, or minded what we did, but if every person we met 'cut us dead,' and acted as if we were non-existing things, a kind of rage and impotent despair would ere long well up in us, from which the cruelest bodily tortures would be a relief; for these would make us feel that, however bad might be our plight, we had not sunk to such a depth as to be unworthy of attention at all.

Properly speaking, *a man has as many social selves as there are individuals who recognize him* and carry an image of him in their mind. To wound any one of these his images is to wound him. But as the individuals who carry the images fall naturally into classes, we may practically say that he has as many different social selves as there are distinct *groups* of persons about whose opinion he cares. He generally shows a different side of himself to each of these different groups. Many a youth who is demure enough before his parents and teachers, swears and swaggers like a pirate among his 'tough' young friends. We do not show ourselves to our children as to our club-companions, to our customers as to the laborers we employ, to our own masters and employers as to our intimate friends. From this there results what practically is a division of the man into several selves; and this may be a discordant splitting, as where one is afraid to let one set of his acquaintances know him as he is elsewhere; or it may be a perfectly harmonious division of labor, as where one tender to his children is stern to the soldiers or prisoners under his command.

The most peculiar social self which one is apt to have is in the mind of the person one is in love with. The good or bad fortunes of this self cause the most intense elation and dejection unreasonable enough as measured by every other standard than that of the organic feeling of the individual. To his own consciousness he *is* not, so long as this particular social self fails to get recognition, and when it is recognized his contentment passes all bounds.

A man's *fame*, good or bad, and his *honor* or dishonor, are names for one of his social selves. The particular social self of a man called his honor is usually the result of one of those splittings of which we have spoken. It is his image in the eyes of his own 'set,' which exalts or condemns him as he conforms or not to certain requirements that may not be made of one in another walk of life. Thus a layman may abandon a city infected with cholera; but a priest or a doctor would think such an act incompatible with his honor. A soldier's honor requires him to fight or to die under circumstances where another man can apologize or run away with no stain upon his social self. A judge, a statesman, are in like manner debarred by the honor of their cloth from entering into pecuniary relations perfectly honorable to persons in private life. Nothing is commoner than to hear people discriminate between their different selves of this sort: "As a man I pity you, but as an official I must show you no mercy"; "As a politician I regard him as an ally, but as a moralist I loathe him"; etc., etc. What may be called 'club-opinion' is one of the very strongest forces in life. The thief must not steal from other thieves; the gambler must pay his gambling-debts, though he pay no other debts in the world. The code of honor of fashionable society has throughout history been full of permissions as well as of vetoes, the only reason for following either of which is that so we best serve one of our social selves. You must not lie in general, but you may lie as much as you please if asked about your relations with a lady; you must accept a challenge from an equal, but if challenged by an inferior you may laugh him to scorn: these are examples of what is meant.

The Spiritual Me. By the 'spiritual me,' so far as it belongs to the empirical self, I mean no one of my passing states of consciousness. I mean rather the entire collection of my states of consciousness, my psychic faculties and dispositions taken concretely. This collection can at any moment become an object to my thought at that moment and awaken emotions like those awakened by any of the other portions of the Me. When *we think of ourselves as thinkers*, all the other ingredients of our Me seem relatively external possessions. Even within the spiritual *Me* some ingredients seem more external than others. Our capacities for sensation, for example, are less intimate possessions, so to speak, than our emotions and desires; our intellectual processes are less intimate than our volitional decisions. The more *active-feeling* states of consciousness are thus the more central portions of the spiritual Me. The very core and nucleus of our self, as we know it, the very sanctuary of our life, is the sense of activity which certain inner states possess. This sense of activity is often held to be a direct revelation of the living substance of our Soul. Whether this be so or not is an ulterior question. I wish now only to lay down the peculiar *internality* of whatever states possess this quality of seeming to be active. It is as if they *went out to meet* all the other elements of our experience. In thus feeling about them probably all men agree.

*   *   *   *

B) THE SELF AS KNOWER

The I, or 'pure ego,' is a very much more difficult subject of inquiry than the Me. It is that which at any given moment *is* conscious, whereas the Me is only one of the things which it is conscious *of*. In other words, it is the *Thinker*; and the question immediately comes up, *what* is the thinker? Is it the passing state of consciousness itself, or is it something deeper and less mutable? The passing state we have seen to be the very embodiment of change (see p. 155 ff. [this volume p. 70 ff.]). Yet each of us spontaneously considers that by 'I,' he means something always the same. This has led most philosophers to postulate behind the passing state of consciousness a permanent Substance or Agent whose modification or act it is. This Agent is the thinker; the 'state' is only its instrument or means. 'Soul,' 'transcendental Ego,' 'Spirit,' are so many names for this more permanent sort of Thinker. Not discriminating them just yet, let us proceed to define our idea of the passing state of consciousness more clearly.

  The Unity of the Passing Thought. Already, in speaking of 'sensations,' from the point of view of Fechner's idea of measuring them, we saw that there was no ground for calling them compounds. But what is true of sensations cognizing simple qualities is also true of thoughts with complex objects composed of many parts. This proposition unfortunately runs counter to a wide-spread prejudice, and will have to be defended at some length. Common-sense, and psychologists of almost every school, have agreed that whenever an object of thought contains many elements, the thought itself must be made up of just as many ideas, one idea for each element, all fused together in appearance, but really separate.

"There can be no difficulty in admitting that association *does* form the ideas of an indefinite number of individuals into one complex idea," says James Mill, "because it is an acknowledged fact. Have we not the idea of an army? And is not that precisely the ideas of an indefinite number of men formed into one idea?"

Similar quotations might be multiplied, and the reader's own first impressions probably would rally to their support. Suppose, for example, he thinks that "the pack of cards is on the table." If he begins to reflect, he is as likely as not to say: "Well, isn't that a thought of the pack of cards? Isn't it of the cards as included in the pack? Isn't it of the table? And of the legs of the table as well? Hasn't my thought, then, all these parts—one part for the pack and another for the table? And within the pack-part a part for each card, as within the table-part a part for each leg? And isn't each of these parts an idea? And can thought, then, be anything but an assemblage or pack of ideas, each answering to some element of what it knows?"

Plausible as such considerations may seem, it is astonishing how little force they have. In assuming a pack of ideas, each cognizant of some one element of the fact one has assumed, nothing has been assumed which knows the whole fact *at once*. The idea which, on the hypothesis of the pack of ideas, knows, *e.g.*, the ace of spades must be ignorant of the leg of the table, since to account for that knowledge another special idea is by the same hypothesis invoked; and so on with the rest of the ideas, all equally ignorant of each other's objects. And yet in the actual living human mind what knows the cards also knows the table, its legs, etc., for all these things are known in relation to each other and at once. Our notion of the abstract numbers eight, four, two is as truly one feeling of the mind as our notion of simple unity. Our idea of a couple is not a couple of ideas. "But," the reader may say, "is not the taste of lemonade composed of that of lemon plus that of sugar?" No! I reply, this is taking the combining of objects for that of feelings. The physical lemonade contains both the lemon and the sugar, but its taste does not contain their tastes; for if there are any two things which are certainly *not* present in the taste of lemonade, those are the pure lemon-sour on the one hand and the pure sugar-sweet on the other. These tastes are absent utterly. A taste somewhat *like* both of them is there, but that is a distinct state of mind altogether.

Distinct mental states cannot 'fuse.' But not only is the notion that our ideas are combinations of smaller ideas improbable, it is logically unintelligible; it leaves out the essential features of all the 'combinations' which we actually know.

All the 'combinations' which we actually know are EFFECTS, wrought by the units said to be 'combined,' UPON SOME ENTITY OTHER THAN THEMSELVES. Without this feature of a medium or vehicle, the notion of combination has no sense.

In other words, no possible number of entities (call them as you like, whether forces, material particles, or mental elements) can sum *themselves* together. Each remains, in the sum, what it always was; and the sum itself exists only *for a bystander* who happens to overlook the units and to apprehend the sum as such; or else it exists in the shape of some other effect on an entity external to the sum itself. When H_2 and O are said to combine into 'water,' and thenceforward to exhibit new properties, the 'water' is just the old atoms in the new position, H-O-H; the 'new properties' are just their combined *effects*, when in this position, upon external media, such as our sense-organs and the various reagents on which water may exert its properties and be known. Just so, the strength of many men may combine when they pull upon one rope, of many muscular fibres when they pull upon one tendon.

In the parallelogram of forces, the 'forces' do not combine *themselves* into the diagonal resultant; a *body* is needed on which they may impinge, to exhibit their resultant effect. No more do musical sounds combine *per se* into concords or discords. Concord and discord are names for their combined effects on that external medium, the *ear*.

Where the elemental units are supposed to be feelings, the case is in no wise altered. Take a hundred of them, shuffle them and pack them as close together as you can (whatever that may mean); still each remains the same feeling it always was, shut in its own skin, windowless, ignorant of what the other feelings are and mean. There would be a hundred-and-first feeling there, if, when a group or series of such feelings were set up, a consciousness *belonging to the group as such* should emerge, and this one hundred and first feeling would be a totally new fact. The one hundred original feelings might, by a curious physical law, be a signal for its *creation*, when they came together—we often have to learn things separately before we know them as a sum—but they would have no substantial identity with the new feeling, nor it with them; and one could never deduce the one from the others, or (in any intelligible sense) say that they *evolved* it out of themselves.

Take a sentence of a dozen words, and take twelve men and tell to each one word. Then stand the men in a row or jam them in a bunch, and let each think of his word as intently as he will; nowhere will there be a consciousness of the whole sentence. We talk, it is true, of the 'spirit of the age' and the 'sentiment of the people,' and in various ways we hypostatize 'public opinion.' But we know this to be symbolic speech, and never dream that the spirit, opinion, or sentiment constitutes a consciousness other than, and additional to, that of the several individuals whom the words 'age,' 'people,' or 'public' denote. The private minds do not agglomerate into a higher compound mind. This has always been the invincible contention of the spiritualists against the associationists in psychology. The associationists say the mind is constituted by a multiplicity of distinct 'ideas' *associated* into a unity. There is, they say, an idea of *a*, and also an idea of *b*. Therefore, they say, there is an idea of *a* + *b*, or of *a* and *b* together. Which is like saying that the mathematical square of *a* plus that of *b* is equal to the square of *a* + *b*, a palpable untruth. Idea of *a* + idea of *b* is not identical with idea of (*a* + *b*). It is one, they are two; in it, what knows *a* also knows *b*; in them, what knows *a* is expressly posited as not knowing *b*; etc. In short, the two separate ideas can never by any logic be made to figure as one idea. If one idea (of *a* + *b*, for example) come as a matter of fact after the two separate ideas (of *a* and of *b*), then we must hold it to be as direct a product of the later conditions as the two separate ideas were of the earlier conditions.

The simplest thing, therefore, if we are to assume the existence of a stream of consciousness at all, would be to suppose that things that are known together are known in single pulses of that stream. The things may be many, and may occasion many currents in the brain. But the psychic phenomenon correlative to these many currents is one integral 'state,' transitive or substantive (see p. 161 [this volume p. 76]), to which the many things appear.

The Soul as a Combining Medium. The spiritualists in philosophy have been prompt to see that things which are known together are known by one *something*, but that some thing, they say, is no mere passing thought, but a simple and permanent spiritual being on which many ideas combine their effects. It makes no difference in this connection whether this being be called Soul, Ego, or Spirit, in either case its chief function is that of a combining medium. This is a different vehicle of knowledge from that in which we just said that the mystery of knowing things together might be most simply lodged. Which is the real knower, this permanent being, or our passing state? If we had other grounds, not yet considered, for admitting the Soul into our psychology, then getting there on those grounds, she might turn out to be the knower too. But if there be no *other* grounds for admitting the Soul, we had better cling to our passing 'states' as the exclusive agents of knowledge; for we have to assume their existence anyhow in psychology, and the knowing of many things together is just as well accounted for when we call it one of their functions as when we call it a reaction of the Soul. *Explained* it is not by either conception, and has to figure in psychology as a datum that is ultimate.

But there are other alleged grounds for admitting the Soul into psychology, and the chief of them is

The Sense of Personal Identity. In the last chapter it was stated (see p. 154 [this volume p. 69]) that the thoughts which we actually know to exist do not fly about loose, but seem each to belong to some one thinker and not to another. Each thought, out of a multitude of other thoughts of which it may think, is able to distinguish those which belong to it from those which do not. The former have a warmth and intimacy about them of which the latter are completely devoid, and the result is a Me of yesterday, judged to be in some peculiarly subtle sense the *same* with the I who now make the judgment. As a mere subjective phenomenon the judgment presents no special mystery. It belongs to the great class of judgments of sameness; and there is nothing more remarkable in making a judgment of sameness in the first person than in the second or the third. The intellectual operations seem essentially alike, whether 'I say I am the same as I was,' or whether I say 'the pen is the same as it was, yesterday.' It is as easy to think this as to think the opposite and say 'neither of us is the same.' The only question which we have to consider is whether it be a right judgment. *Is the sameness predicated really there?*

Sameness in the Self as Known. If in the sentence "I am the same that I was yesterday" we take the 'I' broadly, it is evident that in many ways I am *not* the same. As a concrete Me, I am somewhat different from what I was: then hungry, now full; then walking, now at rest; then poorer, now richer; then younger, now older; etc. And yet in other ways I *am* the same, and we may call these the essential ways. My name and profession and relations to the world are identical, my face, my faculties and store of memories, are practically indistinguishable, now and then. Moreover the Me of now and the Me of then are *continuous*: the alterations were gradual and never affected the whole of me at once. So far, then, my personal identity is just like the sameness predicated of any other aggregate thing. It is a conclusion grounded either on the resemblance in essential respects, or on the continuity of the phenomena compared. And it must not be taken to mean more than these grounds warrant, or treated as a sort of metaphysical or absolute Unity in which all differences are overwhelmed. The past and present selves compared are the same just so far as they *are* the same, and no farther. They are the same in *kind*. But this generic sameness coexists with generic differences just as real; and if from the one point of view I am one self, from another I am quite as truly many. Similarly of the attribute of continuity: it gives to the self the unity of mere connectedness, or unbrokenness, a perfectly definite phenomenal thing—but it gives not a jot or tittle more.

Sameness in the Self as Knower. But all this is said only of the Me, or Self as known. In the judgment 'I am the same,' etc., the 'I' was taken broadly as the concrete person. Suppose, however, that we take it narrowly as the *Thinker*, as '*that to which*' all the concrete determinations of the Me belong and are known: does there not then appear an absolute identity at different times? That something which at every moment goes out and knowingly appropriates the *Me* of the past, and discards the non-me as foreign, is it not a permanent abiding principle of spiritual activity identical with itself wherever found?

That it is such a principle is the reigning doctrine both of philosophy and common-sense, and yet reflection finds it difficult to justify the idea. *If there were no passing states of consciousness*, then indeed we might suppose an abiding principle, absolutely one with itself, to be the ceaseless thinker in each one of us. But if the states of consciousness be accorded as realities, no such 'substantial' identity in the thinker need be supposed. Yesterday's and today's states of consciousness have no *substantial* identity, for when one is here the other is irrevocably dead and gone. But they have a *functional* identity, for both know the same objects, and so far as the by-gone me is one of those objects, they react upon it in an identical way, greeting it and calling it *mine*, and opposing it to all the other things they know. This functional identity seems really the only sort of identity in the thinker which the facts require us to suppose. Successive thinkers, numerically distinct, but all aware of the same past in the same way, form an adequate vehicle for all the experience of personal unity and sameness which we actually have. And just such a train of successive thinkers is the stream of mental states (each with its complex object cognized and emotional and selective reaction thereupon) which psychology treated as a natural science has to assume (see p. 2).

The logical conclusion seems then to be that *the states of consciousness are all that psychology needs to do her work with. Metaphysics or theology may prove the Soul to exist; but for psychology the hypothesis of such a substantial principle of unity is superfluous.*

How the I appropriates the Me. But *why* should each successive mental state appropriate the same past Me? I spoke a while ago of my own past experiences appearing to me with a 'warmth and intimacy' which the experiences thought of by me as having occurred to other people lack. This leads us to the answer sought. My present Me is felt with warmth and intimacy. The heavy warm mass of my body is there, and the nucleus of the 'spiritual me,' the sense of intimate activity (p. 184 [this volume p. 93]), is there. We cannot realize our present self without simultaneously feeling one or other of these two things. Any other object of thought which brings these two things with it into consciousness will be thought with a warmth and an intimacy like those which cling to the present me.

Any *distant* object which fulfills this condition will be thought with such warmth and intimacy. But which distant objects *do* fulfill the condition, when represented?

Obviously those, and only those, which fulfilled it when they were alive. *Them* we shall still represent with the animal warmth upon them; to them may possibly still cling the flavor of the inner activity taken in the act. And by a natural consequence, we shall assimilate them to each other and to the warm and intimate self we now feel within us as we think, and separate them as a collection from whatever objects have not this mark, much as out of a herd of cattle let loose for the winter on some wide Western prairie the owner picks out and sorts together, when the round-up comes in the spring, all the beasts on which he finds his own particular brand. Well, just such objects are the past experiences which I now call mine. Other men's experiences, no matter how much I may know about them, never bear this vivid, this peculiar brand. This is why Peter, awakening in the same bed with Paul, and recalling what both had in mind before they went to sleep, re-identifies and appropriates the 'warm' ideas as his, and is never tempted to confuse them with those cold and pale-appearing ones which he ascribes to Paul. As well might he confound Paul's body, which he only sees, with his own body, which he sees but also feels. Each of us when he awakens says, Here's the same old Me again, just as he says, Here's the same old bed, the same old room, the same old world.

And similarly in our waking hours, though each pulse of consciousness dies away and is replaced by another, yet that other, among the things it knows, knows its own predecessor, and finding it "warm," in the way we have described, greets it, saying: "Thou art *mine*, and part of the same self with me." Each later thought, knowing and including thus the thoughts that went before, is the final receptacle—and appropriating them is the final owner—of all that they contain and own. As Kant says, it is as if elastic balls were to have not only motion but knowledge of it, and a first ball were to transmit both its motion and its consciousness to a second, which took both up into *its* consciousness and passed them to a third, until the last ball held all that the other balls had held, and realized it as its own. It is this trick which the nascent thought has of immediately taking up the expiring thought and 'adopting' it, which leads to the appropriation of most of the remoter constituents of the self. Who owns the last self owns the self before the last, for what possesses the possessor possesses the possessed. It is impossible to discover any *verifiable* features in personal identity which this sketch does not contain, impossible to imagine how any transcendent principle of Unity (were such a principle there) could shape matters to any other result, or be known by any other fruit, than just this production of a stream of consciousness each successive part of which should know, and knowing, hug to itself and adopt, all those that went before, thus standing as the *representative* of an entire past stream with which it is in no wise to be identified.

*   *   *   *

Review, and Psychological Conclusion. To sum up this long chapter: The consciousness of Self involves a stream of thought, each part of which as 'I' can remember those which went before, know the things they knew, and care paramountly for certain ones among them as '*Me*,' and *appropriate to these* the rest. This Me is an empirical aggregate of things objectively known. The *I* which knows them cannot itself be an aggregate; neither for psychological purposes need it be an unchanging metaphysical entity like the Soul, or a principle like the transcendental Ego, viewed as 'out of time.' It is a *thought*, at each moment different from that of the last moment, but *appropriative* of the latter, together with all that the latter called its own. All the experiential facts find their place in this description, unencumbered with any hypothesis save that of the existence of passing thoughts or states of mind.

If passing thoughts be the directly verifiable existents which no school has hitherto doubted them to be, then they are the only 'Knower' of which Psychology, treated as a natural science, need take any account. The only pathway that I can discover for bringing in a more transcendental Thinker would be to deny that we have any such *direct* knowledge of the existence of our states of consciousness as common-sense supposes us to possess. The existence of the 'states' in question would then be a mere hypothesis, or one way of asserting that there *must be* a knower correlative to all this known; but the problem *who that knower is* would have become a metaphysical problem. With the question once stated in these terms, the notion either of a Spirit of the world which thinks through us, or that of a set of individual substantial souls, must be considered as *prima facie* on a par with our own 'psychological' solution and discussed impartially. I myself believe that room for much future inquiry lies in this direction. The 'states of mind' which every psychologist believes in are by no means clearly apprehensible, if distinguished from their objects. But to doubt them lies beyond the scope of our natural-science (see p. 1) point of view. And in this book the provisional solution which we have reached must be the final word: the thoughts themselves are the thinkers.

4

Does 'Consciousness' Exist?

'Thoughts' and 'things' are names for two sorts of object, which common sense will always find contrasted and will always practically oppose to each other. Philosophy, reflecting on the contrast, has varied in the past in her explanations of it, and may be expected to vary in the future. At first, 'spirit and matter,' 'soul and body,' stood for a pair of equipollent substances quite on a par in weight and interest. But one day Kant undermined the soul and brought in the transcendental ego, and ever since then the bipolar relation has been very much off its balance. The transcendental ego seems nowadays in rationalist quarters to stand for everything, in empiricist quarters for almost nothing. In the hands of such writers as Schuppe, Rehmke, Natorp, Münsterberg—at any rate in his earlier writings, Schubert-Soldern and others, the spiritual principle attenuates itself to a thoroughly ghostly condition, being only a name for the fact that the 'content' of experience *is known*. It loses personal form and activity—these passing over to the content— becomes a bare *Bewusstheit* or *Bewusstsein überhaupt*, of which in its own right absolutely nothing can be said.

I believe that 'consciousness,' when once it has evaporated to this estate of pure diaphaneity, is on the point of disappearing altogether. It is the name of a nonentity, and has no right to a place among first principles. Those who still cling to it are clinging to a mere echo, the faint rumor left behind by the disappearing 'soul' upon the air of philosophy. During the past year, I have read a number of articles whose authors seemed just on the point of abandoning the notion of consciousness,[1] and substituting for it that of an absolute experience not due to two factors. But they were not quite radical enough, not quite daring enough in their negations. For twenty years past I have mistrusted "consciousness" as an entity; for seven or eight years past I have suggested its non-existence to my students, and tried to give them its pragmatic equivalent in realities of experience. It seems to me that the hour is ripe for it to be openly and universally discarded.

To deny plumply that 'consciousness' exists seems so absurd on the face of it—for undeniably 'thoughts' do exist—that I fear some readers will follow me no farther. Let me then immediately explain that I mean only to deny that the word stands for an entity, but to insist most emphatically that it does stand for a function. There is, I mean, no aboriginal stuff or quality of being, contrasted with that of which material objects are made, out of which our thoughts of them are made; but there is a function in experience which thoughts perform, and for the performance of which this quality of being is invoked. That function is *knowing*. 'Consciousness' is supposed necessary to explain the fact that things not only are, but get reported, are known. Whoever blots out the notion of consciousness from his list of first principles must still provide in some way for that function's being carried on.

I

My thesis is that if we start with the supposition that there is only one primal stuff or material in the world, a stuff of which everything is composed, and if we call that stuff 'pure experience,' then knowing can easily be explained as a particular sort of relation towards one another into which portions of pure experience may enter. The relation itself is a part of pure experience; one of its 'terms' becomes the subject or bearer of the knowledge, the knower,[2] the other becomes the object known. This will need much explanation before it can be understood. The best way to get it understood is to contrast it with the alternative view; and for that we may take the recentest alternative, that in which the evaporation of the definite soul-substance has proceeded as far as it can go without being yet complete. If neo-Kantism has expelled earlier forms of dualism, we shall have expelled all forms if we are able to expel neo-Kantism in its turn.

For the thinkers I call neo-Kantian, the word consciousness to-day does no more than signalize the fact that experience is indefeasibly dualistic in structure. It means that not subject, not object, but object-plus-subject is the minimum that can actually be. The subject-object distinction meanwhile is entirely different from that between mind and matter, from that between body and soul. Souls were detachable, had separate destinies; things could happen to them. To consciousness as such nothing can happen, for, timeless itself, it is only a witness of happenings in time, in which it plays no part. It is, in a word, but the logical correlative of 'content' in an Experience of which the peculiarity is that *fact comes to light* in it, that *awareness of content* takes place. Consciousness as such is entirely impersonal—'self' and its activities belong to the content. To say that I am self-conscious, or conscious of putting forth volition, means only that certain contents, for which 'self' and 'effort of will' are the names, are not without witness as they occur.

Thus, for these belated drinkers at the Kantian spring, we should have to admit consciousness as an 'epistemological' necessity, even if we had no direct evidence of its being there.

But in addition to this, we are supposed by almost every one to have an immediate consciousness of consciousness itself. When the world of outer fact ceases to be materially present, and we merely recall it in memory, or fancy it, the consciousness is believed to stand out and to be felt as a kind of impalpable inner flowing, which, once known in this sort of experience, may equally be detected in presentations of the outer world. "The moment we try to fix our attention upon consciousness and to see *what*, distinctly, it is," says a recent writer, "it seems to vanish: it seems as if we had before us a mere emptiness. When we try to introspect the sensation of blue, all we can see is the blue: the other element is as if it were diaphanous. Yet it *can* be distinguished if we look attentively enough, and if we know that there is something to look for."[3] "Consciousness" (*Bewusstheit*), says another philosopher, "is inexplicable and hardly describable, yet all conscious experiences have this in common that what we call their content has this peculiar reference to a centre for which 'self' is the name, in virtue of which reference alone the content is subjectively given, or appears. . . . While in this way consciousness, or reference to a self, is the only thing which distinguishes a conscious content from any sort of being that might be there with no one conscious of it, yet this only ground of the distinction defies all closer explanations. The existence of consciousness, although it is the fundamental fact of psychology, can indeed be laid down as certain, can be brought out by analysis, but can neither be defined nor deduced from anything but itself."[4]

"Can be brought out by analysis," this author says. This supposes that the consciousness is one element, moment, factor—call it what you like—of an experience of essentially dualistic inner constitution, from which, if you abstract the content, the consciousness will remain revealed to its own eye. Experience, at this rate, would be much like a paint of which the world pictures were made. Paint has a dual constitution, involving, as it does, a menstruum[5] (oil, size or what not) and a mass of content in the form of pigment suspended therein. We can get the pure menstruum by letting the pigment settle, and the pure pigment by pouring off the size or oil. We operate here by physical subtraction; and the usual view is, that by mental subtraction we can separate the two factors of experience in an analogous way—not isolating them entirely, but distinguishing them enough to know that they are two.

II

Now my contention is exactly the reverse of this. *Experience, I believe, has no such inner duplicity; and the separation of it into consciousness and content comes, not by way of subtraction, but by way of addition*—the addition, to a given concrete piece of it, of other sets of experiences, in connection with which severally its use or function may be of two different kinds. The paint will also serve here as an illustration. In a pot in a paint-shop, along with other paints, it serves in its entirety as so much saleable matter. Spread on a canvas, with other paints around it, it represents, on the contrary, a feature in a picture and performs a spiritual function. Just so, I maintain, does a given undivided portion of experience, taken in one context of associates, play the part of a knower, of a state of mind, of 'consciousness'; while in a different context the same undivided bit of experience plays the part of a thing known, of an objective 'content.' In a word, in one group it figures as a thought, in another group as a thing. And, since it can figure in both groups simultaneously we have every right to speak of it as subjective and objective both at once. The dualism connoted by such double-barreled terms as 'experience,' 'phenomenon,' 'datum,' '*Vorfindung*'—terms which, in philosophy at any rate, tend more and more to replace the single-barreled terms of 'thought' and 'thing'—that dualism, I say, is still preserved in this account, but reinterpreted, so that, instead of being mysterious and elusive, it becomes verifiable and concrete. It is an affair of relations, it falls outside, not inside, the single experience considered, and can always be particularized and defined.

The entering wedge for this more concrete way of understanding the dualism was fashioned by Locke when he made the word 'idea' stand indifferently for thing and thought, and by Berkeley when he said that what common sense means by realities is exactly what the philosopher means by ideas. Neither Locke nor Berkeley thought his truth out into perfect clearness, but it seems to me that the conception I am defending does little more than consistently carry out the 'pragmatic' method which they were the first to use.

If the reader will take his own experiences, he will see what I mean. Let him begin with a perceptual experience, the 'presentation,' so called, of a physical object, his actual field of vision, the room he sits in, with the book he is reading as its center; and let him for the present treat this complex object in the commonsense way as being 'really' what it seems to be, namely, a collection of physical things cut out from an environing world of other physical things with which these physical things have actual or potential relations. Now at the same time it is just *those self-same things* which his mind, as we say, perceives; and the whole philosophy of perception from Democritus's time downwards has been just one long wrangle over the paradox that what is evidently one reality should be in two places at once, both in outer space and in a person's mind. 'Representative' theories of perception avoid the logical paradox, but on the other hand they violate the reader's sense of life, which knows no intervening mental image but seems to see the room and the book immediately just as they physically exist.

The puzzle of how the one identical room can be in two places is at bottom just the puzzle of how one identical point can be on two lines. It can, if it be situated at their intersection; and similarly, if the 'pure experience' of the room were a place of intersection of two processes, which connected it with different groups of associates respectively, it could be counted twice over, as belonging to either group, and spoken of loosely as existing in two places, although it would remain all the time a numerically single thing.

Well, the experience is a member of diverse processes that can be followed away from it along entirely different lines. The one self-identical thing has so many relations to the rest of experience that you can take it in disparate systems of association, and treat it as belonging with opposite contexts. In one of these contexts it is your 'field of consciousness'; in another it is 'the room in which you sit,' and it enters both contexts in its wholeness, giving no pretext for being said to attach itself to consciousness by one of its parts or aspects, and to outer reality by another. What are the two processes, now, into which the room-experience simultaneously enters in this way?

One of them is the reader's personal biography, the other is the history of the house of which the room is part. The presentation, the experience, the *that* in short (for until we have decided what it is it must be a mere *that*) is the last term of a train of sensations, emotions, decisions, movements, classifications, expectations, etc., ending in the present, and the first term of a series of similar 'inner' operations extending into the future, on the reader's part. On the other hand, the very same *that* is the *terminus ad quem* of a lot of previous physical operations, carpentering, papering, furnishing, warming, etc., and the *terminus a quo* of a lot of future ones, in which it will be concerned when undergoing the destiny of a physical room. The physical and the mental operations form curiously incompatible groups. As a room, the experience has occupied that spot and had that environment for thirty years. As your field of consciousness it may never have existed until now. As a room, attention will go on to discover endless new details in it. As your mental state merely, few new ones will emerge under attention's eye. As a room, it will take an earthquake, or a gang of men, and in any case a certain amount of time, to destroy it. As your subjective state, the closing of your eyes, or any instantaneous play of your fancy will suffice. In the real world, fire will consume it. In your mind, you can let fire play over it without effect. As an outer object, you must pay so much a month to inhabit it. As an inner content, you may occupy it for any length of time rent-free. If, in short, you follow it in the mental direction, taking it along with events of personal biography solely, all sorts of things are true of it which are false, and false of it which are true if you treat it as a real thing experienced, follow it in the physical direction, and relate it to associates in the outer world.

III

So far, all seems plain sailing, but my thesis will probably grow less plausible to the reader when I pass from percepts to concepts, or from the case of things presented to that of things remote. I believe, nevertheless, that here also the same law holds good. If we take conceptual manifolds, or memories, or fancies, they also are in their first intention mere bits of pure experience, and, as such, are single *thats* which act in one context as objects, and in another context figure as mental states. By taking them in their first intention, I mean ignoring their relation to possible perceptual experiences with which they may be connected, which they may lead to and terminate in, and which then they may be supposed to 'represent.' Taking them in this way first, we confine the problem to a world merely 'thought of' and not directly felt or seen. This world, just like the world of percepts, comes to us at first as a chaos of experiences, but lines of order soon get traced. We find that any bit of it which we may cut out as an example is connected with distinct groups of associates, just as our perceptual experiences are, that these associates link themselves with it by different relations,[6] and that one forms the inner history of a person, while the other acts as an impersonal 'objective' world, either spatial and temporal, or else merely logical or mathematical, or otherwise 'ideal.'

The first obstacle on the part of the reader to seeing that these non-perceptual experiences have objectivity as well as subjectivity will probably be due to the intrusion into his mind of *percepts*, that third group of associates with which the non-perceptual experiences have relations, and which, as a whole, they 'represent,' standing to them as thoughts to things. This important function of the non-perceptual experiences complicates the question and confuses it; for, so used are we to treat percepts as the sole genuine realities that, unless we keep them out of the discussion, we tend altogether to overlook the objectivity that lies in non-perceptual experiences by themselves. We treat them, 'knowing' percepts as they do, as through and through subjective, and say that they are wholly constituted of the stuff called consciousness, using this term now for a kind of entity, after the fashion which I am seeking to refute.[7]

Abstracting, then, from percepts altogether, what I maintain is, that any single non-perceptual experience tends to get counted twice over, just as a perceptual experience does, figuring in one context as an object or field of objects, in another as a state of mind: and all this without the least internal self-diremption on its own part into consciousness and content. It is all consciousness in one taking; and, in the other, all content.

I find this objectivity of non-perceptual experiences, this complete parallelism in point of reality between the presently felt and the remotely thought, so well set forth in a page of Münsterberg's *Grundzüge*, that I will quote it as it stands.

"I may only think of my objects," says Professor Münsterberg; "yet, in my living thought they stand before me exactly as perceived objects would do, no matter how different the two ways of apprehending them may be in their genesis. The book here lying on the table before me, and the book in the next room of which I think and which I mean to get, are both in the same sense given realities for me, realities which I acknowledge and of which I take account. If you agree that the perceptual object is not an idea within me, but that percept and thing, as indistinguishably one, are really experienced *there, outside*, you ought not to believe that the merely thought-of object is hid away inside of the thinking subject. The object of which I think, and of whose existence I take cognizance without letting it now work upon my senses, occupies its definite place in the outer world as much as does the object which I directly see."

"What is true of the here and the there, is also true of the now and the then. I know of the thing which is present and perceived, but I know also of the thing which yesterday was but is no more, and which I only remember. Both can determine my present conduct, both are parts of the reality of which I keep account. It is true that of much of the past I am uncertain, just as I am uncertain of much of what is present if it be but dimly perceived. But the interval of time does not in principle alter my relation to the object, does not transform it from an object known into a mental state. . . . The things in the room here which I survey, and those in my distant home of which I think, the things of this minute and those of my long-vanished boyhood, influence and decide me alike, with a reality which my experience of them directly feels. They both make up my real world, they make it directly, they do not have first to be introduced to me and mediated by ideas which now and here arise within me. . . . This not-me character of my recollections and expectations does not imply that the external objects of which I am aware in those experiences should necessarily be there also for others. The objects of dreamers and hallucinated persons are wholly without general validity. But even were they centaurs and golden mountains, they still would be 'off there,' in fairy land, and not 'inside' of ourselves."[8]

This certainly is the immediate, primary, naïf, or practical way of taking our thought-of- world. Were there no perceptual world to serve as its 'reductive,' in Taine's sense, by being 'stronger' and more genuinely 'outer' (so that the whole merely thought-of world seems weak and inner in comparison), our world of thought would be the only world, and would enjoy complete reality in our belief. This actually happens in our dreams, and in our day-dreams so long as percepts do not interrupt them.

And yet, just as the seen room (to go back to our late example) is *also* a field of consciousness, so the conceived or recollected room is *also* a state of mind; and the doubling-up of the experience has in both cases similar grounds.

The room thought-of, namely, has many thought-of couplings with many thought-of-things. Some of these couplings are inconstant, others are stable. In the reader's personal history the room occupies a single date—he saw it only once perhaps, a year ago. Of the house's history, on the other hand, it forms a permanent ingredient. Some couplings have the curious stubbornness, to borrow Royce's term, of fact; others show the fluidity of fancy—we let them come and go as we please. Grouped with the rest of its house, with the name of its town, of its owner, builder, value, decorative plan, the room maintains a definite foothold, to which, if we try to loosen it, it tends to return, and to reassert itself with force.[9] With these associates, in a word, it coheres, while to other houses, other towns, other owners, etc., it shows no tendency to cohere at all. The two collections, first of its cohesive, and, second, of its loose associates, inevitably come to be contrasted. We call the first collection the system of external realities, in the midst of which the room, as 'real,' exists; the other we call the stream of our internal thinking, in which, as a 'mental image,' it for a moment floats.[10] The room thus again gets counted twice over. It plays two different roles, being *Gedanke* and *Gedachtes*, the thought-of-an-object, and the object-thought-of, both in one; and all this without paradox or mystery, just as the same material thing may be both low and high, or small and great, or bad and good, because of its relations to opposite parts of an environing world.

As 'subjective' we say that the experience represents; as 'objective' it is represented. What represents and what is represented is here numerically the same; but we must remember that no dualism of being represented and representing resides in the experience *per se*. In its pure state, or when isolated, there is no self-splitting of it into consciousness and what the consciousness is 'of.' Its subjectivity and objectivity are functional attributes solely, realized only when the experience is 'taken,' *i.e.*, talked-of, twice, considered along with its two differing contexts respectively, by a new retrospective experience, of which that whole past complication now forms the fresh content.

The instant field of the present is at all times what I call the 'pure' experience. It is only virtually or potentially either object or subject as yet. For the time being, it is plain, unqualified actuality, or existence, a simple *that*. In this *naïf* immediacy it is of course *valid*; it is *there*, we *act* upon it; and the doubling of it in retrospection into a state of mind and a reality intended thereby, is just one of the acts. The 'state of mind,' first treated explicitly as such in retrospection, will stand corrected or confirmed, and the retrospective experience in its turn will get a similar treatment; but the immediate experience in its passing is always 'truth,'[11] practical truth, *something to act on*, at its own movement. If the world were then and there to go out like a candle, it would remain truth absolute and objective, for it would be 'the last word,' would have no critic, and no one would ever oppose the thought in it to the reality intended.[12]

I think I may now claim to have made my thesis clear. Consciousness connotes a kind of external relation, and does not denote a special stuff or way of being. *The peculiarity of our experiences, that they not only are, but are known, which their 'conscious' quality is invoked to explain, is better explained by their relations—these relations themselves being experiences— to one another.*

IV

Were I now to go on to treat of the knowing of perceptual by conceptual experiences, it would again prove to be an affair of external relations. One experience would be the knower, the other the reality known; and I could perfectly well define, without the notion of 'consciousness,' what the knowing actually and practically amounts to—leading-towards, namely, and terminating-in percepts, through a series of transitional experiences which the world supplies. But I will not treat of this, space being insufficient.[13] I will rather consider a few objections that are sure to be urged against the entire theory as it stands.

V

First of all, this will be asked: "If experience has not 'conscious' existence, if it be not partly made of 'consciousness,' of what then is it made? Matter we know, and thought we know, and conscious content we know, but neutral and simple 'pure experience' is something we know not at all. Say *what* it consists of—for it must consist of something—or be willing to give it up!"

To this challenge the reply is easy. Although for fluency's sake I myself spoke early in this article of a stuff of pure experience, I have now to say that there is no *general* stuff of which experience at large is made. There are as many stuffs as there are 'natures' in the things experienced. If you ask what any one bit of pure experience is made of, the answer is always the same: "It is made of *that*, of just what appears, of space, of intensity, of flatness, brownness, heaviness, or what not." Shadworth Hodgson's analysis here leaves nothing to be desired. Experience is only a collective name for all these sensible natures, and save for time and space (and, if you like, for 'being') there appears no universal element of which all things are made.

VI

The next objection is more formidable, in fact it sounds quite crushing when one hears it first.

"If it be the self-same piece of pure experience, taken twice over, that serves now as thought and now as thing"—so the objection runs—"how comes it that its attributes should differ so fundamentally in the two takings. As thing, the experience is extended; as thought, it occupies no space or place. As thing, it is red, hard, heavy; but who ever heard of a red, hard or heavy thought? Yet even now you said that an experience is made of just what appears, and what appears is just such adjectives. How can the one experience in its thing-function be made of them, consist of them, carry them as its own attributes, while in its thought-function it disowns them and attributes them elsewhere. There is a self-contradiction here from which the radical dualism of thought and thing is the only truth that can save us. Only if the thought is one kind of being can the adjectives exist in it 'intentionally' (to use the scholastic term); only if the thing is another kind, can they exist in it constitutively and energetically. No simple subject can take the same adjectives and at one time be qualified by it, and at another time be merely 'of' it, as of something only meant or known."

The solution insisted on by this objector, like many other common-sense solutions, grows the less satisfactory the more one turns it in one's mind. To begin with, *are* thought and thing as heterogeneous as is commonly said?

No one denies that they have some categories in common. Their relations to time are identical. Both, moreover, may have parts (for psychologists in general treat thoughts as having them); and both may be complex or simple. Both are of kinds, can be compared, added and subtracted and arranged in serial orders. All sorts of adjectives qualify our thoughts which appear incompatible with consciousness, being as such a bare diaphaneity. For instance, they are natural and easy, or laborious. They are beautiful, happy, intense, interesting, wise, idiotic, focal, marginal, insipid, confused, vague, precise, rational, casual, general, particular, and many things besides. Moreover, the chapters on 'Perception' in the psychology-books are full of facts that make for the essential homogeneity of thought with thing. How, if 'subject' and 'object' were separated 'by the whole diameter of being,' and had no attributes in common, could it be so hard to tell, in a presented and recognized material object, what part comes in through the sense-organs and what part comes 'out of one's own head'? Sensations and apperceptive ideas fuse here so intimately that you can no more tell where one begins and the other ends, than you can tell, in those cunning circular panoramas that have lately been exhibited, where the real foreground and the painted canvas join together.[14]

Descartes for the first time defined thought as the absolutely unextended, and later philosophers have accepted the description as correct. But what possible meaning has it to say that, when we think of a footrule or a square yard, extension is not attributable to our thought? Of every extended object the *adequate* mental picture must have all the extension of the object itself. The difference between objective and subjective extension is one of relation to a context solely. In the mind the various extents maintain no necessarily stubborn order relatively to each other, while in the physical world they bound each other stably, and, added together, make the great enveloping Unit which we believe in and call real Space. As 'outer,' they carry themselves adversely, so to speak, to one another, exclude one another and maintain their distances; while, as 'inner,' their order is loose, and they form a *durcheinander* in which unity is lost.[15] But to argue from this that inner experience is absolutely inextensive seems to me little short of absurd. The two worlds differ, not by the presence or absence of extension, but by the relations of the extensions which in both worlds exist.

Does not this case of extension now put us on the track of truth in the case of other qualities? It does; and I am surprised that the facts should not have been noticed long ago. Why, for example, do we call a fire hot, and water wet, and yet refuse to say that our mental state, when it is 'of' these objects, is either wet or hot? 'Intentionally,' at any rate, and when the mental state is a vivid image, hotness and wetness are in it just as much as they are in the physical experience. The reason is this, that, as the general chaos of all our experiences gets sifted, we find that there are some fires that will always burn sticks and always warm our bodies, and that there are some waters that will always put out fires; while there are other fires and waters that will not act at all. The general group of experiences that *act*, that do not only possess their natures intrinsically, but wear them adjectively and energetically, turning them against one another, comes inevitably to be contrasted with the group whose members, having identically the same natures, fail to manifest them in the 'energetic' way. I make for myself now an experience of blazing fire; I place it near my body; but it does not warm me in the least. I lay a stick upon it, and the stick either burns or remains green, as I please. I call up water, and pour it on the fire, and absolutely no difference ensues. I account for all such facts by calling this whole train of experiences unreal, a mental train. Mental fire is what won't burn real sticks; mental water is what won't necessarily (though of course it may) put out even a mental fire. Mental knives may be sharp, but they won't cut real wood. Mental triangles are pointed, but their points won't wound. With 'real' objects, on the contrary, consequences always accrue; and thus the real experiences get sifted from the mental ones, the things from our thoughts of them, fanciful or true, and precipitated together as the stable part of the whole experience-chaos, under the name of the physical world. Of this our perceptual experiences are the nucleus, they being the originally *strong* experiences. We add a lot of conceptual experiences to them, making these strong also in imagination, and building out the remoter parts of the physical world by their means; and around this core of reality the world of laxly connected fancies and mere rhapsodical objects floats like a bank of clouds. In the clouds, all sorts of rules are violated which in the core are kept. Extensions there can be indefinitely located; motion there obeys no Newton's laws.

VII

There is a peculiar class of experiences to which, whether we take them as subjective or as objective, we *assign* their several natures as attributes, because in both contexts they affect their associates actively, though in neither quite as 'strongly' or as sharply as things affect one another by their physical energies. I refer here to *appreciations*, which form an ambiguous sphere of being, belonging with emotion on the one hand, and having objective 'value' on the other, yet seeming not quite inner nor quite outer, as if a diremption had begun but had not made itself complete.

Experiences of painful objects, for example, are usually also painful experiences; perceptions of loveliness, of ugliness, tend to pass muster as lovely or as ugly perceptions; intuitions of the morally lofty are lofty intuitions. Sometimes the adjective wanders as if uncertain where to fix itself. Shall we speak of seductive visions or of visions of seductive things? Of wicked desires or of desires for wickedness? Of healthy thoughts or of thoughts of healthy objects? Of good impulses, or of impulses towards the good? Of feelings of anger, or of angry feelings? Both in the mind and in the thing, these natures modify their context, exclude certain associates and determine others, have their mates and incompatibles. Yet not as stubbornly as in the case of physical qualities, for beauty and ugliness, love and hatred, pleasant and painful can, in certain complex experiences, coexist.

If one were to make an evolutionary construction of how a lot of originally chaotic pure experiences became gradually differentiated into an orderly inner and outer world, the whole theory would turn upon one's success in explaining how or why the quality of an experience, once active, could become less so, and, from being an energetic attribute in some cases, elsewhere lapse into the status of an inert or merely internal 'nature.' This would be the 'evolution' of the psychical from the bosom of the physical, in which the esthetic, moral and otherwise emotional experiences would represent a halfway stage.

VIII

But a last cry of *non possumus* will probably go up from many readers. "All very pretty as a piece of ingenuity," they will say, "but our consciousness itself intuitively contradicts you. We, for our part, *know* that we are conscious. We *feel* our thought, flowing as a life within us, in absolute contrast with the objects which it so unremittingly escorts. We can not be faithless to this immediate intuition. The dualism is a fundamental *datum*: Let no man join what God has put asunder."

My reply to this is my last word, and I greatly grieve that to many it will sound materialistic. I cannot help that, however, for I, too, have my intuitions and I must obey them. Let the case be what it may in others, I am as confident as I am of anything that, in myself, the stream of thinking (which I recognize emphatically as a phenomenon) is only a careless name for what, when scrutinized, reveals itself to consist chiefly of the stream of my breathing. The 'I think' which Kant said must be able to accompany all my objects, is the 'I breathe' which actually does accompany them. There are other internal facts besides breathing (intra-cephalic muscular adjustments, etc., of which I have said a word in my larger Psychology), and these increase the assets of 'consciousness,' so far as the latter is subject to immediate perception; but breath, which was ever the original of 'spirit,' breath moving outwards, between the glottis and the nostrils, is, I am persuaded, the essence out of which philosophers have constructed the entity known to them as consciousness. *That entity is fictitious, while thoughts in the concrete are fully real. But thoughts in the concrete are made of the same stuff as things are.*

I wish I might believe myself to have made that plausible in this article. In another article I shall try to make the general notion of a world composed of pure experiences still more clear.

5

A World of Pure Experience

It is difficult not to notice a curious unrest in the philosophic atmosphere of the time, a loosening of old landmarks, a softening of oppositions, a mutual borrowing from one another on the part of systems anciently closed, and an interest in new suggestions, however vague, as if the one thing sure were the inadequacy of the extant school-solutions. The dissatisfaction with these seems due for the most part to a feeling that they are too abstract and academic. Life is confused and superabundant, and what the younger generation appears to crave is more of the temperament of life in its philosophy, even though it were at some cost of logical rigor and of formal purity. Transcendental idealism is inclining to let the world wag incomprehensibly, in spite of its Absolute Subject and his unity of purpose. Berkeleyan idealism is abandoning the principle of parsimony and dabbling in panpsychic speculations. Empiricism flirts with teleology; and, strangest of all, natural realism, so long decently buried, raises its head above the turf, and finds glad hands outstretched from the most unlikely quarters to help it to its feet again. We are all biased by our personal feelings, I know, and I am personally discontented with extant solutions; so I seem to read the signs of a great unsettlement, as if the upheaval of more real conceptions and more fruitful methods were imminent, as if a true landscape might result, less clipped, straight-edged and artificial.

If philosophy be really on the eve of any considerable rearrangement, the time should be propitious for anyone who has suggestions of his own to bring forward. For many years past my mind has been growing into a certain type of *Weltanshauung*. Rightly or wrongly, I have got to the point where I can hardly see things in any other pattern. I propose, therefore, to describe the pattern as clearly as I can consistently with great brevity, and to throw my description into the bubbling vat of publicity where, jostled by rivals and torn by critics, it will eventually either disappear from notice, or else, if better luck befall it, quietly subside to the profundities, and serve as a possible ferment of new growths or a nucleus of new crystallization.

I. RADICAL EMPIRICISM

I give the name of 'radical empiricism' to my *Weltanschauung*. Empiricism is known as the opposite of rationalism. Rationalism tends to emphasize universals and to make wholes prior to parts in the order of logic as well as in that of being. Empiricism, on the contrary, lays the explanatory stress upon the part, the element, the individual, and treats the whole as a collection and the universal as an abstraction. My description of things, accordingly, starts with the parts and makes of the whole being of the second order. It is essentially a mosaic philosophy, a philosophy of plural facts, like that of Hume and his descendants, who refer these facts neither to Substances in which they inhere nor to an Absolute Mind that creates them as its objects. But it differs from the Humian type of empiricism in one particular which makes me add the epithet radical.

To be radical, an empiricism must neither admit into its constructions any element that is not directly experienced, nor exclude from them any element that is directly experienced. For such a philosophy, *the relations that connect experiences must themselves be experienced relations, and any kind of relation experienced must be accounted as 'real' as anything else in the system.* Elements may indeed be redistributed, the original placing of things getting corrected, but a real place must be found for every kind of thing experienced, whether term or relation, in the final philosophic arrangement.

Now, ordinary empiricism, in spite of the fact that conjunctive and disjunctive relations present themselves as being fully co-ordinate parts of experience, has always shown a tendency to do away with the connections of things, and to insist most on the disjunctions. Berkeley's nominalism, Hume's statement that whatever things we distinguish are as 'loose and separate' as if they had 'no manner of connection,' James Mill's denial that similars have anything 'really' in common, the resolution of the causal tie into habitual sequence, John Mill's account of both physical things and selves as composed of discontinuous possibilities, and the general pulverization of all Experience by association and the mind-dust theory, are examples of what I mean.

The natural result of such a world-picture has been the efforts of rationalism to correct its incoherencies by the addition of trans-experiential agents of unification, substances, intellectual categories and powers, or Selves; whereas, if empiricism had only been radical and taken everything that comes without disfavor, conjunction as well as separation, each at its face value, the results would have called for no such artificial correction. *Radical empiricism*, as I understand it, *does full justice to conjunctive relations*, without, however, treating them as rationalism always tends to treat them, as being true in some supernal way, as if the unity of things and their variety belonged to different orders of truth and vitality altogether.

II. CONJUNCTIVE RELATIONS

Relations are of different degrees of intimacy. Merely to be 'with' one another in a universe of discourse is the most external relation that terms can have, and seems to involve nothing whatever as to farther consequences. Simultaneity and time-interval come next, and then space-adjacency and distance. After them, similarity and difference, carrying the possibility of many inferences. Then relations of activity, tying terms into series involving change, tendency, resistance, and the causal order generally. Finally, the relation experienced between terms that form states of mind, and are immediately conscious of continuing each other. The organization of the Self as a system of memories, purposes, strivings, fulfillments or disappointments, is incidental to this most intimate of all relations, the terms of which seem in many cases actually to compenetrate and suffuse each other's being.

Philosophy has always turned on grammatical particles. With, near, next, like, from, towards, against, because, for, through, my—these words designate types of conjunctive relation arranged in a roughly ascending order of intimacy and inclusiveness. *A priori*, we can imagine a universe of withness but no nextness; or one of nextness but no likeness, or of likeness with no activity, or of activity with no purpose, or of purpose with no ego. These would be universes, each with its own grade, of unity. The universe of human experience is, by one or another of its parts, of each and all these grades. Whether or not it possibly enjoys some still more absolute grade of union does not appear upon the surface.

Taken as it does appear, our universe is to a large extent chaotic. No one single type of connection runs through all the experiences that compose it. If we take space-relations, they fail to connect minds into any regular system. Causes and purposes obtain only among special series of facts. The self-relation seems extremely limited and does not link two different selves together. *Prima facie*, if you should liken the universe of absolute idealism to an aquarium, a crystal globe in which goldfish are swimming, you would have to compare the empiricist universe to something more like one of those dried human heads with which the Dyaks of Borneo deck their lodges. The skull forms a solid nucleus; but innumerable feathers, leaves, strings, beads, and loose appendices of every description float and dangle from it, and, save that they terminate in it, seem to have nothing to do with one another. Even so my experiences and yours float and dangle, terminating, it is true, in a nucleus of common perception, but for the most part out of sight and irrelevant and unimaginable to one another. This imperfect intimacy, this bare relation of *withness* between some parts of the sum total of experience and other parts, is the fact that ordinary empiricism over-emphasizes against rationalism, the latter always tending to ignore it unduly. Radical empiricism, on the contrary, is fair to both the unity and the disconnection. It finds no reason for treating either as illusory. It allots to each its definite sphere of description, and agrees that there appear to be actual forces at work which tend, as time goes on, to make the unity greater.

The conjunctive relation that has given most trouble to philosophy is *the co-conscious transition*, so to call it, by which one experience passes into another when both belong to the same self. About the facts there is no question. My experiences and your experiences are 'with' each other in various external ways, but mine pass into mine, and yours pass into yours in a way in which yours and mine never pass into one another. Within each of our personal histories, subject, object, interest and purpose *are continuous or maybe continuous*.[1] Personal histories are processes of change in time, and *the change itself is one of the things immediately experienced*. 'Change' in this case means continuous as opposed to discontinuous transition. But continuous transition is one sort of a conjunctive relation; and to be a radical empiricist means to hold fast to this conjunctive relation of all others, for this is the strategic point, the position through which, if a hole be made, all the corruptions of dialectics and all the metaphysical fictions pour into our philosophy. The holding fast to this relation means taking it at its face value, neither less nor more; and to take it at its face value means first of all to take it just as we feel it, and not to confuse ourselves with abstract talk *about* it, involving words that drive us to invent secondary conceptions in order to neutralize their suggestions and to make our actual experience again seem rationally possible.

What I do feel simply when a later moment of my experience succeeds an earlier one is that though they are two moments, the transition from the one to the other is *continuous*. Continuity here is a definite sort of experience; just as definite as is the *discontinuity-experience* which I find it impossible to avoid when I seek to make the transition from an experience of my own to one of yours. In this latter case I have to get on and off again, to pass from a thing lived to another thing only conceived, and the break is positively experienced and noted. Though the functions exerted by my experience and by yours may be the same (*e.g.*, the same objects known and the same purposes followed), yet the sameness has in this case to be ascertained expressly (and often with difficulty and uncertainty) after the break has been felt; whereas in passing from one of my own moments to another the sameness of object and interest is unbroken, and both the earlier and the later experience are of things directly lived.

There is no other *nature*, no other whatness than this absence of break and this sense of continuity in that most intimate of all conjunctive relations, the passing of one experience into another when they belong to the same self. And this whatness is real empirical 'content,' just as the whatness of separation and discontinuity is real content in the contrasted case. Practically to experience one's personal continuum in this living way is to know the originals of the ideas of continuity and of sameness, to know what the words stand for concretely, to own all that they can ever mean. But all experiences have their conditions; and over-subtle intellects, thinking about the facts here, and asking how they are possible, have ended by substituting a lot of static objects of conception for the direct perceptual experiences. "Sameness," they have said, "must be a stark numerical identity; it can't run on from next to next. Continuity can't mean mere absence of gap; for if you say two things are in immediate contact, at the contact how can they be two? If, on the other hand, you put a relation of transition between them, that itself is a third thing, and needs to be related or hitched to its terms. An infinite series is involved," and so on. The result is that from difficulty to difficulty, the plain conjunctive experience has been discredited by both schools, the empiricists leaving things permanently disjoined, and the rationalists remedying the looseness by their Absolutes or Substances, or whatever other fictitious agencies of union they may have employed. From all which artificiality we can be saved by a couple of simple reflections: first, that conjunctions and separations are, at all events, co-ordinate phenomena which, if we take experiences at their face value, must be accounted equally real; and second, that if we insist on treating things as really separate when they are given as continuously joined, invoking, when union is required, transcendental principles to overcome the separateness we have assumed, then we ought to stand ready to perform the converse act. We ought to invoke higher principles of *dis*union, also, to make our merely experienced disjunctions more truly real. Failing thus, we ought to let the originally given continuities stand on their own bottom. We have no right to be lopsided or to blow capriciously hot and cold.

III. THE COGNITIVE RELATION

The first great pitfall from which such a radical standing by experience will save us is an artificial conception of the *relations between knower and known*. Throughout the history of philosophy the subject and its object have been treated as absolutely discontinuous entities; and thereupon the presence of the latter to the former, or the 'apprehension' by the former of the latter, has assumed a paradoxical character which all sorts of theories had to be invented to overcome. Representative theories put a mental 'representation,' 'image,' or 'content' into the gap, as a sort of intermediary. Common-sense theories left the gap untouched, declaring our mind able to clear it by a self-transcending leap. Transcendentalist theories left it impassible in the finite realm, and brought an Absolute in to perform the saltatory act. All the while, in the very bosom of the finite experience, every conjunction required to make the relation intelligible is given in full. Either the knower and the known are:

(1) the self-same piece of experience taken twice over in different contexts; or they are

(2) two pieces of *actual* experience belonging to the same subject, with definite tracts of conjunctive transitional experience between them; or

(3) the known is a *possible* experience either of that subject or another, to which the said conjunctive transitions *would* lead, if sufficiently prolonged.

To discuss all the ways in which one experience may function as the knower of another, would be incompatible with the limits of this essay.[2]

I have just treated of type 1, the kind of knowledge called perception, in an article in this Journal for September 1, 1904. This is the type of case in which the mind enjoys direct 'acquaintance' with a present object. In the other types the mind has 'knowledge-about' an object not immediately there. Of type 2, the simplest sort of conceptual knowledge, I have given some account in two articles, published respectively in *Mind*, vol. X, p. 27, 1885, and in the *Psychological Review*, vol. II, p. 105, 1895.[3] Type 3 can always formally and hypothetically be reduced to type 2, so that a brief description of that type will put the present reader sufficiently at my point of view, and make him see what the actual meanings of the mysterious cognitive relation may be.

Suppose me to be sitting here in my library at Cambridge, at ten minutes' walk from 'Memorial Hall,' and to be thinking truly of the latter object. My mind may have before it only the name, or it may have a clear image, or it may have a very dim image of the hall, but such intrinsic differences in the image make no difference in its cognitive function. Certain *extrinsic* phenomena, special experiences of conjunction, are what impart to the image, be it what it may, its knowing office.

For instance, if you ask me what hall I mean by my image, and I can tell you nothing; or if I fail to point or lead you towards the Harvard Delta; or if, being led by you, I am uncertain whether the Hall I see be what I had in mind or not; you would rightly deny that I had 'meant' that particular hall at all, even though my mental image might to some degree have resembled it. The resemblance would count in that case as coincidental merely, for all sorts of things of a kind resemble one another in this world without being held for that reason to take cognizance of one another.

On the other hand, if I can lead you to the hall, and tell you of its history and present uses; if in its presence I feel my idea, however bad it may have been, to be now *terminated*; if the associates of the image and of the felt hall run parallel, so that each term of the one context corresponds serially, as I walk, with an answering term of the other; why then my soul was prophetic, and my idea must be, and by common consent would be, called cognizant of reality. That percept was what I *meant*, for into it my idea has passed by conjunctive experiences of sameness and fulfilled intention. Nowhere is there jar, but every later moment continues and corroborates an earlier.

In this continuing and corroborating, taken in no transcendental sense, but denoting definitely felt transitions, *lies all that the knowing of a percept by an idea can possibly contain or signify.* Wherever such transitions are felt, the first experience *knows* the last one. Where they do not, or where even as possibles they cannot, intervene, there can be no pretence of knowing. In this latter case the extremes will be connected, if connected at all, by inferior relations—bare likeness or succession, or by 'withness' alone. Knowledge of sensible realities thus comes to life in the tissue of experience. It is *made*; and made by relations that unroll themselves in time. Whenever certain intermediaries are given, such that, as they develop towards their terminus, there is experience from point to point of one direction followed, and finally of one process fulfilled, the result is that *their starting point thereby becomes a knower and their terminus an object meant or known.* That is all that knowing (in the simple case considered) can be known-as, that is the whole of its nature, put into experiential terms. Whenever such is the sequence of our experiences we may freely say that we had the terminal object 'in mind' from the outset, even although *at* the outset nothing was there in us but a flat piece of substantive experience like any other, with no self-transcendency about it, and no mystery save the mystery of coming into existence and of being gradually followed by other pieces of substantive experience, with conjunctively transitional experiences between. That is what we *mean* here by being 'in mind.' Of any deeper more real way of being in mind we have no positive conception, and we have no right to discredit our actual experience by talking of such a way at all.

I know that many a reader will rebel at this. "Mere intermediaries," he will say, "even though they be feelings of continuously growing fulfillment, only *separate* the knower from the known, whereas what we have in knowledge is a kind of immediate touch of the one by the other, an 'apprehension' in the etymological sense of the word, a leaping of the chasm as by lightning, an act by which two terms are smitten into one over the head of the distinctness of its terms. All these dead intermediaries of yours are out of each other, and outside of their termini still."

But do not such dialectic difficulties remind us of the dog dropping his bone and snapping at its image in the water? If we knew any more real kind of union *aliunde*, we might be entitled to brand all our empirical unions as a sham. But unions by continuous transition are the only ones we know of, whether in this matter of a knowledge-about that terminates in an acquaintance, whether in personal identity, in logical predication through the copula 'is,' or elsewhere. If anywhere there were more absolute unions realized, they could only reveal themselves to us by just such conjunctive results. These are what the unions are *worth*, these are all that *we can ever practically mean* by union, by continuity. Is it not time to repeat what Lotze said of substances, that to *act like one* is to *be* one? Should we not say here that to be experienced as continuous is to be really continuous, in a world where experience and reality come to the same thing? In a picture gallery a painted hook will serve to hang a painted chain by, a painted cable will hold a painted ship. In a world where both the terms and their distinctions are affairs of experience, the conjunctions which we experience must be at least as real as anything else. They will be 'absolutely' real conjunctions, if we have no transphenomenal Absolute ready, to derealize the whole experienced world by, at a stroke. If, on the other hand, we had such an Absolute, not one of our opponents' theories of knowledge could remain standing any better than ours could; for the distinctions as well as the conjunctions of experience would impartially fall its prey. The whole question of how 'one' thing can know 'another' would cease to be a real one at all in a world where otherness itself was an illusion.[4]

So much for the essentials of the cognitive relation where the knowledge is conceptual in type, or forms knowledge 'about' an object. It consists in intermediary experiences (possible, if not actual) of continuously developing progress, and, finally, of fulfillment, when the sensible percept which is the object is reached. The percept here not only *verifies* the concept, proves its function of knowing that percept to be true, but the percept's existence as the terminus of the chain of intermediaries *creates* the function. Whatever terminates that chain was, because it now is, what the concept 'had in mind.'

The towering importance for human life of this kind of knowing lies in the fact that an experience that knows another can figure as its *representative*, not in any quasi-miraculous 'epistemological' sense, but in the definite practical sense of being its *substitute* in various operations, sometimes physical and sometimes mental, which lead us to its associates and results. By experimenting on our ideas of reality, we may save ourselves the trouble of experimenting on the real experiences which they severally mean. The ideas form related systems, corresponding point for point to the systems which the realities form; and by letting an ideal term call up its associates systematically, we may be led to a terminus which the corresponding real term would have led to in case we had operated on the real world. This brings us to the general question of substitution, and some remarks on that subject seem to be the next thing in order.

IV. SUBSTITUTION

In Taine's brilliant book on 'Intelligence,' substitution was for the first time named as a cardinal logical function, though of course the facts had always been familiar enough. What, exactly, in a system of experiences, does the 'substitution' of one of them for another mean?

According to my view, experience as a whole is a process in time, whereby innumerable particular terms lapse and are superseded by others that follow upon them by transitions which, whether disjunctive or conjunctive in content, are themselves experiences, and must in general be accounted at least as real as the terms which they relate. What the nature of the event called 'superseding' signifies, depends altogether on the kind of transition that obtains. Some experiences simply abolish their predecessors without continuing them in any way. Others are felt to increase or to enlarge their meaning, to carry out their purpose, or to bring us nearer to their goal. They 'represent' them, and may fulfill their function better than they fulfilled it themselves. But to 'fulfill a function' in a world of pure experience can be conceived and defined in only one possible way. In such a world transitions and arrivals (or terminations) are the only events that happen, though they happen by so many sorts of path. The only function that one experience can perform is to lead into another experience; and the only fulfillment we can speak of is the reaching of a certain experienced end. When one experience leads to (or can lead to) the same end as another, they agree in function. But the whole system of experiences as they are immediately given presents itself as a quasi-chaos through which one can pass out of an initial term in many directions and yet end in the same terminus, moving from next to next by a great many alternative paths.

Either one of these paths might be a functional substitute for another, and to follow one rather than another might on occasion be an advantageous thing to do. As a matter of fact, and in a general way, the paths that run through conceptual experiences, that is, through 'thoughts' or 'ideas' that 'know' the things in which they terminate, are highly advantageous paths to follow. Not only do they yield inconceivably rapid transitions; but, owing to the 'universal' character[5] which they frequently possess, and to their capacity for association with one another in great systems, they outstrip the tardy consecutions of the things themselves, and sweep us on towards our ultimate termini in a far more labor-saving way than the following of trains of sensible perception ever could. Wonderful are the new cuts and the short-circuits the thought-paths make. Most thought-paths, it is true, are substitutes for nothing actual; they end outside the real world altogether, in wayward fancies, utopias, fictions or mistakes. But where they do re-enter reality and terminate therein, we substitute them always; and with these substitutes we pass the greater number of our hours.

This is why I called our experiences, taken all together, a quasi-chaos. There is vastly more discontinuity in the sum total of experiences than we commonly suppose. The objective nucleus of every man's experience, his own body, is, it is true, a continuous percept; and equally continuous as a percept (though we may be inattentive to it) is the material environment of that body, changing by gradual transition when the body moves. But the distant parts of the physical world are at all times absent from us, and form conceptual objects merely, into the perceptual reality of which our life inserts itself at points discrete and relatively rare. Round their several objective nuclei, partly common and partly discrete, of the real physical world, innumerable thinkers, pursuing their several lines of physically true cogitation, trace paths that intersect one another only at discontinuous perceptual points, and the rest of the time are quite incongruent; and around all the nuclei of shared 'reality,' as around the Dyak's head of my late metaphor, floats the vast *nimbus* of experiences that are wholly subjective, that are non-substitutional, that find not even an eventual ending for themselves in the perceptual world—the mere day-dreams and joys and sufferings and wishes of the individual minds. These exist *with* one another, indeed, and with the objective nuclei, but out of them it is probable that to all eternity no interrelated system of any kind will ever be made.

This notion of the purely substitutional or conceptual physical world brings us to the most critical of all the steps in the development of a philosophy of pure experience. The paradox of self-transcendency in knowledge comes back upon us here, but I think that our notions of pure experience and of substitution, and our radically empirical view of conjunctive transitions, are *Denkmittel* that will carry us safely through the pass.

V. WHAT OBJECTIVE REFERENCE IS

Whosoever feels his experience to be something substitutional, even while he has it, may be said to have an experience that reaches beyond itself. From inside of its own entity it says 'more,' and postulates reality existing elsewhere. For the transcendentalist, who holds knowing to consist in a *salto mortale* across an 'epistemological chasm,' such an idea presents no difficulty; but it seems at first sight as if it might be inconsistent with an empiricism like our own. Have we not explained that conceptual knowledge is made such wholly by the existence of things that fall outside of the knowing experience itself—by intermediary experiences and by a terminus that fulfils? Can the knowledge be there before these elements that constitute its being have come? And, if knowledge be not there, how can objective reference occur?

The key to this difficulty lies in the distinction between knowing as verified and completed, and the same knowing as in transit and on its way. To recur to the Memorial Hall example lately used, it is only when our idea of the Hall has actually terminated in the percept that we know 'for certain' that from the beginning it was truly cognitive of *that*. Until established by the end of the process, its quality of knowing that, or indeed of knowing anything, could still be doubted; and yet the knowing really was there, as the result now shows. We were *virtual* knowers of the Hall long before we were certified to have been its actual knowers by the percept's retroactive validating power. Just so we are 'mortal' all the time, by reason of the virtuality of the inevitable event which will make it so when it shall have come.

Now the immensely greater part of all our knowing never gets beyond this virtual stage. It never is completed or nailed down. I speak not merely of our ideas of imperceptibles like ether-waves or dissociated 'ions,' or of 'ejects' like the contents of our neighbors' minds; I speak also of ideas which we might verify if we would take the trouble, but which we hold for true although unterminated perceptually, because nothing says 'no' to us, and there is no contradicting truth in sight. *To continue thinking unchallenged is, ninety-nine times out of a hundred, our practical substitute for knowing in the completed sense.* As each experience runs by cognitive transition into the next one, and we nowhere feel a collision with what we elsewhere count as truth or fact, we commit ourselves to the current as if the port were sure. We live, as it were, upon the front edge of an advancing wave-crest, and our sense of a determinate direction in falling forward is all we cover of the future of our path. It is as if a differential quotient should be conscious and treat itself as an adequate substitute for a traced-out curve. Our experience, *inter alia*, is of variations of rate and of direction, and lives in these transitions more than in the journey's end. The experiences of tendency are sufficient to act upon—what more could we have *done* at those moments even if the later verification comes complete?

This is what, as a radical empiricist, I say to the charge that the objective reference which is so flagrant a character of our experiences involves a chasm and a mortal leap. A positively conjunctive transition involves neither chasm nor leap. Being the very original of what we mean by continuity, it makes a continuum wherever it appears. I know full well that such brief words as these will leave the hardened transcendentalist unshaken. Conjunctive experiences *separate* their terms, he will still say: they are third things interposed, that have themselves to be conjoined by new links, and to invoke them makes our trouble infinitely worse. To 'feel' our motion forward is impossible. Motion implies terminus; and how can terminus be felt before we have arrived? The barest start and sally forwards, the barest tendency to leave the instant, involves the chasm and the leap. Conjunctive transitions are the most superficial of appearances, illusions of our sensibility which philosophical reflection pulverizes at a touch. Conception is our only trustworthy instrument, conception and the Absolute working hand in hand. Conception disintegrates experience utterly, but its disjunctions are easily overcome again when the Absolute takes up the task.

Such transcendentalists I must leave, provisionally at least, in full possession of their creed. I have no space for polemics in this article, so I shall simply formulate the empiricist doctrine as my hypothesis, leaving it to work or not work as it may.

Objective reference, I say then, is an incident of the fact that so much of our experience comes as an insufficient and consists of process and transition. Our fields of experience have no more definite boundaries than have our fields of view. Both are fringed forever by a *more* that continuously develops, and that continuously supersedes them as life proceeds. The relations, generally speaking, are as real here as the terms are, and the only complaint of the transcendentalist's with which I could at all sympathize would be his charge that, by first making knowledge to consist in external relations as I have done, and by then confessing that nine-tenths of the time these are not actually but only virtually there, I have knocked the solid bottom out of the whole business, and palmed off a substitute of knowledge for the genuine thing. Only the admission, such a critic might say, that our ideas are self-transcendent and 'true' already, in advance of the experiences that are to terminate them, can bring solidity back to knowledge in a world like this, in which transitions and terminations are only by exception fulfilled.

This seems to me an excellent place for applying the pragmatic method. What would the self-transcendency affirmed to exist in advance of all experiential mediation or termination, be *known-as*? What would it practically result in for *us*, were it true?

It could only result in our orientation, in the turning of our expectations and practical tendencies into the right path; and the right path here, so long as we and the object are not yet face to face (or can never get face to face, as in the case of ejects), would be the path that led us into the object's nearest neighborhood. Where direct acquaintance is lacking, 'knowledge about' is the next best thing, and an acquaintance with what actually lies about the object, and is most closely related to it, puts such knowledge within our grasp. Ether-waves and your anger, for example, are things in which my thoughts will never *perceptually* terminate, but my concepts of them lead me to their very brink, to the chromatic fringes and to the hurtful words and deeds which are their really next effects.

Even if our ideas did in themselves carry the postulated self-transcendency, it would still remain true that their putting us into possession of such really next effects *would be the sole cash-value of the self-transcendency for us*. And this cash-value, it is needless to say, is *verbatim et literatim* what our empiricist account pays in. On pragmatist principles therefore, a dispute over self-transcendency is a pure logomachy. Call our concepts of ejective things self-transcendent or the reverse, it makes no difference, so long as we don't differ about the nature of that exalted virtue's fruits—fruits for us, of course, humanistic fruits.

If an Absolute were proved to exist for other reasons, it might well appear that *his* knowledge is terminated in innumerable cases where ours is still incomplete. That, however, would be a fact indifferent to our knowledge. The latter would grow neither worse nor better, whether we acknowledged such an Absolute or left him out.

So the notion of a knowledge still *in transitu* and on its way joins hands here with that notion of a 'pure experience' which I tried to explain in my recent article entitled "Does 'Consciousness' Exist?" The instant field of the present is always experience in its 'pure' state, plain unqualified actuality, a simple *that*, as yet undifferentiated into thing and thought, and only virtually classifiable as objective fact or as someone's opinion about fact. This is as true when the field is conceptual as when it is perceptual. 'Memorial Hall' is 'there' in my idea as much as when I stand before it. I proceed to act on its account in either case. Only in the later experience that supersedes the present one is this *naïf* immediacy retrospectively split into two parts, a 'consciousness' and its 'content,' and the content corrected or confirmed. While still pure, or present, any experience—mine, for example, of what I write about in these very lines—passes for 'truth.' The morrow may reduce it to 'opinion.' The transcendentalist in all his particular knowledges is as liable to this reduction as I am: his Absolute does not save him. Why, then, need he quarrel with an account of knowledge that insists on naming this effect? Why not treat the working of the idea from next to next as the essence of its self-transcendency? Why insist that knowing is a static relation out of time when it practically seems so much a function of our active life? For a thing to be valid, says Lotze, is the same as to make itself valid. When the whole universe seems only to be making itself valid and to be still incomplete (else why its ceaseless changing?) why, of all things, should knowing be exempt? Why should it not be making itself valid like everything else? That some parts of it may be already valid or verified beyond dispute, the empirical philosopher, of course, like any one else, may always hope.

VI. THE CONTERMINOUSNESS OF DIFFERENT MINDS

With transition and prospect thus enthroned in pure experience, it is impossible to subscribe to the idealism of the English school. Radical empiricism has, in fact, more affinities with natural realism than with the views of Berkeley or of Mill, and this can be easily shown.

For the Berkeleyan school, ideas (the verbal equivalent of what I term experiences) are discontinuous. The content of each is wholly immanent, and there are no transitions with which they are consubstantial and through which their beings may unite. Your Memorial Hall and mine, even when both are percepts, are wholly out of connection with each other. Our lives are a congeries of solipsisms, out of which in strict logic only a God could compose a universe even of discourse. No dynamic currents run between my objects and your objects. Never can our minds meet in the *same*.

The incredibility of such a philosophy is flagrant. It is 'cold, strained, and unnatural' in a supreme degree; and it may be doubted whether even Berkeley himself, who took it so religiously, really believed, when walking through the streets of London, that his spirit and the spirits of his fellow wayfarers had absolutely different towns in view.

To me the decisive reason in favor of our minds meeting in *some* common objects at least is that, unless I make that supposition, I have no motive for assuming that your mind exists at all. Why do I postulate your mind? Because I see your body acting in a certain way. Its gestures, facial movements, words and conduct generally, are 'expressive,' so I deem it actuated as my own is, by an inner life like mine. This argument from analogy is my *reason*, whether an instinctive belief runs before it or not. But what is 'your body' here but a percept in *my* field? It is only as animating *that* object, *my* object, that I have any occasion to think of you at all. If the body that you actuate be not the very body that I see there, but some duplicate body of your own with which that has nothing to do, we belong to different universes, you and I, and for me to speak of you is folly. Myriads of such universes even now may coexist, irrelevant to one another; my concern is solely with the universe with which my own life is connected.

In that perceptual part of *my* universe which I call *your* body, your mind and my mind meet and may be called conterminous. Your mind actuates that body and mine sees it; my thoughts pass into it as into their harmonious cognitive fulfillment; your emotions and volitions pass into it as causes into their effects.

But that percept hangs together with all our other physical percepts. They are of one stuff with it; and if it be our common possession, they must be so likewise. For instance, your hand lays hold of one end of a rope and my hand lays hold of the other end. We pull against each other. Can our two hands be mutual objects in this experience, and the rope not be mutual also? What is true of the rope is true of any other percept. Your objects are over and over again the same as mine. If I ask you *where* some object of yours is, our old Memorial Hall, for example, you point to *my* Memorial Hall with *your* hand which *I* see. If you alter an object in your world, put out a candle, for example, when I am present, *my* candle *ipso facto* goes out. It is only as altering my objects that I guess you to exist. If your objects do not coalesce with my objects, if they be not identically where mine are, they must be proved to be positively somewhere else. But no other location can be assigned for them, so their place must be what it seems to be, the same.[6]

Practically, then, our minds meet in a world of objects which they share in common, which would still be there, if one or several of the minds were destroyed. I can see no formal objection to this supposition's being literally true. On the principles which I am defending, a 'mind' or 'personal consciousness' is the name for a series of experiences run together by certain definite transitions, and an objective reality is a series of similar experiences knit by different transitions. If one and the same experience can figure twice, once in a mental and once in a physical context (as I have tried, in my article on 'Consciousness,' to show that it can), one does not see why it might not figure thrice, or four times, or any number of times, by running into as many different mental contexts, just as the same point, lying at their intersection, can be continued into many different lines. Abolishing any number of contexts would not destroy the experience itself or its other contexts, any more than abolishing some of the point's linear continuations would destroy the others, or destroy the point itself.

I well know the subtle dialectic which insists so that a term taken in another relation must needs be an intrinsically different term. The crux is always the old Greek one, that the same man can't be tall in relation to one neighbor, and short in relation to another, for that would make him tall and short at once. In this essay I can not stop to refute this dialectic, so I pass on, leaving my flank for the time exposed. But if my reader will only allow that the same '*now*' both ends his past and begins his future; or that, when he buys an acre of land from his neighbor, it is the same acre that successively figures in the two estates; or that when I pay him a dollar, the same dollar goes into his pocket that came out of mine; he will also in consistency have to allow that the same object may conceivably play a part in, as being related to the rest of, any number of otherwise entirely different minds. This is enough for my present point: the common-sense notion of minds sharing the same object offers no special logical or epistemological difficulties of its own; it stands or falls with the general possibility of things being in conjunctive relation with other things at all.

In principle, then, let natural realism pass for possible. Your mind and mine *may* terminate in the same percept, not merely against it, as if it were a third external thing, but by inserting themselves into it and coalescing with it, for such is the sort of conjunctive union that appears to be experienced when a perceptual terminus 'fulfils.' Even so, two hawsers may embrace the same pile, and yet neither one of them touch any other part except that pile, of what the other hawser is attached to.

It is therefore not a formal question, but a question of empirical fact solely, whether, when you and I are said to know the 'same' Memorial Hall, our minds do terminate at or in a numerically identical percept. Obviously, as a plain matter of fact, they do *not*. Apart from color-blindness and such possibilities, we see the Hall in different perspectives. You may be on one side of it and I on another. The percept of each of us, as he sees the surface of the Hall, is moreover only his provisional terminus. The next thing beyond my percept is not your mind, but more percepts of my own into which my first percept develops, the interior of the Hall, for instance, or the inner structure of its bricks and mortar. If our minds were in a literal sense *con*terminous, neither could get beyond the percept which they had in common, it would be an ultimate barrier between them—unless indeed they flowed over it and became 'co-

conscious' over a still larger part of their content, which (thought-transference apart) is not supposed to be the case. In point of fact the ultimate common barrier can always be pushed, by both minds, farther than any actual percept of either, until at last it resolves itself into the mere notion of imperceptibles like atoms or ether, so that, where we do terminate in percepts, our knowledge is only speciously completed, being, in theoretic strictness, only a virtual knowledge of those remoter objects which conception carries out.

Is natural realism, permissible in logic, refuted then by empirical fact? Do our minds have no object in common after all?

Yes, they certainly have *space* in common. On pragmatic principles we are obliged to predicate sameness wherever we can predicate no assignable point of difference. If two named things have every quality and function indiscernible, and are at the same time in the same place, they must be written down as numerically one thing under two different names. But there is no test discoverable, so far as I know, by which it can be shown that the place occupied by your percept of Memorial Hall differs from the place occupied by mine. The percepts themselves may be shown to differ; but if each of us be asked to point out where his percept is, we point to an identical spot. All the relations, whether geometrical or causal, of the Hall originate or terminate in that spot wherein our hands meet, and where each of us begins to work if he wishes to make the Hall change before the other's eyes. Just so it is with our bodies. That body of yours which you actuate and feel from within must be in the same spot as the body of yours which I see or touch from without. 'There' for me means where I place my finger. If you do not feel my finger's contact to be 'there' in *my* sense, when I place it on your body, where then do you feel it? Your inner actuations of your body also meet my finger *there*: it is *there* that you resist its push, or shrink back, or sweep the finger aside with your hand. Whatever farther knowledge either of us may acquire of the real constitution of the body which we thus feel, you from within and I from without, it is in that same place that the newly conceived or perceived constituents have to be located, and it is *through* that space that your and my mental intercourse with each other has always to be carried on, by the mediation of impressions which I convey thither, and of the reactions thence which those impressions may provoke from you.

In general terms, then, whatever differing contents our minds may eventually fill a place with, the place itself is a numerically identical content of the two minds, a piece of common property in which, through which, and over which they join. The receptacle of certain of our experiences being thus common, the experiences themselves might some day become common also. If that day ever did come, our thoughts would terminate in a complete empirical identity, there would be an end, so far as *those* experiences went, to our discussions about truth. No points of difference appearing, they would have to count as the same.

VII. CONCLUSION

With this we have the outlines of a philosophy of pure experience before us. At the outset of my essay, I called it a mosaic philosophy. In actual mosaics the pieces are held together by their bedding, for which bedding the substances, transcendental egos, or absolutes of other philosophies may be taken to stand. In radical empiricism there is no bedding; it is as if the pieces clung together by their edges, the transitions experienced between them forming their cement. Of course such a metaphor is misleading, for in actual experience the more substantive and the more transitive parts run into each other continuously, there is in general no separateness needing to be overcome by an external cement; and whatever separateness is actually experienced is not overcome, it stays and counts as separateness to the end. But the metaphor serves to symbolize the fact that experience itself, taken at large, can grow by its edges. That one moment of it proliferates into the next by transitions which, whether conjunctive or disjunctive, continue the experiential tissue, cannot, I contend, be denied. Life is in the transitions as much as in the terms connected; often, indeed, it seems to be there more emphatically, as if our spurts and sallies forward were the real firing-line of the battle, were like the thin line of flame advancing across the dry autumnal field which the farmer proceeds to burn. In this line we live prospectively as well as retrospectively. It is 'of' the past, inasmuch as it comes expressly as the past's continuation; it is 'of' the future in so far as the future, when it comes, will have continued *it*.

These relations of continuous transition experienced are what make our experiences cognitive. In the simplest and completest cases the experiences are cognitive of one another. When one of them terminates a previous series of them with a sense of fulfillment, it, we say, is what those other experiences 'had in view.' The knowledge, in such a case, is verified; the truth is 'salted down.' Mainly, however, we live on speculative investments, or on our prospects only. But living on things *in posse* is as good as living in the actual, so long as our credit remains good. It is evident that for the most part it is good, and that the universe seldom protests our drafts.

In this sense we at every moment can continue to believe in an existing *beyond*. It is only in special cases that our confident rush forward gets rebuked. The beyond must, of course, always in our philosophy be itself of an experiential nature. If not a future experience of our own or a present one of our neighbor, it must be a thing in itself in Dr. Prince's and Professor Strong's sense of the term—that is, it must be an experience *for* itself whose relation to other things we translate into the action of molecules, ether-waves, or whatever else the physical symbols may be.[7] This opens the chapter of the relations of radical empiricism to panpsychism, into which I can not enter now.

The beyond can in any case exist simultaneously—for it can be experienced *to have existed* simultaneously—with the experience that practically postulates it by looking in its direction, or by turning or changing in the direction of which it is the goal. Pending that actuality of union, in the virtuality of which the 'truth,' even now, of the postulation consists, the beyond and its knower are entities split off from each other. The world is in so far forth a pluralism of which the unity is not fully experienced as yet. But, as fast as verifications come, trains of experience, once separate, run into one another; and that is why I said, earlier in my article, that the unity of the world is on the whole undergoing increase.

The universe continually grows in quantity by new experiences that graft themselves upon the older mass; but these very new experiences often help the mass to a more consolidated form.

These are the main features of a philosophy of pure experience. It has innumerable other aspects and arouses innumerable questions, but the points I have touched on seem enough to make an entering wedge. In my own mind such a philosophy harmonizes best with a radical pluralism, with novelty and indeterminism, moralism and theism, and with the 'humanism' lately sprung upon us by the Oxford and the Chicago schools.[8] I cannot, however, be sure that all these doctrines are its necessary and indispensable allies. It presents so many points of difference, both from the common sense and from the idealism that have made our philosophic language, that it is almost as difficult to state it as it is to think it out clearly, and if it is ever to grow into a respectable system, it will have to be built up by the contributions of many cooperating minds. It seems to me, as I said at the outset of this essay, that many minds are, in point of fact, now turning in a direction that points towards radical empiricism. If they are carried farther by my words, and if then they add their stronger voices to my feebler one, the publication of this essay will have been worth while.

6

How Two Minds
Can Know One Thing

In an article in this Journal entitled "Does 'Consciousness' Exist?"[1] I have tried to show that when we call an experience 'conscious,' that does not mean that it is suffused throughout with a peculiar modality of being ('psychic' being) as stained glass may be suffused with light, but rather that it stands in certain determinate relations to other portions of experience extraneous to itself. These form one peculiar 'context' for it; while, taken in another context of experiences, we class it as a fact in the physical world. This 'pen,' for example, is, in the first instance, a bald *that*, a datum, fact, phenomenon, content, or whatever other neutral or ambiguous name you may prefer to apply. I called it in that article a 'pure experience.' To get classed either as a physical pen or as someone's percept of a pen, it must assume a *function*, and that can only happen in a more complicated world. So far as in that world it is a stable feature, holds ink, marks paper and obeys the guidance of a hand, it is a physical pen. That is what we mean by being 'physical,' in a pen. So far as it is instable, on the contrary, coming and going with the movements of my eyes, altering with what I call my fancy, continuous with subsequent experiences of its 'having been' (in the past tense), it is the percept of a pen in my mind. Those peculiarities are what we mean by being 'conscious,' in a pen.

In Section VI of another article[2] I tried to show that the same *that*, the same numerically identical pen of pure experience, can enter simultaneously into many conscious contexts, or, in other words, be an object for many different minds. I admitted that I had not space to treat of certain possible objections in that article; but in a subsequent article[3] I took some of the objections up. At the end of that article I said that still more formidable-sounding objections remained; so, to leave my pure experience theory in as strong a state as possible, I propose to consider those objections now.

I

The objections I previously tried to dispose of were purely logical or dialectical. No one identical term, whether physical or psychical, it had been said, could be the subject of two relations at once. This thesis I sought to prove unfounded. The objections that now confront us arise from the nature supposed to inhere in psychic facts specifically. Whatever may be the case with physical objects, a fact of consciousness, it is alleged (and indeed very plausibly), cannot, without self-contradiction, be treated as a portion of two different minds, and for the following reasons.

In the physical world we make with impunity the assumption that one and the same material object can figure in an indefinitely large number of different processes at once. When, for instance, a sheet of rubber is pulled at its four corners, a unit of rubber in the middle of the sheet is affected by all four of the pulls. It *transmits* them each, as if it pulled in four different ways at once itself. So, an air-particle or an ether-particle 'compounds' the different directions of movement imprinted on it without obliterating their several individualities. It delivers them distinct, on the contrary, at as many several 'receivers' (ear, eye or what not) as may be 'tuned' to that effect. The apparent paradox of a distinctness like this surviving in the midst of compounding is a thing which, I fancy, the analyses made by physicists have by this time sufficiently cleared up.

But if, on the strength of these analogies, one should ask: "Why, if two or more lines can run through one and the same geometrical point, or if two or more distinct processes of activity can run through one and the same physical thing so that it simultaneously plays a role in each and every process, might not two or more streams of personal consciousness include one and the same unit of experience so that it would simultaneously be a part of the experience of all the different minds?" one would be checked by thinking of a certain peculiarity by which phenomena of consciousness differ from physical things.

While physical things, namely, are supposed to be permanent and to have their 'states,' a fact of consciousness exists but once and *is* a state. Its *esse* is *sentiri*; it is only so far as it is felt; and it is unambiguously and unequivocally exactly *what* is felt. The hypothesis under consideration would, however, oblige it to be felt equivocally, felt now as part of my mind and again at the same time *not* as a part of my mind, but of yours (for my mind is *not* yours), and this would seem impossible without doubling it into two distinct things, or, in other words, without reverting to the ordinary dualistic philosophy of insulated minds each knowing its object representatively as a third thing,—and that would be to give up the pure experience scheme altogether.

Can we see, then, any way in which a unit of pure experience might enter into and figure in two diverse streams of consciousness without turning itself into the two units which, on our hypothesis, it must not be?

II

There is a way; and the first step towards it is to see more precisely how the unit enters into either one of the streams of consciousness alone. Just what, from being 'pure,' does its becoming 'conscious' *once* mean?

It means, first, that new experiences have supervened; and, second, that they have borne a certain assignable relation to the unit supposed. Continue, if you please, to speak of the pure unit as 'the pen.' So far as the pen's successors do but repeat the pen or, being different from it, are 'energetically'[4] related to it, it and they will form a group of stably existing physical things. So far, however, as its successors differ from it in another well-determined way, the pen will figure in their context, not as a physical, but as a mental fact. It will become a passing 'percept,' my percept of that pen. What now is that decisive well-determined way?

In the chapter on 'The Self,' in my *Principles of Psychology*, I explained the continuous identity of each personal consciousness as a name for the practical fact that new experiences[5] come which look back on the old ones, find them 'warm,' and greet and appropriate them as 'mine.' These operations mean, when analyzed empirically, several tolerably definite things, viz.:

1. That the new experience has past time for its 'content,' and in that time a pen that 'was';
2. That 'warmth' was also about the pen: in the sense of a group of feelings ('interest' aroused, 'attention' turned, 'eyes' employed, etc.) that were closely connected with it and that now recur and evermore recur with unbroken vividness, though from the pen of now which may be only an image all such vividness may have gone;
3. That these feelings are the nucleus of 'me';
4. That whatever once was associated with them was, at least for that one moment, 'mine'—my implement if associated with hand-feelings, my 'percept' only, if only eye-feelings and attention-feelings were involved.

The pen, realized in this retrospective way as my percept, thus figures as a fact of 'conscious' life. But it does so only so far as 'appropriation' has occurred; and appropriation is *part of the content of a later experience* wholly additional to the originally 'pure' pen. *That* pen, virtually both objective and subjective, is at its own moment actually and intrinsically neither. It has to be looked back upon and *used*, in order to be classed in either distinctive way. But its use, so called, is in the hands of the other experience, while *it* stands, throughout the operation, passive and unchanged.

If this pass muster as an intelligible account of how an experience originally pure can enter into one consciousness, the next question is as to how it might conceivably enter into two.

III

Obviously no new kind of condition would have to be supplied. All that we should have to postulate would be a second subsequent experience, collateral and contemporary with the first subsequent one, in which a similar act of appropriation should occur. The two acts would interfere neither with one another nor with the originally pure pen. It would sleep undisturbed in its own past, no matter how many such successors went through their several appropriative acts. Each would know it as 'my' percept, each would class it as a 'conscious' fact.

Nor need their so classing it interfere in the least with their classing it at the same time as a physical pen. Since the classing in both cases depends upon the taking of it in one group or another of associates, if the superseding experience were of wide enough 'span' it could think the pen in both groups simultaneously, and yet distinguish the two groups. It would then see the whole situation conformably to what we call 'the representative theory of cognition,' and that is what we all spontaneously do. As a man philosophizing 'popularly,' I believe that what I see myself writing with is double—I think it in its relations to physical nature, and also in its relations to my personal life; I see that it is in my mind, but that it also is a physical pen.

The paradox of the same experience figuring in two consciousnesses seems thus no paradox at all. To be 'conscious' means not simply to be, but to be reported, known, to have awareness of one's being added to that being; and this is just what happens when the appropriative experience supervenes. The pen-experience in its original immediacy is not aware of itself, it simply *is*, and the second experience is required for what we call awareness of it to occur.[6] The difficulty of understanding what happens here is, therefore, not a logical difficulty: there is no contradiction involved. It is an ontological difficulty rather. Experiences come on an enormous scale, and if we take them all together, they come in a chaos of incommensurable relations that we can not straighten out. We have to abstract different groups of them, and handle these separately if we are to talk of them at all. But how the experiences ever *get themselves made*, or *why* their characters and relations are just such as appear, we cannot begin to understand. Granting, however, that, by hook or crook, they *can* get themselves made, and can appear in the successions that I have so schematically described, then we have to confess that even although (as I began by quoting from the adversary) 'a feeling only is as it is felt,' there is still nothing absurd in the notion of its being felt in two different ways at once, as yours, namely, and as mine. It is, indeed, 'mine' only as it is felt as mine, and 'yours' only as it is felt as yours. But it is felt as neither *by itself*, but only when 'owned' by our two several remembering experiences, just as one undivided estate is owned by several heirs.

IV

One word, now, before I close, about the corollaries of the views set forth. Since the acquisition of conscious quality on the part of an experience depends upon a context coming to it, it follows that the sum total of all experiences, having no context, cannot strictly be called conscious at all. It is a *that*, an Absolute, a 'pure' experience on an enormous scale, undifferentiated and undifferentiable into thought and thing. This the post-Kantian idealists have always practically acknowledged by calling their doctrine an *Identitätsphilosophie*. The question of the *Beseelung* of the All of things ought not, then, even to be asked. No more ought the question of its *truth* to be asked, for truth is a relation inside of the sum total, obtaining between thoughts and something else, and thoughts, as we have seen, can only be contextual things. In these respects the pure experiences of our philosophy are, in themselves considered so many little absolutes, the philosophy of pure experience being only a more comminuted *Identitätsphilosophie*.

Meanwhile, a pure experience can be postulated with any amount whatever of span or field. If it exert the retrospective and appropriative function on any other piece of experience, the latter thereby enters into its own conscious stream. And in this operation time intervals make no essential difference. After sleeping, my retrospection is as perfect as it is between two successive waking moments of my time. Accordingly if, millions of years later, a similarly retrospective experience should anyhow come to birth, my present thought would form a genuine portion of its long-span conscious life. 'Form a portion,' I say, but not in the sense that the two things could be entitatively or substantively one— they cannot, for they are numerically discrete facts—but only in the sense that the *functions* of my present thought, its knowledge, its purpose, its content and 'consciousness,' in short, being inherited, would be continued practically unchanged. Speculations like Fechner's, of an Earth-soul, of wider spans of consciousness enveloping narrower ones throughout the cosmos, are, therefore, philosophically quite in order, provided they distinguish the functional from the entitative point of view, and do not treat the minor consciousness under discussion as a kind of standing material of which the wider ones *consist*.

Part Two

Knowledge and Action

7

The Will to Believe

In the recently published *Life* by Leslie Stephen of his brother, Fitz-james, there is an account of a school to which the latter went when he was a boy. The teacher, a certain Mr. Guest, used to converse with his pupils in this wise: "Gurney, what is the difference between justification and sanctification?—Stephen, prove the omnipotence of God!" etc. In the midst of our Harvard freethinking and indifference we are prone to imagine that here at your good old orthodox College conversation continues to be somewhat upon this order; and to show you that we at Harvard have not lost all interest in these vital subjects, I have brought with me tonight something like a sermon on justification by faith to read to you—I mean an essay in justification *of* faith, a defense of our right to adopt a believing attitude in religious matters, in spite of the fact that our merely logical intellect may not have been coerced. "The Will to Believe," accordingly, is the title of my paper.

I have long defended to my own students the lawfulness of voluntarily adopted faith; but as soon as they have got well imbued with the logical spirit, they have as a rule refused to admit my contention to be lawful philosophically, even though in point of fact they were personally all the time chock-full of some faith or other themselves. I am all the while, however, so profoundly convinced that my own position is correct, that your invitation has seemed to me a good occasion to make my statements more clear. Perhaps your minds will be more open than those with which I have hitherto had to deal. I will be as little technical as I can, though I must begin by setting up some technical distinctions that will help us in the end.

I

Let us give the name of *hypothesis* to anything that may be proposed to our belief; and just as the electricians speak of live and dead wires, let us speak of any hypothesis as either *live* or *dead*. A live hypothesis is one which appeals as a real possibility to him to whom it is proposed. If I ask you to believe in the Mahdi, the notion makes no electric connection with your nature—it refuses to scintillate with any credibility at all. As an hypothesis it is completely dead. To an Arab, however (even if he be not one of the Mahdi's followers), the hypothesis is among the mind's possibilities: it is alive. This shows that deadness and liveness in an hypothesis are not intrinsic properties, but relations to the individual thinker. They are measured by his willingness to act. The maximum of liveness in an hypothesis means willingness to act irrevocably. Practically, that means belief; but there is some believing tendency wherever there is willingness to act at all.

Next, let us call the decision between two hypotheses an *option*. Options may be of several kinds. They may be—1, *living* or *dead*; 2, *forced* or *avoidable*; 3, *momentous* or *trivial*; and for our purposes we may call an option a *genuine* option when it is of the forced, living, and momentous kind.

1. A living option is one in which both hypotheses are live ones. If I say to you: "Be a theosophist or be a Mohammedan," it is probably a dead option, because for you neither hypothesis is likely to be alive. But if I say: "Be an agnostic or be a Christian," it is otherwise: trained as you are, each hypothesis makes some appeal, however small, to your belief.

2. Next, if I say to you: "Choose between going out with your umbrella or without it," I do not offer you a genuine option, for it is not forced. You can easily avoid it by not going out at all. Similarly, if I say, "Either love me or hate me," "Either call my theory true or call it false," your option is avoidable. You may remain indifferent to me, neither loving nor hating, and you may decline to offer any judgment as to my theory. But if I say, "Either accept this truth or go without it," I put on you a forced option, for there is no standing place outside of the alterna-

tive. Every dilemma based on a complete logical disjunction, with no possibility of not choosing, is an option of this forced kind.

3. Finally, if I were Dr. Nansen and proposed to you to join my North Pole expedition, your option would be momentous; for this would probably be your only similar opportunity, and your choice now would either exclude you from the North Pole sort of immortality altogether or put at least the chance of it into your hands. He who refuses to embrace a unique opportunity loses the prize as surely as if he tried and failed. *Per contra*, the option is trivial when the opportunity is not unique, when the stake is insignificant, or when the decision is reversible if it later prove unwise. Such trivial options abound in the scientific life. A chemist finds an hypothesis live enough to spend a year in its verification: he believes in it to that extent. But if his experiments prove inconclusive either way, he is quit for his loss of time, no vital harm being done.

It will facilitate our discussion if we keep all these distinctions well in mind.

II

The next matter to consider is the actual psychology of human opinion. When we look at certain facts, it seems as if our passional and volitional nature lay at the root of all our convictions. When we look at others, it seems as if they could do nothing when the intellect had once said its say. Let us take the latter facts up first.

Does it not seem preposterous on the very face of it to talk of our opinions being modifiable at will? Can our will either help or hinder our intellect in its perceptions of truth? Can we, by just willing it, believe that Abraham Lincoln's existence is a myth, and that the portraits of him in *McClure's Magazine* are all of some one else? Can we, by any effort of our will, or by any strength of wish that it were true, believe ourselves well and about when we are roaring with rheumatism in bed, or feel certain that the sum of the two one-dollar bills in our pocket must be a hundred dollars? We can *say* any of these things, but we are absolutely impotent to believe them; and of just such things is the whole fabric of the truths that we do believe in made up—matters of fact, immediate or remote, as Hume said, and relations between ideas, which are either there or not there for us if we see them so, and which if not there cannot be put there by any action of our own.

In Pascal's *Thoughts* there is a celebrated passage known in literature as Pascal's wager. In it he tries to force us into Christianity by reasoning as if our concern with truth resembled our concern with the stakes in a game of chance. Translated freely his words are these: You must either believe or not believe that God is—which will you do? Your human reason cannot say. A game is going on between you and the nature of things which at the day of judgment will bring out either heads or tails. Weigh what your gains and your losses would be if you should stake all you have on heads, or God's existence: if you win in such case, you gain eternal beatitude; if you lose, you lose nothing at all. If there were an infinity of chances, and only one for God in this wager, still you ought to stake your all on God; for though you surely risk a finite loss by this procedure, any finite loss is reasonable, even a certain one is reasonable, if there is but the possibility of infinite gain. Go, then, and take holy water, and have masses said; belief will come and stupefy your scruples—*Cela vous fera croire et vous abêtira.* Why should you not? At bottom, what have you to lose?

You probably feel that when religious faith expresses itself thus, in the language of the gaming-table, it is put to its last trumps. Surely Pascal's own personal belief in masses and holy water had far other springs; and this celebrated page of his is but an argument for others, a last desperate snatch at a weapon against the hardness of the unbelieving heart. We feel that a faith in masses and holy water adopted willfully after such a mechanical calculation would lack the inner soul of faith's reality; and if we were ourselves in the place of the Deity, we should probably take particular pleasure in cutting off believers of this pattern from their infinite reward. It is evident that unless there be some pre-existing tendency to believe in masses and holy water, the option offered to the will by Pascal is not a living option. Certainly no Turk ever took to masses and holy water on its account; and even to us Protestants these means of salvation seem such foregone impossibilities that Pascal's logic, invoked for them specifically, leaves us unmoved. As well might the Mahdi write to us, saying, "I am the Expected One whom God has created in his effulgence. You shall be infinitely happy if you confess me; otherwise you shall be cut off from the light of the sun. Weigh, then, your infinite gain if I am genuine against your finite sacrifice if I am not!" His logic would be that of Pascal; but he would vainly use it on us, for the hypothesis he offers us is dead. No tendency to act on it exists in us to any degree.

The talk of believing by our volition seems, then, from one point of view, simply silly. From another point of view it is worse than silly, it is vile. When one turns to the magnificent edifice of the physical sciences, and sees how it was reared; what thousands of disinterested moral lives of men lie buried in its mere foundations; what patience and postponement, what choking down of preference, what submission to the icy laws of outer fact are wrought into its very stones and mortar; how absolutely impersonal it stands in its vast augustness—then how besotted and contemptible seems every little sentimentalist who comes blowing his voluntary smoke-wreaths, and pretending to decide things from out of his private dream! Can we wonder if those bred in the rugged and manly school of science should feel like spewing such subjectivism out of their mouths? The whole system of loyalties which grow up in the schools of science go dead against its toleration; so that it is only natural that those who have caught the scientific fever should pass over to the opposite extreme, and write sometimes as if the incorruptibly truthful intellect ought positively to prefer bitterness and unacceptableness to the heart in its cup.

> "It fortifies my soul to know
> That, though I perish, Truth is so—"

sings Clough, while Huxley exclaims: "My only consolation lies in the reflection that, however bad our posterity may become, so far as they hold by the plain rule of not pretending to believe what they have no reason to believe, because it may be to their advantage so to pretend [the word 'pretend' is surely here redundant], they will not have reached the lowest depth of immorality." And that delicious *enfant terrible* Clifford writes: "Belief is desecrated when given to unproved and unquestioned statements for the solace and private pleasure of the believer.... Whoso would deserve well of his fellows in this matter will guard the purity of his belief with a very fanaticism of jealous care, lest at any time it should rest on an unworthy object, and catch a stain which can never be wiped away.... If [a] belief has been accepted on insufficient evidence [even though the belief be true, as Clifford on the same page explains] the pleasure is a stolen one.... It is sinful, because it is stolen in defiance of our duty to mankind. That duty is to guard ourselves from such beliefs as from a pestilence which may shortly master our own body and then spread to the rest of the town.... It is wrong always, everywhere, and for anyone, to believe anything upon insufficient evidence."

III

All this strikes one as healthy, even when expressed, as by Clifford, with somewhat too much of robustious pathos in the voice. Free-will and simple wishing do seem, in the matter of our credences, to be only fifth wheels to the coach. Yet if any one should thereupon assume that intellectual insight is what remains after wish and will and sentimental preference have taken wing, or that pure reason is what then settles our opinions, he would fly quite as directly in the teeth of the facts.

It is only our already dead hypotheses that our willing nature is unable to bring to life again. But what has made them dead for us is for the most part a previous action of our willing nature of an antagonistic kind. When I say "willing nature," I do not mean only such deliberate volitions as may have set up habits of belief that we cannot now escape from—I mean all such factors of belief as fear and hope, prejudice and passion, imitation and partisanship, the circumpressure of our caste and set. As a matter of fact we find ourselves believing, we hardly know how or why. Mr. Balfour gives the name of "authority" to all those influences, born of the intellectual climate, that make hypotheses possible or impossible for us, alive or dead. Here in this room, we all of us believe in molecules and the conservation of energy, in democracy and necessary progress, in Protestant Christianity and the duty of fighting for 'the doctrine of the immortal Monroe,' all for no reasons worthy of the name. We see into these matters with no more inner clearness, and probably with much less, than any disbeliever in them might possess. His unconventionality would probably have some grounds to show for its conclusions; but for us, not insight, but the *prestige* of the opinions, is what makes the spark shoot from them and light up our sleeping magazines of faith. Our reason is quite satisfied, in nine hundred and ninety-nine cases out of every thousand of us, if it can find a few arguments that will do to recite in case our credulity is criticized by someone else. Our faith is faith in someone else's faith, and in the greatest matters this is most the case. Our belief in truth itself, for instance, that there is a truth, and that our minds and it are made for each other—what is it but a passionate affirmation of desire, in which our social system backs us up? We want to have a truth; we want to believe that our experiments and studies and discussions must put us in a continually better and better position towards it; and on this line we agree to fight out our thinking lives. But if a pyrrhonistic sceptic asks us *how we know* all this, can our logic find a reply? No! certainly it cannot. It is just one volition against another—we willing to go in for life upon a trust or assumption which he, for his part, does not care to make.[1]

As a rule we disbelieve all facts and theories for which we have no use. Clifford's cosmic emotions find no use for Christian feelings. Huxley belabors the bishops because there is no use for sacerdotalism in his scheme of life. Newman, on the contrary, goes over to Romanism, and finds all sorts of reasons good for staying there, because a priestly system is for him an organic need and delight. Why do so few "scientists" even look at the evidence for telepathy, so-called? Because they think, as a leading biologist, now dead, once said to me, that even if such a thing were true, scientists ought to band together to keep it suppressed and concealed. It would undo the uniformity of Nature and all sorts of other things without which scientists cannot carry on their pursuits. But if this very man had been shown something which as a scientist he might *do* with telepathy, he might not only have examined the evidence, but even have found it good enough. This very law which the logicians would impose upon us—if I may give the name of logicians to those who would rule out our willing nature here—is based on nothing but their own natural wish to exclude all elements for which they, in their professional quality of logicians, can find no use.

Evidently, then, our non-intellectual nature does influence our convictions. There are passional tendencies and volitions which run before and others which come after belief, and it is only the latter that are too late for the fair; and they are not too late when the previous passional work has been already in their own direction. Pascal's argument, instead of being powerless, then seems a regular clincher, and is the last stroke needed to make our faith in masses and holy water complete. The state of things is evidently far from simple; and pure insight and logic, whatever they might do ideally, are not the only things that really do produce our creeds.

IV

Our next duty, having recognized this mixed-up state of affairs, is to ask whether it be simply reprehensible and pathological, or whether, on the contrary, we must treat it as a normal element in making up our minds. The thesis I defend is, briefly stated, this: *Our passional nature not only lawfully may, but must, decide an option between propositions, whenever it is a genuine option that cannot by its nature be decided on intellectual grounds; for to say, under such circumstances, "Do not decide, but leave the question open," is itself a passional decision—just like deciding yes or no— and is attended with the same risk of losing the truth.* The thesis thus abstractly expressed will, I trust, soon become quite clear. But I must first indulge in a bit more of preliminary work.

V

It will be observed that for the purposes of this discussion we are on 'dogmatic' ground—ground, I mean, which leaves systematic philosophical scepticism altogether out of account. The postulate that there is truth, and that it is the destiny of our minds to attain it, we are deliberately resolving to make, though the sceptic will not make it. We part company with him, therefore, absolutely, at this point. But the faith that truth exists, and that our minds can find it, may be held in two ways. We may talk of the *empiricist* way and of the *absolutist* way of believing in truth. The absolutists in this matter say that we not only can attain to knowing truth, but we can *know when* we have attained to knowing it; while the empiricists think that although we may attain it, we cannot infallibly know when. To *know* is one thing, and to know for certain *that* we know is another. One may hold to the first being possible without the second; hence the empiricists and the absolutists, although neither of them is a sceptic in the usual philosophic sense of the term, show very different degrees of dogmatism in their lives.

If we look at the history of opinions, we see that the empiricist tendency has largely prevailed in science, while in philosophy the absolutist tendency has had everything its own way. The characteristic sort of happiness, indeed, which philosophies yield has mainly consisted in the conviction felt by each successive school or system that by it bottom-certitude had been attained. "Other philosophies are collections of opinions, mostly false; *my* philosophy gives standing-ground forever"—who does not recognize in this the key-note of every system worthy of the name? A system, to be a system at all, must come as a *closed* system, reversible in this or that detail, perchance, but in its essential features never!

Scholastic orthodoxy, to which one must always go when one wishes to find perfectly clear statement, has beautifully elaborated this absolutist conviction in a doctrine which it calls that of 'objective evidence.' If, for example, I am unable to doubt that I now exist before you, that two is less than three, or that if all men are mortal then I am mortal too, it is because these things illumine my intellect irresistibly. The final ground of this objective evidence possessed by certain propositions is the *adaequatio intellectûs nostri cum rê.* The certitude it brings involves an *aptitudinem ad extorquendum certum assensum* on the part of the truth envisaged, and on the side of the subject a *quietem in cognitione,* when once the object is mentally received, that leaves no possibility of doubt behind; and in the whole transaction nothing operates but the *entitas ipsa* of the object and the *entitas ipsa* of the mind. We slouchy modern thinkers dislike to talk in Latin—indeed, we dislike to talk in set terms at all; but at bottom our own state of mind is very much like this whenever we uncritically abandon ourselves: You believe in objective evidence, and I do. Of some things we feel that we are certain: we know, and we know that we do know. There is something that gives a click inside of us, a bell that strikes twelve, when the hands of our mental clock have swept the dial and meet over the meridian hour. The greatest empiricists among us are only empiricists on reflection: when left to their instincts, they dogmatize like infallible popes. When the Cliffords tell us how sinful it is to be Christians on such 'insufficient evidence,' insufficiency is really the last thing they have in mind. For them the evidence is absolutely sufficient, only it makes the other way. They believe so completely in an anti-christian order of the universe that there is no living option: Christianity is a dead hypothesis from the start.

VI

But now, since we are all such absolutists by instinct, what in our quality of students of philosophy ought we to do about the fact? Shall we espouse and indorse it? Or shall we treat it as a weakness of our nature from which we must free ourselves, if we can?

I sincerely believe that the latter course is the only one we can follow as reflective men. Objective evidence and certitude are doubtless very fine ideals to play with, but where on this moonlit and dream-visited planet are they found? I am, therefore, myself a complete empiricist so far as my theory of human knowledge goes. I live, to be sure, by the practical faith that we must go on experiencing and thinking over our experience, for only thus can our opinions grow more true; but to hold any one of them—I absolutely do not care which—as if it never could be reinterpretable or corrigible, I believe to be a tremendously mistaken attitude, and I think that the whole history of philosophy will bear me out. There is but one indefectibly certain truth, and that is the truth that pyrrhonistic scepticism itself leaves standing—the truth that the present phenomenon of consciousness exists. That, however, is the bare starting-point of knowledge, the mere admission of a stuff to be philosophized-about. The various philosophies are but so many attempts at expressing what this stuff really is. And if we repair to our libraries what disagreement do we discover! Where is a certainly true answer found? Apart from abstract propositions of comparison (such as two and two are the same as four), propositions which tell us nothing by themselves about concrete reality, we find no proposition ever regarded by anyone as evidently certain that has not either been called a falsehood, or at least had its truth sincerely questioned by someone else. The transcending of the axioms of geometry, not in play but in earnest, by certain of our contemporaries (as Zöllner and Charles H. Hinton), and the rejection of the whole Aristotelian logic by the Hegelians, are striking instances in point.

No concrete test of what is really true has ever been agreed upon. Some make the criterion external to the moment of perception, putting it either in revelation, the *consensus gentium*, the instincts of the heart, or the systematized experience of the race. Others make the perceptive moment its own test—Descartes, for instance, with his clear and distinct ideas guaranteed by the veracity of God; Reid with his 'common-sense'; and Kant with his forms of synthetic judgment *a priori*. The inconceivability of the opposite; the capacity to be verified by sense; the possession of complete organic unity or self-relation, realized when a thing is its own other—are standards which, in turn, have been used. The much lauded objective evidence is never triumphantly there; it is a mere aspiration or *Grenzbegriff*, marking the infinitely remote ideal of our thinking life. To claim that certain truths now possess it, is simply to say that when you think them true and they *are* true, then their evidence is objective, otherwise it is not. But practically one's conviction that the evidence one goes by is of the real objective brand, is only one more subjective opinion added to the lot. For what a contradictory array of opinions have objective evidence and absolute certitude been claimed! The world is rational through and through—its existence is an ultimate brute fact; there is a personal God—a personal God is inconceivable; there is an extra-mental physical world immediately known—the mind can only know its own ideas; a moral imperative exists—obligation is only the resultant of desires; a permanent spiritual principle is in everyone—there are only shifting states of mind; there is an endless chain of causes—there is an absolute first cause; an eternal necessity—a freedom; a purpose—no purpose; a primal One—a primal Many; a universal continuity—an essential discontinuity in things; an infinity—no infinity. There is this—there is that; there is indeed nothing which someone has not thought absolutely true, whilst his neighbor deemed it absolutely false; and not an absolutist among them seems ever to have considered that the trouble may all the time be essential, and that the intellect, even with truth directly in its grasp, may have no infallible signal for knowing whether it be truth or no. When, indeed, one remembers that the most striking practical application to life of the doctrine of objective certitude has been the conscientious labors of the Holy Office of the Inquisition, one feels less tempted than ever to lend the doctrine a respectful ear.

But please observe, now, that when as empiricists we give up the doctrine of objective certitude, we do not thereby give up the quest or hope of truth itself. We still pin our faith on its existence, and still believe that we gain an ever better position towards it by systematically continuing to roll up experiences and think. Our great difference from the scholastic lies in the way we face. The strength of his system lies in the principles, the origin, the *terminus a quo* of his thought; for us the strength is in the outcome, the upshot, the *terminus ad quem.* Not where it comes from but what it leads to is to decide. It matters not to an empiricist from what quarter an hypothesis may come to him: he may have acquired it by fair means or by foul; passion may have whispered or accident suggested it; but if the total drift of thinking continues to confirm it, that is what he means by its being true.

VII

One more point, small but important, and our preliminaries are done. There are two ways of looking at our duty in the matter of opinion—ways entirely different, and yet ways about whose difference the theory of knowledge seems hitherto to have shown very little concern. *We must know the truth*; and *we must avoid error*—these are our first and great commandments as would-be knowers; but they are not two ways of stating an identical commandment, they are two separable laws. Although it may indeed happen that when we believe the truth *A*, we escape as an incidental consequence from believing the falsehood *B*, it hardly ever happens that by merely disbelieving *B* we necessarily believe *A*. We may in escaping *B* fall into believing other falsehoods, *C* or *D*, just as bad as *B*; or we may escape *B* by not believing anything at all, not even *A*.

Believe truth! Shun error!—these, we see, are two materially different laws; and by choosing between them we may end by coloring differently our whole intellectual life. We may regard the chase for truth as paramount, and the avoidance of error as secondary; or we may, on the other hand, treat the avoidance of error as more imperative, and let truth take its chance. Clifford, in the instructive passage which I have quoted, exhorts us to the latter course. Believe nothing, he tells us, keep your mind in suspense forever, rather than by closing it on insufficient evidence incur the awful risk of believing lies. You, on the other hand, may think that the risk of being in error is a very small matter when compared with the blessings of real knowledge, and be ready to be duped many times in your investigation rather than postpone indefinitely the chance of guessing true. I myself find it impossible to go with Clifford. We must remember that these feelings of our duty about either truth or error are in any case only expressions of our passional life. Biologically considered, our minds are as ready to grind out falsehood as veracity, and he who says "Better go without belief forever than believe a lie!" merely shows his own preponderant private horror of becoming a dupe. He may be critical of many of his desires and fears, but this fear he slavishly obeys. He cannot imagine any one questioning its binding force. For my own part,

I have also a horror of being duped; but I can believe that worse things than being duped may happen to a man in this world: so Clifford's exhortation has to my ears a thoroughly fantastic sound. It is like a general informing his soldiers that it is better to keep out of battle forever than to risk a single wound. Not so are victories either over enemies or over nature gained. Our errors are surely not such awfully solemn things. In a world where we are so certain to incur them in spite of all our caution, a certain lightness of heart seems healthier than this excessive nervousness on their behalf. At any rate, it seems the fittest thing for the empiricist philosopher.

VIII

And now, after all this introduction, let us go straight at our question. I have said, and now repeat it, that not only as a matter of fact do we find our passional nature influencing us in our opinions, but that there are some options between opinions in which this influence must be regarded both as an inevitable and as a lawful determinant of our choice.

I fear here that some of you my hearers will begin to scent danger, and lend an inhospitable ear. Two first steps of passion you have indeed had to admit as necessary—we must think so as to avoid dupery, and we must think so as to gain truth; but the surest path to those ideal consummations, you will probably consider, is from now onwards to take no further passional step.

Well, of course, I agree as far as the facts will allow. Wherever the option between losing truth and gaining it is not momentous, we can throw the chance of *gaining truth* away, and at any rate save ourselves from any chance of *believing falsehood*, by not making up our minds at all till objective evidence has come. In scientific questions, this is almost always the case; and even in human affairs in general, the need of acting is seldom so urgent that a false belief to act on is better than no belief at all. Law courts, indeed, have to decide on the best evidence attainable for the moment, because a judge's duty is to make law as well as to ascertain it, and (as a learned judge once said to me) few cases are worth spending much time over: the great thing is to have them decided on *any* acceptable principle, and got out of the way. But in our dealings with objective nature we obviously are recorders, not makers, of the truth; and decisions for the mere sake of deciding promptly and getting on to the next business would be wholly out of place. Throughout the breadth of physical nature facts are what they are quite independently of us, and seldom is there any such hurry about them that the risks of being duped by believing a premature theory need be faced. The questions here are always trivial options, the hypotheses are hardly living (at any rate not living for us spectators), the choice between believing truth or falsehood is seldom forced. The attitude of sceptical balance is therefore the absolutely wise one if we would escape mistakes. What difference, indeed, does it make to most of us whether we have or have not a theory of the Röntgen rays, whether we believe or not in mind-stuff, or have a conviction about the causality of conscious states? It makes no difference. Such options are not forced on us. On every account it is better not to make them, but still keep weighing reasons *pro et contra* with an indifferent hand.

I speak, of course, here of the purely judging mind. For purposes of discovery such indifference is to be less highly recommended, and science would be far less advanced than she is if the passionate desires of individuals to get their own faiths confirmed had been kept out of the game. See for example the sagacity which Spencer and Weismann now display. On the other hand, if you want an absolute duffer in an investigation, you must, after all, take the man who has no interest whatever in its results: he is the warranted incapable, the positive fool. The most useful investigator, because the most sensitive observer, is always he whose eager interest in one side of the question is balanced by an equally keen nervousness lest he become deceived.[2] Science has organized this nervousness into a regular *technique,* her so-called method of verification; and she has fallen so deeply in love with the method that one may even say she has ceased to care for truth by itself at all. It is only truth as technically verified that interests her. The truth of truths might come in merely affirmative form, and she would decline to touch it. Such truth as that, she might repeat with Clifford, would be stolen in defiance of her duty to mankind. Human passions, however, are stronger than technical rules. "Le coeur a ses raisons," as Pascal says, "que la raison ne connaît pas"; and however indifferent to all but the bare rules of the game the umpire, the abstract intellect, may be, the concrete players who furnish him the materials to judge of are usually, each one of them, in love with some pet 'live hypothesis' of his own. Let us agree, however, that wherever there is no forced option, the dispassionately judicial intellect with no pet hypothesis, saving us, as it does, from dupery at any rate, ought to be our ideal.

The question next arises: Are there not somewhere forced options in our speculative questions, and can we (as men who may be interested at least as much in positively gaining truth as in merely escaping dupery) always wait with impunity till the coercive evidence shall have arrived? It seems *a priori* improbable that the truth should be so nicely adjusted to our needs and powers as that. In the great boarding-house of nature, the cakes and the butter and the syrup seldom come out so even and leave the plates so clean. Indeed, we should view them with scientific suspicion if they did.

IX

Moral questions immediately present themselves as questions whose solution cannot wait for sensible proof. A moral question is a question not of what sensibly exists, but of what is good, or would be good if it did exist. Science can tell us what exists; but to compare the *worths*, both of what exists and of what does not exist, we must consult not science, but what Pascal calls our heart. Science herself consults her heart when she lays it down that the infinite ascertainment of fact and correction of false belief are the supreme goods for man. Challenge the statement and science can only repeat it oracularly, or else prove it by showing that such ascertainment and correction bring man all sorts of other goods which man's heart in turn declares. The question of having moral beliefs at all or not having them is decided by our will. Are our moral preferences true or false, or are they only odd biological phenomena, making things good or bad for *us*, but in themselves indifferent? How can your pure intellect decide? If your heart does not *want* a world of moral reality, your head will assuredly never make you believe in one. Mephistophelian scepticism, indeed, will satisfy the head's play-instincts much better than any rigorous idealism can. Some men (even at the student age) are so naturally cool-hearted that the moralistic hypothesis never has for them any pungent life, and in their supercilious presence the hot young moralist always feels strangely ill at ease. The appearance of knowingness is on their side, of *naïveté* and gullibility on his. Yet, in the inarticulate heart of him, he clings to it that he is not a dupe, and that there is a realm in which (as Emerson says) all their wit and intellectual superiority is no better than the cunning of a fox. Moral scepticism can no more be refuted or proved by logic than intellectual scepticism can. When we stick to it that there *is* truth (be it of either kind), we do so with our whole nature, and resolve to stand or fall by the results. The sceptic with his whole nature adopts the doubting attitude; but which of us is the wiser, Omniscience only knows.

Turn now from these wide questions of good to a certain class of questions of fact, questions concerning personal relations, states of mind between one man and another. *Do you like me or not?*—for example. Whether you do or not depends, in countless instances, on whether I meet you half-way, am willing to assume that you must like me, and show you trust and expectation. The previous faith on my part in your liking's existence is in such cases what makes your liking come. But if I stand aloof, and refuse to budge an inch until I have objective evidence, until you shall have done something apt, as the absolutists say, *ad extorquendum assensum meum*, ten to one your liking never comes. How many women's hearts are vanquished by the mere sanguine insistence of some man that they *must* love him! he will not consent to the hypothesis that they cannot. The desire for a certain kind of truth here brings about that special truth's existence; and so it is in innumerable cases of other sorts. Who gains promotions, boons, appointments, but the man in whose life they are seen to play the part of live hypotheses, who discounts them, sacrifices other things for their sake before they have come, and takes risks for them in advance? His faith acts on the powers above him as a claim, and creates its own verification.

A social organism of any sort whatever, large or small, is what it is because each member proceeds to his own duty with a trust that the other members will simultaneously do theirs. Wherever a desired result is achieved by the co-operation of many independent persons, its existence as a fact is a pure consequence of the precursive faith in one another of those immediately concerned. A government, an army, a commercial system, a ship, a college, an athletic team, all exist on this condition, without which not only is nothing achieved, but nothing is even attempted. A whole train of passengers (individually brave enough) will be looted by a few highwaymen, simply because the latter can count on one another, while each passenger fears that if he makes a movement of resistance, he will be shot before any one else backs him up. If we believed that the whole car-full would rise at once with us, we should each severally rise, and train-robbing would never even be attempted. There are, then, cases where a fact cannot come at all unless a preliminary faith exists in its coming. *And where faith in a fact can help create the fact,* that would be an insane logic which should say that faith running ahead of scientific evidence is the "lowest kind of immorality" into which a thinking being can fall. Yet such is the logic by which our scientific absolutists pretend to regulate our lives!

X

In truths dependent on our personal action, then, faith based on desire is certainly a lawful and possibly an indispensable thing.

But now, it will be said, these are all childish human cases, and have nothing to do with great cosmical matters, like the question of religious faith. Let us then pass on to that. Religions differ so much in their accidents that in discussing the religious question we must make it very generic and broad. What then do we now mean by the religious hypothesis? Science says things are; morality says some things are better than other things; and religion says essentially two things.

First, she says that the best things are the more eternal things, the overlapping things, the things in the universe that throw the last stone, so to speak, and say the final word. "Perfection is eternal"—this phrase of Charles Secrétan seems a good way of putting this first affirmation of religion, an affirmation which obviously cannot yet be verified scientifically at all. The second affirmation of religion is that we are better off even now if we believe her first affirmation to be true.

Now, let us consider what the logical elements of this situation are *in case the religious hypothesis in both its branches be really true.* (Of course, we must admit that possibility at the outset. If we are to discuss the question at all, it must involve a living option. If for any of you religion be a hypothesis that cannot, by any living possibility be true, then you need go no farther. I speak to the 'saving remnant' alone.) So proceeding, we see, first, that religion offers itself as a *momentous* option. We are supposed to gain, even now, by our belief, and to lose by our non-belief, a certain vital good. Secondly, religion is a *forced* option, so far as that good goes. We cannot escape the issue by remaining sceptical and waiting for more light, because, although we do avoid error in that way *if religion be untrue,* we lose the good, *if it be true,* just as certainly as if we positively chose to disbelieve. It is as if a man should hesitate indefinitely to ask a certain woman to marry him because he was not perfectly sure that she would prove an angel after he brought her home. Would he not cut himself off from that particular angel-possibility as decisively as if he went and married some one else? Scepticism, then, is not avoidance of option; it is option of a certain particular kind of risk. *Better risk loss of truth than chance of error*—that is your faith-vetoer's exact position. He is actively playing his stake as much as the believer is; he is backing the field against the religious hypothesis, just as the believer is backing the religious hypothesis against the field. To preach scepticism to us as a duty until 'sufficient evidence' for religion be found, is tantamount therefore to telling us, when in presence of the religious hypothesis, that to yield to our fear of its being error is wiser and better than to yield to our hope that it may be true. It is not intellect against all passions, then; it is only intellect with one passion laying down its law. And by what, forsooth, is the supreme wisdom of this passion warranted? Dupery for dupery, what proof is there that dupery through hope is so much worse than dupery through fear? I, for one, can see no proof; and I simply refuse obedience to the scientist's command to imitate his kind of option, in a case where my own stake is important enough to give me the right to choose my own form of risk. If religion be true and the evidence for it be still insufficient, I do not wish, by putting your extinguisher upon my nature (which feels to me as if it had after all some business in this matter), to forfeit my sole chance in life of getting upon the winning side—that chance depending, of course, on my willingness to run the risk of acting as if my passional need of taking the world religiously might be prophetic and right.

All this is on the supposition that it really may be prophetic and right, and that, even to us who are discussing the matter, religion is a live hypothesis which may be true. Now, to most of us religion comes in a still farther way that makes a veto on our active faith even more illogical. The more perfect and more eternal aspect of the universe is represented in our religions as having personal form. The universe is no longer a mere *It* to us, but a *Thou*, if we are religious; and any relation that may be possible from person to person might be possible here. For instance, although in one sense we are passive portions of the universe, in another we show a curious autonomy, as if we were small active centers on our own account. We feel, too, as if the appeal of religion to us were made to our own active good-will, as if evidence might be forever withheld from us unless we met the hypothesis half-way. To take a trivial illustration: just as a man who in a company of gentlemen made no advances, asked a warrant for every concession, and believed no one's word without proof, would cut himself off by such churlishness from all the social rewards that a more trusting spirit would earn—so here, one who should shut himself up in snarling logicality and try to make the gods extort his recognition willy-nilly, or not get it at all, might cut himself off forever from his only opportunity of making the gods' acquaintance. This feeling, forced on us we know not whence, that by obstinately believing that there are gods (although not to do so would be so easy both for our logic and our life) we are doing the universe the deepest service we can, seems part of the living essence of the religious hypothesis. If the hypothesis *were* true in all its parts, including this one, then pure intellectualism, with its veto on our making willing advances, would be an absurdity; and some participation of our sympathetic nature would be logically required. I, therefore, for one, cannot see my way to accepting the agnostic rules for truth-seeking, or wilfully agree to keep my willing nature out of the game. I cannot do so for this plain reason, that *a rule of thinking which would absolutely prevent me from acknowledging certain kinds of truth if those kinds of truth were really there, would be an irrational rule.* That for me is the long and short of the formal logic of the situation, no matter what the kinds of truth might materially be.

I confess I do not see how this logic can be escaped. But sad experience makes me fear that some of you may still shrink from radically saying with me, *in abstracto*, that we have the right to believe at our own risk any hypothesis that is live enough to tempt our will. I suspect, however, that if this is so, it is because you have got away from the abstract logical point of view altogether, and are thinking (perhaps without realizing it) of some particular religious hypothesis which for you is dead. The freedom to 'believe what we will' you apply to the case of some patent superstition; and the faith you think of is the faith defined by the schoolboy when he said, "Faith is when you believe something that you know ain't true." I can only repeat that this is misapprehension. *In concreto*, the freedom to believe can only cover living options which the intellect of the individual cannot by itself resolve; and living options never seem absurdities to him who has them to consider. When I look at the religious question as it really puts itself to concrete men, and when I think of all the possibilities which both practically and theoretically it involves, then this command that we shall put a stopper on our heart, instincts, and courage, and *wait*—acting of course meanwhile more or less as if religion were *not* true[3]—till doomsday, or till such time as our intellect and senses working together may have raked in evidence enough—this command, I say, seems to me the queerest idol ever manufactured in the philosophic cave. Were we scholastic absolutists, there might be more excuse. If we had an infallible intellect with its objective certitudes, we might feel ourselves disloyal to such a perfect organ of knowledge in not trusting to it exclusively, in not waiting for its releasing word. But if we are empiricists, if we believe that no bell in us tolls to let us know for certain when truth is in our grasp, then it seems a piece of idle fantasticality to preach so solemnly our duty of waiting for the bell. Indeed we *may* wait if we will—I hope you do not think that I am denying that—but if we do so, we do so at our peril as much as if we believed. In either case we *act,* taking our life in our hands. No one of us ought to issue vetoes to the other, nor should we bandy words of abuse. We ought, on the contrary, delicately and profoundly to respect one another's mental freedom—then only shall we bring about the intellectual republic; then only shall we have that spirit of inner tolerance without which all our outer tolerance is soulless, and which is empiricism's glory; then only shall we live and let live, in speculative as well as in practical things.

I began by a reference to Fitzjames Stephen; let me end by a quotation from him. "What do you think of yourself? What do you think of the world? . . . These are questions with which all must deal as it seems good to them. They are riddles of the Sphinx, and in some way or other we must deal with them. . . . In all important transactions of life we have to take a leap in the dark. . . . If we decide to leave the riddles unanswered, that is a choice; if we waver in our answer, that, too, is a choice; but whatever choice we make, we make it at our peril. If a man chooses to turn his back altogether on God and the future, no one can prevent him; no one can show beyond reasonable doubt that he is mistaken. If a man thinks otherwise, and acts as he thinks, I do not see how any one can prove that *he* is mistaken. Each must act as he thinks best, and if he is wrong so much the worse for him. We stand on a mountain pass in the midst of whirling snow and blinding mist, through which we get glimpses now and then of paths which may be deceptive. If we stand still, we shall be frozen to death. If we take the wrong road we shall be dashed to pieces. We do not certainly know whether there is any right one. What must we do? 'Be strong and of a good courage.' Act for the best, hope for the best, and take what comes. . . . If death ends all, we cannot meet death better."[4]

8

The Function of Cognition

The following inquiry is (to use a distinction familiar to readers of Mr. Shadworth Hodgson) not an inquiry into the 'how it comes,' but into the 'what it is' of cognition. What we call acts of cognition are evidently realized through what we call brains and their events, whether there be 'souls' dynamically connected with the brains or not. But with neither brains nor souls has this essay any business to transact. In it we shall simply assume that cognition *is* produced, somehow, and limit ourselves to asking what elements it contains, what factors it implies. In other words, our task is a purely analytic and introspective one; less important, possibly, than would be a successful research into the *causes* of cognition, but still interesting enough in its way.

Cognition is a function of consciousness. The first factor it implies is therefore a state of consciousness wherein the cognition shall take place. Having elsewhere used the word 'feeling' to designate generically all states of consciousness considered subjectively, or without respect to their possible function, I shall then say that, whatever elements an act of cognition may imply besides, it at least implies the existence of a *feeling*. [If the reader share the current antipathy to the word 'feeling,' he may substitute for it, wherever I use it, the word 'idea,' taken in the old broad Lockian sense, or he may use the clumsy phrase 'state of consciousness,' or finally he may say 'thought' instead.]

Now it is to be observed that the common consent of mankind has agreed that some feelings are cognitive and some are simple facts having a subjective or, what one might almost call a physical, existence, but no such self-transcendent function as would be implied in their being pieces of knowledge. Our task is again limited here. We are not to ask, "How is self-transcendence possible?" We are only to ask, How comes it that common sense has assigned a number of cases in which it is assumed not only to be possible but actual? And what are the marks used by common sense to distinguish those cases from the rest? In short, our inquiry is a chapter in descriptive psychology—hardly anything more.

Condillac embarked on a quest similar to this by his famous hypothesis of a statue to which various feelings were successively imparted. Its first feeling was supposed to be one of fragrance. But to avoid all possible complication with the question of genesis, let us not attribute even to a statue the possession of our imaginary feeling. Let us rather suppose it attached to no matter, nor localized at any point in space, but left swinging *in vacuo*, as it were, by the direct creative *fiat* of a god. And let us also, to escape entanglement with difficulties about the physical or psychical nature of its 'object,' not call it a feeling of fragrance or of any other determinate sort, but limit ourselves to assuming that it is a feeling of q. What is true of it under this abstract name will be no less true of it in any more particular shape (such as fragrance, pain, hardness) the reader may suppose.

Now, if this feeling of q be the only creation of the god, it will of course form the entire universe. And if, to escape the cavils of that large class of persons who believe that *semper idem sentire ac non sentire* are the same,[1] we allow the feeling to be of as short a duration as they like, that universe will only need to last an infinitesimal part of a second. The feeling in question will thus be reduced to its fighting weight, and all that befalls it in the way of a cognitive function must be held to befall in the brief instant of its quickly snuffed-out life,—a life, it will also be noticed, that has no other moment of consciousness either preceding or following it.

Well now, can our little feeling, thus left alone in the universe,—for the god and we psychological critics may be supposed left out of the account,—can the feeling, I say, be said to have any sort of a cognitive function? For it to *know*, there must be something to be known. What is there, on the present supposition? One may reply, "the feeling's content *q.*" But does it not seem more proper to call this the feeling's *quality* than its content? Does not the word 'content' suggest that the feeling itself has already been discriminated as an act from its content as an object? And would it be quite safe to assume so promptly that the quality *q* of a feeling is one and the same thing with a feeling of the quality *q*? The quality *q*, so far, is an entirely subjective fact which the feeling carries in its pocket, so to speak, endogenously. If anyone pleases to dignify so simple a fact as this by the name of knowledge, of course nothing can prevent him. But let us keep closer to the path of common usage, and reserve the name knowledge for the cognition of 'realities,' meaning by realities things that exist independently of the feeling through which their cognition occurs. If the content of the feeling occur nowhere in the universe outside of the feeling itself, and perish with the feeling, common usage refuses to call it a reality, and brands it as a subjective feature of the feeling's constitution, or at the most as the feeling's *dream*.

For the feeling to be cognitive in the specific sense, then, it must be self-transcendent; and we must prevail upon the god to create a reality outside of it to correspond to its intrinsic quality *q*. Thus only can it be redeemed from the condition of being a solipsism. If now the new-created reality *resemble* the feeling's quality *q*, I say that the feeling may be held by us *to be cognizant of that reality.*

This first installment of my thesis is sure to be attacked. But one word before defending it. 'Reality' has become our warrant for calling a feeling cognitive; but what becomes our warrant for calling anything reality? The only reply is—the faith of the present critic or inquirer. At every moment of his life he finds himself subject to a belief in *some* realities, even though his realities of this year should prove to be his illusions of the next. Whenever he finds that the feeling he is studying contemplates what he himself regards as a reality, he must of course admit the feeling itself to be truly cognitive. We are ourselves the critics here; and we shall find our burden much lightened by being allowed to take reality in this relative and provisional way. Every science must make some assumptions. *Erkenntnisstheoretiker* are but fallible mortals. When they study the function of cognition, they do it by means of the same function in themselves. And knowing that the fountain cannot go higher than its source, we should promptly confess that our results in this field are affected by our own liability to err. *The most we can claim is, that what we say about cognition may be counted as true as what we say about anything else.* If our hearers agree with us about what are to be held 'realities,' they will perhaps also agree to our doctrine of the way in which they are known. We cannot ask for more.

Our terminology shall follow the spirit of these remarks. We will deny the function of knowledge to any feeling whose quality or content we do not ourselves believe to exist outside of that feeling as well as in it. We may call such a feeling a dream if we like; we shall have to see later on whether we can call it a fiction or an error.

To revert now to our thesis. Followers of Berkeley and Reid will immediately cry out, "How *can* a reality resemble a feeling?" Here we find how wise we were to name the quality of the feeling by an algebraic letter q. We flank the whole difficulty of resemblance between an inner state and an outward reality, by leaving it free to anyone to postulate as the reality whatever sort of thing he thinks *can* resemble a feeling,—if not an outward thing, then another feeling like the first one,—the mere feeling q in the critic's mind for example. Evading thus this objection, we turn to another which is sure to be urged.

It will come from those philosophers to whom 'thought,' in the sense of a knowledge of relations, is the all in all of mental life; and who hold a merely feeling consciousness to be no better—one would sometimes say from their utterances, a good deal worse—than no consciousness at all. Such phrases as these, for example, are common today in the mouths of those who claim to walk in the footprints of Kant and Hegel rather than in the ancestral English paths: "A perception detached from all others, 'left out of the heap we call a mind,' being out of all relation, has no qualities— is simply nothing. We can no more consider it than we can see vacancy." "It is simply in itself—fleeting, momentary, unnamable (because while we name it, it has become another), and for the very same reason unknowable, the very negation of knowability." "Exclude from what we have considered real all qualities constituted by relation, we find that none are left."

Although such citations as these from the late Professor Green might be multiplied almost indefinitely, it would hardly repay the pains of collection, so egregiously false is the doctrine they teach. Our little supposed feeling, whatever it may be, from the cognitive point of view, whether a bit of knowledge or a dream, is certainly no psychical zero. It is a most positively and definitely qualified inner fact, with a complexion all its own. Of course there are many mental facts which it is *not*. It knows *q*, if *q* be a reality, with a very minimum of knowledge. It neither dates nor locates it. It neither classes nor names it. And it neither knows itself as a feeling, nor contrasts itself with other feelings, nor estimates its own duration or intensity. It is, in short, if there is no more of it than this, a most dumb and helpless and useless kind of thing.

But if we must describe it by so many negations, and if it can say nothing *about* itself or *about* anything else, by what right do we deny that it is a psychical zero? And may not the 'relationists' be right after all?

In the innocent looking word 'about' lies the solution of this riddle; and a simple enough solution it is when frankly looked at. A quotation from a too seldom quoted book, the *Exploratio Philosophica* of John Grote (London, 1865), p. 60, will form the best introduction to it.

"Our knowledge," writes Grote, "may be contemplated in either of two ways, or, to use other words, we may speak in a double manner of the 'object' of knowledge. That is, we may either use language thus: we *know* a thing, a man, etc.; or we may use it thus: we know such and such things *about* the thing, the man, etc. Language in general, following its true logical instinct, distinguishes between these two applications of the notion of knowledge, the one being γνῶναι, *noscere, kennen, connaître,* the other being εἰδέναι, *scire, wissen, savoir.* In the origin, the former may be considered more what I have called phenomenal—it is the notion of knowledge as *acquaintance* or familiarity with what is known; which notion is perhaps more akin to the phenomenal bodily communication, and is less purely intellectual than the other: it is the kind of knowledge which we have of a thing by the presentation to the senses or the representation of it in picture or type, a '*vorstellung*.' The other, which is what we express in judgments or propositions, what is embodied in 'begriffe' or concepts without any necessary imaginative representation, is in its origin the more *intellectual* notion of knowledge. There is no reason however why we should not express our knowledge, whatever its kind, in either manner, provided only we do not confusedly express it, in the same proposition or piece of reasoning, in both."

Now obviously if our supposed feeling of q is (if knowledge at all) only knowledge of the mere acquaintance-type, it is milking a he-goat, as the ancients would have said, to try to extract from it any deliverance *about* anything under the sun, even about itself. And it is as unjust, after our failure, to turn upon it and call it a psychical nothing, as it would be, after our fruitless attack upon the billy-goat, to proclaim the non-lactiferous character of the whole goat-tribe. But the entire industry of the Hegelian school in trying to shove simple sensation out of the pale of philosophic recognition is founded on this false issue. It is always the 'speechlessness' of sensation, its inability to make any 'statement,'[2] that is held to make the very notion of it meaningless, and to justify the student of knowledge in scouting it out of existence. 'Significance,' in the sense of standing as the sign of other mental states, is taken to be the sole function of what mental states we have; and from the perception that our little primitive sensation has as yet no significance in this literal sense, it is an easy step to call it first meaningless, next senseless, then vacuous, and finally to brand it as absurd and inadmissible. But in this universal liquidation, this everlasting slip, slip, slip, of direct acquaintance into knowledge-*about*, until at last nothing is left between which the knowledge can be supposed to obtain, does not all 'significance' depart from the situation? And when our knowledge about things has reached its never so complicated perfection, must there not needs abide alongside of it and inextricably mixed in with it some acquaintance with *what* things all this knowledge is about?

Now, our supposed little feeling gives a *what*; and if other feelings should succeed which remember the first, its *what* may stand as subject or predicate of some piece of knowledge-about, of some judgment, perceiving relations between it and other *whats* which the other feelings may know. The hitherto dumb q will then receive a name and be no longer speechless. But every name, as students of logic know, has its 'denotation'; and the denotation always means some reality or content, relationless *ab extra* or with its internal relations unanalyzed, like the *q* which our primitive sensation is supposed to know. No relation-expressing proposition is possible except on the basis of a preliminary acquaintance with such 'facts,' with such contents, as this. Let the *q* be fragrance, let it be toothache, or let it be a more complex kind of feeling, like that of the full-moon swimming in her blue abyss, it must first come in that simple shape, and be held fast in that first intention, before any knowledge *about* it can be attained. The knowledge *about* it is *it* with a context added. Undo *it*, and what is added cannot be *con*text.[3]

Let us say no more then about this objection, but enlarge our thesis, thus: If there be in the universe a *q* other than the *q* in the feeling, the latter has acquaintance with an entity ejective to itself; an acquaintance moreover, which, as mere acquaintance, it is hard to imagine susceptible either of improvement or increase, being in its way complete; and which obliges us (so long as we refuse not to call acquaintance knowledge) to say not only that the feeling is cognitive, but that all qualities of feeling, *so long as there is anything outside of them which they resemble*, are feelings *of* qualities of existence, and perceptions of outward truth.

The point of this vindication of the cognitive function of the first feeling lies, it will be noticed, in the discovery that *q* does exist elsewhere than in it. In case this discovery were not made, we could not be sure the feeling was cognitive; and in case there were nothing outside to be discovered, we should have to call the feeling a dream. But the feeling itself cannot make the discovery. Its own *q* is the only *q* it grasps; and its own nature is not a particle altered by having the self-transcendent function of cognition either added to it or taken away. The function is accidental; synthetic, not analytic; and falls outside and not inside its being.[4]

A feeling feels as a gun shoots. If there be nothing to be felt or hit, they discharge themselves *ins blaue hinein*. If, however, something starts up opposite them, they no longer simply shoot or feel, they hit and know.

But with this arises a worse objection than any yet made. We the critics look on and see a real *q* and a feeling of *q*; and because the two resemble each other, we say the one knows the other. But what right have we to say this until we know that the feeling of q means to stand for or represent just that *same* other q? Suppose, instead of one q, a number of real q's in the field. If the gun shoots and hits, we can easily see which one of them it hits. But how can we distinguish which one the feeling knows? It knows the one it stands for. But which one *does* it stand for? It declares no intention in this respect. It merely resembles; it resembles all indifferently; and resembling, *per se*, is not necessarily representing or standing-for at all. Eggs resemble each other, but do not on that account represent, stand for, or know each other. And if you say this is because neither of them is a *feeling*, then imagine the world to consist of nothing but toothaches, which *are* feelings, feelings resembling each other exactly,— would they know each other the better for all that?

The case of q being a bare quality like that of toothache-pain is quite different from that of its being a concrete individual thing. There is practically no test for deciding whether the feeling of a bare quality means to represent it or not. It can *do* nothing to the quality beyond resembling it, simply because an abstract quality is a thing to which nothing can be done. Being without context or environment or *principium individuationis*, a quiddity with no haecceity, a Platonic idea, even duplicate editions of such a quality (were they possible), would be indiscernible, and no sign could be given, no result altered, whether the feeling meant to stand for this edition or for that, or whether it simply resembled the quality without meaning to stand for it at all.

If now we grant a genuine pluralism of editions to the quality q, by assigning to each a *context* which shall distinguish it from its mates, we may proceed to explain which edition of it the feeling knows, by extending our principle of resemblance to the context too, and saying the feeling knows the particular q whose context it most exactly duplicates. But here again the theoretic doubt recurs: duplication and coincidence, are they knowledge? The gun shows which q it points to and hits, by *breaking* it. Until the feeling can show us which q it points to and knows, by some equally flagrant token, why are we not free to deny that it either points to or knows any one of the *real* q's at all, and to affirm that the word 'resemblance' exhaustively describes its relation to the reality?

Well, as a matter of fact, every actual feeling *does* show us, quite as flagrantly as the gun, which q it points to; and practically in concrete cases the matter is decided by an element we have hitherto left out. Let us pass from abstractions to possible instances, and ask our obliging *deus ex machina* to frame for us a richer world. Let him send me, for example, a dream of the death of a certain man, and let him simultaneously cause the man to die. How would our practical instinct spontaneously decide whether this were a case of cognition of the reality, or only a sort of marvelous coincidence of a resembling reality with my dream? Just such puzzling cases as this are what the 'society for psychical research' is busily collecting and trying to interpret in the most reasonable way.

If my dream were the only one of the kind I ever had in my life, if the context of the death in the dream differed in many particulars from the real death's context, and if my dream led me to no action about the death, unquestionably we should all call it a strange coincidence, and naught besides. But if the death in the dream had a long context, agreeing point for point with every feature that attended the real death; if I were constantly having such dreams, all equally perfect, and if on awaking I had a habit of acting immediately as if they were true and so getting 'the start' of my more tardily instructed neighbors,—we should probably all have to admit that I had some mysterious kind of clairvoyant power, that my dreams in an inscrutable way meant just those realities they figured, and that the word 'coincidence' failed to touch the root of the matter. And whatever doubts anyone preserved would completely vanish, if it should appear that from the midst of my dream I had the power of *interfering* with the course of the reality, and making the events in it turn this way or that, according as I dreamed they should. Then at least it would be certain that my waking critics and my dreaming self were dealing with the *same*.

And thus do men invariably decide such a question. *The falling of the dream's practical consequences* into the real world, and the *extent* of the resemblance between the two worlds are the criteria they instinctively use.[5] All feeling is for the sake of action, all feeling results in action,—today no argument is needed to prove these truths. But by a most singular disposition of nature which we may conceive to have been different, *my feelings act upon the realities within my critic's world*. Unless, then, my critic can prove that my feeling does not 'point to' those realities which it acts upon, how can he continue to doubt that he and I are alike cognizant of one and the same real world? If the action is performed in one world, that must be the world the feeling intends; if in another world, *that* is the world the feeling has in mind. If your feeling bear no fruits in my world, I call it utterly detached from my world; I call it a solipsism, and call its world a dream-world. If your toothache do not prompt you to *act* as if I had a toothache, nor even as if I had a separate existence; if you neither say to me, "I know now how you must suffer!" nor tell me of a remedy, I deny that your feeling, however it may resemble mine, is really cognizant of mine. It gives no *sign* of being cognizant, and such a sign is absolutely necessary to my admission that it is.

Before I can think you to mean my world, you must affect my world; before I can think you to mean much of it, you must affect much of it; and before I can be sure you mean it *as I do*, you must affect it *just as I should* if I were in your place. Then I, your critic, will gladly believe that we are thinking, not only of the same reality, but that we are thinking it *alike*, and thinking of much of its extent.

Without the practical effects of our neighbor's feelings on our own world, we should never suspect the existence of our neighbor's feelings at all, and of course should never find ourselves playing the critic as we do in this article. The constitution of nature is very peculiar. In the world of each of us are certain objects called human bodies, which move about and act on all the other objects there, and the occasions of their action are in the main what the occasions of our action would be, were they our bodies. They use words and gestures, which, if we used them, would have thoughts behind them,—no mere thoughts *überhaupt*, however, but strictly determinate thoughts. I think you have the notion of fire in general, because I see you act towards this fire in my room just as I act towards it,—poke it and present your person towards it, and so forth. But that binds me to believe that if you feel 'fire' at all, *this* is the fire you feel. As a matter of fact, whenever we constitute ourselves into psychological critics, it is not by dint of discovering which reality a feeling 'resembles' that we find out which reality it means. We become first aware of which one it means, and then we suppose that to be the one it resembles. We see each other looking at the same objects, pointing to them and turning them over in various ways, and thereupon we hope and trust that all of our several feelings resemble the reality and each other. But this is a thing of which we are never theoretically sure. Still, it would practically be a case of *grübelsucht*, if a ruffian were assaulting and drubbing my body, to spend much time in subtle speculation either as to whether his vision of my body resembled mine, or as to whether the body he really *meant* to insult were not some body in his mind's eye, altogether other from my own. The practical point of view brushes such metaphysical cobwebs away. If what he have in mind be not *my* body, why call we it a body at all? His mind is inferred as a term, to whose existence we trace the things that happen. The inference is quite void if the term, once inferred, be separated from its connection with the body that made me infer it, and connected with others that are no objects of mine at all. No matter for the metaphysical puzzle of how our two minds, the ruffian's and mine, *can* mean the same bodies. Men who see each other's bodies sharing the same space, treading the same earth, splashing the same water, making the same air resonant, and pursuing the same game and eating out of the same dish, will never practically believe in a pluralism of solipsistic worlds.

Where, however, the actions of one mind seem to take no effect in the world of the other, the case is different. This is what happens in poetry and fiction. Everyone knows *Ivanhoe*, for example; but so long as we stick to the story pure and simple without regard to the facts of its production, few would hesitate to admit that there are as many different Ivanhoes as there are different minds cognizant of the story.[6] The fact that all these Ivanhoes *resemble* each other does not prove the contrary. But if an alteration invented by one man in his version were to reverberate immediately through all the other versions, and produce changes therein, we should then easily agree that all these thinkers were thinking the *same* Ivanhoe, and that, fiction or no fiction, it formed a little world common to them all.

Having reached this point, we may take up our thesis and improve it again. Still calling the reality by the name of q and letting the critic's feeling vouch for it, we can say that any other feeling will be held cognizant of q, provided it both resemble q, and refer to q, as shown by its either modifying q directly, or modifying some other reality, p or r, which the critic knows to be continuous with q. Or more shortly, thus: *The feeling of q knows whatever reality it resembles, and either directly or indirectly operates on.* If it resemble without operating, it is a dream; if it operate without resembling, it is an error.[7]

It is to be feared that the reader may consider this formula rather insignificant and obvious, and hardly worth the labor of so many pages, especially when he considers that the only cases to which it applies are *percepts*, and that the whole field of symbolic or conceptual thinking seems to elude its grasp. Where the reality is either a material thing or act, or a state of the critic's consciousness, I may both mirror it in my mind and operate upon it—in the latter case indirectly, of course—as soon as I perceive it. But there are many cognitions, universally allowed to be such, which neither mirror nor operate on their realities.

In the whole field of symbolic thought we are universally held both to intend, to speak of, and to reach conclusions about—to know in short—particular realities, without having in our subjective consciousness any mind-stuff out of which an image of them might be framed. We are instructed about them by language which awakens no substantive consciousness beyond its sound; and we know *which* realities they are by the faintest and most fragmentary glimpse of some remote context they may have and by no direct imagination of themselves. As minds may differ here, let me speak in the first person. I am sure that my own current thinking has *words* for its almost exclusive subjective material, words which are made intelligible by being referred to some reality that lies beyond the horizon of direct consciousness, and of which I am only aware as of a terminal *more* existing in a certain direction to which the words might lead but do not lead yet. The *subject*, or *topic*, of the words is usually something towards which I mentally seem to pitch them in a backward way, almost as I might jerk my thumb over my shoulder to point at something, without looking round, if I were only entirely sure that it was there. The *upshot*, or *conclusion*, of the words is something towards which I seem to incline my head forwards, as if giving assent to its existence, though all my mind's eye catches sight of may be some tatter of an image connected with it, which tatter, however, if only endued with the feeling of familiarity and reality, makes me feel that the whole to which it belongs is rational and real, and fit to be let pass.

Here then is cognitive consciousness on a large scale, and yet what it knows, it hardly resembles in the least degree. The formula last laid down for our thesis must therefore be made more complete. We may now express it thus: *A percept knows whatever reality it directly or indirectly operates on and resembles; a conceptual feeling, or thought, knows*[8] *a reality, whenever it actually or potentially terminates in a percept that operates on or resembles that reality, or is otherwise connected with it or with its context.* The latter percept may be either sensation or sensorial idea; and when I say the thought must *terminate* in such a percept, I mean that it must ultimately be capable of leading up thereto—by the way of practical experience, if the terminal feeling be a sensation; by the way of logical or habitual suggestion, if it be only an image in the mind.

Let an illustration make this plainer. I open the first book I take up, and read the first sentence that meets my eye: "Newton saw the handiwork of God in the heavens as plainly as Paley in the animal kingdom." I immediately look back and try to analyze the subjective state in which I rapidly apprehended this sentence as I read it. In the first place there was an obvious feeling that the sentence was intelligible and rational and related to the world of realities. There was also a sense of agreement or harmony between 'Newton,' 'Paley,' and 'God.' There was no apparent image connected with the words 'heavens,' or 'handiwork,' or 'God'; they were words merely. With 'animal kingdom' I think there was the faintest consciousness (it may possibly have been an image of the steps) of the Museum of Zoology in the town of Cambridge where I write. With 'Paley' there was an equally faint consciousness of a small dark leather book; and with 'Newton' a pretty distinct vision of the right-hand lower corner of a curling periwig. This is all the mind-stuff I can discover in my first consciousness of the meaning of this sentence, and I am afraid that even not all of this would have been present had I come upon the sentence in a genuine reading of the book, and not picked it out for an experiment. And yet my consciousness was truly cognitive. The sentence is 'about' realities which my psychological critic—for we must not forget him—acknowledges to be such, even as he acknowledges my distinct feeling that they *are* realities, and my acquiescence in the general rightness of what I read of them, to be true knowledges on my part.

Now what justifies my critic in being as lenient as this? This singularly inadequate consciousness of mine, made up of symbols that neither resemble nor affect the realities they stand for—how can he be sure it is cognizant of the very realities he has himself in mind?

He is sure because in countless like cases he has seen such inadequate and symbolic thoughts, by developing themselves, terminate in percepts that practically modified and presumably resembled his own. By 'developing' themselves is meant obeying their tendencies, following up the suggestions nascently present in them, working in the direction in which they seem to point, clearing up the penumbra, making distinct the halo, unraveling the fringe, which is part of their composition, and in the midst of which their more substantive kernel of subjective content seems consciously to lie. Thus I may develop my thought in the Paley direction by procuring the brown leather volume and bringing the passages about the animal kingdom before the critic's eyes. I may satisfy him that the words mean for me just what they mean for him, by showing him *in concreto* the very animals and their arrangements, of which the pages treat. I may get Newton's works and portraits; or if I follow the line of suggestion of the wig, I may smother my critic in seventeenth-century matters pertaining to Newton's environment, to show that the word 'Newton' has the same *locus* and relations in both our minds. Finally I may, by act and word, persuade him that what I mean by God and the heavens and the analogy of handiworks, is just what he means also.

My demonstration in the last resort is to his *senses*. My thought makes me act on his senses much as he might himself act on them, were he pursuing the consequences of a perception of his own. Practically then *my* thought terminates in *his* realities. He willingly supposes it, therefore, to be *of* them, and inwardly to *resemble* what his own thought would be, were it of the same symbolic sort as mine. And the pivot and fulcrum and support of his mental persuasion, is the sensible operation which my thought leads me, or may lead, to effect—the bringing of Paley's book, of Newton's portrait, etc., before his very eyes.

In the last analysis, then, we believe that we all know and think about and talk about the same world, because *we believe our PERCEPTS are possessed by us in common*. And we believe this because the percepts of each one of us seem to be changed in consequence of changes in the percepts of someone else. What I am for you is in the first instance a percept of your own. Unexpectedly, however, I open and show you a book, uttering certain sounds the while. These acts are also your percepts, but they so resemble acts of yours with feelings prompting them, that you cannot doubt I have the feelings too, or that the book is one book felt in both our worlds. That it is felt in the same way, that my feelings of it resemble yours, is something of which we never can be sure, but which we assume as the simplest hypothesis that meets the case. As a matter of fact, we never *are* sure of it, and, as *Erkenntnisstheoretiker*, we can only say that of feelings that should *not* resemble each other, both could not know the same thing at the same time in the same way.[9] If each holds to its own percept as the reality, it is bound to say of the other percept, that, though it may *intend* that reality, and prove this by working change upon it, yet, if it do not resemble it, it is all false and wrong.[10]

If this be so of percepts, how much more so of higher modes of thought! Even in the sphere of sensation individuals are probably different enough. Comparative study of the simplest conceptual elements seems to show a wider divergence still. And when it comes to general theories and emotional attitudes towards life, it is indeed time to say with Thackeray, "My friend, a different universe walks about under your hat and under mine."

What can save us at all and prevent us from flying asunder into a chaos of mutually repellent solipsisms? Through what can our several minds commune? Through nothing but the mutual resemblance of those of our feelings which have this strange power of modifying each other, *which are mere dumb knowledges-of-acquaintance*, and which must also resemble their realities or not know them aright at all. In such pieces of knowledge-of-acquaintance all our knowledge-about must end, and carry a sense of this possible termination as part of its content. These percepts, these *termini*, these sensible things, these mere matters-of-acquaintance, are the only realities we ever directly know, and the whole history of our thought is the history of our substitution of one of them for another, and the reduction of the latter to the status of a conceptual sign. Condemned though they be by some thinkers, these sensations are the mother-earth, the anchorage, the stable rock, the first and last limits, the *terminus a quo* and the *terminus ad quem* of the mind. To find such sensational *termini* should be our aim with all our higher thought. They end discussion; they destroy the false conceit of knowledge; and without them we are all at sea with each other's meaning. If two men act alike on a percept, they believe themselves to feel alike about it; if not, they may suspect they know it in differing ways. We can never be sure we understand each other till we are able to bring the matter to this test.[11] This is why metaphysical discussions are so much like fighting with the air; they have no practical issue of a sensational kind. 'Scientific' theories, on the other hand, always terminate in definite percepts. You can deduce a possible sensation from your theory and, taking me into your laboratory, prove that your theory is true of my world by giving me the sensation then and there. Beautiful is the flight of conceptual reason through the upper air of truth. No wonder philosophers are dazzled by it still, and no wonder they look with some disdain at the low earth of feeling from which the goddess launched herself aloft. But woe to her if she return not home to its acquaintance; *Nirgends haften dann die unsicheren Sohlen*—every crazy wind will take her, and, like a fire-balloon at night, she will go out among the stars.

Read before the Aristotelian Society, December 1, 1884, and first published in *Mind*, vol. x (1885).

Note.—The reader will easily see how much of the account of the truth-function developed later in *Pragmatism* was already explicit in this earlier article, and how much came to be defined later. In this earlier article we find distinctly asserted:

1. The reality, external to the true idea;
2. The critic, reader, or epistemologist, with his own belief, as warrant for this reality's existence;
3. The experienceable environment, as the vehicle or medium connecting knower with known, and yielding the cognitive *relation*;
4. The notion of *pointing*, through this medium, to the reality, as one condition of our being said to know it;
5. That of *resembling* it, and eventually *affecting* it, as determining the pointing to *it* and not to something else.
6. The elimination of the 'epistemological gulf,' so that the whole truth-relation falls inside of the continuities of concrete experience, and is constituted of particular processes, varying with every object and subject, and susceptible of being described in detail.

The defects in this earlier account are:

1. The possibly undue prominence given to resembling, which although a fundamental function in knowing truly, is so often dispensed with;
2. The undue emphasis laid upon operating on the object itself, which in many cases is indeed decisive of that being what we refer to, but which is often lacking, or replaced by operations on other things related to the object.
3. The imperfect development of the generalized notion of the *workability* of the feeling or idea as equivalent to that *satisfactory adaptation* to the particular reality, which constitutes the truth of the idea. It is this more generalized notion, as covering all such specifications as pointing, fitting, operating or resembling, that distinguishes the developed view of Dewey, Schiller, and myself.

4. The treatment, on page 39 [this volume p. 194], of percepts as the only realm of reality. I now treat concepts as a co-ordinate realm.

9

What Pragmatism Means

Some years ago, being with a camping party in the mountains, I returned from a solitary ramble to find everyone engaged in a ferocious metaphysical dispute. The *corpus* of the dispute was a squirrel—a live squirrel supposed to be clinging to one side of a tree-trunk; while over against the tree's opposite side a human being was imagined to stand. This human witness tries to get sight of the squirrel by moving rapidly round the tree, but no matter how fast he goes, the squirrel moves as fast in the opposite direction, and always keeps the tree between himself and the man, so that never a glimpse of him is caught. The resultant metaphysical problem now is this: *Does the man go round the squirrel or not?* He goes round the tree, sure enough, and the squirrel is on the tree; but does he go round the squirrel? In the unlimited leisure of the wilderness, discussion had been worn threadbare. Everyone had taken sides, and was obstinate; and the numbers on both sides were even. Each side, when I appeared, therefore appealed to me to make it a majority. Mindful of the scholastic adage that whenever you meet a contradiction you must make a distinction, I immediately sought and found one, as follows: "Which party is right," I said, "depends on what you *practically mean* by 'going round' the squirrel. If you mean passing from the north of him to the east, then to the south, then to the west, and then to the north of him again, obviously the man does go round him, for he occupies these successive positions. But if on the contrary you mean being first in front of him, then on the right of him, then behind him, then on his left, and finally in front again, it is quite as obvious that the man fails to go round him, for by the compensating movements the squirrel makes, he keeps his belly turned towards the man all the time, and his back turned away. Make the distinction, and there is no occasion for any farther dispute. You are both right and both wrong according as you conceive the verb 'to go round' in one practical fashion or the other."

Although one or two of the hotter disputants called my speech a shuffling evasion, saying they wanted no quibbling or scholastic hair-splitting, but meant just plain honest English 'round,' the majority seemed to think that the distinction had assuaged the dispute.

I tell this trivial anecdote because it is a peculiarly simple example of what I wish now to speak of as *the pragmatic method*. The pragmatic method is primarily a method of settling metaphysical disputes that otherwise might be interminable. Is the world one or many?—fated or free?—material or spiritual?—here are notions either of which may or may not hold good of the world; and disputes over such notions are unending. The pragmatic method in such cases is to try to interpret each notion by tracing its respective practical consequences. What difference would it practically make to anyone if this notion rather than that notion were true? If no practical difference whatever can be traced, then the alternatives mean practically the same thing, and all dispute is idle. Whenever a dispute is serious, we ought to be able to show some practical difference that must follow from one side or the other's being right.

A glance at the history of the idea will show you still better what pragmatism means. The term is derived from the same Greek word πράγμα, meaning action, from which our words 'practice' and 'practical' come. It was first introduced into philosophy by Mr. Charles Peirce in 1878. In an article entitled "How to Make Our Ideas Clear," in the *Popular Science Monthly* for January of that year[1] Mr. Peirce, after pointing out that our beliefs are really rules for action, said that, to develop a thought's meaning, we need only determine what conduct it is fitted to produce: that conduct is for us its sole significance. And the tangible fact at the root of all our thought-distinctions, however subtle, is that there is no one of them so fine as to consist in anything but a possible difference of practice. To attain perfect clearness in our thoughts of an object, then, we need only consider what conceivable effects of a practical kind the object may involve—what sensations we are to expect from it, and what reactions we must prepare. Our conception of these effects, whether immediate or remote, is then for us the whole of our conception of the object, so far as that conception has positive significance at all.

This is the principle of Peirce, the principle of pragmatism. It lay entirely unnoticed by anyone for twenty years, until I, in an address before Professor Howison's philosophical union at the University of California, brought it forward again and made a special application of it to religion. By that date (1898) the times seemed ripe for its reception. The word 'pragmatism' spread, and at present it fairly spots the pages of the philosophic journals. On all hands we find the 'pragmatic movement' spoken of, sometimes with respect, sometimes with contumely, seldom with clear understanding. It is evident that the term applies itself conveniently to a number of tendencies that hitherto have lacked a collective name, and that it has 'come to stay.'

To take in the importance of Peirce's principle, one must get accustomed to applying it to concrete cases. I found a few years ago that Ostwald, the illustrious Leipzig chemist, had been making perfectly distinct use of the principle of pragmatism in his lectures on the philosophy of science, though he had not called it by that name.

"All realities influence our practice," he wrote me, "and that influence is their meaning for us. I am accustomed to put questions to my classes in this way: In what respects would the world be different if this alternative or that were true? If I can find nothing that would become different, then the alternative has no sense."

That is, the rival views mean practically the same thing, and meaning, other than practical, there is for us none. Ostwald in a published lecture gives this example of what he means. Chemists have long wrangled over the inner constitution of certain bodies called 'tautomerous.' Their properties seemed equally consistent with the notion that an instable hydrogen atom oscillates inside of them, or that they are instable mixtures of two bodies. Controversy raged; but never was decided. "It would never have begun," says Ostwald, "if the combatants had asked themselves what particular experimental fact could have been made different by one or the other view being correct. For it would then have appeared that no difference of fact could possibly ensue; and the quarrel was as unreal as if, theorizing in primitive times about the raising of dough by yeast, one party should have invoked a 'brownie,' while another insisted on an 'elf' as the true cause of the phenomenon."[2]

It is astonishing to see how many philosophical disputes collapse into insignificance the moment you subject them to this simple test of tracing a concrete consequence. There can *be* no difference anywhere that doesn't *make* a difference elsewhere—no difference in abstract truth that doesn't express itself in a difference in concrete fact and in conduct consequent upon that fact, imposed on somebody, somehow, somewhere and somewhen. The whole function of philosophy ought to be to find out what definite difference it will make to you and me, at definite instants of our life, if this world-formula or that world-formula be the true one.

There is absolutely nothing new in the pragmatic method. Socrates was an adept at it. Aristotle used it methodically. Locke, Berkeley and Hume made momentous contributions to truth by its means. Shadworth Hodgson keeps insisting that realities are only what they are 'known-as.' But these forerunners of pragmatism used it in fragments: they were preluders only. Not until in our time has it generalized itself, become conscious of a universal mission, pretended to a conquering destiny. I believe in that destiny, and I hope I may end by inspiring you with my belief.

Pragmatism represents a perfectly familiar attitude in philosophy, the empiricist attitude, but it represents it, as it seems to me, both in a more radical and in a less objectionable form than it has ever yet assumed. A pragmatist turns his back resolutely and once for all upon a lot of inveterate habits dear to professional philosophers. He turns away from abstraction and insufficiency, from verbal solutions, from bad *a priori* reasons, from fixed principles, closed systems, and pretended absolutes and origins. He turns towards concreteness and adequacy, towards facts, towards action, and towards power. That means the empiricist temper regnant, and the rationalist temper sincerely given up.

It means the open air and possibilities of nature, as against dogma, artificiality and the pretence of finality in truth.

At the same time it does not stand for any special results. It is a method only. But the general triumph of that method would mean an enormous change in what I called in my last lecture the 'temperament' of philosophy. Teachers of the ultra-rationalistic type would be frozen out, much as the courtier type is frozen out in republics, as the ultramontane type of priest is frozen out in protestant lands. Science and metaphysics would come much nearer together, would in fact work absolutely hand in hand.

Metaphysics has usually followed a very primitive kind of quest. You know how men have always hankered after unlawful magic, and you know what a great part, in magic, *words* have always played. If you have his name, or the formula of incantation that binds him, you can control the spirit, genie, afrite, or whatever the power may be. Solomon knew the names of all the spirits, and having their names, he held them subject to his will. So the universe has always appeared to the natural mind as a kind of enigma, of which the key must be sought in the shape of some illuminating or power-bringing word or name. That word names the universe's *principle*, and to possess it is, after a fashion, to possess the universe itself. 'God,' 'Matter,' 'Reason,' 'the Absolute,' 'Energy,' are so many solving names. You can rest when you have them. You are at the end of your metaphysical quest.

But if you follow the pragmatic method, you cannot look on any such word as closing your quest. You must bring out of each word its practical cash-value, set it at work within the stream of your experience. It appears less as a solution, then, than as a program for more work, and more particularly as an indication of the ways in which existing realities may be *changed*.

Theories thus become instruments, not answers to enigmas, in which we can rest. We don't lie back upon them, we move forward, and, on occasion, make nature over again by their aid. Pragmatism unstiffens all our theories, limbers them up and sets each one at work. Being nothing essentially new, it harmonizes with many ancient philosophic tendencies. It agrees with nominalism for instance, in always appealing to particulars; with utilitarianism in emphasizing practical aspects; with positivism in its disdain for verbal solutions, useless questions, and metaphysical abstractions.

All these, you see, are *anti-intellectualist* tendencies. Against rationalism as a pretension and a method, pragmatism is fully armed and militant. But, at the outset, at least, it stands for no particular results. It has no dogmas, and no doctrines save its method. As the young Italian pragmatist Papini has well said, it lies in the midst of our theories, like a corridor in a hotel. Innumerable chambers open out of it. In one you may find a man writing an atheistic volume; in the next someone on his knees praying for faith and strength; in a third a chemist investigating a body's properties. In a fourth a system of idealistic metaphysics is being excogitated; in a fifth the impossibility of metaphysics is being shown. But they all own the corridor, and all must pass through it if they want a practicable way of getting into or out of their respective rooms.

No particular results then, so far, but only an attitude of orientation, is what the pragmatic method means. The attitude of *looking away from first things, principles, 'categories,' supposed necessities; and of looking towards last things, fruits, consequences, facts.*

So much for the pragmatic method! You may say that I have been praising it rather than explaining it to you, but I shall presently explain it abundantly enough by showing how it works on some familiar problems. Meanwhile the word pragmatism has come to be used in a still wider sense, as meaning also a certain *theory of truth*. I mean to give a whole lecture to the statement of that theory, after first paving the way, so I can be very brief now. But brevity is hard to follow, so I ask for your redoubled attention for a quarter of an hour. If much remains obscure, I hope to make it clearer in the later lectures.

One of the most successfully cultivated branches of philosophy in our time is what is called inductive logic, the study of the conditions under which our sciences have evolved. Writers on this subject have begun to show a singular unanimity as to what the laws of nature and elements of fact mean, when formulated by mathematicians, physicists and chemists. When the first mathematical, logical, and natural uniformities, the first *laws*, were discovered, men were so carried away by the clearness, beauty and simplification that resulted, that they believed themselves to have deciphered authentically the eternal thoughts of the Almighty. His mind also thundered and reverberated in syllogisms. He also thought in conic sections, squares and roots and ratios, and geometrized like Euclid. He made Kepler's laws for the planets to follow; he made velocity increase proportionally to the time in falling bodies; he made the law of the sines for light to obey when refracted; he established the classes, orders, families and genera of plants and animals, and fixed the distances between them. He thought the archetypes of all things, and devised their variations; and when we rediscover any one of these his wondrous institutions, we seize his mind in its very literal intention.

But as the sciences have developed farther, the notion has gained ground that most, perhaps all, of our laws are only approximations. The laws themselves, moreover, have grown so numerous that there is no counting them; and so many rival formulations are proposed in all the branches of science that investigators have become accustomed to the notion that no theory is absolutely a transcript of reality, but that any one of them may from some point of view be useful. Their great use is to summarize old facts and to lead to new ones. They are only a man-made language, a conceptual shorthand, as someone calls them, in which we write our reports of nature; and languages, as is well known, tolerate much choice of expression and many dialects.

Thus human arbitrariness has driven divine necessity from scientific logic. If I mention the names of Sigwart, Mach, Ostwald, Pearson, Milhaud, Poincaré, Duhem, Ruyssen, those of you who are students will easily identify the tendency I speak of, and will think of additional names.

Riding now on the front of this wave of scientific logic Messrs. Schiller and Dewey appear with their pragmatistic account of what truth everywhere signifies. Everywhere, these teachers say, 'truth' in our ideas and beliefs means the same thing that it means in science. It means, they say, nothing but this, *that ideas (which themselves are but parts of our experience) become true just in so far as they help us to get into satisfactory relation with other parts of our experience*, to summarize them and get about among them by conceptual short-cuts instead of following the interminable succession of particular phenomena. Any idea upon which we can ride, so to speak; any idea that will carry us prosperously from any one part of our experience to any other part, linking things satisfactorily, working securely, simplifying, saving labor; is true for just so much, true in so far forth, true *instrumentally*. This is the 'instrumental' view of truth taught so successfully at Chicago, the view that truth in our ideas means their power to 'work,' promulgated so brilliantly at Oxford.

Messrs. Dewey, Schiller and their allies, in reaching this general conception of all truth, have only followed the example of geologists, biologists and philologists. In the establishment of these other sciences, the successful stroke was always to take some simple process actually observable in operation—as denudation by weather, say, or variation from parental type, or change of dialect by incorporation of new words and pronunciations—and then to generalize it, making it apply to all times, and produce great results by summating its effects through the ages.

The observable process which Schiller and Dewey particularly singled out for generalization is the familiar one by which any individual settles into *new opinions*. The process here is always the same. The individual has a stock of old opinions already, but he meets a new experience that puts them to a strain. Somebody contradicts them; or in a reflective moment he discovers that they contradict each other; or he hears of facts with which they are incompatible; or desires arise in him which they cease to satisfy. The result is an inward trouble to which his mind till then had been a stranger, and from which he seeks to escape by modifying his previous mass of opinions. He saves as much of it as he can, for in this matter of belief we are all extreme conservatives. So he tries to change first this opinion, and then that (for they resist change very variously), until at last some new idea comes up which he can graft upon the ancient stock with a minimum of disturbance of the latter, some idea that mediates between the stock and the new experience and runs them into one another most felicitously and expediently.

This new idea is then adopted as the true one. It preserves the older stock of truths with a minimum of modification, stretching them just enough to make them admit the novelty, but conceiving that in ways as familiar as the case leaves possible. An *outrée* explanation, violating all our preconceptions, would never pass for a true account of a novelty. We should scratch round industriously till we found something less eccentric. The most violent revolutions in an individual's beliefs leave most of his old order standing. Time and space, cause and effect, nature and history, and one's own biography remain untouched. New truth is always a go-between, a smoother-over of transitions. It marries old opinion to new fact so as ever to show a minimum of jolt, a maximum of continuity. We hold a theory true just in proportion to its success in solving this 'problem of maxima and minima.' But success in solving this problem is eminently a matter of approximation. We say this theory solves it on the whole more satisfactorily than that theory; but that means more satisfactorily to ourselves, and individuals will emphasize their points of satisfaction differently. To a certain degree, therefore, everything here is plastic.

The point I now urge you to observe particularly is the part played by the older truths. Failure to take account of it is the source of much of the unjust criticism leveled against pragmatism. Their influence is absolutely controlling. Loyalty to them is the first principle—in most cases it is the only principle; for by far the most usual way of handling phenomena so novel that they would make for a serious rearrangement of our preconceptions is to ignore them altogether, or to abuse those who bear witness for them.

You doubtless wish examples of this process of truth's growth, and the only trouble is their superabundance. The simplest case of new truth is of course the mere numerical addition of new kinds of facts, or of new single facts of old kinds, to our experience—an addition that involves no alteration in the old beliefs. Day follows day, and its contents are simply added. The new contents themselves are not true, they simply *come* and *are*. Truth is *what we say about* them, and when we say that they have come, truth is satisfied by the plain additive formula.

But often the day's contents oblige a rearrangement. If I should now utter piercing shrieks and act like a maniac on this platform, it would

make many of you revise your ideas as to the probable worth of my philosophy. 'Radium' came the other day as part of the day's content, and
seemed for a moment to contradict our ideas of the whole order of
nature, that order having come to be identified with what is called the
conservation of energy. The mere sight of radium paying heat away
indefinitely out of its own pocket seemed to violate that conservation.
What to think? If the radiations from it were nothing but an escape of
unsuspected 'potential' energy, pre-existent inside of the atoms, the principle of conservation would be saved. The discovery of 'helium' as the
radiation's outcome, opened a way to this belief. So Ramsay's view is generally held to be true, because, although it extends our old ideas of
energy, it causes a minimum of alteration in their nature.

I need not multiply instances. A new opinion counts as 'true' just in
proportion as it gratifies the individual's desire to assimilate the novel in
his experience to his beliefs in stock. It must both lean on old truth and
grasp new fact; and its success (as I said a moment ago) in doing this, is
a matter for the individual's appreciation. When old truth grows, then,
by new truth's addition, it is for subjective reasons. We are in the process
and obey the reasons. That new idea is truest which performs most felicitously its function of satisfying our double urgency. It makes itself true,
gets itself classed as true, by the way it works; grafting itself then upon
the ancient body of truth, which thus grows much as a tree grows by the
activity of a new layer of cambium.

Now Dewey and Schiller proceed to generalize this observation and
to apply it to the most ancient parts of truth. They also once were plastic.
They also were called true for human reasons. They also mediated
between still earlier truths and what in those days were novel observations. Purely objective truth, truth in whose establishment the function
of giving human satisfaction in marrying previous parts of experience
with newer parts played no role whatever, is nowhere to be found. The
reasons why we call things true is the reason why they *are* true, for 'to be
true' *means* only to perform this marriage-function.

The trail of the human serpent is thus over everything. Truth independent; truth that we *find* merely; truth no longer malleable to human

need; truth incorrigible, in a word; such truth exists indeed superabundantly—or is supposed to exist by rationalistically minded thinkers; but then it means only the dead heart of the living tree, and its being there means only that truth also has its paleontology and its 'prescription,' and may grow stiff with years of veteran service and petrified in men's regard by sheer antiquity. But how plastic even the oldest truths nevertheless really are has been vividly shown in our day by the transformation of logical and mathematical ideas, a transformation which seems even to be invading physics. The ancient formulas are reinterpreted as special expressions of much wider principles, principles that our ancestors never got a glimpse of in their present shape and formulation.

Mr. Schiller still gives to all this view of truth the name of 'Humanism,' but, for this doctrine too, the name of pragmatism seems fairly to be in the ascendant, so I will treat it under the name of pragmatism in these lectures.

Such then would be the scope of pragmatism—first, a method; and second, a genetic theory of what is meant by truth. And these two things must be our future topics.

What I have said of the theory of truth will, I am sure, have appeared obscure and unsatisfactory to most of you by reason of its brevity. I shall make amends for that hereafter. In a lecture on 'common sense' I shall try to show what I mean by truths grown petrified by antiquity. In another lecture I shall expatiate on the idea that our thoughts become true in proportion as they successfully exert their go-between function. In a third I shall show how hard it is to discriminate subjective from objective factors in Truth's development. You may not follow me wholly in these lectures; and if you do, you may not wholly agree with me. But you will, I know, regard me at least as serious, and treat my effort with respectful consideration.

You will probably be surprised to learn, then, that Messrs. Schiller's and Dewey's theories have suffered a hailstorm of contempt and ridicule. All rationalism has risen against them. In influential quarters Mr. Schiller, in particular, has been treated like an impudent schoolboy who deserves a spanking. I should not mention this, but for the fact that it throws so much sidelight upon that rationalistic temper to which I have opposed the temper of pragmatism. Pragmatism is uncomfortable away from facts. Rationalism is comfortable only in the presence of abstractions. This pragmatist talk about truths in the plural, about their utility and satisfactoriness, about the success with which they 'work,' etc., suggests to the typical intellectualist mind a sort of coarse lame second-rate makeshift article of truth. Such truths are not real truth. Such tests are merely subjective. As against this, objective truth must be something non-utilitarian, haughty, refined, remote, august, exalted. It must be an absolute correspondence of our thoughts with an equally absolute reality. It must be what we *ought* to think, unconditionally. The conditioned ways in which we *do* think are so much irrelevance and matter for psychology. Down with psychology, up with logic, in all this question!

See the exquisite contrast of the types of mind! The pragmatist clings to facts and concreteness, observes truth at its work in particular cases, and generalizes. Truth, for him, becomes a class-name for all sorts of definite working-values in experience. For the rationalist it remains a pure abstraction, to the bare name of which we must defer. When the pragmatist undertakes to show in detail just *why* we must defer, the rationalist is unable to recognize the concretes from which his own abstraction is taken. He accuses us of *denying* truth; whereas we have only sought to trace exactly why people follow it and always ought to follow it. Your typical ultra-abstractionist fairly shudders at concreteness: other things equal, he positively prefers the pale and spectral. If the two universes were offered, he would always choose the skinny outline rather than the rich thicket of reality. It is so much purer, clearer, nobler.

I hope that as these lectures go on, the concreteness and closeness to facts of the pragmatism which they advocate may be what approves itself to you as its most satisfactory peculiarity. It only follows here the example of the sister-sciences, interpreting the unobserved by the observed. It brings old and new harmoniously together. It converts the absolutely empty notion of a static relation of 'correspondence' (what that may mean we must ask later) between our minds and reality, into that of a rich and active commerce (that anyone may follow in detail and understand) between particular thoughts of ours, and the great universe of other experiences in which they play their parts and have their uses.

But enough of this at present? The justification of what I say must be postponed. I wish now to add a word in further explanation of the claim I made at our last meeting, that pragmatism may be a happy harmonizer of empiricist ways of thinking, with the more religious demands of human beings.

Men who are strongly of the fact-loving temperament, you may remember me to have said, are liable to be kept at a distance by the small sympathy with facts which that philosophy from the present-day fashion of idealism offers them. It is far too intellectualistic. Old fashioned theism was bad enough, with its notion of God as an exalted monarch, made up of a lot of unintelligible or preposterous 'attributes'; but, so long as it held strongly by the argument from design, it kept some touch with concrete realities. Since, however, darwinism has once for all displaced design from the minds of the 'scientific,' theism has lost that foothold; and some kind of an immanent or pantheistic deity working *in* things rather than above them is, if any, the kind recommended to our contemporary imagination. Aspirants to a philosophic religion turn, as a rule, more hopefully nowadays towards idealistic pantheism than towards the older dualistic theism, in spite of the fact that the latter still counts able defenders.

But, as I said in my first lecture, the brand of pantheism offered is hard for them to assimilate if they are lovers of facts, or empirically minded. It is the absolutistic brand, spurning the dust and reared upon pure logic. It keeps no connection whatever with concreteness. Affirming the Absolute Mind, which is its substitute for God, to be the rational presupposition of all particulars of fact, whatever they may be, it remains supremely indifferent to what the particular facts in our world actually are. Be they what they may, the Absolute will father them. Like the sick lion in Esop's fable, all footprints lead into his den, but *nulla vestigia retrorsum*. You cannot redescend into the world of particulars by the Absolute's aid, or deduce any necessary consequences of detail important for your life from your idea of his nature. He gives you indeed the assurance that all is well with *Him*, and for his eternal way of thinking; but thereupon he leaves you to be finitely saved by your own temporal devices.

Far be it from me to deny the majesty of this conception, or its capacity to yield religious comfort to a most respectable class of minds. But from the human point of view, no one can pretend that it doesn't suffer from the faults of remoteness and abstractness. It is eminently a product of what I have ventured to call the rationalistic temper. It disdains empiricism's needs. It substitutes a pallid outline for the real world's richness. It is dapper; it is noble in the bad sense, in the sense in which to be noble is to be inapt for humble service. In this real world of sweat and dirt, it seems to me that when a view of things is 'noble,' that ought to count as a presumption against its truth, and as a philosophic disqualification. The prince of darkness may be a gentleman, as we are told he is, but whatever the God of earth and heaven is, he can surely be no gentleman. His menial services are needed in the dust of our human trials, even more than his dignity is needed in the empyrean.

Now pragmatism, devoted though she be to facts, has no such materialistic bias as ordinary empiricism labors under. Moreover, she has no objection whatever to the realizing of abstractions, so long as you get about among particulars with their aid and they actually carry you somewhere. Interested in no conclusions but those which our minds and our experiences work out together, she has no *a priori* prejudices against theology. *If theological ideas prove to have a value for concrete life, they will be true, for pragmatism, in the sense of being good for so much. For how much more they are true, will depend entirely on their relations to the other truths that also have to be acknowledged.*

What I said just now about the Absolute of transcendental idealism is a case in point. First, I called it majestic and said it yielded religious comfort to a class of minds, and then I accused it of remoteness and sterility. But so far as it affords such comfort, it surely is not sterile; it has that amount of value; it performs a concrete function. As a good pragmatist, I myself ought to call the Absolute true 'in so far forth,' then; and I unhesitatingly now do so.

But what does true *in so far forth* mean in this case? To answer, we need only apply the pragmatic method. What do believers in the Absolute mean by saying that their belief affords them comfort? They mean that since in the Absolute finite evil is 'overruled' already, we may, therefore, whenever we wish, treat the temporal as if it were potentially the eternal, be sure that we can trust its outcome, and, without sin, dismiss our fear and drop the worry of our finite responsibility. In short, they mean that we have a right ever and anon to take a moral holiday, to let the world wag in its own way, feeling that its issues are in better hands than ours and are none of our business.

The universe is a system of which the individual members may relax their anxieties occasionally, in which the don't-care mood is also right for men, and moral holidays in order—that, if I mistake not, is part, at least, of what the Absolute is 'known-as,' that is the great difference in our particular experiences which his being true makes for us, that is part of his cash-value when he is pragmatically interpreted. Farther than that the ordinary lay-reader in philosophy who thinks favorably of absolute idealism does not venture to sharpen his conceptions. He can use the Absolute for so much, and so much is very precious. He is pained at hearing you speak incredulously of the Absolute, therefore, and disregards your criticisms because they deal with aspects of the conception that he fails to follow.

If the Absolute means this, and means no more than this, who can possibly deny the truth of it? To deny it would be to insist that men should never relax, and that holidays are never in order.

I am well aware how odd it must seem to some of you to hear me say that an idea is 'true' so long as to believe it is profitable to our lives. That it is *good*, for as much as it profits, you will gladly admit. If what we do by its aid is good, you will allow the idea itself to be good in so far forth, for we are the better for possessing it. But is it not a strange misuse of the word 'truth,' you will say, to call ideas also 'true' for this reason?

To answer this difficulty fully is impossible at this stage of my account. You touch here upon the very central point of Messrs. Schiller's, Dewey's and my own doctrine of truth, which I cannot discuss with detail until my sixth lecture. Let me now say only this, that truth is *one species of good*, and not, as is usually supposed, a category distinct from good, and co-ordinate with it. *The true is the name of whatever proves itself to be good in the way of belief and good, too, for definite, assignable reasons.* Surely you must admit this, that if there were *no* good for life in true ideas, or if the knowledge of them were positively disadvantageous and false ideas the only useful ones, then the current notion that truth is divine and precious, and its pursuit a duty, could never have grown up or become a dogma. In a world like that, our duty would be to *shun* truth, rather. But in this world, just as certain foods are not only agreeable to our taste, but good for our teeth, our stomach and our tissues; so certain ideas are not only agreeable to think about, or agreeable as supporting other ideas that we are fond of, but they are also helpful in life's practical struggles. If there be any life that it is really better we should lead, and if there be any idea which, if believed in, would help us to lead that life, then it would be really *better for us* to believe in that idea, *unless, indeed, belief in it incidentally clashed with other greater vital benefits.*

"What would be better for us to believe"! This sounds very like a definition of truth. It comes very near to saying 'what we *ought* to believe'; and in *that* definition none of you would find any oddity. Ought we ever not to believe what it is *better for us* to believe? And can we then keep the notion of what is better for us, and what is true for us, permanently apart?

Pragmatism says no, and I fully agree with her. Probably you also agree, so far as the abstract statement goes, but with a suspicion that if we practically did believe everything that made for good in our own personal lives, we should be found indulging all kinds of fancies about this world's affairs, and all kinds of sentimental superstitions about a world hereafter. Your suspicion here is undoubtedly well founded, and it is evident that something happens when you pass from the abstract to the concrete, that complicates the situation.

I said just now that what is better for us to believe is true *unless the belief incidentally clashes with some other vital benefit.* Now in real life what vital benefits is any particular belief of ours most liable to clash with? What indeed except the vital benefits yielded by *other beliefs* when these prove incompatible with the first ones? In other words, the greatest enemy of any one of our truths may be the rest of our truths. Truths have once for all this desperate instinct of self-preservation and of desire to extinguish whatever contradicts them. My belief in the Absolute, based on the good it does me, must run the gauntlet of all my other beliefs. Grant that it may be true in giving me a moral holiday. Nevertheless, as I conceive it—and let me speak now confidentially, as it were, and merely in my own private person—it clashes with other truths of mine whose benefits I hate to give up on its account. It happens to be associated with a kind of logic of which I am the enemy, I find that it entangles me in metaphysical paradoxes that are inacceptable, etc., etc. But as I have enough trouble in life already without adding the trouble of carrying these intellectual inconsistencies, I personally just give up the Absolute. I just *take* my moral holidays; or else as a professional philosopher, I try to justify them by some other principle.

If I could restrict my notion of the Absolute to its bare holiday-giving value, it wouldn't clash with my other truths. But we can not easily thus restrict our hypotheses. They carry supernumerary features, and these it is that clash so. My disbelief in the Absolute means then disbelief in those other supernumerary features, for I fully believe in the legitimacy of taking moral holidays.

You see by this what I meant when I called pragmatism a mediator and reconciler and said, borrowing the word from Papini, that she 'unstiffens' our theories. She has in fact no prejudices whatever, no obstructive dogmas, no rigid canons of what shall count as proof. She is completely genial. She will entertain any hypothesis, she will consider any evidence. It follows that in the religious field she is at a great advantage both over positivistic empiricism, with its anti-theological bias, and over religious rationalism, with its exclusive interest in the remote, the noble, the simple, and the abstract in the way of conception.

In short, she widens the field of search for God. Rationalism sticks to logic and the empyrean. Empiricism sticks to the external senses. Pragmatism is willing to take anything, to follow either logic or the senses, and to count the humblest and most personal experiences. She will count mystical experiences if they have practical consequences. She will take a God who lives in the very dirt of private fact—if that should seem a likely place to find him.

Her only test of probable truth is what works best in the way of leading us, what fits every part of life best and combines with the collectivity of experience's demands, nothing being omitted. If theological ideas should do this, if the notion of God, in particular, should prove to do it, how could pragmatism possibly deny God's existence? She could see no meaning in treating as 'not true' a notion that was pragmatically so successful. What other kind of truth could there be, for her, than all this agreement with concrete reality?

In my last lecture I shall return again to the relations of pragmatism with religion. But you see already how democratic she is. Her manners are as various and flexible, her resources as rich and endless, and her conclusions as friendly as those of mother nature.

10

Pragmatism's Conception of Truth

W hen Clerk Maxwell was a child it is written that he had a mania for having everything explained to him, and that when people put him off with vague verbal accounts of any phenomenon he would interrupt them impatiently by saying, "Yes; but I want you to tell me the *particular go* of it!" Had his question been about truth, only a pragmatist could have told him the particular go of it. I believe that our contemporary pragmatists, especially Messrs. Schiller and Dewey, have given the only tenable account of this subject. It is a very ticklish subject, sending subtle rootlets into all kinds of crannies, and hard to treat in the sketchy way that alone befits a public lecture. But the Schiller-Dewey view of truth has been so ferociously attacked by rationalistic philosophers, and so abominably misunderstood, that here, if anywhere, is the point where a clear and simple statement should be made.

I fully expect to see the pragmatist view of truth run through the classic stages of a theory's career. First, you know, a new theory is attacked as absurd; then it is admitted to be true, but obvious and insignificant; finally it is seen to be so important that its adversaries claim that they themselves discovered it. Our doctrine of truth is at present in the first of these three stages, with symptoms of the second stage having begun in certain quarters. I wish that this lecture might help it beyond the first stage in the eyes of many of you.

Truth, as any dictionary will tell you, is a property of certain of our ideas. It means their 'agreement,' as falsity means their disagreement, with 'reality.' Pragmatists and intellectualists both accept this definition as a matter of course. They begin to quarrel only after the question is raised as to what may precisely be meant by the term 'agreement,' and what by the term 'reality,' when reality is taken as something for our ideas to agree with.

In answering these questions the pragmatists are more analytic and painstaking, the intellectualists more offhand and irreflective. The popular notion is that a true idea must copy its reality. Like other popular views, this one follows the analogy of the most usual experience. Our true ideas of sensible things do indeed copy them. Shut your eyes and think of yonder clock on the wall, and you get just such a true picture or copy of its dial. But your idea of its 'works' (unless you are a clock-maker) is much less of a copy, yet it passes muster, for it in no way clashes with the reality. Even though it should shrink to the mere word 'works,' that word still serves you truly; and when you speak of the 'time-keeping function' of the clock, or of its spring's 'elasticity,' it is hard to see exactly what your ideas can copy.

You perceive that there is a problem here. Where our ideas cannot copy definitely their object, what does agreement with that object mean? Some idealists seem to say that they are true whenever they are what God means that we ought to think about that object. Others hold the copy-view all through, and speak as if our ideas possessed truth just in proportion as they approach to being copies of the Absolute's eternal way of thinking.

These views, you see, invite pragmatistic discussion. But the great assumption of the intellectualists is that truth means essentially an inert static relation. When you've got your true idea of anything, there's an end of the matter. You're in possession; you *know*; you have fulfilled your thinking destiny. You are where you ought to be mentally; you have obeyed your categorical imperative; and nothing more need follow on that climax of your rational destiny. Epistemologically you are in stable equilibrium.

Pragmatism, on the other hand, asks its usual question. "Grant an idea or belief to be true," it says, "what concrete difference will its being true make in anyone's actual life? How will the truth be realized? What experiences will be different from those which would obtain if the belief were false? What, in short, is the truth's cash-value in experiential terms?"

The moment pragmatism asks this question, it sees the answer: *True ideas are those that we can assimilate, validate, corroborate and verify. False ideas are those that we cannot.* That is the practical difference it makes to us to have true ideas; that, therefore, is the meaning of truth, for it is all that truth is known-as.

This thesis is what I have to defend. The truth of an idea is not a stagnant property inherent in it. Truth *happens* to an idea. It *becomes* true, is *made* true by events. Its verity *is* in fact an event, a process: the process namely of its verifying itself, its veri-*fication*. Its validity is the process of its valid-*ation*.

But what do the words verification and validation themselves pragmatically mean? They again signify certain practical consequences of the verified and validated idea. It is hard to find any one phrase that characterizes these consequences better than the ordinary agreement formula—just such consequences being what we have in mind whenever we say that our ideas 'agree' with reality. They lead us, namely, through the acts and other ideas which they instigate, into or up to, or towards, other parts of experience with which we feel all the while such feeling being among our potentialities—that the original ideas remain in agreement. The connections and transitions come to us from point to point as being progressive, harmonious, satisfactory. This function of agreeable leading is what we mean by an idea's verification. Such an account is vague and it sounds at first quite trivial, but it has results which it will take the rest of my hour to explain.

Let me begin by reminding you of the fact that the possession of true thoughts means everywhere the possession of invaluable instruments of action; and that our duty to gain truth, so far from being a blank command from out of the blue, or a 'stunt' self-imposed by our intellect, can account for itself by excellent practical reasons.

The importance to human life of having true beliefs about matters of fact is a thing too notorious. We live in a world of realities that can be infinitely useful or infinitely harmful. Ideas that tell us which of them to expect count as the true ideas in all this primary sphere of verification, and the pursuit of such ideas is a primary human duty. The possession of truth, so far from being here an end in itself, is only a preliminary means towards other vital satisfactions. If I am lost in the woods and starved, and find what looks like a cow-path, it is of the utmost importance that I should think of a human habitation at the end of it, for if I do so and follow it, I save myself. The true thought is useful here because the house which is its object is useful. The practical value of true ideas is thus primarily derived from the practical importance of their objects to us. Their objects are, indeed, not important at all times. I may on another occasion have no use for the house; and then my idea of it, however verifiable, will be practically irrelevant, and had better remain latent. Yet since almost any object may some day become temporarily important, the advantage of having a general stock of *extra* truths, of ideas that shall be true of merely possible situations, is obvious. We store such extra truths away in our memories, and with the overflow we fill our books of reference. Whenever such an extra truth becomes practically relevant to one of our emergencies, it passes from cold-storage to do work in the world, and our belief in it grows active. You can say of it then either that 'it is useful because it is true' or that 'it is true because it is useful.' Both these phrases mean exactly the same thing, namely that here is an idea that gets fulfilled and can be verified. True is the name for whatever idea starts the verification-process, useful is the name for its completed function in experience. True ideas would never have been singled out as such, would never have acquired a class-name, least of all a name suggesting value, unless they had been useful from the outset in this way.

From this simple cue pragmatism gets her general notion of truth as something essentially bound up with the way in which one moment in our experience may lead us towards other moments which it will be worth while to have been led to. Primarily, and on the common-sense level, the truth of a state of mind means this function of *a leading that is worth while*. When a moment in our experience, of any kind whatever, inspires us with a thought that is true, that means that sooner or later we dip by that thought's guidance into the particulars of experience again and make advantageous connection with them. This is a vague enough statement, but I beg you to retain it, for it is essential.

Our experience meanwhile is all shot through with regularities. One bit of it can warn us to get ready for another bit, can 'intend' or 'be significant of' that remoter object. The object's advent is the significance's verification. Truth, in these cases, meaning nothing but eventual verification, is manifestly incompatible with waywardness on our part. Woe to him whose beliefs play fast and loose with the order which realities follow in his experience: they will lead him nowhere or else make false connexions.

By 'realities' or 'objects' here, we mean either things of common sense, sensibly present, or else common-sense relations, such as dates, places, distances, kinds, activities. Following our mental image of a house along the cow-path, we actually come to see the house; we get the image's full verification. *Such simply and fully verified leadings are certainly the originals and prototypes of the truth-process.* Experience offers indeed other forms of truth-process, but they are all conceivable as being primary verifications arrested, multiplied or substituted one for another.

Take, for instance, yonder object on the wall. You and I consider it to be a 'clock,' although no one of us has seen the hidden works that make it one. We let our notion pass for true without attempting to verify. If truths mean verification-process essentially, ought we then to call such unverified truths as this abortive? No, for they form the overwhelmingly large number of the truths we live by. Indirect as well as direct verifications pass muster. Where circumstantial evidence is sufficient, we can go without eye-witnessing. Just as we here assume Japan to exist without ever having been there, because it *works* to do so, everything we know conspiring with the belief, and nothing interfering, so we assume that thing to be a clock. We *use* it as a clock, regulating the length of our lecture by it. The verification of the assumption here means its leading to no frustration or contradiction. Verifi*ability* of wheels and weights and pendulum is as good as verification. For one truth-process completed there are a million in our lives that function in this state of nascency. They turn us *towards* direct verification; lead us into the *surroundings* of the objects they envisage; and then, if everything runs on harmoniously, we are so sure that verification is possible that we omit it, and are usually justified by all that happens.

Truth lives, in fact, for the most part on a credit system. Our thoughts and beliefs 'pass,' so long as nothing challenges them, just as bank-notes pass so long as nobody refuses them. But this all points to direct face-to-face verifications somewhere, without which the fabric of truth collapses like a financial system with no cash-basis whatever. You accept my verification of one thing, I yours of another. We trade on each other's truth. But beliefs verified concretely by *somebody* are the posts of the whole superstructure.

Another great reason—beside economy of time—for waiving complete verification in the usual business of life is that all things exist in kinds and not singly. Our world is found once for all to have that peculiarity. So that when we have once directly verified our ideas about one specimen of a kind, we consider ourselves free to apply them to other specimens without verification. A mind that habitually discerns the kind of thing before it, and acts by the law of the kind immediately, without pausing to verify, will be a 'true' mind in ninety-nine out of a hundred emergencies, proved so by its conduct fitting everything it meets, and getting no refutation.

Indirectly or only potentially verifying processes may thus be true as well as full verification-processes. They work as true processes would work, give us the same advantages, and claim our recognition for the same reasons. All this on the common-sense level of matters of fact, which we are alone considering.

But matters of fact are not our only stock in trade. *Relations among purely mental ideas* form another sphere where true and false beliefs obtain, and here the beliefs are absolute, or unconditional. When they are true they bear the name either of definitions or of principles. It is either a principle or a definition that 1 and 1 make 2, that 2 and 1 make 3, and so on; that white differs less from gray than it does from black; that when the cause begins to act the effect also commences. Such propositions hold of all possible 'ones,' of all conceivable 'whites' and 'grays' and 'causes.' The objects here are mental objects. Their relations are perceptually obvious at a glance, and no sense-verification is necessary. Moreover, once true, always true, of those same mental objects. Truth here has an 'eternal' character. If you can find a concrete thing anywhere that is 'one' or 'white' or 'gray,' or an 'effect,' then your principles will everlastingly apply to it. It is but a case of ascertaining the kind, and then applying the law of its kind to the particular object. You are sure to get truth if you can but name the kind rightly, for your mental relations hold good of everything of that kind without exception. If you then, nevertheless, failed to get truth concretely, you would say that you had classed your real objects wrongly.

In this realm of mental relations, truth again is an affair of leading. We relate one abstract idea with another, framing in the end great systems of logical and mathematical truth, under the respective terms of which the sensible facts of experience eventually arrange themselves, so that our eternal truths hold good of realities also. This marriage of fact and theory is endlessly fertile. What we say is here already true in advance of special verification, *if we have subsumed our objects rightly*. Our ready-made ideal framework for all sorts of possible objects follows from the very structure of our thinking. We can no more play fast and loose with these abstract relations than we can do so with our sense-experiences. They coerce us; we must treat them consistently, whether or not we like the results. The rules of addition apply to our debts as rigorously as to our assets. The hundredth decimal of π, the ratio of the circumference to its diameter, is predetermined ideally now, though no one may have computed it. If we should ever need the figure in our dealings with an actual circle we should need to have it given rightly, calculated by the usual rules; for it is the same kind of truth that those rules elsewhere calculate.

Between the coercions of the sensible order and those of the ideal order, our mind is thus wedged tightly. Our ideas must agree with realities, be such realities concrete or abstract, be they facts or be they principles, under penalty of endless inconsistency and frustration.

So far, intellectualists can raise no protest. They can only say that we have barely touched the skin of the matter.

Realities mean, then, either concrete facts, or abstract kinds of things and relations perceived intuitively between them. They furthermore and thirdly mean, as things that new ideas of ours must no less take account of, the whole body of other truths already in our possession. But what now does 'agreement' with such threefold realities mean?—to use again the definition that is current.

Here it is that pragmatism and intellectualism begin to part company. Primarily, no doubt, to agree means to copy, but we saw that the mere word 'clock' would do instead of a mental picture of its works, and that of many realities our ideas can only be symbols and not copies. 'Past time,' 'power,' 'spontaneity'—how can our mind copy such realities?

To 'agree' in the widest sense with a reality, *can only mean to be guided either straight up to it or into its surroundings, or to be put into such working touch with it as to handle either it or something connected with it better than if we disagreed.* Better either intellectually or practically! And often agreement will only mean the negative fact that nothing contradictory from the quarter of that reality comes to interfere with the way in which our ideas guide us elsewhere. To copy a reality is, indeed, one very important way of agreeing with it, but it is far from being essential. The essential thing is the process of being guided. Any idea that helps us to *deal*, whether practically or intellectually, with either the reality or its belongings, that doesn't entangle our progress in frustrations, that *fits*, in fact, and adapts our life to the reality's whole setting, will agree sufficiently to meet the requirement. It will hold true of that reality.

Thus, *names* are just as 'true' or 'false' as definite mental pictures are. They set up similar verification-processes, and lead to fully equivalent practical results.

All human thinking gets discursified; we exchange ideas; we lend and borrow verifications, get them from one another by means of social intercourse. All truth thus gets verbally built out, stored up, and made available for everyone. Hence, we must *talk* consistently just as we must *think* consistently: for both in talk and thought we deal with kinds. Names are arbitrary, but once understood they must be kept to. We mustn't now call Abel 'Cain' or Cain 'Abel.' If we do, we ungear ourselves from the whole book of Genesis, and from all its connections with the universe of speech and fact down to the present time. We throw ourselves out of whatever truth that entire system of speech and fact may embody.

The overwhelming majority of our true ideas admit of no direct or face-to-face verification—those of past history, for example, as of Cain and Abel. The stream of time can be remounted only verbally, or verified indirectly by the present prolongations or effects of what the past harbored. Yet if they agree with these verbalities and effects, we can know that our ideas of the past are true. *As true as past time itself was*, so true was Julius Caesar, so true were antediluvian monsters, all in their proper dates and settings. That past time itself was, is guaranteed by its coherence with everything that's present. True as the present *is*, the past *was* also.

Agreement thus turns out to be essentially an affair of leading—leading that is useful because it is into quarters that contain objects that are important. True ideas lead us into useful verbal and conceptual quarters as well as directly up to useful sensible termini. They lead to consistency, stability and flowing human intercourse. They lead away from excentricity and isolation, from foiled and barren thinking. The untrammeled flowing of the leading-process, its general freedom from clash and contradiction, passes for its indirect verification; but all roads lead to Rome, and in the end and eventually, all true processes must lead to the face of directly verifying sensible experiences *somewhere*, which somebody's ideas have copied.

Such is the large loose way in which the pragmatist interprets the word agreement. He treats it altogether practically. He lets it cover any process of conduction from a present idea to a future terminus, provided only it run prosperously. It is only thus that 'scientific' ideas, flying as they do beyond common sense, can be said to agree with their realities. It is, as I have already said, *as if* reality were made of ether, atoms or electrons, but we mustn't think so literally. The term 'energy' doesn't even pretend to stand for anything 'objective.' It is only a way of measuring the surface of phenomena so as to string their changes on a simple formula.

Yet in the choice of these man-made formulas we cannot be capricious with impunity any more than we can be capricious on the common-sense practical level. We must find a theory that will *work*; and that means something extremely difficult; for our theory must mediate between all previous truths and certain new experiences. It must derange common sense and previous belief as little as possible, and it must lead to some sensible terminus or other that can be verified exactly. To 'work' means both these things; and the squeeze is so tight that there is little loose play for any hypothesis. Our theories are wedged and controlled as nothing else is. Yet sometimes alternative theoretic formulas are equally compatible with all the truths we know, and then we choose between them for subjective reasons. We choose the kind of theory to which we are already partial; we follow 'elegance' or 'economy.' Clerk Maxwell somewhere says it would be "poor scientific taste" to choose the more complicated of two equally well-evidenced conceptions; and you will all agree with him. Truth in science is what gives us the maximum possible sum of satisfactions, taste included, but consistency both with previous truth and with novel fact is always the most imperious claimant.

I have led you through a very sandy desert. But now, if I may be allowed so vulgar an expression, we begin to taste the milk in the cocoanut. Our rationalist critics here discharge their batteries upon us, and to reply to them will take us out from all this dryness into full sight of a momentous philosophical alternative.

Our account of truth is an account of truths in the plural, of processes of leading, realized in *rebus*, and having only this quality in common, that they *pay*. They pay by guiding us into or towards some part of a system that dips at numerous points into sense-percepts, which we may copy mentally or not, but with which at any rate we are now in the kind of commerce vaguely designated as verification. Truth for us is simply a collective name for verification-processes, just as health, wealth, strength, etc., are names for other processes connected with life, and also pursued because it pays to pursue them. Truth is *made*, just as health, wealth and strength are made, in the course of experience.

Here rationalism is instantaneously up in arms against us. I can imagine a rationalist to talk as follows:

"Truth is not made," he will say; "it absolutely obtains, being a unique relation that does not wait upon any process, but shoots straight over the head of experience, and hits its reality every time. Our belief that yon thing on the wall is a clock is true already, although no one in the whole history of the world should verify it. The bare quality of standing in that transcendent relation is what makes any thought true that possesses it, whether or not there be verification. You pragmatists put the cart before the horse in making truth's being reside in verification-processes. These are merely signs of its being, merely our lame ways of ascertaining after the fact, which of our ideas already has possessed the wondrous quality. The quality itself is timeless, like all essences and natures. Thoughts partake of it directly, as they partake of falsity or of irrelevancy. It can't be analyzed away into pragmatic consequences."

The whole plausibility of this rationalist tirade is due to the fact to which we have already paid so much attention. In our world, namely abounding as it does in things of similar kinds and similarly associated, one verification serves for others of its kind, and one great use of knowing things is to be led not so much to them as to their associates, especially to human talk about them. The quality of truth, obtaining *ante rem*, pragmatically means, then, the fact that in such a world innumerable ideas work better by their indirect or possible than by their direct and actual verification. Truth *ante rem* means only verifiability, then; or else it is a case of the stock rationalist trick of treating the *name* of a concrete phenomenal reality as an independent prior entity, and placing it behind the reality as its explanation. Professor Mach quotes somewhere an epigram of Lessing's:

> Sagt Hänschen Schlau zu Vetter Fritz,
> "Wie kommt es, Vetter Fritzen,
> Dass grad' die Reichsten in der Welt,
> Das meiste Geld besitzen?"

Hänschen Schlau here treats the principle 'wealth' as something distinct from the facts denoted by the man's being rich. It antedates them; the facts become only a sort of secondary coincidence with the rich man's essential nature.

In the case of 'wealth' we all see the fallacy. We know that wealth is but a name for concrete processes that certain men's lives play a part in, and not a natural excellence found in Messrs. Rockefeller and Carnegie, but not in the rest of us.

Like wealth, health also lives *in rebus*. It is a name for processes, as digestion, circulation, sleep, etc., that go on happily, though in this instance we are more inclined to think of it as a principle and to say the man digests and sleeps so well *because* he is so healthy.

With 'strength' we are, I think, more rationalistic still, and decidedly inclined to treat it as an excellence pre-existing in the man and explanatory of the herculean performances of his muscles.

With 'truth' most people go over the border entirely, and treat the rationalistic account as self-evident. But really all these words in *th* are exactly similar. Truth exists *ante rem* just as much and as little as the other things do.

The scholastics, following Aristotle, made much of the distinction between habit and act. Health *in actu* means, among other things, good sleeping and digesting. But a healthy man need not always be sleeping, or always digesting, any more than a wealthy man need be always handling money or a strong man always lifting weights. All such qualities sink to the status of 'habits' between their times of exercise; and similarly truth becomes a habit of certain of our ideas and beliefs in their intervals of rest from their verifying activities. But those activities are the root of the whole matter, and the condition of there being any habit to exist in the intervals.

'The true,' to put it very briefly, is only the expedient in the way of our thinking, just as 'the right' is only the expedient in the way of our behaving. Expedient in almost any fashion; and expedient in the long run and on the whole of course; for what meets expediently all the experience in sight won't necessarily meet all farther experiences equally satisfactorily. Experience, as we know, has ways of *boiling over*, and making us correct our present formulas.

The 'absolutely' true, meaning what no farther experience will ever alter, is that ideal vanishing-point towards which we imagine that all our temporary truths will some day converge. It runs on all fours with the perfectly wise man, and with the absolutely complete experience; and, if these ideals are ever realized, they will all be realized together. Meanwhile we have to live to-day by what truth we can get to-day, and be ready to-morrow to call it falsehood. Ptolemaic astronomy, euclidean space, aristotelian logic, scholastic metaphysics, were expedient for centuries, but human experience has boiled over those limits, and we now call these things only relatively true, or true within those borders of experience. 'Absolutely' they are false; for we know that those limits were casual, and might have been transcended by past theorists just as they are by present thinkers.

When new experiences lead to retrospective judgments, using the past tense, what these judgments utter *was* true, even though no past thinker had been led there. We live forwards, a Danish thinker has said, but we understand backwards. The present sheds a backward light on the world's previous processes. They may have been truth-processes for the actors in them. They are not so for one who knows the later revelations of the story.

This regulative notion of a potential better truth to be established later, possibly to be established some day absolutely, and having powers of retroactive legislation, turns its face, like all pragmatist notions, towards concreteness of fact, and towards the future. Like the half-truths, the absolute truth will have to be *made*, made is a relation incidental to the growth of a mass of verification-experience, to which the half-true ideas are all along contributing their quota.

I have already insisted on the fact that truth is made largely out of previous truths. Men's beliefs at any time are so much experience *funded*. But the beliefs are themselves parts of the sum total of the world's experience, and become matter, therefore, for the next day's funding operations. So far as reality means experienceable reality, both it and the truths men gain about it are everlastingly in process of mutation—mutation towards a definite goal, it may be—but still mutation.

Mathematicians can solve problems with two variables. On the Newtonian theory, for instance, acceleration varies with distance, but distance also varies with acceleration. In the realm of truth-processes facts come independently and determine our beliefs provisionally. But these beliefs make us act, and as fast as they do so, they bring into sight or into existence new facts which re-determine the beliefs accordingly. So the whole coil and ball of truth, as it rolls up, is the product of a double influence. Truths emerge from facts; but they dip forward into facts again and add to them; which facts again create or reveal new truth (the word is indifferent) and so on indefinitely. The 'facts' themselves meanwhile are not *true*. They simply *are*. Truth is the function of the beliefs that start and terminate among them.

The case is like a snowball's growth, due as it is to the distribution of the snow on the one hand, and to the successive pushes of the boys on the other, with these factors co-determining each other incessantly.

The most fateful point of difference between being a rationalist and being a pragmatist is now fully in sight. Experience is in mutation, and our psychological ascertainments of truth are in mutation—so much rationalism will allow; but never that either reality itself or truth itself is mutable. Reality stands complete and ready-made from all eternity, rationalism insists, and the agreement of our ideas with it is that unique unanalyzable virtue in them of which she has already told us. As that intrinsic excellence, their truth has nothing to do with our experiences. It adds nothing to the content of experience. It makes no difference to reality itself; it is supervenient, inert, static, a reflection merely. It doesn't *exist*, it *holds* or *obtains*, it belongs to another dimension from that of either facts or fact-relations, belongs, in short, to the epistemological dimension—and with that big word rationalism closes the discussion.

Thus, just as pragmatism faces forward to the future, so does rationalism here again face backward to a past eternity. True to her inveterate habit, rationalism reverts to 'principles,' and thinks that when an abstraction once is named, we own an oracular solution.

The tremendous pregnancy in the way of consequences for life of this radical difference of outlook will only become apparent in my later lectures. I wish meanwhile to close this lecture by showing that rationalism's sublimity does not save it from inanity.

When, namely, you ask rationalists, instead of accusing pragmatism of desecrating the notion of truth, to define it themselves by saying exactly what *they* understand by it, the only positive attempts I can think of are these two:

1. "Truth is just the system of propositions which have an unconditional claim to be recognized as valid."[1]
2. Truth is a name for all those judgments which we find ourselves under obligation to make by a kind of imperative duty.[2]

The first thing that strikes one in such definitions is their unutterable triviality. They are absolutely true, of course, but absolutely insignificant until you handle them pragmatically. What do you mean by 'claim' here, and what do you mean by 'duty'? As summary names for the concrete reasons why thinking in true ways is overwhelmingly expedient and good for mortal men, it is all right to talk of claims on reality's part to be agreed with, and of obligations on our part to agree. We feel both the claims and the obligations, and we feel them for just those reasons.

But the rationalists who talk of claim and obligation *expressly say that they have nothing to do with our practical interests or personal reasons.* Our reasons for agreeing are psychological facts, they say, relative to each thinker, and to the accidents of his life. They are his evidence merely, they are no part of the life of truth itself. That life transacts itself in a purely logical or epistemological, as distinguished from a psychological, dimension, and its claims antedate and exceed all personal motivations whatsoever. Though neither man nor God should ever ascertain truth, the word would still have to be defined as that which *ought* to be ascertained and recognized.

There never was a more exquisite example of an idea abstracted from the concretes of experience and then used to oppose and negate what it was abstracted from.

Philosophy and common life abound in similar instances. The 'sentimentalist fallacy' is to shed tears over abstract justice and generosity, beauty, etc., and never to know these qualities when you meet them in the street, because there the circumstances make them vulgar. Thus I read in the privately printed biography of an eminently rationalistic mind: "It was strange that with such admiration for beauty in the abstract, my brother had no enthusiasm for fine architecture, for beautiful painting, or for flowers." And in almost the last philosophic work I have read, I find such passages as the following: "Justice is ideal, solely ideal. Reason conceives that it ought to exist, but experience shows that it cannot. . . . Truth, which ought to be, cannot be. . . . Reason is deformed by experience. As soon as reason enters experience, it becomes contrary to reason."

The rationalist's fallacy here is exactly like the sentimentalist's. Both extract a quality from the muddy particulars of experience, and find it so pure when extracted that they contrast it with each and all its muddy instances as an opposite and higher nature. All the while it is *their* nature. It is the nature of truths to be validated, verified. It pays for our ideas to be validated. Our obligation to seek truth is part of our general obligation to do what pays. The payments true ideas bring are the sole why of our duty to follow them.

Identical whys exist in the case of wealth and health. Truth makes no other kind of claim and imposes no other kind of ought than health and wealth do. All these claims are conditional; the concrete benefits we gain are what we mean by calling the pursuit a duty. In the case of truth, untrue beliefs work as perniciously in the long run as true beliefs work beneficially. Talking abstractly, the quality 'true' may thus be said to grow absolutely precious, and the quality 'untrue' absolutely damnable: the one may be called good, the other bad, unconditionally. We ought to think the true, we ought to shun the false, imperatively.

But if we treat all this abstraction literally and oppose it to its mother soil in experience, see what a preposterous position we work ourselves into.

We cannot then take a step forward in our actual thinking. When shall I acknowledge this truth and when that? Shall the acknowledgment be loud?—or silent? If sometimes loud, sometimes silent, which *now*? When may a truth go into cold-storage in the encyclopedia? and when shall it come out for battle? Must I constantly be repeating the truth 'twice two are four' because of its eternal claim on recognition? or is it sometimes irrelevant? Must my thoughts dwell night and day on my personal sins and blemishes, because I truly have them?—or may I sink and ignore them in order to be a decent social unit, and not a mass of morbid melancholy and apology?

It is quite evident that our obligation to acknowledge truth, so far from being unconditional, is tremendously conditioned. Truth with a big T, and in the singular, claims abstractly to be recognized, of course; but concrete truths in the plural need be recognized only when their recognition is expedient. A truth must always be preferred to a falsehood when both relate to the situation; but when neither does, truth is as little of a duty as falsehood. If you ask me what o'clock it is and I tell you that I live at 95 Irving Street, my answer may indeed be true, but you don't see why it is my duty to give it. A false address would be as much to the purpose.

With this admission that there are conditions that limit the application of the abstract imperative, *the pragmatistic treatment of truth sweeps back upon us in its fullness.* Our duty to agree with reality is seen to be grounded in a perfect jungle of concrete expediencies.

When Berkeley had explained what people meant by matter, people thought that he denied matter's existence. When Messrs. Schiller and Dewey now explain what people mean by truth, they are accused of denying *its* existence. These pragmatists destroy all objective standards, critics say, and put foolishness and wisdom on one level. A favorite formula for describing Mr. Schiller's doctrines and mine is that we are persons who think that by saying whatever you find it pleasant to say and calling it truth you fulfill every pragmatistic requirement.

I leave it to you to judge whether this be not an impudent slander. Pent in, as the pragmatist more than anyone else sees himself to be, between the whole body of funded truths squeezed from the past and the coercions of the world of sense about him, who so well as he feels the immense pressure of objective control under which our minds perform their operations? If anyone imagines that this law is lax, let him keep its commandment one day, says Emerson. We have heard much of late of the uses of the imagination in science. It is high time to urge the use of a little imagination in philosophy. The unwillingness of some of our critics to read any but the silliest

of possible meanings into our statements is as discreditable to their imaginations as anything I know in recent philosophic history. Schiller says the
true is that which 'works.' Thereupon he is treated as one who limits verification to the lowest material utilities. Dewey says truth is what gives 'satisfaction.' He is treated as one who believes in calling everything true
which, if it were true, would be pleasant.

Our critics certainly need more imagination of realities. I have honestly tried to stretch my own imagination and to read the best possible
meaning into the rationalist conception, but I have to confess that it still
completely baffles me. The notion of a reality calling on us to 'agree' with
it, and that for no reasons, but simply because its claim is 'unconditional'
or 'transcendent,' is one that I can make neither head nor tail of. I try to
imagine myself as the sole reality in the world, and then to imagine what
more I would 'claim' if I were allowed to. If you suggest the possibility of
my claiming that a mind should come into being from out of the void
inane and stand and *copy* me, I can indeed imagine what the copying
might mean, but I can conjure up no motive. What good it would do me
to be copied, or what good it would do that mind to copy me, if farther
consequences are expressly and in principle ruled out as motives for the
claim (as they are by our rationalist authorities) I cannot fathom. When
the Irishman's admirers ran him along to the place of banquet in a sedan
chair with no bottom, he said, "Faith, if it wasn't for the honor of the
thing, I might as well have come on foot." So here: but for the honor of
the thing, I might as well have remained uncopied. Copying is one
genuine mode of knowing (which for some strange reason our contemporary transcendentalists seem to be tumbling over each other to
repudiate); but when we get beyond copying, and fall back on unnamed
forms of agreeing that are expressly denied to be either copyings or leadings or fittings, or any other processes pragmatically definable, the *what*
of the 'agreement' claimed becomes as unintelligible as the why of it.
Neither content nor motive can be imagined for it. It is an absolutely
meaningless abstraction.[3]

Surely in this field of truth it is the pragmatists and not the rationalists who are the more genuine defenders of the universe's rationality.

11

The Pragmatist Account of Truth and Its Misunderstanders

The account of truth given in my volume entitled *Pragmatism*, continues to meet with such persistent misunderstanding that I am tempted to make a final brief reply. My ideas may well deserve refutation, but they can get none till they are conceived of in their proper shape. The fantastic character of the current misconceptions shows how unfamiliar is the concrete point of view which pragmatism assumes. Persons who are familiar with a conception move about so easily in it that they understand each other at a hint, and can converse without anxiously attending to their P's and Q's. I have to admit, in view of the results, that we have assumed too ready an intelligence, and consequently in many places used a language too slipshod. We should never have spoken elliptically. The critics have boggled at every word they could boggle at, and refused to take the spirit rather than the letter of our discourse. This seems to show a genuine unfamiliarity in the whole point of view. It also shows, I think, that the second stage of opposition, which has already begun to express itself in the stock phrase that 'what is new is not true, and what is true not new,' in pragmatism, is insincere. If we said nothing in any degree new, why was our meaning so desperately hard to catch? The blame cannot be laid wholly upon our obscurity of speech, for in other subjects we have attained to making ourselves understood. But recriminations are tasteless; and, as far as I personally am concerned, I am sure that some of the misconception I complain of is due to my doctrine of truth being surrounded in that volume of popular lectures by a lot of other opinions not necessarily implicated with it, so that a reader may very naturally have grown confused. For this I am to blame—likewise for omitting certain explicit cautions, which the pages that follow will now in part supply.

FIRST MISUNDERSTANDING: PRAGMATISM IS ONLY A RE-EDITING OF POSITIVISM.

This seems the commonest mistake. Scepticism, positivism, and agnosticism agree with ordinary dogmatic rationalism in presupposing that everybody knows what the word 'truth' means, without further explanation. But the former doctrines then either suggest or declare that real truth, absolute truth, is inaccessible to us, and that we must fain put up with relative or phenomenal truth as its next best substitute. By scepticism this is treated as an unsatisfactory state of affairs, while positivism and agnosticism are cheerful about it, call real truth sour grapes, and consider phenomenal truth quite sufficient for all our 'practical' purposes.

In point of fact, nothing could be farther from all this than what pragmatism has to say of truth. Its thesis is an altogether previous one. It leaves off where these other theories begin, having contented itself with the word truth's *definition*. "No matter whether any mind extant in the universe possess truth or not," it asks, "what does the notion of truth signify *ideally*?" "What kind of things would true judgments be *in case* they existed?" The answer which pragmatism offers is intended to cover the most complete truth that can be conceived of, 'absolute' truth if you like, as well as truth of the most relative and imperfect description. This question of what truth would be like if it did exist, belongs obviously to a purely speculative field of inquiry. It is not a theory about any sort of reality, or about what kind of knowledge is actually possible; it abstracts from particular terms altogether, and defines the nature of a possible relation between two of them.

As Kant's question about synthetic judgments had escaped previous philosophers, so the pragmatist question is not only so subtle as to have escaped attention hitherto, but even so subtle, it would seem, that when openly broached now, dogmatists and sceptics alike fail to apprehend it, and deem the pragmatist to be treating of something wholly different. He insists, they say (I quote an actual critic), "that the greater problems are insoluble by human intelligence, that our need of knowing truly is artificial and illusory, and that our reason, incapable of reaching the foundations of reality, must turn itself exclusively towards *action*." There could not be a worse misapprehension.

SECOND MISUNDERSTANDING: PRAGMATISM IS PRIMARILY AN APPEAL TO ACTION.

The name 'pragmatism,' with its suggestions of action, has been an unfortunate choice, I have to admit, and has played into the hands of this mistake. But no word could protect the doctrine from critics so blind to the nature of the inquiry that, when Dr. Schiller speaks of ideas 'working' well, the only thing they think of is their immediate workings in the physical environment, their enabling us to make money, or gain some similar 'practical' advantage. Ideas do work thus, of course, immediately or remotely; but they work indefinitely inside of the mental world also. Not crediting us with this rudimentary insight, our critics treat our view as offering itself exclusively to engineers, doctors, financiers, and men of action generally, who need some sort of a rough and ready *weltanschauung*, but have no time or wit to study genuine philosophy. It is usually described as a characteristically American movement, a sort of bobtailed scheme of thought, excellently fitted for the man on the street, who naturally hates theory and wants cash returns immediately.

It is quite true that, when the refined theoretic question that pragmatism begins with is once answered, secondary corollaries of a practical sort follow. Investigation shows that, in the function called truth, previous realities are not the only independent variables. To a certain extent our ideas, being realities, are also independent variables, and, just as they follow other reality and fit it, so, in a measure, does other reality follow and fit them. When they add themselves to being, they partly redetermine the existent, so that reality as a whole appears incompletely definable unless ideas also are kept account of. This pragmatist doctrine, exhibiting our ideas as complemental factors of reality, throws open (since our ideas are instigators of our action) a wide window upon human action, as well as a wide license to originality in thought. But few things could be sillier than to ignore the prior epistemological edifice in which the window is built, or to talk as if pragmatism began and ended at the window. This, nevertheless, is what our critics do almost without exception. They ignore our primary step and its motive, and make the relation to action, which is our secondary achievement, primary.

THIRD MISUNDERSTANDING: PRAGMATISTS CUT THEMSELVES OFF FROM THE RIGHT TO BELIEVE IN EJECTIVE REALITIES.

They do so, according to the critics, by making the truth of our beliefs consist in their verifiability, and their verifiability in the way in which they do work for us. Professor Stout, in his otherwise admirable and hopeful review of Schiller in *Mind* for October, 1897, considers that this ought to lead Schiller (could he sincerely realize the effects of his own doctrine) to the absurd consequence of being unable to believe genuinely in another man's headache, even were the headache there. He can only "postulate" it for the sake of the working value of the postulate to himself. The postulate guides certain of his acts and leads to advantageous consequences; but the moment he understands fully that the postulate is true *only* (!) in this sense, it ceases (or should cease) to be true for him that the other man really *has* a headache. All that makes the postulate most precious then evaporates: his interest in his fellow-man "becomes a veiled form of self-interest, and his world grows cold, dull, and heartless."

Such an objection makes a curious muddle of the pragmatist's universe of discourse. Within that universe the pragmatist finds some one with a headache or other feeling, and some one else who postulates that feeling. Asking on what condition the postulate is 'true,' the pragmatist replies that, for the postulator at any rate, it is true just in proportion as to believe in it works in him the fuller sum of satisfactions. What is it that is satisfactory here? Surely to *believe* in the postulated object, namely, in the really existing feeling of the other man. But how (especially if the postulator were himself a thoroughgoing pragmatist) could it ever be satisfactory to him *not* to believe in that feeling, so long as, in Professor Stout's words, disbelief "made the world seem to him cold, dull, and heartless"? Disbelief would seem, on pragmatist principles, quite out of the question under such conditions, unless the heartlessness of the world were made probable already on other grounds. And since the belief in the headache, true for the subject assumed in the pragmatist's universe of discourse, is also true for the pragmatist who for his epistemologizing purposes has assumed that entire universe, why is it not true in that universe absolutely? The headache believed in is a reality there, and no extant mind disbelieves it, neither the critic's mind nor his subject's! Have our opponents any better brand of truth in this real universe of ours that they can show us?[1]

So much for the third misunderstanding, which is but one specification of the following still wider one.

FOURTH MISUNDERSTANDING: NO PRAGMATIST CAN BE A REALIST IN HIS EPISTEMOLOGY.

This is supposed to follow from his statement that the truth of our beliefs consists in general in their giving satisfaction. Of course satisfaction *per se* is a subjective condition; so the conclusion is drawn that truth falls wholly inside of the subject, who then may manufacture it at his pleasure. True beliefs become thus wayward affections, severed from all responsibility to other parts of experience.

It is difficult to excuse such a parody of the pragmatist's opinion, ignoring as it does every element but one of his universe of discourse. The terms of which that universe consists positively forbid any non-realistic interpretation of the function of knowledge defined there. The pragmatizing epistemologist posits there a reality and a mind with ideas. What, now, he asks, can make those ideas true of that reality? Ordinary epistemology contents itself with the vague statement that the ideas must 'correspond' or 'agree'; the pragmatist insists on being more concrete, and asks what such 'agreement' may mean in detail. He finds first that the ideas must point to or lead towards *that* reality and no other, and then that the pointings and leadings must yield satisfaction as their result. So far the pragmatist is hardly less abstract than the ordinary slouchy epistemologist; but as he defines himself farther, he grows more concrete. The entire quarrel of the intellectualist with him is over his concreteness, intellectualism contending that the vaguer and more abstract account is here the more profound. The concrete pointing and leading are conceived by the pragmatist to be the work of other portions of the same universe to which the reality and the mind belong, intermediary verifying bits of experience with which the mind at one end, and the reality at the other, are joined. The 'satisfaction,' in turn, is no abstract satisfaction *überhaupt*, felt by an unspecified being, but is assumed to consist of such satisfactions (in the plural) as concretely existing men actually do find in their beliefs. As we humans are constituted in point of fact, we find that to believe in other men's minds, in independent physical realities, in past events, in eternal logical relations, is satisfactory. We find hope satisfactory. We often find it satisfactory to cease to doubt. Above all we find *consistency* satisfactory, consistency between the present idea and the entire rest of our mental equipment, including the whole order of our sensations, and that of our intuitions of likeness and difference, and our whole stock of previously acquired truths.

The pragmatist, being himself a man, and imagining in general no contrary lines of truer belief than ours about the 'reality' which he has laid at the base of his epistemological discussion, is willing to treat our satisfactions as possibly really true guides to it, not as guides true solely for *us*. It would seem here to be the duty of his critics to show with some explicitness why, being our subjective feelings, these satisfactions can *not* yield 'objective' truth. The beliefs which they accompany 'posit' the assumed reality, 'correspond' and 'agree' with it, and 'fit' it in perfectly definite and assignable ways, through the sequent trains of thought and action which form their verification, so merely to insist on using these words abstractly instead of concretely is no way of driving the pragmatist from the field—his more concrete account virtually includes his critic's. If our critics have any definite idea of a truth more objectively grounded than the kind we propose, why do they not show it more articulately? As they stand, they remind one of Hegel's man who wanted 'fruit,' but rejected cherries, pears, and grapes, because they were not fruit in the abstract. We offer them the full quart-pot, and they cry for the empty quart-capacity.

But here I think I hear some critic retort as follows: "If satisfactions are all that is needed to make truth, how about the notorious fact that errors are so often satisfactory? And how about the equally notorious fact that certain true beliefs may cause the bitterest dissatisfaction? Isn't it clear that not the satisfaction which it gives, but the relation of the belief *to the reality* is all that makes it true? Suppose there were no such reality, and that the satisfactions yet remained: would they not then effectively work falsehood? Can they consequently be treated distinctively as the truth-builders? It is the *inherent relation to reality* of a belief that gives us that specific *truth*-satisfaction, compared with which all other satisfactions are the hollowest humbug. The satisfaction of *knowing truly* is thus the only one which the pragmatist ought to have considered. As a *psychological sentiment*, the anti-pragmatist gladly concedes it to him, but then only as a concomitant of truth, not as a constituent. What *constitutes* truth is not the sentiment, but the purely logical or objective function of rightly cognizing the reality, and the pragmatist's failure to reduce this function to lower values is patent."

Such anti-pragmatism as this seems to me a tissue of confusion. To begin with, when the pragmatist says 'indispensable,' it confounds this with 'sufficient.' The pragmatist calls satisfactions indispensable for truth-building, but I have everywhere called them insufficient unless reality be also incidentally led to. If the reality assumed were cancelled from the pragmatist's universe of discourse, he would straightway give the name of falsehoods to the beliefs remaining, in spite of all their satisfactoriness. For him, as for his critic, there can be no truth if there is nothing to be true about. Ideas are so much flat psychological surface unless some mirrored matter gives them cognitive lustre. This is why as a pragmatist I have so carefully posited 'reality' *ab initio*, and why, throughout my whole discussion, I remain an epistemological realist.[2]

The anti-pragmatist is guilty of the further confusion of imagining that, in undertaking to give him an account of what truth formally means, we are assuming at the same time to provide a warrant for it, trying to define the occasions when he can be sure of materially possessing it. Our making it hinge on a reality so 'independent' that when it comes, truth comes, and when it goes, truth goes with it, disappoints this naive expectation, so he deems our description unsatisfactory. I suspect that under this confusion lies the still deeper one of not discriminating sufficiently between the two notions, truth and reality. Realities are not *true*, they *are*; and beliefs are true *of* them. But I suspect that in the anti-pragmatist mind the two notions sometimes swap their attributes. The reality itself, I fear, is treated as if 'true,' and conversely. Whoso tells us of the one, it is then supposed, must also be telling us of the other; and a true idea must in a manner *be*, or at least *yield* without extraneous aid, the reality it cognitively is possessed of.

To this absolute-idealistic demand pragmatism simply opposes its *non possumus*. If there is to be truth, it says, both realities and beliefs about them must conspire to make it; but whether there ever is such a thing, or how anyone can be sure that his own beliefs possess it, it never pretends to determine. That truth-satisfaction *par excellence* which may tinge a belief unsatisfactory in other ways, it easily explains as the feeling of consistency with the stock of previous truths, or supposed truths, of which one's whole past experience may have left one in possession.

But are not all pragmatists sure that their own belief is right? their enemies will ask at this point; and this leads me to the

FIFTH MISUNDERSTANDING: WHAT PRAGMATISTS SAY IS INCONSISTENT WITH THEIR SAYING SO.

A correspondent puts this objection as follows: "When you say to your audience, 'pragmatism is the truth concerning truth,' the first truth is different from the second. About the first you and they are not to be at odds; you are not giving them liberty to take or leave it according as it works satisfactorily or not for their private uses. Yet the second truth, which ought to describe and include the first, affirms this liberty. Thus the *intent* of your utterance seems to contradict the *content* of it."

General scepticism has always received this same classic refutation. "You have to dogmatize," the rationalists say to the sceptics, "whenever you express the sceptical position; so your lives keep contradicting your thesis." One would suppose that the impotence of so hoary an argument to abate in the slightest degree the amount of general scepticism in the world might have led some rationalists themselves to doubt whether these instantaneous logical refutations are such fatal ways, after all, of killing off live mental attitudes. General scepticism is the live mental attitude of refusing to conclude. It is a permanent torpor of the will, renewing itself in detail towards each successive thesis that offers, and you can no more kill it off by logic than you can kill off obstinacy or practical joking. This is why it is so irritating. Your consistent sceptic never puts his scepticism into a formal proposition—he simply chooses it as a habit. He provokingly hangs back when he might so easily join us in saying yes, but he is not illogical or stupid—on the contrary, he often impresses us by his intellectual superiority. This is the *real* scepticism that rationalists have to meet, and their logic does not even touch it.

No more can logic kill the pragmatist's behavior: his act of utterance, so far from contradicting, accurately exemplifies the matter which he utters. What is the matter which he utters? In part, it is this, that truth, concretely considered, is an attribute of our beliefs, and that these are attitudes that follow satisfactions. The ideas around which the satisfactions cluster are primarily only hypotheses that challenge or summon a belief to come and take its stand upon them. The pragmatist's idea of truth is just such a challenge. He finds it ultra-satisfactory to accept it, and takes his own stand accordingly. But, being gregarious as they are, men seek to spread their beliefs, to awaken imitation, to infect others. Why should not *you* also find the same belief satisfactory? thinks the pragmatist, and forthwith endeavors to convert you. You and he will then believe similarly; you will hold up your subject-end of a truth, which will be a truth objective and irreversible if the reality holds up the object-end by being itself present simultaneously. What there is of self-contradiction in all this I confess I cannot discover. The pragmatist's conduct in his own case seems to me on the contrary admirably to illustrate his universal formula; and of all epistemologists, he is perhaps the only one who is irreproachably self-consistent.

SIXTH MISUNDERSTANDING: PRAGMATISM EXPLAINS NOT WHAT TRUTH IS, BUT ONLY HOW IT IS ARRIVED AT.

In point of fact it tells us both, tells us what it is incidentally to telling us how it is arrived at—for what *is* arrived at except just what the truth is? If I tell you how to get to the railroad station, don't I implicitly introduce you to the *what*, to the being and nature of that edifice? It is quite true that the abstract *word* 'how' hasn't the same meaning as the abstract *word* 'what,' but in this universe of concrete facts you cannot keep hows and whats asunder. The reasons why I find it satisfactory to believe that any idea is true, the *how* of my arriving at that belief, may be among the very reasons why the idea *is* true in reality. If not, I summon the anti-pragmatist to explain the impossibility articulately.

His trouble seems to me mainly to arise from his fixed inability to understand how a concrete statement can possibly mean as much, or be as valuable, as an abstract one. I said above that the main quarrel between us and our critics was that of concreteness *versus* abstractness. This is the place to develop that point farther.

In the present question, the links of experience sequent upon an idea, which mediate between it and a reality, form and for the pragmatist indeed *are*, the *concrete* relation of truth that may obtain between the idea and that reality. They, he says, are all that we mean when we speak of the idea 'pointing' to the reality, 'fitting' it, 'corresponding' with it, or 'agreeing' with it—they or other similar mediating trains of verification. Such mediating events *make* the idea 'true.' The idea itself, if it exists at all, is also a concrete event: so pragmatism insists that truth in the singular is only a collective name for truths in the plural, these consisting always of series of definite events; and that what intellectualism calls *the* truth, the *inherent* truth, of any one such series is only the abstract name for its truthfulness in act, for the fact that the ideas there do lead to the supposed reality in a way that we consider satisfactory.

The pragmatist himself has no objection to abstractions. Elliptically, and 'for short,' he relies on them as much as any one, finding upon innumerable occasions that their comparative emptiness makes of them useful substitutes for the overfulness of the facts he meets with. But he never ascribes to them a higher grade of reality. The full reality of a truth for him is always some process of verification, in which the abstract property of connecting ideas with objects truly is workingly embodied. Meanwhile it is endlessly serviceable to be able to talk of properties abstractly and apart from their working, to find them the same in innumerable cases, to take them 'out of time,' and to treat of their relations to other similar abstractions. We thus form whole universes of platonic ideas *ante rem*, universes *in posse*, tho none of them exists effectively except *in rebus*. Countless relations obtain there which nobody experiences as obtaining—as, in the eternal universe of musical relations, for example, the notes of Aennchen von Tharau were a lovely melody long ere mortal ears ever heard them. Even so the music of the future sleeps now, to be awakened hereafter. Or, if we take the world of geometrical relations, the thousandth decimal of π sleeps there, though no one may ever try to compute it. Or, if we take the universe of 'fitting,' countless coats 'fit' backs, and countless boots 'fit' feet, on which they are not practically *fitted*; countless stones 'fit' gaps in walls into which no one seeks to fit them actually. In the same way countless opinions 'fit' realities, and countless truths are valid, though no thinker ever thinks them.

For the anti-pragmatist these prior timeless relations are the presupposition of the concrete ones, and possess the profounder dignity and value. The actual workings of our ideas in verification-processes are as naught in comparison with the 'obtainings' of this discarnate truth within them.

For the pragmatist, on the contrary, all discarnate truth is static, impotent, and relatively spectral, full truth being the truth that energizes and does battle. Can any one suppose that the sleeping quality of truth would ever have been abstracted or have received a name, if truths had remained forever in that storage-vault of essential timeless 'agreements' and had never been embodied in any panting struggle of men's live ideas for verification? Surely no more than the abstract property of 'fitting' would have received a name, if in our world there had been no backs or feet or gaps in walls to be actually fitted. *Existential* truth is incidental to the actual competition of opinions. *Essential* truth, the truth of the intellectualists, the truth with no one thinking it, is like the coat that fits though no one has ever tried it on, like the music that no ear has listened to. It is less real, not more real, than the verified article; and to attribute a superior degree of glory to it seems little more than a piece of perverse abstraction-worship. As well might a pencil insist that the outline is the essential thing in all pictorial representation, and chide the paint-brush and the camera for omitting it, forgetting that *their* pictures not only contain the whole outline, but a hundred other things in addition. Pragmatist truth contains the whole of intellectualist truth and a hundred other things in addition. Intellectualist truth is then only pragmatist truth *in posse*. That on innumerable occasions men do substitute truth *in posse* or verifiability, for verification or truth in act, is a fact to which no one attributes more importance than the pragmatist: he emphasizes the practical utility of such a habit. But he does not on that account consider truth *in posse*—truth not alive enough ever to have been asserted or questioned or contradicted—to be the metaphysically prior thing, to which truths in act are tributary and subsidiary. When intellectualists do this, pragmatism charges them with inverting the real relation. Truth *in posse* *means* only truths in act; and he insists that these latter take precedence in the order of logic as well as in that of being.

SEVENTH MISUNDERSTANDING: PRAGMATISM IGNORES THE THEORETIC INTEREST.

This would seem to be an absolutely wanton slander, were not a certain excuse to be found in the linguistic affinities of the word 'pragmatism,' and in certain offhand habits of speech of ours which assumed too great a generosity on our reader's part. When we spoke of the meaning of ideas consisting in their 'practical' consequences, or of the 'practical' differences which our beliefs make to us; when we said that the truth of a belief consists in its 'working' value, etc.; our language evidently was too careless, for by 'practical' we were almost unanimously held to mean *opposed* to theoretical or genuinely cognitive, and the consequence was punctually drawn that a truth in our eyes could have no relation to any independent reality, or to any other truth, or to anything whatever but the acts which we might ground on it or the satisfactions they might bring. The mere existence of the idea, all by itself, if only its results were satisfactory, would give full truth to it, it was charged, in our absurd pragmatist epistemology. The solemn attribution of this rubbish to us was also encouraged by two other circumstances. First, ideas *are* practically useful in the narrow sense, false ideas sometimes, but most often ideas which we can verify by the sum total of all their leadings, and the reality of whose objects may thus be considered established beyond doubt. That these ideas should be true in advance of and apart from their utility, that, in other words, their objects should be really there, is the very condition of their having that kind of utility—the objects they connect us with are so important that the ideas which serve as the objects' substitutes grow important also. This manner of their practical working was the first thing that made truths good in the eyes of primitive men;

and buried among all the other good workings by which true beliefs are characterized, this kind of subsequential utility remains.

The second misleading circumstance was the emphasis laid by Schiller and Dewey on the fact that, unless a truth be relevant to the mind's momentary predicament, unless it be germane to the 'practical' situation—meaning by this the quite particular perplexity—it is no good to urge it. It doesn't meet our interests any better than a falsehood would under the same circumstances. But why our predicaments and perplexities might not be theoretical here as well as narrowly practical, I wish that our critics would explain. They simply assume that no pragmatist *can* admit a genuinely theoretic interest. Having used the phrase 'cash-value' of an idea, I am implored by one correspondent to alter it, "for every one thinks you mean only pecuniary profit and loss." Having said that the true is 'the expedient in our thinking,' I am rebuked in this wise by another learned correspondent: "The word expedient has no other meaning than that of self-interest. The pursuit of this has ended by landing a number of officers of national banks in penitentiaries. A philosophy that leads to such results must be unsound."

But the word 'practical' is so habitually loosely used that more indulgence might have been expected. When one says that a sick man has now practically recovered, or that an enterprise has practically failed, one usually means just the opposite of practically in the literal sense. One means that, although untrue in strict practice, what one says is true in theory, true virtually, *certain to be* true. Again, by the practical one often means the distinctively concrete, the individual, particular, and effective, as opposed to the abstract, general, and inert. To speak for myself, whenever I have emphasized the practical nature of truth, this is mainly what has been in my mind. 'Pragmata' are things in their plurality; and in that early California address, when I described pragmatism as holding that "the meaning of any proposition can always be brought down to some particular consequence in our future practical experience, whether passive or active," I expressly added these qualifying words: "the point lying rather in the fact that the experience must be particular than in the fact that it must be active"—by 'active' meaning here 'practical' in the narrow literal sense.[3] But particular consequences can perfectly well be of a theoretic nature. Every remote fact which we infer from an idea is a particular theoretic consequence which our mind practically works towards. The loss of every old opinion of ours which we see that we shall have to give up if a new opinion be true, is a particular theoretic as well as a particular practical consequence. After man's interest in breathing freely, the greatest of all his interests (because it never fluctuates or remits, as most of his physical interests do), is his interest in *consistency*, in feeling that what he now thinks goes with what he thinks on other occasions. We tirelessly compare truth with truth for this sole purpose. Is the present candidate for belief perhaps contradicted by principle number one? Is it compatible with fact number two? and so forth. The particular operations here are the purely logical ones of analysis, deduction, comparison, etc.; and although general terms may be used *ad libitum*, the satisfactory *practical working* of the candidate-idea consists in the consciousness yielded by each successive theoretic consequence in particular. It is therefore simply idiotic to repeat that pragmatism takes no account of purely theoretic interests. All it insists on is that verity in act means *verifications*, and that these are always particulars. Even in exclusively theoretic matters, it insists that vagueness and generality serve to verify nothing.

EIGHTH MISUNDERSTANDING: PRAGMATISM IS SHUT UP TO SOLIPSISM.

I have already said something about this misconception under the third and fourth heads, above, but a little more may be helpful. The objection is apt to clothe itself in words like these: "You make truth to consist in every value except the cognitive value proper; you always leave your knower at many removes (or, at the uttermost, at one remove) from his real object; the best you do is to let his ideas carry him towards it; it remains forever outside of him," etc.

I think that the leaven working here is the rooted intellectualist persuasion that, to know a reality, an idea must in some inscrutable fashion possess or be it.[4] For pragmatism this kind of coalescence is inessential. As a rule our cognitions are only processes of mind off their balance and in motion towards real termini; and the reality of the termini, believed in by the states of mind in question, can be *guaranteed* only by some wider knower.[5] But if there is no reason extant in the universe why they should be doubted, the beliefs are true in the only sense in which anything can be true anyhow: they are practically and concretely true, namely. True in the mystical mongrel sense of an *identitätsphilosophie* they need not be; nor is there any intelligible reason why they ever need be true otherwise than verifiably and practically. It is reality's part to possess its own existence; it is thought's part to get into 'touch' with it by innumerable paths of verification.

I fear that the 'humanistic' developments of pragmatism may cause a certain difficulty here. We get at one truth only through the rest of truth; and the reality, everlastingly postulated as that which all our truth must keep in touch with, may never be given to us save in the form of truth other than that which we are now testing. But since Dr. Schiller has shown that all our truths, even the most elemental, are affected by race-inheritance with a human coefficient, reality *per se* thus may appear only as a sort of limit; it may be held to shrivel to the mere *place* for an object, and what is known may be held to be only matter of our psyche that we fill the place with.

It must be confessed that pragmatism, worked in this humanistic way, is *compatible* with solipsism. It joins friendly hands with the agnostic part of Kantism, with contemporary agnosticism, and with idealism generally. But worked thus, it is a metaphysical theory about the matter of reality, and flies far beyond pragmatism's own modest analysis of the nature of the knowing function, which analysis may just as harmoniously be combined with less humanistic accounts of reality. One of pragmatism's merits is that it is so purely epistemological. It must assume realities; but it prejudges nothing as to their constitution, and the most diverse metaphysics can use it as their foundation. It certainly has no special affinity with solipsism.

As I look back over what I have written, much of it gives me a queer impression, as if the obvious were set forth so condescendingly that readers might well laugh at my pomposity. It may be, however, that concreteness as radical as ours is not so obvious. The whole originality of pragmatism, the whole point in it, is its use of the concrete way of seeing. It begins with concreteness, and returns and ends with it. Dr. Schiller, with his two 'practical' aspects of truth, (1) relevancy to situation, and (2) subsequential utility, is only filling the cup of concreteness to the brim for us. Once seize that cup, and you cannot misunderstand pragmatism. It seems as if the power of imagining the world concretely *might* have been common enough to let our readers apprehend us better, as if they might have read between our lines, and, in spite of all our infelicities of expression, guessed a little more correctly what our thought was. But alas! this was not on fate's programme, so we can only think, with the German ditty:

> "Es wär' zu schön gewesen,
> Es hat nicht sollen sein."

12

The Meaning of the Word Truth

My account of truth is realistic, and follows the epistemological dualism of common sense. Suppose I say to you "The thing exists"—is that true or not? How can you tell? Not till my statement has developed its meaning farther is it determined as being true, false, or irrelevant to reality altogether. But if now you ask "what thing?" and I reply "a desk"; if you ask "where?" and I point to a place; if you ask "does it exist materially, or only in imagination?" and I say "materially"; if moreover I say "I mean that desk," and then grasp and shake a desk which you see just as I have described it, you are willing to call my statement true. But you and I are commutable here; we can exchange places; and, as you go bail for my desk, so I can go bail for yours.

This notion of a reality independent of either of us, taken from ordinary social experience, lies at the base of the pragmatist definition of truth. With some such reality any statement, in order to be counted true, must agree. Pragmatism defines 'agreeing' to mean certain ways of 'working,' be they actual or potential. Thus, for my statement "the desk exists" to be true of a desk recognized as real by you, it must be able to lead me to shake your desk, to explain myself by words that suggest that desk to your mind, to make a drawing that is like the desk you see, etc. Only in such ways as this is there sense in saying it agrees with *that* reality, only thus does it gain for me the satisfaction of hearing you corroborate me. Reference then to something determinate, and some sort of adaptation to it worthy of the name of agreement, are thus constituent elements in the definition of any statement of mine as 'true.'

You cannot get at either the reference or the adaptation without using the notion of the workings. *That* the thing is, *what* it is, and *which* it is (of all the possible things with that what) are points determinable only by the pragmatic method. The 'which' means a possibility of pointing, or of otherwise singling out the special object; the 'what' means choice on our part of an essential aspect to conceive it by (and this is always relative to what Dewey calls our own 'situation'); and the 'that' means our assumption of the attitude of belief, the reality recognizing attitude. Surely for understanding what the word 'true' means as applied to a statement, the mention of such workings is indispensable. Surely if we leave them out the subject and the object of the cognitive relation float—in the same universe, 'tis true—but vaguely and ignorantly and without mutual contact or mediation.

Our critics nevertheless call the workings inessential. No functional possibilities 'make' our beliefs true, they say; they are true inherently, true positively, born 'true' as the Count of Chambord was born 'Henri-Cinq.' Pragmatism insists, on the contrary, that statements and beliefs are thus inertly and statically true only by courtesy: they practically pass for true; but you *cannot define what you mean* by calling them true without referring to their functional possibilities. These give its whole *logical content* to that relation to reality on a belief's part to which the name 'truth' is applied, a relation which otherwise remains one of mere coexistence or bare witness.

The foregoing statements reproduce the essential content of the lecture on Truth in my book *Pragmatism*. Schiller's doctrine of 'humanism,' Dewey's *Studies in Logical Theory*, and my own 'radical empiricism,' all involve this general notion of truth as 'working,' either actual or conceivable. But they envelop it as only one detail in the midst of much wider theories that aim eventually at determining the notion of what 'reality' at large is in its ultimate nature and constitution.

Part Three

Ethics and Religion

13

The Dilemma of Determinism

A common opinion prevails that the juice has ages ago been pressed out of the free-will controversy, and that no new champion can do more than warm up stale arguments which everyone has heard. This is a radical mistake. I know of no subject less worn out, or in which inventive genius has a better chance of breaking open new ground—not, perhaps, of forcing a conclusion or of coercing assent, but of deepening our sense of what the issue between the two parties really is, of what the ideas of fate and of free will imply. At our very side almost, in the past few years, we have seen falling in rapid succession from the press works that present the alternative in entirely novel lights. Not to speak of the English disciples of Hegel, such as Green and Bradley; not to speak of Hinton and Hodgson, nor of Hazard here—we see in the writings of Renouvier, Fouillée, and Delboeuf[1] how completely changed and refreshed is the form of all the old disputes. I cannot pretend to vie in originality with any of the masters I have named, and my ambition limits itself to just one little point. If I can make two of the necessarily implied corollaries of determinism clearer to you than they have been made before, I shall have made it possible for you to decide for or against that doctrine with a better understanding of what you are about. And if you prefer not to decide at all, but to remain doubters, you will at least see more plainly what the subject of your hesitation is. I thus disclaim openly on the threshold all pretension to prove to you that the freedom of the will is true. The most I hope is to induce some of you to follow my own example in assuming it true, and acting as if it were true. If it be true, it seems to me that this is involved in the strict logic of the case. Its truth ought not to be forced willy-nilly down our indifferent throats. It ought to be freely espoused by men who can equally well turn their backs upon it. In other words, our first act of freedom, if we are free, ought in all inward propriety to be to affirm that we are free. This should exclude, it seems to me, from the free-will side of the question all hope of a coercive demonstration,—a demonstration which I, for one, am perfectly contented to go without.

With thus much understood at the outset, we can advance. But not without one more point understood as well. The arguments I am about to urge all proceed on two suppositions: first, when we make theories about the world and discuss them with one another, we do so in order to attain a conception of things which shall give us subjective satisfaction; and, second, if there be two conceptions, and the one seems to us, on the whole, more rational than the other, we are entitled to suppose that the more rational one is the truer of the two. I hope that you are all willing to make these suppositions with me; for I am afraid that if there be any of you here who are not, they will find little edification in the rest of what I have to say. I cannot stop to argue the point; but I myself believe that all the magnificent achievements of mathematical and physical science—our doctrines of evolution, of uniformity of law, and the rest—proceed from our indomitable desire to cast the world into a more rational shape in our minds than the shape into which it is thrown there by the crude order of our experience. The world has shown itself, to a great extent, plastic to this demand of ours for rationality. How much farther it will show itself plastic no one can say. Our only means of finding out is to try; and I, for one, feel as free to try conceptions of moral as of mechanical or of logical rationality. If a certain formula for expressing the nature of the world violates my moral demand, I shall feel as free to throw it overboard, or at least to doubt it, as if it disappointed my demand for uniformity of sequence, for example; the one demand being, so far as I can see, quite as subjective and emotional as the other is. The principle of causality, for example—what is it but a postulate, an empty name covering simply a demand that the sequence of events shall some day manifest a deeper kind of belonging of one thing with another than the mere arbitrary juxtaposition which now phenomenally appears? It is as much an altar to an unknown god as the one that Saint Paul found at Athens. All our scientific and philosophic ideals are altars to unknown gods. Uniformity is as much so as is free-will. If this be admitted, we can debate on even terms. But if anyone pretends that while freedom and variety are, in the first instance, subjective demands, necessity and uniformity are something altogether different, I do not see how we can debate at all.[2]

To begin, then, I must suppose you acquainted with all the usual arguments on the subject. I cannot stop to take up the old proofs from causation, from statistics, from the certainty with which we can foretell one another's conduct, from the fixity of character, and all the rest. But there are two *words* which usually encumber these classical arguments, and which we must immediately dispose of if we are to make any progress. One is the eulogistic word *freedom*, and the other is the opprobrious word *chance*. The word "chance" I wish to keep, but I wish to get rid of the word "freedom." Its eulogistic associations have so far overshadowed all the rest of its meaning that both parties claim the sole right to use it, and determinists today insist that they alone are freedom's champions. Old-fashioned determinism was what we may call *hard* determinism. It did not shrink from such words as fatality, bondage of the will, necessitation, and the like. Nowadays, we have a *soft* determinism which abhors harsh words, and, repudiating fatality, necessity, and even predetermination, says that its real name is freedom; for freedom is only necessity understood, and bondage to the highest is identical with true freedom. Even a writer as little used to making capital out of soft words as Mr. Hodgson hesitates not to call himself a 'free-will determinist.'

Now, all this is a quagmire of evasion under which the real issue of fact has been entirely smothered. Freedom in all these senses presents simply no problem at all. No matter what the soft determinist means by it—whether he means the acting without external constraint; whether he means the acting rightly, or whether he means the acquiescing in the law of the whole—who cannot answer him that sometimes we are free and sometimes we are not? But there is a problem, an issue of fact and not of words, an issue of the most momentous importance, which is often decided without discussion in one sentence—nay, in one clause of a sentence—by those very writers who spin out whole chapters in their efforts to show what 'true' freedom is; and that is the question of determinism, about which we are to talk tonight.

Fortunately, no ambiguities hang about this word or about its opposite, indeterminism. Both designate an outward way in which things may happen, and their cold and mathematical sound has no sentimental associations that can bribe our partiality either way in advance. Now, evidence of an external kind to decide between determinism and indeterminism is, as I intimated a while back, strictly impossible to find. Let us look at the difference between them and see for ourselves. What does determinism profess?

It professes that those parts of the universe already laid down absolutely appoint and decree what the other parts shall be. The future has no ambiguous possibilities bidden in its womb; the part we call the present is compatible with only one totality. Any other future complement than the one fixed from eternity is impossible. The whole is in each and every part, and welds it with the rest into an absolute unity, an iron block, in which there can be no equivocation or shadow of turning.

> "With earth's first clay they did the last man knead,
> And there of the last harvest sowed the seed.
> And the first morning of creation wrote
> What the last dawn of reckoning shall read."

Indeterminism, on the contrary, says that the parts have a certain amount of loose play on one another, so that the laying down of one of them does not necessarily determine what the others shall be. It admits that possibilities may be in excess of actualities, and that things not yet revealed to our knowledge may really in themselves be ambiguous. Of two alternative futures which we conceive, both may now be really possible; and the one becomes impossible only at the very moment when the other excludes it by becoming real itself. Indeterminism thus denies the world to be one unbending unit of fact. It says there is a certain ultimate pluralism in it; and, so saying, it corroborates our ordinary unsophisticated view of things. To that view, actualities seem to float in a wider sea of possibilities from out of which they are chosen; and, *somewhere*, indeterminism says, such possibilities exist, and form a part of truth.

Determinism, on the contrary, says they exist *nowhere*, and that necessity on the one hand and impossibility on the other are the sole categories of the real. Possibilities that fail to get realized are, for determinism, pure illusions: they never were possibilities at all. There is nothing inchoate, it says, about this universe of ours, all that was or is or shall be actual in it having been from eternity virtually there. The cloud of alternatives our minds escort this mass of actuality withal is a cloud of sheer deceptions, to which 'impossibilities' is the only name that rightfully belongs.

The issue, it will be seen, is a perfectly sharp one, which no eulogistic terminology can smear over or wipe out. The truth *must* lie with one side or the other, and its lying with one side makes the other false.

The question relates solely to the existence of possibilities, in the strict sense of the term, as things that may, but need not, be. Both sides admit that a volition, for instance, has occurred. The indeterminists say another volition might have occurred in its place: the determinists swear that nothing could possibly have occurred in its place. Now, can science be called in to tell us which of these two point-blank contradicters of each other is right? Science professes to draw no conclusions but such as are based on matters of fact, things that have actually happened; but how can any amount of assurance that something actually happened give us the least grain of information as to whether another thing might or might not have happened in its place? Only facts can be proved by other facts. With things that are possibilities and not facts, facts have no concern. If we have no other evidence than the evidence of existing facts, the possibility-question must remain a mystery never to be cleared up.

And the truth is that facts practically have hardly anything to do with making us either determinists or indeterminists. Sure enough, we make a flourish of quoting facts this way or that; and if we are determinists, we talk about the infallibility with which we can predict one another's conduct; while if we are indeterminists, we lay great stress on the fact that it is just because we cannot foretell one another's conduct, either in war or statecraft or in any of the great and small intrigues and businesses of men, that life is so intensely anxious and hazardous a game. But who does not see the wretched insufficiency of this so-called objective testimony on both sides? What fills up the gaps in our minds is something not objective, not external. What divides us into possibility men and anti-possibility men is different faiths or postulates—postulates of rationality. To this man the world seems more rational with possibilities in it—to that man more rational with possibilities excluded; and talk as we will about having to yield to evidence, what makes us monists or pluralists, determinists or indeterminists, is at bottom always some sentiment like this.

The stronghold of the deterministic sentiment is the antipathy to the idea of chance. As soon as we begin to talk indeterminism to our friends, we find a number of them shaking their heads. This notion of alternative possibilities, they say, this admission that any one of several things may come to pass, is, after all, only a roundabout name for chance; and chance is something the notion of which no sane mind can for an instant tolerate in the world. What is it, they ask, but barefaced crazy unreason, the negation of intelligibility and law? And if the slightest particle of it exists anywhere, what is to prevent the whole fabric from falling together, the stars from going out, and chaos from recommencing her topsy-turvy reign?

Remarks of this sort about chance will put an end to discussion as quickly as anything one can find. I have already told you that 'chance' was a word I wished to keep and use. Let us then examine exactly what it means, and see whether it ought to be such a terrible bugbear to us. I fancy that squeezing the thistle boldly will rob it of its sting.

The sting of the word 'chance' seems to lie in the assumption that it means something positive, and that if anything happens by chance, it must needs be something of an intrinsically irrational and preposterous sort. Now, chance means nothing of the kind. It is a purely negative and relative term,[3] giving us no information about that of which it is predicated, except that it happens to be disconnected with something else—not controlled, secured, or necessitated by other things in advance of its own actual presence. As this point is the most subtle one of the whole lecture, and at the same time the point on which all the rest hinges, I beg you to pay particular attention to it. What I say is that it tells us nothing about what a thing may be in itself to call it 'chance.' It may be a bad thing, it may be a good thing. It may be lucidity, transparency, fitness incarnate, matching the whole system of other things, when it has once befallen, in an unimaginably perfect way. All you mean by calling it 'chance' is that this is not guaranteed, that it may also fall out otherwise. For the system of other things has no positive hold on the chance-thing. Its origin is in a certain fashion negative: it escapes, and says, Hands off! coming, when it comes, as a free gift, or not at all.

This negativeness, however, and this opacity of the chance-thing when thus considered *ab extra*, or from the point of view of previous things or distant things, do not preclude its having any amount of positiveness and luminosity from within, and at its own place and moment. All that its chance-character asserts about it is that there is something in it really of its own, something that is not the unconditional property of the whole. If the whole wants this property, the whole must wait till it can get it, if it be a matter of chance. That the universe may actually be a sort of joint-stock society of this sort, in which the sharers have both limited liabilities and limited powers, is of course a simple and conceivable notion.

Nevertheless, many persons talk as if the minutest dose of disconnectedness of one part with another, the smallest modicum of independence, the faintest tremor of ambiguity about the future, for example, would ruin everything, and turn this goodly universe into a sort of insane sand-heap or nulliverse, no universe at all. Since future human volitions are as a matter of fact the only ambiguous things we are tempted to believe in, let us stop for a moment to make ourselves sure whether their independent and accidental character need be fraught with such direful consequences to the universe as these.

What is meant by saying that my choice of which way to walk home after the lecture is ambiguous and matter of chance as far as the present moment is concerned? It means that both Divinity Avenue and Oxford Street are called; but that only one, and that one *either* one, shall be chosen. Now, I ask you seriously to suppose that this ambiguity of my choice is real; and then to make the impossible hypothesis that the choice is made twice over, and each time falls on a different street. In other words, imagine that I first walk through Divinity Avenue, and then imagine that the powers governing the universe annihilate ten minutes of time with all that it contained, and set me back at the door of this hall just as I was before the choice was made. Imagine then that, everything else being the same, I now make a different choice and traverse Oxford Street. You, as passive spectators, look on and see the two alternative universes—one of them with me walking through Divinity Avenue in it, the other with the same me walking through Oxford Street. Now, if you are determinists you believe one of these universes to have been from eternity impossible: you believe it to have been impossible because of the intrinsic irrationality or accidentality somewhere involved in it. But looking outwardly at these universes, can you say which is the impossible and accidental one, and which the rational and necessary one? I doubt if the most ironclad determinist among you could have the slightest glimmer of light on this point. In other words, either universe *after the fact* and once there would, to our means of observation and understanding, appear just as rational as the other. There would be absolutely no criterion by which we might judge one necessary and the other matter of chance. Suppose now we relieve the gods of their hypothetical task and assume my choice, once made, to be made forever. I go through Divinity Avenue for good and all. If, as good determinists, you now begin to affirm, what all good determinists punctually do affirm, that in the nature of things I *couldn't* have gone through Oxford Street—had I done so it would have been chance, irrationality, insanity, a horrid gap in nature—I simply call your attention to this, that your affirmation is what the Germans call a *Machtspruch*, a mere conception fulminated as a dogma and based on no insight into details. Before my choice, either street seemed as natural to you as to me. Had I happened to take Oxford Street, Divinity Avenue would have figured in your philosophy as the gap in nature; and you would have so proclaimed it with the best deterministic conscience in the world.

But what a hollow outcry, then, is this against a chance which, if it were presented to us, we could by no character whatever distinguish from a rational necessity! I have taken the most trivial of examples, but no possible example could lead to any different result. For what are the alternatives which, in point of fact, offer themselves to human volition? What are those futures that now seem matters of chance? Are they not one and all like the Divinity Avenue and Oxford Street of our example? Are they not all of them *kinds* of things already here and based in the existing frame of nature? Is anyone ever tempted to produce an *absolute* accident, something utterly irrelevant to the rest of the world? Do not all the motives that assail us, all the futures that offer themselves to our choice, spring equally from the soil of the past; and would not either one of them, whether realized through chance or through necessity, the moment it was realized, seem to us to fit that past, and in the completest and most continuous manner to interdigitate with the phenomena already there?[4]

The more one thinks of the matter, the more one wonders that so empty and gratuitous a hubbub as this outcry against chance should have found so great an echo in the hearts of men. It is a word which tells us absolutely nothing about what chances, or about the *modus operandi* of the chancing; and the use of it as a war-cry shows only a temper of intellectual absolutism, a demand that the world shall be a solid block, subject to one control—which temper, which demand, the world may not be found to gratify at all. In every outwardly verifiable and practical respect, a world in which the alternatives that now actually distract *your* choice were decided by pure chance would be by *me* absolutely undistinguished from the world in which I now live. I am, therefore, entirely willing to call it, so far as your choices go, a world of chance for me. To *yourselves*, it is true, those very acts of choice, which to me are so blind, opaque, and external, are the opposites of this, for you are within them and effect them. To you they appear as decisions; and decisions, for him who makes them, are altogether peculiar psychic facts. Self-luminous and self-justifying at the living moment at which they occur, they appeal to no outside moment to put its stamp upon them or make them continuous with the rest of nature. Themselves it is rather who seem to make nature continuous; and in their strange and intense function of granting consent to one possibility and withholding it from another, to transform an equivocal and double future into an unalterable and simple past.

But with the psychology of the matter we have no concern this evening. The quarrel which determinism has with chance fortunately has nothing to do with this or that psychological detail. It is a quarrel altogether metaphysical. Determinism denies the ambiguity of future volitions, because it affirms that nothing future can be ambiguous. But we have said enough to meet the issue. Indeterminate future volitions *do* mean chance. Let us not fear to shout it from the house-tops if need be; for we now know that the idea of chance is, at bottom, exactly the same thing as the idea of gift—the one simply being a disparaging, and the other a eulogistic, name for anything on which we have no effective *claim*. And whether the world be the better or the worse for having either chances or gifts in it will depend altogether on *what* these uncertain and unclaimable things turn out to be.

And this at last brings us within sight of our subject. We have seen what determinism means: we have seen that indeterminism is rightly described as meaning chance; and we have seen that chance, the very name of which we are urged to shrink from as from a metaphysical pestilence, means only the negative fact that no part of the world, however big, can claim to control absolutely the destinies of the whole. But although, in discussing the word 'chance,' I may at moments have seemed to be arguing for its real existence, I have not meant to do so yet. We have not yet ascertained whether this be a world of chance or no; at most, we have agreed that it seems so. And I now repeat what I said at the outset, that, from any strict theoretical point of view, the question is insoluble. To deepen our theoretic sense of the *difference* between a world with chances in it and a deterministic world is the most I can hope to do; and this I may now at last begin upon, after all our tedious clearing of the way.

I wish first of all to show you just what the notion that this is a deterministic world implies. The implications I call your attention to are all bound up with the fact that it is a world in which we constantly have to make what I shall, with your permission, call judgments of regret. Hardly an hour passes in which we do not wish that something might be otherwise; and happy indeed are those of us whose hearts have never echoed the wish of Omar Khayam—

> "That we might clasp, ere closed, the book of fate,
> And make the writer on a fairer leaf
> Inscribe our names, or quite obliterate.
>
> "Ah! Love, could you and I with fate conspire
> To mend this sorry scheme of things entire,
> Would we not shatter it to bits, and then
> Remold it nearer to the heart's desire?"

Now, it is undeniable that most of these regrets are foolish, and quite on a par in point of philosophic value with the criticisms on the universe of that friend of our infancy, the hero of the fable "The Atheist and the Acorn"—

> "Fool! had that bough a pumpkin bore,
> Thy whimsies would have worked no more," etc.

Even from the point of view of our own ends, we should probably make a botch of remodeling the universe. How much more then from the point of view of ends we cannot see! Wise men therefore regret as little as they can. But still some regrets are pretty obstinate and hard to stifle—regrets for acts of wanton cruelty or treachery, for example, whether performed by others or by ourselves. Hardly anyone can remain *entirely* optimistic after reading the confession of the murderer at Brockton the other day: how, to get rid of the wife whose continued existence bored him, he inveigled her into a desert spot, shot her four times, and then, as she lay on the ground and said to him, "You didn't do it on purpose, did you, dear?" replied, "No, I didn't do it on purpose," as he raised a rock and smashed her skull. Such an occurrence, with the mild sentence and self-satisfaction of the prisoner, is a field for a crop of regrets, which one need not take up in detail. We feel that, although a perfect mechanical fit to the rest of the universe, it is a bad moral fit, and that something else would really have been better in its place.

But for the deterministic philosophy the murder, the sentence, and the prisoner's optimism were all necessary from eternity; and nothing else for a moment had a ghost of a chance of being put in their place. To admit such a chance, the determinists tell us, would be to make a suicide of reason; so we must steel our hearts against the thought. And here our plot thickens, for we see the first of those difficult implications of determinism and monism, which it is my purpose to make you feel. If this Brockton murder was called for by the rest of the universe, if it had to come at its preappointed hour, and if nothing else would have been consistent with the sense of the whole, what are we to think of the universe? Are we stubbornly to stick to our judgment of regret, and say, though it *couldn't* be, yet it *would* have been a better universe with something different from this Brockton murder in it? That, of course, seems the natural and spontaneous thing for us to do; and yet it is nothing short of deliberately espousing a kind of pessimism. The judgment of regret calls the murder bad. Calling a thing bad means, if it means anything at all, that the thing ought not to be, that something else ought to be in its stead. Determinism, in denying that anything else can be in its stead, virtually defines the universe as a place in which what ought to be is impossible—in other words, as an organism whose constitution is afflicted with an incurable taint, an irremediable flaw. The pessimism of a Schopenhauer says no more than this—that the murder is a symptom; and that it is a vicious symptom because it belongs to a vicious whole, which can express its nature no otherwise than by bringing forth just such a symptom as that at this particular spot. Regret for the murder must transform itself, if we are determinists and wise, into a larger regret.

It is absurd to regret the murder alone. Other things being what they are, *it* could not be different. What we should regret is that whole frame of things of which the murder is one member. I see no escape whatever from this pessimistic conclusion if, being determinists, our judgment of regret is to be allowed to stand at all.

The only deterministic escape from pessimism is everywhere to abandon the judgment of regret. That this can be done, history shows to be not impossible. The devil, *quoad existentiam*, may be good. That is, although he be a *principle* of evil, yet the universe, with such a principle in it, may practically be a better universe than it could have been without. On every hand, in a small way, we find that a certain amount of evil is a condition by which a higher form of good is brought. There is nothing to prevent anybody from generalizing this view, and trusting that if we could but see things in the largest of all ways, even such matters as this Brockton murder would appear to be paid for by the uses that follow in their train. An optimism *quand même*, a systematic and infatuated optimism like that ridiculed by Voltaire in his *Candide*, is one of the possible ideal ways in which a man may train himself to look on life. Bereft of dogmatic hardness and lit up with the expression of a tender and pathetic hope, such an optimism has been the grace of some of the most religious characters that ever lived.

> "Throb thine with Nature's throbbing breast,
> And all is clear from east to west."

Even cruelty and treachery may be among the absolutely blessed fruits of time, and to quarrel with any of their details may be blasphemy. The only real blasphemy, in short, may be that pessimistic temper of the soul which lets it give way to such things as regrets, remorse, and grief.

Thus, our deterministic pessimism may become a deterministic optimism at the price of extinguishing our judgments of regret.

But does not this immediately bring us into a curious logical predicament? Our determinism leads us to call our judgments of regret wrong, because they are pessimistic in implying that what is impossible yet ought to be. But how then about the judgments of regret themselves? If they are wrong, other judgments, judgments of approval presumably, ought to be in their place. But as they are necessitated, nothing else *can* be in their place; and the universe is just what it was before—namely, a place in which what ought to be appears impossible. We have got one foot out of the pessimistic bog, but the other one sinks all the deeper. We have rescued our actions from the bonds of evil, but our judgments are now held fast. When murders and treacheries cease to be sins, regrets are theoretic absurdities and errors. The theoretic and the active life thus play a kind of see-saw with each other on the ground of evil. The rise of either sends the other down. Murder and treachery cannot be good without regret being bad: regret cannot be good without treachery and murder being bad. Both, however, are supposed to have been fore-doomed; so something must be fatally unreasonable, absurd, and wrong in the world. It must be a place of which either sin or error forms a necessary part. From this dilemma there seems at first sight no escape. Are we then so soon to fall back into the pessimism from which we thought we had emerged? And is there no possible way by which we may, with good intellectual consciences, call the cruelties and treacheries, the reluctances and the regrets, *all* good together?

Certainly there is such a way, and you are probably most of you ready to formulate it yourselves. But, before doing so, remark how inevitably the question of determinism and indeterminism slides us into the question of optimism and pessimism, or, as our fathers called it, 'the question of evil.' The theological form of all these disputes is the simplest and the deepest, the form from which there is the least escape—not because, as some have sarcastically said, remorse and regret are clung to us with a morbid fondness by the theologians as spiritual luxuries, but because they are existing facts of the world, and as such must be taken into account in the deterministic interpretation of all that is fated to be. If they are fated to be error, does not the bat's wing of irrationality still cast its shadow over the world?

The refuge from the quandary lies, as I said, not far off. The necessary acts we erroneously regret may be good, and yet our error in so regretting them may be also good, on one simple condition; and that condition is this: The world must not be regarded as a machine whose final purpose is the making real of any outward good, but rather as a contrivance for deepening the theoretic consciousness of what goodness and evil in their intrinsic natures are. Not the doing either of good or evil is what nature cares for, but the knowing of them. Life is one long eating of the fruit of the tree of *knowledge*. I am in the habit, in thinking to myself, of calling this point of view the *gnostical* point of view. According to it, the world is neither an optimism nor a pessimism, but a *gnosticism*. But as this term may perhaps lead to some misunderstandings, I will use it as little as possible here, and speak rather of *subjectivism*, and the *subjectivistic* point of view.

Subjectivism has three great branches—we may call them scientificism, sentimentalism, and sensualism, respectively. They all agree essentially about the universe, in deeming that what happens there is subsidiary to what we think or feel about it. Crime justifies its criminality by awakening our intelligence of that criminality, and eventually our remorses and regrets; and the error included in remorses and regrets, the error of supposing that the past could have been different, justifies itself by its use. Its use is to quicken our sense of *what* the irretrievably lost is. When we think of it as that which might have been ("the saddest words of tongue or pen"), the quality of its worth speaks to us with a wilder sweetness; and, conversely, the dissatisfaction wherewith we think of what seems to have driven it from its natural place gives us the severer pang. Admirable artifice of nature! we might be tempted to exclaim—deceiving us in order the better to enlighten us, and leaving nothing undone to accentuate to our consciousness the yawning distance of those opposite poles of good and evil between which creation swings.

We have thus clearly revealed to our view what may be called the dilemma of determinism, so far as determinism pretends to think things out at all. A merely mechanical determinism, it is true, rather rejoices in not thinking them out. It is very sure that the universe must satisfy its postulate of a physical continuity and coherence, but it smiles at anyone who comes forward with a postulate of moral coherence as well. I may suppose, however, that the number of purely mechanical or hard determinists among you this evening is small. The determinism to whose seductions you are most exposed is what I have called soft determinism—the determinism which allows considerations of good and bad to mingle with those of cause and effect in deciding what sort of a universe this may rationally be held to be. The dilemma of this determinism is one whose left horn is pessimism and whose right horn is subjectivism. In other words, if determinism is to escape pessimism, it must leave off looking at the goods and ills of life in a simple objective way, and regard them as materials, indifferent in themselves, for the production of consciousness, scientific and ethical, in us.

To escape pessimism is, as we all know, no easy task. Your own studies have sufficiently shown you the almost desperate difficulty of making the notion that there is a single principle of things, and that principle absolute perfection, rhyme together with our daily vision of the facts of life. If perfection be the principle, how comes there any imperfection here? If God be good, how came he to create—or, if he did not create, how comes he to permit—the devil? The evil facts must be explained as seeming: the devil must be whitewashed, the universe must be disinfected, if neither God's goodness nor his unity and power are to remain impugned. And of all the various ways of operating the disinfection, and making bad seem less bad, the way of subjectivism appears by far the best.[5]

For, after all, is there not something rather absurd in our ordinary notion of external things being good or bad in themselves? Can murders and treacheries, considered as mere outward happenings, or motions of matter, be bad without anyone to feel their badness? And could paradise properly be good in the absence of a sentient principle by which the goodness was perceived? Outward goods and evils seem practically indistinguishable except in so far as they result in getting moral judgments made about them. But then the moral judgments seem the main thing, and the outward facts mere perishing instruments for their production. This is subjectivism. Everyone must at some time have wondered at that strange paradox of our moral nature, that, though the pursuit of outward good is the breath of its nostrils, the attainment of outward good would seem to be its suffocation and death. Why does the painting of any paradise or utopia, in heaven or on earth, awaken such yawnings for nirvana and escape? The white-robed harp-playing heaven of our sabbath-schools, and the ladylike tea-table elysium represented in Mr. Spencer's *Data of Ethics*, as the final consummation of progress, are exactly on a par in this respect—lubberlands, pure and simple, one and all.[6] We look upon them from this delicious mess of insanities and realities, strivings and deadnesses, hopes and fears, agonies and exultations, which forms our present state, and *tedium vitae* is the only sentiment they awaken in our breasts. To our crepuscular natures, born for the conflict, the Rembrandtesque moral chiaroscuro, the shifting struggle of the sunbeam in the gloom, such pictures of light upon light are vacuous and expressionless, and neither to be enjoyed nor understood. If *this* be the whole fruit of the victory, we say; if the generations of mankind suffered and laid down their lives; if prophets confessed and martyrs sang in the fire, and all the sacred tears were shed for no other end than that a race of creatures of such unexampled insipidity should succeed, and protract *in* saecula saeculorum their contented and inoffensive lives—why, at such a rate, better lose than win the battle, or at all events better ring down the curtain before the last act of the play, so that a business that began so importantly may be saved from so singularly flat a winding-up.

All this is what I should instantly say, were I called on to plead for gnosticism; and its real friends, of whom you will presently perceive I am not one, would say without difficulty a great deal more. Regarded as a stable finality, every outward good becomes a mere weariness to the flesh. It must be menaced, be occasionally lost, for its goodness to be fully felt as such. Nay, more than occasionally lost. No one knows the worth of innocence till he knows it is gone forever, and that money cannot buy it back. Not the saint, but the sinner that repenteth, is he to whom the full length and breadth, and height and depth, of life's meaning is revealed. Not the absence of vice, but vice there, and virtue holding her by the throat, seems the ideal human state. And there seems no reason to suppose it not a permanent human state. There is a deep truth in what the school of Schopenhauer insists on—the illusoriness of the notion of moral progress. The more brutal forms of evil that go are replaced by others more subtle and more poisonous. Our moral horizon moves with us as we move, and never do we draw nearer to the far-off line where the black waves and the azure meet. The final purpose of our creation seems most plausibly to be the greatest possible enrichment of our ethical consciousness, through the intensest play of contrasts and the widest diversity of characters. This of course obliges some of us to be vessels of wrath, while it calls others to be vessels of honor. But the subjectivist point of view reduces all these outward distinctions to a common denominator. The wretch languishing in the felon's cell may be drinking draughts of the wine of truth that will never pass the lips of the so-called favorite of fortune. And the peculiar consciousness of each of them is an indispensable note in the great ethical concert which the centuries as they roll are grinding out of the living heart of man.

So much for subjectivism! If the dilemma of determinism be to choose between it and pessimism, I see little room for hesitation from the strictly theoretical point of view. Subjectivism seems the more rational scheme. And the world may, possibly, for aught I know, be nothing else. When the healthy love of life is on one, and all its forms and its appetites seem so unutterably real; when the most brutal and the most spiritual things are lit by the same sun, and each is an integral part of the total richness—why, then it seems a grudging and sickly way of meeting so robust a universe to shrink from any of its facts and wish them not to be. Rather take the strictly dramatic point of view, and treat the whole thing as a great unending romance which the spirit of the universe, striving to realize its own content, is eternally thinking out and representing to itself.[7]

No one, I hope, will accuse me, after I have said all this, of underrating the reasons in favor of subjectivism. And now that I proceed to say why those reasons, strong as they are, fail to convince my own mind, I trust the presumption may be that my objections are stronger still.

I frankly confess that they are of a practical order. If we practically take up subjectivism in a sincere and radical manner and follow its consequences, we meet with some that make us pause. Let a subjectivism begin in never so severe and intellectual a way, it is forced by the law of its nature to develop another side of itself and end with the corruptest curiosity. Once dismiss the notion that certain duties are good in themselves, and that we are here to do them, no matter how we feel about them; once consecrate the opposite notion that our performances and our violations of duty are for a common purpose, the attainment of subjective knowledge and feeling, and that the deepening of these is the chief end of our lives—and at what point on the downward slope are we to stop? In theology, subjectivism develops as its 'left wing' antinomianism. In literature, its left wing is romanticism. And in practical life it is either a nerveless sentimentality or a sensualism without bounds.

Everywhere it fosters the fatalistic mood of mind. It makes those who are already too inert more passive still; it renders wholly reckless those whose energy is already in excess. All through history we find how subjectivism, as soon as it has a free career, exhausts itself in every sort of spiritual, moral, and practical license. Its optimism turns to an ethical indifference, which infallibly brings dissolution in its train. It is perfectly safe to say now that if the Hegelian gnosticism, which has begun to show itself here and in Great Britain, were to become a popular philosophy, as it once was in Germany, it would certainly develop its left wing here as there, and produce a reaction of disgust. Already I have heard a graduate of this very school express in the pulpit his willingness to sin like David, if only he might repent like David. You may tell me he was only sowing his wild, or rather his tame, oats; and perhaps he was. But the point is that in the subjectivistic or gnostical philosophy oat-sowing, wild or tame, becomes a systematic necessity and the chief function of life. After the pure and classic truths, the exciting and rancid ones must be experienced; and if the stupid virtues of the philistine herd do not then come in and save society from the influence of the children of light, a sort of inward putrefaction becomes its inevitable doom.

Look at the last runnings of the romantic school, as we see them in that strange contemporary Parisian literature, with which we of the less clever countries are so often driven to rinse out our minds after they have become clogged with the dullness and heaviness of our native pursuits.

The romantic school began with the worship of subjective sensibility and the revolt against legality of which Rousseau was the first great prophet: and through various fluxes and refluxes, right wings and left wings, it stands today with two men of genius, M. Renan and M. Zola, as its principal exponents—one speaking with its masculine, and the other with what might be called its feminine, voice. I prefer not to think now of less noble members of the school, and the Renan I have in mind is of course the Renan of latest dates. As I have used the term gnostic, both he and Zola are gnostics of the most pronounced sort. Both are athirst for the facts of life, and both think the facts of human sensibility to be of all facts the most worthy of attention. Both agree, moreover, that sensibility seems to be there for no higher purpose—certainly not, as the Philistines say, for the sake of bringing mere outward rights to pass and frustrating outward wrongs. One dwells on the sensibilities for their energy, the other for their sweetness; one speaks with a voice of bronze, the other with that of an Æolian harp; one ruggedly ignores the distinction of good and evil, the other plays the coquette between the craven unmanliness of his Philosophic Dialogues and the butterfly optimism of his *Souvenirs de Jeunesse*. But under the pages of both there sounds incessantly the hoarse bass of *vanitas vanitatum, omnia vanitas*, which the reader may hear, whenever he will, between the lines. No writer of this French romantic school has a word of rescue from the hour of satiety with the things of life—the hour in which we say, "I take no pleasure in them"—or from the hour of terror at the world's vast meaningless grinding, if perchance such hours should come. For terror and satiety are facts of sensibility like any others; and at their own hour they reign in their own right. The heart of the romantic utterances, whether poetical, critical, or historical, is this inward remedilessness, what Carlyle calls this far-off whimpering of wail and woe. And from this romantic state of mind there is absolutely no possible *theoretic* escape. Whether, like Renan, we look upon life in a more refined way, as a romance of the spirit; or whether, like the friends of M. Zola, we pique ourselves on our 'scientific' and 'analytic' character, and prefer to be cynical, and call the world a 'roman expérimental' on an infinite scale—in either case the world appears to us potentially as what the same Carlyle once called it, a vast, gloomy, solitary Golgotha and mill of death.

The only escape is by the practical way. And since I have mentioned the nowadays much-reviled name of Carlyle, let me mention it once more, and say it is the way of his teaching. No matter for Carlyle's life, no matter for a great deal of his writing. What was the most important thing he said to us? He said: "Hang your sensibilities! Stop your snivelling complaints, and your equally snivelling raptures! Leave off your general emotional tomfoolery, and get to WORK like men!" But this means a complete rupture with the subjectivist philosophy of things. It says conduct, and not sensibility, is the ultimate fact for our recognition. With the vision of certain works to be done, of certain outward changes to be wrought or resisted, it says our intellectual horizon terminates. No matter how we succeed in doing these outward duties, whether gladly and spontaneously, or heavily and unwillingly, do them we somehow must; for the leaving of them undone is perdition. No matter how we feel; if we are only faithful in the outward act and refuse to do wrong, the world will in so far be safe, and we quit of our debt toward it. Take, then, the yoke upon our shoulders; bend our neck beneath the heavy legality of its weight; regard something else than our feeling as our limit, our master, and our law; be willing to live and die in its service—and, at a stroke, we have passed from the subjective into the objective philosophy of things, much as one awakens from some feverish dream, full of bad lights and noises, to find one's self bathed in the sacred coolness and quiet of the air of the night.

But what is the essence of this philosophy of objective conduct, so old-fashioned and finite, but so chaste and sane and strong, when compared with its romantic rival? It is the recognition of limits, foreign and opaque to our understanding. It is the willingness, after bringing about some external good, to feel at peace; for our responsibility ends with the performance of that duty, and the burden of the rest we may lay on higher powers.[8]

> "Look to thyself, O Universe,
> Thou are better and not worse,"

we may say in that philosophy, the moment we have done our stroke of conduct, however small. For in the view of that philosophy the universe belongs to a plurality of semi-independent forces, each one of which may help or hinder, and be helped or hindered by, the operations of the rest.

But this brings us right back, after such a long detour, to the question of indeterminism and to the conclusion of all I came here to say tonight. For the only consistent way of representing a pluralism and a world whose parts may affect one another through their conduct being either good or bad is the indeterministic way. What interest, zest, or excitement can there be in achieving the right way, unless we are enabled to feel that the wrong way is also a possible and a natural way—nay, more, a menacing and an imminent way? And what sense can there be in condemning ourselves for taking the wrong way, unless we need have done nothing of the sort, unless the right way was open to us as well? I cannot understand the willingness to act, no matter how we feel, without the belief that acts are really good and bad. I cannot understand the belief that an act is bad, without regret at its happening. I cannot understand regret without the admission of real, genuine possibilities in the world. Only *then* is it other than a mockery to feel, after we have failed to do our best, that an irreparable opportunity is gone from the universe, the loss of which it must forever after mourn.

If you insist that this is all superstition, that possibility is in the eye of science and reason impossibility, and that if I act badly 'tis that the universe was foredoomed to suffer this defect, you fall right back into the dilemma, the labyrinth, of pessimism and subjectivism, from out of whose toils we have just found our way.

Now, we are of course free to fall back, if we please. For my own part, though, whatever difficulties may beset the philosophy of objective right and wrong, and the indeterminism it seems to imply, determinism, with its alternative of pessimism or romanticism, contains difficulties that are greater still. But you will remember that I expressly repudiated a while ago the pretension to offer any arguments which could be coercive in a so-called scientific fashion in this matter. And I consequently find myself, at the end of this long talk, obliged to state my conclusions in an altogether personal way. This personal method of appeal seems to be among the very conditions of the problem; and the most anyone can do is to confess as candidly as he can the grounds for the faith that is in him, and leave his example to work on others as it may.

Let me, then, without circumlocution say just this. The world is enigmatical enough in all conscience, whatever theory we may take up toward it. The indeterminism I defend, the free-will theory of popular sense based on the judgment of regret, represents that world as vulnerable, and liable to be injured by certain of its parts if they act wrong. And it represents their acting wrong as a matter of possibility or accident, neither inevitable nor yet to be infallibly warded off. In all this, it is a theory devoid either of transparency or of stability. It gives us a pluralistic, restless universe, in which no single point of view can ever take in the whole scene; and to a mind possessed of the love of unity at any cost, it will, no doubt, remain forever unacceptable. A friend with such a mind once told me that the thought of my universe made him sick, like the sight of the horrible motion of a mass of maggots in their carrion bed.

But while I freely admit that the pluralism and the restlessness are repugnant and irrational in a certain way, I find that every alternative to them is irrational in a deeper way. The indeterminism with its maggots, if you please to speak so about it, offends only the native absolutism of my intellect—an absolutism which, after all, perhaps, deserves to be snubbed and kept in check. But the determinism with its necessary carrion, to continue the figure of speech, and with no possible maggots to eat the latter up, violates my sense of moral reality through and through. When, for example, I imagine such carrion as the Brockton murder, I cannot conceive it as an act by which the universe, as a whole, logically and necessarily expresses its nature without shrinking from complicity with such a whole. And I deliberately refuse to keep on terms of loyalty with the universe by saying blankly that the murder, since it does flow from the nature of the whole, is not carrion. There are *some* instinctive reactions which I, for one, will not tamper with. The only remaining alternative, the attitude of gnostical romanticism, wrenches my personal instincts in quite as violent a way. It falsifies the simple objectivity of their deliverance. It makes the goose-flesh the murder excites in me a sufficient reason for the perpetration of the crime. It transforms life from a tragic reality into an insincere melodramatic exhibition, as foul or as tawdry as anyone's diseased curiosity pleases to carry it out. And with its consecration of the 'roman naturaliste' state of mind, and its enthronement of the baser crew of Parisian *littérateurs* among the eternally indispensable organs by which the infinite spirit of things attains to that subjective illumination which is the task of its life, it leaves me in presence of a sort of subjective carrion considerably more noisome than the objective carrion I called it in to take away.

No! better a thousand times, than such systematic corruption of our moral sanity, the plainest pessimism, so that it be straightforward; but better far than that the world of chance. Make as great an uproar about chance as you please, I know that chance means pluralism and nothing more. If some of the members of the pluralism are bad, the philosophy of pluralism, whatever broad views it may deny me, permits me, at least, to turn to the other members with a clean breast of affection and an unsophisticated moral sense. And if I still wish to think of the world as a totality, it lets me feel that a world with a *chance* in it of being altogether good, even if the chance never come to pass, is better than a world with no such chance at all. That 'chance' whose very notion I am exhorted and conjured to banish from my view of the future as the suicide of reason concerning it, that 'chance' is—what? Just this—the chance that in moral respects the future may be other and better than the past has been. This is the only chance we have any motive for supposing to exist. Shame, rather, on its repudiation and its denial! For its presence is the vital air which lets the world live, the salt which keeps it sweet.

And here I might legitimately stop, having expressed all I care to see admitted by others tonight. But I know that if I do stop here, misapprehensions will remain in the minds of some of you, and keep all I have said from having its effect; so I judge it best to add a few more words.

In the first place, in spite of all my explanations, the word 'chance' will still be giving trouble. Though you may yourselves be adverse to the deterministic doctrine, you wish a pleasanter word than 'chance' to name the opposite doctrine by; and you very likely consider my preference for such a word a perverse sort of a partiality on my part. It certainly *is* a bad word to make converts with; and you wish I had not thrust it so butt-foremost at you—you wish to use a milder term.

Well, I admit there may be just a dash of perversity in its choice. The spectacle of the mere word-grabbing game played by the soft determinists has perhaps driven me too violently the other way; and, rather than be found wrangling with them for the good words, I am willing to take the first bad one which comes along, provided it be unequivocal. The question is of things, not of eulogistic names for them; and the best word is the one that enables men to know the quickest whether they disagree or not about the things. But the word 'chance,' with its singular negativity, is just the word for this purpose. Whoever uses it instead of 'freedom,' squarely and resolutely gives up all pretense to control the things he says are free. For *him*, he confesses that they are no better than mere chance would be. It is a word of *impotence*, and is therefore the only sincere word we can use, if, in granting freedom to certain things, we grant it honestly, and really risk the game. "Who chooses me must give and forfeit all he hath." Any other word permits of quibbling, and lets us, after the fashion of the soft determinists, make a pretense of restoring the caged bird to liberty with one hand, while with the other we anxiously tie a string to its leg to make sure it does not get beyond our sight.

But now you will bring up your final doubt. Does not the admission of such an unguaranteed chance or freedom preclude utterly the notion of a Providence governing the world? Does it not leave the fate of the universe at the mercy of the chance-possibilities, and so far insecure? Does it not, in short, deny the craving of our nature for an ultimate peace behind all tempests, for a blue zenith above all clouds?

To this my answer must be very brief. The belief in free-will is not in the least incompatible with the belief in Providence, provided you do not restrict the Providence to fulminating nothing but *fatal* degrees. If you allow him to provide possibilities as well as actualities to the universe, and to carry on his own thinking in those two categories just as we do ours, chances may be there, uncontrolled even by him, and the course of the universe be really ambiguous; and yet the end of all things may be just what he intended it to be from all eternity.

An analogy will make the meaning of this clear. Suppose two men before a chessboard—the one a novice, the other an expert player of the game. The expert intends to beat. But he cannot foresee exactly what any one actual move of his adversary may be. He knows, however, all the *possible* moves of the latter; and he knows in advance how to meet each of them by a move of his own which leads in the direction of victory. And the victory infallibly arrives, after no matter how devious a course, in the one predestined form of check-mate to the novice's king.

Let now the novice stand for us finite free agents, and the expert for the infinite mind in which the universe lies. Suppose the latter to be thinking out his universe before he actually creates it. Suppose him to say, "I will lead things to a certain end, but I will not *now*[9] decide on all the steps thereto. At various points, ambiguous possibilities shall be left open, *either* of which, at a given instant, may become actual. But whichever branch of these bifurcations becomes real, I know what I shall do at the *next* bifurcation to keep things from drifting away from the final result I intend."[10]

The creator's plan of the universe would thus be left blank as to many of its actual details, but all possibilities would be marked down. The realization of some of these would be left absolutely to chance; that is, would only be determined when the moments of realization came. Other possibilities would be *contingently* determined; that is, their decision would have to wait till it was seen how the matters of absolute chance fell out. But the rest of the plan, including its final upshot, would be rigorously determined once for all. So the creator himself would not need to know all the details of actuality until they came; and at any time his own view of the world would be a view partly of facts and partly of possibilities, exactly as ours is now. Of one thing, however, he might be certain; and that is that his world was safe, and that no matter how much of it might zigzag he could surely bring it home at last.

Now, it is entirely immaterial, in this scheme, whether the creator leave the absolute chance-possibilities to be decided by himself, each when its proper moment arrives, or whether, on the contrary, he alienate this power from himself, and leave the decision out and out to finite creatures such as we men are. The great point is that the possibilities are really *here*. Whether it be we who solve them, or he working through us, at those soul-trying moments when fate's scales seem to quiver, and good snatches the victory from evil or shrinks nerveless from the fight, is of small account, so long as we admit that the issue is decided nowhere else than *here* and *now*. *That* is what gives the palpitating reality to our moral life and makes it tingle, as Mr. Mallock says, with so strange and elaborate an excitement. This reality, this excitement, are what the determinisms, hard and soft alike, suppress by their denial that *anything* is decided here and now, and their dogma that all things were foredoomed and settled long ago. If it be so, may you and I then have been foredoomed to the error of continuing to believe in liberty.[11] It is fortunate for the winding up of controversy that in every discussion with determinism this *argumentum ad hominem* can be its adversary's last word.

14

The Moral Philosopher
and the Moral Life

The main purpose of this paper is to show that there is no such thing possible as an ethical philosophy dogmatically made up in advance. We all help to determine the content of ethical philosophy so far as we contribute to the race's moral life. In other words, there can be no final truth in ethics any more than in physics, until the last man has had his experience and said his say. In the one case as in the other, however, the hypotheses which we now make while waiting, and the acts to which they prompt us, are among the indispensable conditions which determine what that 'say' shall be.

First of all, what is the position of him who seeks an ethical philosophy? To begin with, he must be distinguished from all those who are satisfied to be ethical sceptics. He *will* not be a sceptic; therefore so far from ethical scepticism being one possible fruit of ethical philosophizing, it can only be regarded as that residual alternative to all philosophy which from the outset menaces every would-be philosopher who may give up the quest discouraged, and renounce his original aim. That aim is to find an account of the moral relations that obtain among things, which will weave them into the unity of a stable system, and make of the world what one may call a genuine universe from the ethical point of view. So far as the world resists reduction to the form of unity, so far as ethical propositions seem unstable, so far does the philosopher fail of his ideal. The subject-matter of his study is the ideals he finds existing in the world; the purpose which guides him is this ideal of his own, of getting them into a certain form. This ideal is thus a factor in ethical philosophy whose legitimate presence must never be overlooked; it is a positive contribution which the philosopher himself necessarily makes to the problem. But it is his only positive contribution. At the outset of his inquiry he ought to have no other ideals. Were he interested peculiarly in the triumph of one kind of good, he would *pro tanto* cease to be a judicial investigator, and become an advocate for some limited element of the case.

There are three questions in ethics which must be kept apart. Let them be called respectively the *psychological* question, the *metaphysical* question and the *casuistic* question. The psychological question asks after the historical *origin* of our moral ideas and judgments; the metaphysical question asks what the very *meaning* of the words 'good,' 'ill,' and 'obligation' are; the casuistic question asks what is the *measure* of the various goods and ills which men recognize, so that the philosopher may settle the true order of human obligations.

I

The psychological question is for most disputants the only question. When your ordinary doctor of divinity has proved to his own satisfaction that an altogether unique faculty called 'conscience' must be postulated to tell us what is right and what is wrong; or when your popular-science enthusiast has proclaimed that 'apriorism' is an exploded superstition, and that our moral judgments have gradually resulted from the teaching of the environment, each of these persons thinks that ethics is settled and nothing more is to be said. The familiar pair of names, Intuitionist and Evolutionist, so commonly used now to connote all possible differences in ethical opinion, really refer to the psychological question alone. The discussion of this question hinges so much upon particular details that it is impossible to enter upon it at all within the limits of this paper. I will therefore only express dogmatically my own belief, which is this—that the Benthams, the Mills, and the Bains have done a lasting service in taking so many of our human ideals and showing how they must have arisen from the association with acts of simple bodily pleasures and reliefs from pain. Association with many remote pleasures will unquestionably make a thing significant of goodness in our minds; and the more vaguely the goodness is conceived of, the more mysterious will its source appear to be. But it is surely impossible to explain all our sentiments and preferences in this simple way. The more minutely psychology studies human nature, the more clearly it finds there traces of secondary affections, relating the impressions of the environment with one another and with our impulses in quite different ways from those mere associations of coexistence and succession which are practically all that pure empiricism can admit. Take the love of drunkenness; take bashfulness, the terror of high places, the tendency to sea-sickness, to faint at the sight of blood, the susceptibility to musical sounds; take the emotion of the comical, the passion for poetry, for mathematics, or for metaphysics—no one of these things can be wholly explained by either association or utility. They *go with* other things that can be so explained, no doubt; and some of them are prophetic of future utilities, since there is nothing in us for which some use may not be found. But their origin is in incidental complications to our cerebral structure, a structure whose original features arose with no reference to the perception of such discords and harmonies as these.

Well, a vast number of our moral perceptions also are certainly of this secondary and brain-born kind. They deal with directly felt fitnesses between things, and often fly in the teeth of all the prepossessions of habit and presumptions of utility. The moment you get beyond the coarser and more commonplace moral maxims, the Decalogues and Poor Richard's Almanacs, you fall into schemes and positions which to the eye of common-sense are fantastic and overstrained. The sense for abstract justice which some persons have is as eccentric a variation, from the natural-history point of view, as is the passion for music or for the higher philosophical consistencies which consumes the soul of others. The feeling of the inward dignity of certain spiritual attitudes, as peace, serenity, simplicity, veracity; and of the essential vulgarity of others, as querulousness, anxiety, egoistic fussiness, etc.—are quite inexplicable except by an innate preference of the more ideal attitude for its own pure sake. The nobler thing *tastes* better, and that is all that we can say. "Experience" of consequences may truly teach us what things are *wicked*, but what have consequences to do with what is *mean* and *vulgar*? If a man has shot his wife's paramour, by reason of what subtle repugnancy in things is it that we are so disgusted when we hear that the wife and the husband have made it up and are living comfortably together again? Or if the hypothesis were offered us of a world in which Messrs. Fourier's and Bellamy's and Morris's utopias should all be outdone, and millions kept permanently happy on the one simple condition that a certain lost soul on the far-off edge of things should lead a life of lonely torture, what except a specifical and independent sort of emotion can it be which would make us immediately feel, even though an impulse arose within us to clutch at the happiness so offered, how hideous a thing would be its enjoyment when deliberately accepted as the fruit of such a bargain? To what, once more, but subtle brain-born feelings of discord can be due all these recent protests against the entire race-tradition of retributive justice?—I refer to Tolstoï with his ideas of non-resistance, to Mr. Bellamy with his substitution of oblivion for repentance (in his novel of Dr. Heidenhain's Process), to M. Guyau with his radical condemnation of the punitive ideal. All these subtleties of the moral sensibility go as much beyond what can be ciphered out from the "laws of association" as the delicacies of sentiment possible between a pair of young lovers go beyond such precepts of the "etiquette to be observed during engagement" as are printed in the manuals of social form.

No! Purely inward forces are certainly at work here. All the higher, more penetrating ideals are revolutionary. They present themselves far less in the guise of effects of past experience than in that of probable causes of future experience, factors to which the environment and the lessons it has so far taught us must learn to bend.

This is all I can say of the psychological question now. In the last chapter of a recent work[1] I have sought to prove in a general way the existence, in our thought, of relations which do not merely repeat the couplings of experience. Our ideals have certainly many sources. They are not all explicable as signifying corporeal pleasures to be gained, and pains to be escaped. And for having so constantly perceived this psychological fact, we must applaud the intuitionist school. Whether or not such applause must be extended to that school's other characteristics will appear as we take up the following questions.

The next one in order is the metaphysical question, of what we mean by the words 'obligation,' 'good,' and 'ill.'

II

First of all, it appears that such words can have no application or relevancy in a world in which no sentient life exists. Imagine an absolutely material world, containing only physical and chemical facts, and existing from eternity without a God, without even an interested spectator: would there be any sense in saying of that world that one of its states is better than another? Or if there were two such worlds possible, would there be any rhyme or reason in calling one good and the other bad— good or bad positively, I mean, and apart from the fact that one might relate itself better than the other to the philosopher's private interests? But we must leave these private interests out of the account, for the philosopher is a mental fact, and we are asking whether goods and evils and obligations exist in physical facts *per se*. Surely there is no *status* for good and evil to exist in, in a purely insentient world. How can one physical fact, considered simply as a physical fact, be 'better' than another? Betterness is not a physical relation. In its mere material capacity, a thing can no more be good or bad than it can be pleasant or painful. Good for what? Good for the production of another physical fact, do you say? But what in a purely physical universe demands the production of that other fact? Physical facts simply *are* or are not; and neither when present or absent, can they be supposed to make demands. If they do, they can only do so by having desires; and then they have ceased to be purely physical facts, and have become facts of conscious sensibility. Goodness, badness, and obligation must be *realized* somewhere in order really to exist; and the first step in ethical philosophy is to see that no merely inorganic 'nature of things' can realize them. Neither moral relations nor the moral law can swing *in vacuo*. Their only habitat can be a mind which feels them; and no world composed of merely physical facts can possibly be a world to which ethical propositions apply.

The moment one sentient being, however, is made a part of the universe, there is a chance for goods and evils really to exist. Moral relations now have their *status*, in that being's consciousness. So far as he feels anything to be good, he *makes* it good. It *is* good, for him; and being good for him, is absolutely good, for he is the sole creator of values in that universe, and outside of his opinion things have no moral character at all.

In such a universe as that it would of course be absurd to raise the question of whether the solitary thinker's judgments of good and ill are true or not. Truth supposes a standard outside of the thinker to which he must conform; but here the thinker is a sort of divinity, subject to no higher judge. Let us call the supposed universe which he inhabits a *moral solitude*. In such a moral solitude it is clear that there can be no outward obligation, and that the only trouble the god-like thinker is liable to have will be over the consistency of his own several ideals with one another. Some of these will no doubt be more pungent and appealing than the rest, their goodness will have a profounder, more penetrating taste; they will return to haunt him with more obstinate regrets if violated. So the thinker will have to order his life with them as its chief determinants, or else remain inwardly discordant and unhappy. Into whatever equilibrium he may settle, though, and however he may straighten out his system, it will be a right system; for beyond the facts of his own subjectivity there is nothing moral in the world.

If now we introduce a second thinker with his likes and dislikes into the universe, the ethical situation becomes much more complex, and several possibilities are immediately seen to obtain.

One of these is that the thinkers may ignore each other's attitude about good and evil altogether, and each continue to indulge his own preferences, indifferent to what the other may feel or do. In such a case we have a world with twice as much of the ethical quality in it as our moral solitude, only it is without ethical unity. The same object is good or bad there, according as you measure it by the view which this one or that one of the thinkers takes. Nor can you find any possible ground in such a world for saying that one thinker's opinion is more correct than the other's, or that either has the truer moral sense. Such a world, in short, is not a moral universe but a moral dualism. Not only is there no single point of view within it from which the values of things can be unequivocally judged, but there is not even a demand for such a point of view, since the two thinkers are supposed to be indifferent to each other's thoughts and acts. Multiply the thinkers into a pluralism, and we find realized for us in the ethical sphere something like that world which the antique sceptics conceived of—in which individual minds are the measures of all things, and in which no 'objective' truth, but only a multitude of 'subjective' opinions can be found.

But this is the kind of world with which the philosopher, so long as he holds to the hope of a philosophy, will not put up. Among the various ideals represented, there must be, he thinks, some which have the more truth or authority; and to these the others *ought* to yield, so that system and subordination may reign. Here in the word 'ought' the notion of *obligation* comes emphatically into view, and the next thing in order must be to make its meaning clear.

Since the outcome of the discussion so far has been to show us that nothing can be good or right except so far as some consciousness feels it to be good, or thinks it to be right, we perceive on the very threshold that the real superiority and authority which are postulated by the philosopher to reside in some of the opinions, and the really inferior character which he supposes must belong to others, cannot be explained by any abstract moral "nature of things" existing antecedently to the concrete thinkers themselves with their ideals. Like the positive attributes good and bad, the comparative ones better and worse must be *realized* in order to be real. If one ideal judgment be objectively better than another, that betterness must be made flesh by being lodged concretely in some one's actual perception. It cannot float in the atmosphere, for it is not a sort of meteorological phenomenon, like the aurora borealis or the zodiacal light. Its *esse* is *percipi*, like the *esse* of the ideals themselves between which it obtains. The philosopher, therefore, who seeks to know which ideal ought to have supreme weight and which one ought to be subordinated, must trace the *ought* itself to the *de facto* constitution of some existing consciousness, behind which, as one of the data of the universe, he as a purely ethical philosopher is unable to go. This consciousness must make the one ideal right by feeling it to be right, the other wrong by feeling it to be wrong. But now what particular consciousness in the universe *can* enjoy this prerogative of obliging others to conform to a rule which it lays down?

If one of the thinkers were obviously divine, while all the rest were human, there would probably be no practical dispute about the matter. The divine thought would be the model, to which the others should conform. But still the theoretic question would remain, What is the ground of the obligation, even here?

In our first essays at answering this question, there is an inevitable tendency to slip into an assumption which ordinary men follow when they are disputing with one another about questions of good and bad. They imagine an abstract moral order in which the objective truth resides; and each tries to prove that this pre-existing order is more accurately reflected in his own ideas than in those of his adversary. It is because one disputant is backed by this overarching abstract order that we think the other should submit. Even so, when it is a question no longer of two finite thinkers, but of God and ourselves—we follow our usual habit, and imagine a sort of *de jure* relation, which antedates and overarches the mere facts, and would make it right that we should conform our thoughts to God's thoughts, even though he made no claim to that effect, and though we preferred *de facto* to go on thinking for ourselves.

But the moment we take a steady look at the question, *we see not only that without a claim actually made by some concrete person there can be no obligation, but that there is some obligation wherever there is a claim.* Claim and obligation are, in fact, coextensive terms; they cover each other exactly. Our ordinary attitude of regarding ourselves as subject to an overarching system of moral relations, true 'in themselves,' is therefore either an out-and-out superstition, or else it must be treated as a merely provisional abstraction from that real Thinker in whose actual demand upon us to think as he does our obligation must be ultimately based. In a theistic-ethical philosophy that thinker in question is, of course, the Deity to whom the existence of the universe is due.

I know well how hard it is for those who are accustomed to what I have called the superstitious view, to realize that every *de facto* claim creates in so far forth an obligation. We inveterately think that something which we call the 'validity' of the claim is what gives to it its obligatory character, and that this validity is something outside of the claim's mere existence as a matter of fact. It rains down upon the claim, we think, from some sublime dimension of being, which the moral law inhabits, much as upon the steel of the compass-needle the influence of the Pole rains down from out of the starry heavens. But again, how can such an inorganic abstract character of imperativeness, additional to the imperativeness which is in the concrete claim itself, *exist*? Take any demand however slight, which any creature, however weak, may make. Ought it not, for its own sake, to be satisfied? If not, prove why not. The only possible kind of proof you could adduce would be the exhibition of another creature who should make a demand that ran the other way. The only possible reason there can be why any phenomenon ought to exist is that such a phenomenon actually is desired. Any desire is imperative to the extent of its amount; it *makes* itself valid by the fact that it exists at all. Some desires, truly enough, are small desires; they are put forward by insignificant persons, and we customarily make light of the obligations which they bring. But the fact that such personal demands as these impose small obligations does not keep the largest obligations from being personal demands.

If we must talk impersonally, to be sure we can say that 'the universe' requires, exacts, or makes obligatory such or such an action, whenever it expresses itself through the desires of such or such a creature. But it is better not to talk about the universe in this personified way, unless we believe in a universal or divine consciousness which actually exists. If there be such a consciousness, then its demands carry the most of obligation simply because they are the greatest in amount. But it is even then not *abstractly* right that we should respect them. It is only *concretely* right—or right after the fact, and by virtue of the fact, that they are actually made. Suppose we do not respect them, as seems largely to be the case in this queer world. That ought not to be, we say; that is wrong. But in what way is this fact of wrongness made more acceptable or intelligible when we imagine it to consist rather in the laceration of an *a priori* ideal order than in the disappointment of a living personal God? Do we, perhaps, think that we cover God and protect him and make his impotence over us less ultimate, when we back him up with this *a priori* blanket from which he may draw some warmth of further appeal? But the only force of appeal to *us*, which either a living God or an abstract ideal order can wield, is found in the 'everlasting ruby vaults' of our own human hearts, as they happen to beat responsive and not irresponsive to the claim. So far as they do feel it when made by a living consciousness, it is life answering to life. A claim thus livingly acknowledged is acknowledged with a solidity and fullness which no thought of an 'ideal' backing can render more complete; while if, on the other hand, the heart's response is withheld, the stubborn phenomenon is there of an impotence in the claims which the universe embodies, which no talk about an eternal nature of things can glaze over or dispel. An ineffective *a priori* order is as impotent a thing as an ineffective God; and in the eye of philosophy it is as hard a thing to explain.

We may now consider that what we distinguished as the metaphysical question in ethical philosophy is sufficiently answered, and that we have learned what the words 'good,' 'bad,' and 'obligation' severally mean. They mean no absolute natures, independent of personal support. They are objects of feeling and desire, which have no foothold or anchorage in Being, apart from the existence of actually living minds.

Wherever such minds exist, with judgments of good and ill, and demands upon one another, there is an ethical world in its essential features. Were all other things, gods and men and starry heavens, blotted out from this universe, and were there left but one rock with two loving souls upon it, that rock would have as thoroughly moral a constitution as any possible world which the eternities and immensities could harbor. It would be a tragic constitution, because the rock's inhabitants would die. But while they lived, there would be real good thing and real bad things in the universe; there would be obligations, claims, and expectations; obediences, refusals, and disappointments; compunctions, and longings for harmony to come again, and inward peace of conscience when it was restored; there would, in short, be a moral life, whose active energy would have no limit but the intensity of interest in each other with which the hero and heroine might be endowed.

We, on this terrestrial globe, so far as the visible facts go, are just like the inhabitants of such a rock. Whether a God exist, or whether no God exist, in yon blue heaven above us bent, we form at any rate an ethical republic here below. And the first reflection which this leads to is that ethics have as genuine and real a foothold in a universe where the highest consciousness is human, as in a universe where there is a God as well. "The religion of humanity" affords a basis for ethics as well as theism does. Whether the purely human system can gratify the philosopher's demand as well as the other is a different question, which we ourselves must answer ere we close.

III

The last fundamental question in Ethics was, it will be remembered, the *casuistic* question. Here we are, in a world where the existence of a divine thinker has been and perhaps always will be doubted by some of the lookers-on, and where, in spite of the presence of a large number of ideals in which human beings agree, there are a mass of others about which no general consensus obtains. It is hardly necessary to present a literary picture of this, for the facts are too well known. The wars of the flesh and the spirit in each man, the concupiscences of different individuals pursuing the same unshareable material or social prizes, the ideals which contrast so according to races, circumstances, temperaments, philosophical beliefs, etc.—all form a maze of apparently inextricable confusion with no obvious Ariadne's thread to lead one out. Yet the philosopher, just because he is a philosopher, adds his own peculiar ideal to the confusion (with which if he were willing to be a sceptic he would be passably content), and insists that over all these individual opinions there is a *system of truth* which he can discover if he only takes sufficient pains.

We stand ourselves at present in the place of that philosopher, and must not fail to realize all the features that the situation comports. In the first place we will not be sceptics; we hold to it that there is a truth to be ascertained. But in the second place we have just gained the insight that that truth cannot be a self-proclaiming set of laws, or an abstract 'moral reason,' but can only exist in act, or in the shape of an opinion held by some thinker really to be found. There is, however, no visible thinker invested with authority. Shall we then simply proclaim our own ideals as the lawgiving ones? No; for if we are true philosophers we must throw our own spontaneous ideals, even the dearest, impartially in with that total mass of ideals which are fairly to be judged. But how then can we as philosophers ever find a test; how avoid complete moral scepticism on the one hand, and on the other escape bringing a wayward personal standard of our own along with us, on which we simply pin our faith?

The dilemma is a hard one, nor does it grow a bit more easy as we revolve it in our minds. The entire undertaking of the philosopher obliges him to seek an impartial test. That test, however, must be incarnated in the demand of some actually existent person; and how can he pick out the person save by an act in which his own sympathies and prepossessions are implied?

One method indeed presents itself, and has as a matter of history been taken by the more serious ethical schools. If the heap of things demanded proved on inspection less chaotic than at first they seemed, if they furnished their own relative test and measure, then the casuistic problem would be solved. If it were found that all goods *qua* goods contained a common essence, then the amount of this essence involved in any one good would show its rank in the scale of goodness, and order could be quickly made; for this essence would be *the* good upon which all thinkers were agreed, the relatively objective and universal good that the philosopher seeks. Even his own private ideals would be measured by their share of it, and find their rightful place among the rest.

Various essences of good have thus been found and proposed as bases of the ethical system. Thus, to be a mean between two extremes; to be recognized by a special intuitive faculty; to make the agent happy for the moment; to make others as well as him happy in the long run; to add to his perfection or dignity; to harm no one; to follow from reason or flow from universal law; to be in accordance with the will of God; to promote the survival of the human species on this planet—are so many tests, each of which has been maintained by somebody to constitute the essence of all good things or actions so far as they are good.

No one of the measures that have been actually proposed has, however, given general satisfaction. Some are obviously not universally present in all cases—*e.g.*, the character of harming no one, or that of following a universal law; for the best course is often cruel; and many acts are reckoned good on the sole condition that they be exceptions, and serve not as examples of a universal law. Other characters, such as following the will of God, are unascertainable and vague. Others again, like survival, are quite indeterminate in their consequences, and leave us in the lurch where we most need their help: a philosopher of the Sioux Nation, for example, will be certain to use the survival-criterion in a very different way from ourselves. The best, on the whole, of these marks and measures of goodness seems to be the capacity to bring happiness. But in order not to break down fatally, this test must be taken to cover innumerable acts and impulses that never *aim* at happiness; so that, after all, in seeking for a universal principle we inevitably are carried onward to the *most* universal principle—that *the essence of good is simply to satisfy demand.* The demand may be for anything under the sun. There is really no more ground for supposing that all our demands can be accounted for by one universal underlying kind of motive than there is ground for supposing that all physical phenomena are cases of a single law. The elementary forces in ethics are probably as plural as those of physics are. The various ideals have no common character apart from the fact that they are ideals. No single abstract principle can be so used as to yield to the philosopher anything like a scientifically accurate and genuinely useful casuistic scale.

A look at another peculiarity of the ethical universe, as we find it, will still further show us the philosopher's perplexities. As a purely theoretic problem, namely, the casuistic question would hardly ever come up at all. If the ethical philosopher were only asking after the best *imaginable* system of goods he would indeed have an easy task; for all demands as such are *prima facie* respectable, and the best simply imaginary world would be one in which *every* demand was gratified as soon as made. Such a world would, however, have to have a physical constitution entirely different from that of the one which we inhabit. It would need not only a space, but a time, "of *n*-dimensions," to include all the acts and experiences incompatible with one another here below, which would then go on in conjunction—such as spending our money, yet growing rich; taking our holiday, yet getting ahead with our work; shooting and fishing, yet doing no hurt to the beasts; gaining no end of experience, yet keeping our youthful freshness of heart; and the like. There can be no question that such a system of things, however brought about, would be the absolutely ideal system; and that if a philosopher could create universes *a priori*, and provide all the mechanical conditions, that is the sort of universe which he should unhesitatingly create.

But this world of ours is made on an entirely different pattern, and the casuistic question here is most tragically practical. The actually possible in this world is vastly narrower than all that is demanded; and there is always a *pinch* between the ideal and the actual which can only be got through by leaving part of the ideal behind. There is hardly a good which we can imagine except as competing for the possession of the same bit of space and time with some other imagined good. Every end of desire that presents itself appears exclusive of some other end of desire. Shall a man drink and smoke, *or* keep his nerves in condition?—he cannot do both. Shall he follow his fancy for Amelia, *or* for Henrietta?—both cannot be the choice of his heart. Shall he have the dear old Republican party, *or* a spirit of unsophistication in public affairs?—he cannot have both, etc. So that the ethical philosopher's demand for the right scale of subordination in ideals is the fruit of an altogether practical need. Some part of the ideal must be butchered, and he needs to know which part. It is a tragic situation, and no mere speculative conundrum, with which he has to deal.

Now *we* are blinded to the real difficulty of the philosopher's task by the fact that we are born into a society whose ideals are largely ordered already. If we follow the ideal which is conventionally highest, the others which we butcher either die and do not return to haunt us; or if they come back and accuse us of murder, every one applauds us for turning to them a deaf ear. In other words, our environment encourages us not to be philosophers but partisans. The philosopher, however, cannot, so long as he clings to his own ideal of objectivity, rule out any ideal from being heard. He is confident, and rightly confident, that the simple taking counsel of his own intuitive preferences would be certain to end in a mutilation of the fullness of the truth. The poet Heine is said to have written "Bunsen" in the place of "Gott" in his copy of that author's work entitled "God in History," so as to make it read "Bunsen in der Geschichte." Now, with no disrespect to the good and learned Baron, is it not safe to say that any single philosopher, however wide his sympathies, must be just such a Bunsen in der Geschichte of the moral world, so soon as he attempts to put his own ideas of order into that howling mob of desires, each struggling to get breathing-room for the ideal to which it clings? The very best of men must not only be insensible, but be ludicrously and peculiarly insensible, to many goods. As a militant, fighting free-handed that the goods to which he *is* sensible may not be submerged and lost from out of life, the philosopher, like every other human being, is in a natural position. But think of Zeno and of Epicurus, think of Calvin and of Paley, think of Kant and Schopenhauer, of Herbert Spencer and John Henry Newman, no longer as one-sided champions of special ideals, but as schoolmasters deciding what all must think—and what more grotesque topic could a satirist wish for on which to exercise his pen? The fabled attempt of Mrs. Partington to arrest the rising tide of the North Atlantic with her broom was a reasonable spectacle compared with their effort to substitute the content of their clean-shaven systems for that exuberant mass of goods with which all human nature is in travail, and groaning to bring to the light of day. Think, furthermore, of such individual moralists, no longer as mere schoolmasters, but as pontiffs armed with the temporal power, and having authority in every concrete case of conflict to order which good shall be butchered and which shall be suffered to survive—and the notion really turns one pale. All one's slumbering revolutionary instincts waken at the thought of any single moralist wielding such powers of life and death. Better chaos forever than an order based on any closet-philosopher's rule, even though he were the most enlightened possible member of his tribe. No! if the philosopher is to keep his judicial position, he must never become of the parties to the fray.

What can he do, then, it will now be asked, except to fall back on scepticism and give up the notion of being a philosopher at all?

But do we not already see a perfectly definite path of escape which is open to him just because he is a philosopher, and not the champion of one particular ideal? Since everything which is demanded is by that fact a good, must not the guiding principle for ethical philosophy (since all demands conjointly cannot be satisfied in this poor world) be simply to satisfy at all times *as many demands as we can*? That act must be the best act, accordingly, which makes for the *best whole*, in the sense of awakening the least sum of dissatisfactions. In the casuistic scale, therefore, those ideals must be written highest which *prevail at the least cost*, or by whose realization the least possible number of other ideals are destroyed. Since victory and defeat there must be, the victory to be philosophically prayed for is that of the more inclusive side—of the side which even in the hour of triumph will to some degree do justice to the ideals in which the vanquished party's interests lay. The course of history is nothing but the story of men's struggles from generation to generation to find the more and more inclusive order. *Invent some manner* of realizing your own ideals which will also satisfy the alien demands—that and that only is the path of peace! Following this path, society has shaken itself into one sort of relative equilibrium after another by a series of social discoveries quite analogous to those of science. Polyandry and polygamy and slavery, private warfare and liberty to kill, judicial torture and arbitrary royal power have slowly succumbed to actually aroused complaints; and though someone's ideals are unquestionably the worse off for each improvement, yet a vastly greater total number of them find shelter in our civilized society than in the older savage ways. So far then, and up to date, the casuistic scale is made for the philosopher already far better than he can ever make it for himself. An experiment of the most searching kind has proved that the laws and usages of the land are what yield the maximum of satisfaction to the thinkers taken all together. The presumption in cases of conflict must always be in favor of the conventionally recognized good. The philosopher must be a conservative, and in the construction of his casuistic scale must put the things most in accordance with the customs of the community on top.

And yet if he be a true philosopher he must see that there is nothing final in any actually given equilibrium of human ideals, but that, as our present laws and customs have fought and conquered other past ones, so they will in their turn be overthrown by any newly discovered order which will hush up the complaints that they still give rise to, without producing others louder still. "Rules are made for man, not man for rules"—that one sentence is enough to immortalize Green's *Prolegomena to Ethics*. And although a man always risks much when he breaks away from established rules and strives to realize a larger ideal whole than they permit, yet the philosopher must allow that it is at all times open to any one to make the experiment, provided he fear not to stake his life and character upon the throw. The pinch is always here. Pent in under every system of moral rules are innumerable persons whom it weighs upon, and goods which it represses; and these are always rumbling and grumbling in the background, and ready for any issue by which they may get free. See the abuses which the institution of private property covers, so that even today it is shamelessly asserted among us that one of the prime functions of the national government is to help the adroiter citizens to grow rich. See the unnamed and unnamable sorrows which the tyranny, on the whole so beneficent, of the marriage-institution brings to so many, both of the married and the unwed. See the wholesale loss of opportunity under our regime of so-called equality and industrialism, with the drummer and the counter-jumper in the saddle, for so many faculties and graces which could flourish in the feudal world. See our kindliness for the humble and the outcast, how it wars with that stern weeding-out which until now has been the condition of every perfection in the breed. See everywhere the struggle and the squeeze; and everlastingly the problem how to make them less. The anarchists, nihilists, and free-lovers; the free-silverites, socialists, and single-tax men; the free-traders and civil-service reformers; the prohibitionists and anti-vivisectionists; the radical darwinians with their idea of the suppression of the weak—these and all the conservative sentiments of society arrayed against them, are simply deciding through actual experiment by what sort of conduct the maximum amount of good can be gained and kept in this world. These experiments are to be judged, not *a priori*, but by actually finding, after the fact of their making, how much more outcry or how much appeasement comes about. What closet-solutions can possibly anticipate the result of trials made on such a scale? Or what can any superficial theorist's judgment be worth, in a world where every one of hundreds of ideals has its special champion already provided in the shape of some genius expressly born to feel it, and to fight to death in its behalf? The pure philosopher can only follow the windings of the spectacle, confident that the line of least resistance will always be towards the richer and the more inclusive arrangement, and that by one tack after another some approach to the kingdom of heaven is incessantly made.

IV

All this amounts to saying that, so far as the casuistic question goes, ethical science is just like physical science, and instead of being deducible all at once from abstract principles, must simply bide its time, and be ready to revise its conclusions from day to day. The presumption of course, in both sciences, always is that the vulgarly accepted opinions are true, and the right casuistic order that which public opinion believes in; and surely it would be folly quite as great, in most of us, to strike out independently and to aim at originality in ethics as in physics. Every now and then, however, someone is born with the right to be original, and his revolutionary thought or action may bear prosperous fruit. He may replace old 'laws of nature' by better ones; he may, by breaking old moral rules in a certain place, bring in a total condition of things more ideal than would have followed had the rules been kept.

On the whole, then, we must conclude that no philosophy of ethics is possible in the old-fashioned absolute sense of the term. Everywhere the ethical philosopher must wait on facts. The thinkers who create the ideals come he knows not whence, their sensibilities are evolved he knows not how; and the question as to which of two conflicting ideals will give the best universe then and there, can be answered by him only through the aid of the experience of other men. I said some time ago, in treating of the 'first' question, that the intuitional moralists deserve credit for keeping most clearly the psychological facts. They do much to spoil this merit on the whole, however, by mixing with it that dogmatic temper which, by absolute distinctions and unconditional "thou shalt nots," changes a growing, elastic, and continuous life into a superstitious system of relics and dead bones. In point of fact, there are no absolute evils, and there are no non-moral goods; and the *highest* ethical life— however few may be called to bear its burdens—consists at all times in the breaking of rules which have grown too narrow for the actual case. There is but one unconditional commandment, which is that we should seek incessantly, with fear and trembling, so to vote and to act as to bring about the very largest total universe of good which we can see. Abstract rules indeed can help; but they help the less in proportion as our intuitions are more piercing, and our vocation is the stronger for the moral life. For every real dilemma is in literal strictness a unique situation; and the exact combination of ideals realized and ideals disappointed which each decision creates is always a universe without a precedent, and for which no adequate previous rule exists. The philosopher, then, *qua* philosopher, is no better able to determine the best universe in the concrete emergency than other men. He sees, indeed, somewhat better than most men what the question always is—not a question of this good or that good simply taken, but of the two total universes with which these goods respectively belong. He knows that he must vote always for the richer universe, for the good which seems most organizable, most fit to enter to complex combinations, most apt to be a member of a more inclusive whole. But which particular universe this is he cannot know for certain in advance; he only knows that if he makes a bad mistake the cries of the wounded will soon inform him of the fact. In all this the philosopher is just like the rest of us non-philosophers, so far as we are just and sympathetic instinctively, and so far as we are open to the voice of complaint. His function is in fact indistinguishable from that of the best kind of statesman at the present day. His books upon ethics, therefore, so far as they truly touch the moral life, must more and more ally themselves with a literature which is confessedly tentative and suggestive rather than dogmatic—I mean with novels and dramas of the deeper sort, with sermons, with books on statecraft and philanthropy and social and economical reform. Treated in this way ethical treatises may be voluminous and luminous as well; but they never can be *final*, except in their abstractest and vaguest features; and they must more and more abandon the old-fashioned, clear-cut, and would-be 'scientific' form.

V

The chief of all the reasons why concrete ethics cannot be final is that they have to wait on metaphysical and theological beliefs. I said some time back that real ethical relations existed in a purely human world. They would exist even in what we called a moral solitude if the thinker had various ideals which took hold of him in turn. His self of one day would make demands on his self of another; and some of the demands might be urgent and tyrannical, while others were gentle and easily put aside. We call the tyrannical demands *imperatives*. If we ignore these we do not hear the last of it. The good which we have wounded returns to plague us with interminable crops of consequential damages, compunctions, and regrets. Obligation can thus exist inside a single thinker's consciousness; and perfect peace can abide with him only so far as he lives according to some sort of a casuistic scale which keeps his more imperative goods on top. It is the nature of these goods to be cruel to their rivals. Nothing shall avail when weighed in the balance against them. They call out all the mercilessness in our disposition, and do not easily forgive us if we are so soft-hearted as to shrink from sacrifice in their behalf.

The deepest difference, practically, in the moral life of man is the difference between the easy-going and the strenuous mood. When in the easy-going mood the shrinking from present ill is our ruling consideration. The strenuous mood, on the contrary, makes us quite indifferent to present ill, if only the greater ideal be attained. The capacity for the strenuous mood probably lies slumbering in every man, but it has more difficulty in some than in others in waking up. It needs the wilder passions to arouse it, the big fears, loves, and indignations; or else the deeply penetrating appeal of some one of the higher fidelities, like justice, truth, or freedom. Strong relief is a necessity of its vision; and a world where all the mountains are brought down and all the valleys are exalted is no congenial place for its habitation. This is why in a solitary thinker this mood might slumber on forever without waking. His various ideals, known to him to be mere preferences of his own, are too nearly of the same denominational value; he can play fast and loose with them at will. This too is why, in a merely human world without a God, the appeal to our moral energy falls short of its maximal stimulating power. Life, to be sure, is even in such a world a genuinely ethical symphony; but it is played in the compass of a couple of poor octaves, and the infinite scale of values fails to open up. Many of us, indeed—like Sir James Stephen in those eloquent *Essays by a Barrister*—would openly laugh at the very idea of the strenuous mood being awakened in us by those claims of remote posterity which constitute the last appeal of the religion of humanity. We do not love these men of the future keenly enough; and we love them perhaps the less the more we hear of their evolutionized perfection, their high average longevity and education, their freedom from war and crime, their relative immunity from pain and zymotic disease, and all their other negative superiorities. This is all too finite, we say; we see too well the vacuum beyond. It lacks the note of infinitude and mystery, and may all be dealt with in the don't-care mood. No need of agonizing ourselves or making others agonize for these good creatures just at present.

When, however, we believe that a God is there, and that he is one of the claimants, the infinite perspective opens out. The scale of the symphony is incalculably prolonged. The more imperative ideals now begin to speak with an altogether new objectivity and significance, and to utter the penetrating, shattering, tragically challenging note of appeal. They ring out like the call of Victor Hugo's alpine eagle, "qui parle au précipice et que le gouffre entend," and the strenuous mood awakens at the sound. It saith among the trumpets, ha, ha! it smelleth the battle afar off, the thunder of the captains and the shouting. Its blood is up; and cruelty to the lesser claims, so far from being a deterrent element, does but add to the stern joy with which it leaps to answer to the greater. All through history, in the periodical conflicts of puritanism with the don't-care temper, we see the antagonism of the strenuous and genial moods, and the contrast between the ethics of infinite and mysterious obligation from on high, and those of prudence and the satisfaction of merely finite need.

The capacity of the strenuous mood lies so deep down among our natural human possibilities that even if there were no metaphysical or traditional grounds for believing in a God, men would postulate one simply as a pretext for living hard, and getting out of the game of existence its keenest possibilities of zest. Our attitude towards concrete evils is entirely different in a world where we believe there are none but finite demanders, from what it is in one where we joyously face tragedy for an infinite demanders' sake. Every sort of energy and endurance, of courage and capacity for handling life's evils, is set free in those who have religious faith. For this reason the strenuous type of character will on the battle-field of human history always outwear the easy-going type, and religion will drive irreligion to the wall.

It would seem, too—and this is my final conclusion—that the stable and systematic moral universe for which the ethical philosopher asks is fully possible only in a world where there is a divine thinker with all-enveloping demands. If such a thinker existed, his way of subordinating the demands to one another would be the finally valid casuistic scale; his claims would be the most appealing; his ideal universe would be the most inclusive realizable whole. If he now exist, then actualized in his thought already must be that ethical philosophy which we seek as the pattern which our own must evermore approach.[2] In the interest of our own ideal of systematically unified moral truth, therefore, we, as would-be philosophers, must postulate a divine thinker, and pray for the victory of the religious cause. Meanwhile, exactly what the thought of the infinite thinker may be is hidden from us even were we sure of his existence; so that our postulation of him after all serves only to let loose in us the strenuous mood. But this is what it does in all men, even those who have no interest in philosophy. The ethical philosopher, therefore, whenever he ventures to say which course of action is the best, is on no essentially different level from the common man. "See, I have set before thee this day life and good, and death and evil; therefore choose life that thou and thy seed may live"—when this challenge comes to us, it is simply our total character and personal genius that are on trial; and if we invoke any so-called philosophy, our choice and use of that also are but revelations of our personal aptitude or incapacity for moral life. From this unsparing practical ordeal no professor's lectures and no array of books can save us. The solving word, for the learned and the unlearned man alike, lies in the last resort in the dumb willingnesses and unwillingnesses of their interior characters, and nowhere else. It is not in heaven, neither is it beyond the sea; but the word is very nigh unto thee, in thy mouth and in thy heart, that thou mayest do it.

15

The Energies of Men

We habitually hear much nowadays of the difference between structural and functional psychology. I am not sure that I understand the difference, but it probably has something to do with what I have privately been accustomed to distinguish as the analytical and the clinical points of view in psychological observation. Professor Sanford, in a recently published "Sketch of a Beginner's Course in Psychology," recommended "the physician's attitude" in that subject as the thing the teacher should first of all try to impart to the pupil. I fancy that few of you can have read Professor Pierre Janet's masterly works in mental pathology without being struck by the little use he makes of the machinery usually relied on by psychologists, and by his own reliance on conceptions which in the laboratories and in scientific publications we never hear of at all.

Discriminations and associations, the rise and fall of thresholds, impulses and inhibitions, fatigue—these are the terms into which our inner life is analyzed by psychologists who are not doctors, and in which, by hook or crook, its aberrations from normality have to be expressed. They can indeed be described, after the fact, in such terms, but always lamely; and everyone must feel how much is unaccounted for, how much left out.

When we turn to Janet's pages, we find entirely other forms of thought employed. Oscillations of the level of mental energy, differences of tension, splittings of consciousness, sentiments of insufficiency and of unreality, substitutions, agitations and anxieties, depersonalizations—such are the elementary conceptions which the total view of his patient's life imposes on this clinical observer. They have little or nothing to do with the usual laboratory categories. Ask a scientific psychologist to predict what symptoms a patient must have when his 'supply of mental energy' diminishes, and he can utter only the word 'fatigue.' He could never predict such consequences as Janet subsumes under his one term 'psychasthenia'—the most bizarre obsessions and agitations, the most complete distortions of the relation between the self and the world.

I do not vouch for Janet's conceptions being valid, and I do not say that the two ways of looking at the mind contradict each other or are mutually incongruous; I simply say that they are incongru*ent*. Each covers so little of our total mental life that they do not even interfere or jostle. Meanwhile the clinical conceptions, though they may be vaguer than the analytic ones, are certainly more adequate, give the concreter picture of the way the whole mind works, and are of far more urgent practical importance. So the 'physician's attitude,' the 'functional psychology,' is assuredly the thing most worthy of general study to-day.

I wish to spend this hour on one conception of functional psychology, a conception never once mentioned or heard of in laboratory circles, but used perhaps more than any other by common, practical men—I mean the conception of the *amount of energy available* for running one's mental and moral operations by. Practically every one knows in his own person the difference between the days when the tide of this energy is high in him and those when it is low, though no one knows exactly what reality the term energy covers when used here, or what its tides, tensions, and levels are in themselves. This vagueness is probably the reason why our scientific psychologists ignore the conception altogether. It undoubtedly connects itself with the energies of the nervous system, but it presents fluctuations that cannot easily be translated into neural terms. It offers itself as the notion of a quantity, but its ebbs and floods produce extraordinary qualitative results. To have its level raised is the most important thing that can happen to a man, yet in all my reading I know of no single page or paragraph of a scientific psychology book in which it receives mention—the psychologists have left it to be treated by the moralists and mind-curers and doctors exclusively.

Everyone is familiar with the phenomenon of feeling more or less alive on different days. Everyone knows on any given day that there are energies slumbering in him which the incitements of that day do not call forth, but which he might display if these were greater. Most of us feel as if we lived habitually with a sort of cloud weighing on us, below our highest notch of clearness in discernment, sureness in reasoning, or firmness in deciding. Compared with what we ought to be, we are only half awake. Our fires are damped, our drafts are checked. We are making use of only a small part of our possible mental and physical resources. In some persons this sense of being cut off from their rightful resources is extreme, and we then get the formidable neurasthenic and psychasthenic conditions, with life grown into one tissue of impossibilities, that the medical books describe.

Part of the imperfect vitality under which we labor can be explained by scientific psychology. It is the result of the inhibition exerted by one part of our ideas on other parts. Conscience makes cowards of us all. Social conventions prevent us from telling the truth, after the fashion of the heroes and heroines of Bernard Shaw. Our scientific respectability keeps us from exercising the mystical portions of our nature freely. If we are doctors, our mind-cure sympathies, if we are mind-curists, our medical sympathies, are tied up. We all know persons who are models of excellence, but who belong to the extreme philistine type of mind. So deadly is their intellectual respectability that we can't converse about certain subjects at all, can't let our minds play over them, can't even mention them in their presence. I have numbered among my dearest friends persons thus inhibited intellectually, with whom I would gladly have been able to talk freely about certain interests of mine, certain authors, say, as Bernard Shaw, Chesterton, Edward Carpenter, H. G. Wells, but it wouldn't do, it made them too uncomfortable, they wouldn't play, I had to be silent. An intellect thus tied down by literality and decorum makes on one the same sort of impression that an able-bodied man would who should habituate himself to do his work with only one of his fingers, locking up the rest of his organism and leaving it unused.

In few of us are functions not tied-up by the exercise of other functions. G. T. Fechner is an extraordinary exception that proves the rule. He could use his mystical faculties while being scientific. He could be both critically keen and devout. Few scientific men can pray, I imagine. Few can carry on any living commerce with 'God.' Yet many of us are well aware how much freer in many directions and abler our lives would be, were such important forms of energizing not sealed up. There are in everyone potential forms of activity that actually are shunted out from use.

The existence of reservoirs of energy that habitually are not tapped is most familiar to us in the phenomenon of 'second wind.' Ordinarily we stop when we meet the first effective layer, so to call it, of fatigue. We have then walked, played, or worked 'enough,' and desist. That amount of fatigue is an efficacious obstruction, on this side of which our usual life is cast. But if an unusual necessity forces us to press onward, a surprising thing occurs. The fatigue gets worse up to a certain critical point, when gradually or suddenly it passes away, and we are fresher than before. We have evidently tapped a level of new energy, masked until then by the fatigue-obstacle usually obeyed. There may be layer after layer of this experience. A third and a fourth 'wind' may supervene. Mental activity shows the phenomenon as well as physical, and in exceptional cases we may find, beyond the very extremity of fatigue-distress, amounts of ease and power that we never dreamed ourselves to own, sources of strength habitually not taxed at all, because habitually we never push through the obstruction, never pass those early critical points.

When we do pass, what makes us do so?

Either some unusual stimulus fill us with emotional excitement, or some unusual idea of necessity induces us to make an extra effort of will. *Excitements, ideas, and efforts*, in a word, are what carry us over the dam.

In those hyperesthetic conditions which chronic invalidism so often brings in its train, the dam has changed its normal place. The pain-threshold is abnormally near. The slightest functional exercise gives a distress which the patient yields to and stops. In such cases of 'habit-neurosis' a new range of power often comes in consequence of the bullying-treatment, of efforts which the doctor obliges the patient, against his will, to make. First comes the very extremity of distress, then follows unexpected relief. There seems no doubt that we are each and all of us to some extent victims of habit-neurosis. We have to admit the wider potential range and the habitually narrow actual use. We live subject to inhibition by degrees of fatigue which we have come only from habit to obey. Most of us may learn to push the barrier farther off, and to live in perfect comfort on much higher levels of power.

Country people and city people, as a class, illustrate this difference. The rapid rate of life, the number of decisions in an hour, the many things to keep account of, in a busy city-man's or woman's life, seem monstrous to a country-brother. He doesn't see how we live at all. But settle him in town; and in a year or two, if not too old, he will have trained himself to keep the pace as well as any of us, getting more out of himself in any week than he ever did in ten weeks at home. The physiologists show how one can be in nutritive equilibrium, neither losing nor gaining weight, on astonishingly different quantities of food. So one can be in what I might call 'efficiency-equilibrium' (neither gaining nor losing power when once the equilibrium is reached), on astonishingly different quantities of work, no matter in what dimension the work may be measured. It may be physical work, intellectual work, moral work, or spiritual work.

Of course there are limits: the trees don't grow into the sky. But the plain fact remains that men the world over possess amounts of resource, which only very exceptional individuals push to their extremes of use.

The excitements that carry us over the usually effective dam are most often the classic emotional ones, love, anger, crowd-contagion, or despair. Life's vicissitudes bring them in abundance. A new position of responsibility, if it do not crush a man, will often, nay, one may say, will usually, show him to be a far stronger creature than was supposed. Even here we are witnessing (some of us admiring, some deploring—I must class myself as admiring) the dynamogenic effects of a very exalted political office upon the energies of an individual who had already manifested a healthy amount of energy before the office came.

Mr. Sydney Olivier has given us a fine fable of the dynamogenic effects of love in a late story called "The Empire Builder," in the *Con-*

temporary Review for May, 1905. A young naval officer falls in love at sight with a missionary's daughter on a lost island, which his ship accidentally touches. From that day onward he must see her again; and he so moves Heaven and earth and the Colonial Office and the Admiralty to get sent there once more, that the island finally is annexed to the empire in consequence of the various fusses he is led to make. People must have been appalled lately in San Francisco to find the stores of bottled up energy and endurance they possessed.

Wars, of course, and shipwrecks, are the great revealers of what men and women are able to do and bear. Cromwell's and Grant's careers are the stock examples of how war will wake a man up. I owe to Professor Norton's kindness the permission to read to you part of a letter from Colonel Baird-Smith, written shortly after the six weeks' siege of Delhi in 1857, for the victorious issue of which that excellent officer was chiefly to be thanked. He writes as follows:—

... "My poor wife had some reason to think that war and disease between them had left very little of a husband to take under nursing when she got him again. An attack of camp-scurvy had filled my mouth with sores, shaken every joint in my body, and covered me all over with sores and livid spots so that I was marvelously unlovely to look upon. A smart knock on the ankle-joint from the splinter of a shell that burst in my face, in itself a mere bagatelle of a wound, had been of necessity neglected under the pressing and incessant calls upon me, and had grown worse and worse till the whole foot below the ankle became a black mass and seemed to threaten mortification. I insisted however on being allowed to use it till the place was taken, mortification or no; and tho' the pain was sometimes horrible, I carried my point and kept up to the last. On the day after the assault I had an unlucky fall on some bad ground; and it was an open question for a day or two whether I hadn't broken my arm at the elbow. Fortunately it turned out to be only a very severe sprain, but I am still conscious of the wrench it gave me. To crown the whole pleasant catalogue, I was worn to a shadow by a constant diarrhea, and consumed as much opium as would have done credit to my father-in-law.[1] However, thank God I have a good share of Tapleyism in me and come out strong under difficulties. I think I may confidently say that no man ever saw me out of heart, or ever heard one croaking word from me even when our prospects were gloomiest. We were sadly scourged by the cholera and it was almost appalling to me to find that out of twenty-seven officers present, I could only muster fifteen for the operations of the attack. However, it was done, and after it was done came the collapse. Don't be horrified when I tell you that for the whole of the actual siege, and in truth for some little time before, I almost lived on brandy. Appetite for food I had none, but I forced myself to eat just sufficient to sustain life, and I had an incessant craving for brandy as the strongest stimulant I could get. Strange to say, I was quite unconscious of its affecting me in the slightest degree. *The excitement of the work was so great that no lesser one seemed to have any chance against it, and I certainly never found my intellect clearer or my nerves stronger in my life.* It was only my wretched body that was weak, and the moment the real work was done by our becoming complete masters of Delhi, I broke down without delay and discovered that if I wished to live I must continue no longer the system that had kept me up until the crisis was past. With it passed away as if in a moment all desire to stimulate, and a perfect loathing of my late staff of life took possession of me."

Such experiences show how profound is the alteration in the manner in which, under excitement, our organism will sometimes perform its physiological work. The metabolisms become different when the reserves have to be used, and for weeks and months the deeper use may go on.

Morbid cases, here as elsewhere, lay the normal machinery bare. In the first number of Dr. Morton Prince's *Journal of Abnormal Psychology,* Dr. Janet has discussed five cages of morbid impulse, with an explanation that is precious for my present point of view. One is a girl who eats, eats, eats, all day. Another walks, walks, walks, and gets her food from an automobile that escorts her. Another is a dipsomaniac. A fourth pulls out her hair. A fifth wounds her flesh and burns her skin. Hitherto such freaks of impulse have received Greek names (as bulimia, dromomania, etc.) and been sci-entifically disposed of as "episodic syndromata of hereditary degeneration." But it turns out that Janet's cases are all what he calls psychasthenics, or victims of a chronic sense of weakness, torpor, lethargy, fatigue, insufficiency, impossibility, unreality, and powerlessness of will; and that in each and all of them the particular activity pursued, deleterious though it be, has the temporary result of raising the sense of vitality and making the patient feel alive again. These things reanimate; they would reanimate *us*; but it happens that in each patient the particular freak-activity chosen is the only thing that does reanimate; and therein lies the morbid state. The way to treat such persons is to discover to them more usual and useful ways of throwing their stores of vital energy into gear.

Colonel Baird-Smith, needing to draw on altogether extraordinary stores of energy, found that brandy and opium were ways of throwing them into gear.

Such cases are humanly typical. We are all to some degree oppressed, unfree. We don't come to our own. It is there, but we don't get at it. The threshold must be made to shift. Then many of us find that an eccentric activity—a 'spree,' say—relieves. There is no doubt that to some men sprees and excesses of almost any kind are medicinal, temporarily at any rate, in spite of what the moralists and doctors say.

But when the normal tasks and stimulations of life don't put a man's deeper levels of energy on tap, and he requires distinctly deleterious excitements, his constitution verges on the abnormal. The normal opener of deeper and deeper levels of energy is the will. The difficulty is to use it; to make the effort which the word volition implies. But if we *do* make it (or if a god, though he were only the god Chance, makes it through us), it will act dynamogenically on us for a month. It is notorious that a single successful effort of moral volition, such as saying 'no' to some habitual temptation, or performing some courageous act, will launch a man on a higher level of energy for days and weeks, will give him a new range of power.

The emotions and excitements due to usual situations are the usual inciters of the will. But these act discontinuously; and in the intervals the shallower levels of life tend to close in and shut us off. Accordingly the best practical knowers of the human soul have invented the thing known as methodical ascetic discipline to keep the deeper levels constantly in reach. Beginning with easy tasks, passing to harder ones, and exercising day by day, it is, I believe, admitted that disciples of asceticism can reach very high levels of freedom and power of will.

Ignatius Loyola's spiritual exercises must have produced this result in innumerable devotees. But the most venerable ascetic system, and the one whose results have the most voluminous experimental corroboration is undoubtedly the Yoga system in Hindostan. From time immemorial, by Hatha Yoga, Raja Yoga, Karma Yoga, or whatever code of practice it might be, Hindu aspirants to perfection have trained themselves, month in and out, for years. The result claimed, and certainly in many cases accorded by impartial judges, is strength of character, personal power, unshakability of soul. But it is not easy to disentangle fact from tradition in Hindu affairs. So I am glad to have a European friend who has submitted to Hatha Yoga training, and whose account of the results I am privileged to quote. I think you will appreciate the light it throws on the question of our unused reservoirs of power.

My friend is an extraordinarily gifted man, both morally and intellectually, but has an instable nervous system, and for many years has lived in a circular process of alternate lethargy and over-animation: something like three weeks of extreme activity, and then a week of prostration in bed. An unpromising condition, which the best specialists in Europe had failed to relieve; so he tried Hatha Yoga, partly out of curiosity, and partly with a sort of desperate hope. What follows is a short extract from a letter sixty pages long which he addressed me a year ago.

"Thus I decided to follow Vivekananda's advice: 'Practice hard: whether you live or die by it doesn't matter.' My improvised chela and I began with starvation. I do not know whether you did try it ever . . . but voluntary starvation is very different from involuntary, and implies more temptations. We reduced first our meals to twice a day and then to once a day. The best authorities agree that in order to control the body fasting is essential, and even in the Gospel the worst spirits are said to obey only those who fast and pray. We reduced very much the amount of food, disregarding chemical theories about the need of albumen, sometimes living on olive oil and bread; or on fruits alone; or on milk and rice; in very small quantities—much less than I formerly ate at one meal. I began to get lighter every day, and lost 20 pounds in a few weeks; but this could not stop such a desperate undertaking... rather starve than live as a slave! Then besides we practiced *asana* or postures, breaking almost our limbs. Try to sit down on the floor and to kiss your knees without bending them, or to join your hands on the usually unapproachable upper part of your back, or to bring the toe of your right foot to your left ear without bending the knees... these are easy samples of posture for a Yogi.

"All the time also breathing exercises: keeping the breath in and out up to two minutes, breathing in different rhythms and positions. Also very much prayer and Roman Catholic practices combined with the Yoga, in order to leave nothing untried and, to be protected against the tricks of Hindu devils! Then concentration of thought on different parts of the body, and on the processes going on within them. Exclusion of all emotions, dry logical reading, as intellectual diet, and working out logical problems.... I wrote a Handbook of Logic as a *Nebenprodukt* of the whole experiment.[2]

"After a few weeks I broke down and had to interrupt everything, in a worse state of prostration than ever.... My younger chela went on unshaken by my fate; and as soon as I arose from bed I tried again decided to fight it out, even feeling a kind of determination such as I had never felt before, a certain absolute will of victory at any price and faith in it. Whether it is my own merit or a divine grace, I can not judge for certain, but I prefer to admit the latter. I had been ill for seven years, and some people say this is a term for many punishments. However base and vile a sinner I had been, perhaps my sins were about to be forgiven, and Yoga was only an exterior opportunity, an object for concentration of will. I do not yet pretend to explain much of what I have gone through, but the fact is that since I arose from bed on August 20, no new crisis of prostration came again, and I have now the strongest conviction that no crisis will ever return. If you consider that for the past years there has not been a single month without this lethargy, you will grant that even to an outside observer four successive months of increasing health are an objective test.

In this time I underwent very severe penances, reducing sleep and food and increasing the task of work and exercise. My intuition was developed by these practices: there came a sense of certainty, never known before, as to the things needed by the body and the mind, and the body came to obey like a wild horse tamed. Also the mind learned to obey, and the current of thought and feeling was shaped according to my will. I mastered sleep and hunger, and the flights of thought, and came to know a peace never known before, an inner rhythm of unison with a deeper rhythm above or beyond. Personal wishes ceased, and the consciousness of being the instrument of a superior power arose. A calm certainty of indubitable success in every undertaking imparts great and real power. I often guessed the thoughts of my companion . . . we observed generally the greatest isolation and silence. We both felt an unspeakable joy in the simplest natural impressions, light, air, landscape, any kind of simplest food; and above everything in rhythmical respiration, which produces a state of mind without thought or feeling, and still very intense, indescribable.

"These results began to be more evident in the fourth month of uninterrupted training. We felt quite happy, never tired, sleeping only from 8 p.m. to midnight, and rising with joy from our sleep to another day's work of study and exercise. . . .

"I am now in Palermo, and have had to neglect the exercises in the last few days, but I feel as fresh as if I were in full training and see the sunny side of all things. I am not in a hurry, rushing to complete—."

And here my friend mentions a certain life-work of his own about which I had better be silent. He goes on to analyze the exercises and their effects in an extremely practical way, but at too great length for me to entertain you with. Repetition, alteration, periodicity, parallelism (or the association of the idea of some desirable vital or spiritual effect with each movement), etc., are laws which he deems highly important. "I am sure," he continues, "that everybody who is able to concentrate thought and will, and to eliminate superfluous emotions, sooner or later becomes a master of his body and can overcome every kind of illness. This is the truth at the bottom of all mind-cures. Our thoughts have a plastic power over the body."

You will be relieved, I doubt not, to hear my eccentric correspondent here make connection at last with something you know by heart, namely, 'suggestive therapeutics.' Call his whole performance, if you like, an experiment in methodical self-suggestion. That only makes it more valuable as an illustration of what I wish to impress in as many ways as possible upon your minds, that we habitually live inside our limits of power. Suggestion, especially under hypnosis, is now universally recognized as a means, exceptionally successful in certain persons, of concentrating consciousness, and, in others, of influencing their bodies' states. It throws into gear energies of imagination, of will, and of mental influence over physiological processes, that usually lie dormant, and that can only be thrown into gear at all in chosen subjects. It is, in short, dynamogenic; and the cheapest terms in which to deal with our amateur Yogi's experience is to call it auto-suggestive.

I wrote to him that I couldn't possibly attribute any sacramental value to the particular Hatha Yoga processes, the postures, breathings, fastings and the like, and that they seemed to me but so many manners, available in his case and his chela's, but not for everybody, of breaking through the barriers which life's routine had concreted round the deeper strata of the will, and gradually bringing its unused energies into action.

He replied as follows: "You are quite right that the Yoga exercises are nothing else than a methodical way of increasing our will. Because we are unable to will at once the most difficult things, we must imagine steps leading to them. Breathing being the easiest of the bodily activities, it is very natural that it offers a good scope for exercise of will. The control of thought could be gained without breathing-discipline, but it is simply easier to control thought simultaneously with the control of breath. Anyone who can think clearly and persistently of one thing needs not breathing exercises. You are quite right that we are not using all our power and that we often learn how much we *can* only when we *must*. . . . The power that we do not use up completely can be brought [more and more] into use by what we call *faith*. Faith is like the manometer of the will, registering its pressure. If I could believe that I can levitate, I could do it. But I can not believe, and therefore I am clumsily sticking to earth.

...Now this faith, this power of credulity, can be educated by small efforts. I can breathe at the rate of say twelve times a minute. I can easily believe that I can breathe ten times a minute. When I have accustomed myself to breathe ten times a minute, I learn to believe it will be easy to breathe six times a minute. Thus I have actually learned to breathe at the rate of once a minute. How far I shall progress I do not know.... The Yogi goes on in his activity in an even way, without fits of too much or too little, and he is eliminating more and more every unrest, every worry—growing into the infinite by regular training, by small additions to a task which has grown familiar.... But you are quite right that religious crises, love-crises, indignation-crises, may awaken in a very short time powers similar to those reached by years of patient Yoga practice.... The Hindus themselves admit that Samadhi can be reached in many ways end with complete disregard of every physical training."

Allowance made for every enthusiasm and exaggeration, there can be no doubt of my friend's regeneration—relatively, at any rate. The second letter, written six months later than the first (ten months after beginning Yoga practice, therefore), says the improvement holds good. He has undergone material trials with indifference, traveled third-class on Mediterranean steamers, and fourth-class on African trains, living with the poorest Arabs and sharing their unaccustomed food, all with equanimity. His devotion to certain interests has been put to heavy strain, and nothing is more remarkable to me than the changed moral tone with which he reports the situation. Compared with certain earlier letters, these read as if written by a different man, patient and reasonable instead of vehement, self-subordinating instead of imperious. The new tone persists in a communication received only a fortnight ago (fourteen months after beginning training)—there is, in fact, no doubt that profound modification has occurred in the running of his mental machinery. The gearing has changed, and his will is available otherwise than it was. Available without any new ideas, beliefs, or emotions, so far as I can make out, having been implanted in him. He is simply more balanced where he was more unbalanced.

You will remember that he speaks of faith, calling it a 'manometer' of the will. It sounds more natural to call our will the manometer of our faiths. Ideas set free beliefs, and the beliefs set free our wills (I use these terms with no pretension to be 'psychological'), so the will-acts register the faith-pressure within. Therefore, having considered the liberation of our stored-up energy by emotional excitements and by efforts, whether methodical or unmethodical, I must now say a word about *ideas* as our third great dynamogenic agent. Ideas contradict other ideas and keep us from believing them. An idea that thus negates a first idea may itself in turn be negated by a third idea, and the first idea may thus regain its natural influence over our belief and determine our behavior. Our philosophic and religious development proceeds thus by credulities, negations, and the negating of negations.

But whether for arousing or for stopping belief, ideas may fail to be efficacious, just as a wire at one time alive with electricity, may at another time be dead. Here our insight into causes fails us, and we can only note results in general terms. In general, whether a given idea shall be a live idea, depends more on the person into whose mind it is injected than on the idea itself. The whole history of 'suggestion' opens out here. Which are the suggestive ideas for this person, and which for that? Beside the susceptibilities determined by one's education and by one's original peculiarities of character, there are lines along which men simply as men tend to be inflammable by ideas. As certain objects naturally awaken love, anger, or cupidity, so certain ideas naturally awaken the energies of loyalty, courage, endurance, or devotion. When these ideas are effective in an individual's life, their effect is often very great indeed. They may transfigure it, unlocking innumerable powers which, but for the idea would never have come into play. 'Fatherland,' 'The Union,' 'Holy Church,' the 'Monroe Doctrine,' 'Truth,' 'Science,' 'Liberty,' Garibaldi's phrase 'Rome or Death,' etc., are so many examples of energy-releasing abstract ideas. The *social* nature of all such phrases is an essential factor of their dynamic power. They are forces of detent in situations in which no other force produces equivalent effects, and each is a force of detent only in a specific group of men.

The memory that an oath or vow has been made will nerve one to abstinences and efforts otherwise impossible: witness the 'pledge' in the history of the temperance movement. A mere promise to his sweetheart will clean up a youth's life all over—at any rate for a time. For such effects an educated susceptibility is required. The idea of one's 'honour,' for example, unlocks energy only in those who have had the education of a gentleman, so called.

That delightful being, Prince Pueckler-Muskau, writes to his wife from England that he has invented "a sort of artificial resolution respecting things that are difficult of performance." "My device," he says, "is this: I give my word of honour most solemnly to myself to do or to leave undone this or that. I am of course extremely cautious in the use of this expedient... but when once the word is given, even though I afterwards think I have been precipitate or mistaken, I hold it to be perfectly irrevocable, whatever inconveniences I foresee likely to result. ... If I were capable of breaking my word after such mature consideration, I should lose all respect for myself—and what man of sense would not prefer death to such an alternative? ... [When the mysterious formula is pronounced,] no alteration in my own views, nothing short of physical impossibility, must, for the welfare of my soul, alter my will. ... I find something very satisfactory in the thought that man has the power of framing such props and weapons out of the most trivial materials, indeed out of nothing, merely by the force of his will, which thereby truly deserves the name of omnipotent."[3]

Conversions, whether they be political, scientific, philosophic, or religious, form another way in which bound energies are let loose. They unify, and put a stop to ancient mental interferences. The result is freedom, and often a great enlargement of power. A belief that thus settles upon an individual always acts as a challenge to his will. But, for the particular challenge to operate, he must be the right challeng*ee*. In religious conversions we have so fine an adjustment that the idea may be in the mind of the challengee for years before it exerts effects; and why it should do so then is often so far from obvious that the event is taken for a miracle of grace, and not a natural occurrence. Whatever it is, it may be a highwater mark of energy, in which 'noes,' once impossible, are easy, and in which a new range of 'yeses' gain the right of way.

We are just now witnessing—but our scientific education has unfitted most of us for comprehending the phenomenon—a very copious unlocking of energies by ideas, in the persons of those converts to 'New Thought,' 'Christian Science,' 'Metaphysical Healing,' or other forms of spiritual philosophy, who are so numerous among us today. The ideas here are healthy-minded and optimistic; and it is quite obvious that a wave of religious activity, analogous in some respects to the spread of early Christianity, Buddhism, and Mohammedanism is passing over our American world. The common feature of these optimistic faiths is that they all tend to the suppression of what Mr. Horace Fletcher has termed "fear thought." Fear thought he defines as "the self-suggestion of inferiority"; so that one may say that these systems all operate by the suggestion of power. And the power, small or great, comes in various shapes to the individual, power, as he will tell you, not to 'mind' things that used to vex him, power to concentrate his mind, good cheer, good temper; in short, to put it mildly, a firmer, more elastic moral tone. The most genuinely saintly person I have ever known is a friend of mine now suffering from cancer of the breast. I do not assume to judge of the wisdom or unwisdom of her disobedience to the doctors, and I cite her here solely as an example of what ideas can do. Her ideas have kept her a practically well woman for months after she should have given up and gone to bed. They have annulled all pain and weakness and given her a cheerful active life, unusually beneficent to others to whom she has afforded help.

How far the mind-cure movement is destined to extend its influence, or what intellectual modifications it may yet undergo, no one can foretell. Being a religious movement, it will certainly outstrip the purviews of its rationalist critics, such as we here may be supposed to be.

I have thus brought a pretty wide induction to bear upon my thesis, and it appears to hold good. The human individual lives usually far within his limits; he possesses powers of various sorts which he habitually fails to use. He energizes below his maximum, and he behaves below his optimum. In elementary faculty, in coordination, in power of inhibition and control, in every conceivable way, his life is contracted like the field of vision of an hysteric subject—but with less excuse, for the poor hysteric is diseased, while in the rest of us it is only an inveterate *habit*—the habit of inferiority to our full self—that is bad.

Expressed in this vague manner, everyone must admit my thesis to be true. The terms have to remain vague; for though every man of woman born knows what is meant by such phrases as having a good vital tone, a high tide of spirits, an elastic temper, as living energetically, working easily, deciding firmly, and the like, we should all be put to our trumps if asked to explain in terms of scientific psychology just what such expressions mean. We can draw some child-like psychophysical diagrams, and that is all. In physics the conception of 'energy' is perfectly defined. It is correlated with the conception of 'work.' But mental work and moral work, although we cannot live without talking about them, are terms as yet hardly analyzed, and doubtless mean several heterogeneous elementary things. Our muscular work is a voluminous physical quantity, but our ideas and volitions are minute forces of release, and by 'work' here we mean the substitution of higher *kinds* for lower *kinds* of detent. Higher and lower here are qualitative terms, not translatable immediately into quantities, unless indeed they should prove to mean newer or older forms of cerebral organization, and unless newer should then prove to mean cortically more superficial, older, cortically more deep. Some anatomists, as you know, have pretended this; but it is obvious that the intuitive or popular idea of mental work, fundamental and absolutely indispensable as it is in our lives, possesses no degree whatever of scientific clearness today.

Here, then, is the first problem that emerges from our study. Can any one of us refine upon the conceptions of mental work and mental energy, so as later to be able to throw some definitely analytic light on what we mean by "having a more elastic moral tone," or by "using higher levels of power and will"? I imagine that we may have to wait long before progress in this direction is made. The problem is too homely; one doesn't see just how to get in the electric keys and revolving drums that alone make psychology scientific today.

My fellow-pragmatist in Florence, G. Papini, has adopted a new conception of philosophy. He calls it the *doctrine of action* in the widest sense, the study of all human powers and means (among which latter, *truths* of every kind whatsoever figure, of course, in the first rank). From this point of view philosophy is a *Pragmatic*, comprehending, as tributary departments of itself, the old disciplines of logic, metaphysic, physic, and ethic.

And here, after our first problem, two other problems burst upon our view. My belief that these two problems form a program of work well worthy of the attention of a body as learned and earnest as this audience, is, in fact, what has determined me to choose this subject, and to drag you through so many familiar facts during the hour that has sped.

The first of the two problems is *that of our powers*, the second *that of our means*. We ought somehow to get a topographic survey made of the limits of human power in every conceivable direction, something like an ophthalmologist's chart of the limits of the human field of vision; and we ought then to construct a methodical inventory of the paths of access, or keys, differing with the diverse types of individual, to the different kinds of power. This would be an absolutely concrete study, to be carried on by using historical and biographical material mainly. The limits of power must be limits that have been realized in actual persons, and the various ways of unlocking the reserves of power must have been exemplified in individual lives. Laboratory experimentation can play but a small part. Your psychologist's *Versuchsthier*, outside of hypnosis, can never be called on to tax his energies in ways as extreme as those which the emergencies of life will force on him.

So here is a program of concrete individual psychology, at which anyone in some measure may work. It is replete with interesting facts, and points to practical issues superior in importance to anything we know. I urge it therefore upon your consideration. In some shape we have all worked at it in a more or less blind and fragmentary way; yet before Papini mentioned it I had never thought of it, or heard it broached by anyone, in the generalized form of a program such as I now suggest, a program that might with proper care be made to cover the whole field of psychology, and might show us parts of it in a very fresh light.

It is just the generalizing of the problem that seems to me to make so strong an appeal. I hope that in some of you the conception may unlock unused reservoirs of investigating power.

16

Philosophy

The subject of Saintliness left us face to face with the question, Is the sense of divine presence a sense of anything objectively true? We turned first to mysticism for an answer, and found that although mysticism is entirely willing to corroborate religion, it is too private (and also too various) in its utterances to be able to claim a universal authority. But philosophy publishes results which claim to be universally valid if they are valid at all, so we now turn with our question to philosophy. Can philosophy stamp a warrant of veracity upon the religious man's sense of the divine?

I imagine that many of you at this point begin to indulge in guesses at the goal to which I am tending. I have undermined the authority of mysticism, you say, and the next thing I shall probably do is to seek to discredit that of philosophy. Religion, you expect to hear me conclude, is nothing but an affair of faith, based either on vague sentiment, or on that vivid sense of the reality of things unseen of which in my second lecture and in the lecture on Mysticism I gave so many examples. It is essentially private and individualistic; it always exceeds our powers of formulation; and although attempts to pour its contents into a philosophic mould will probably always go on, men being what they are, yet these attempts are always secondary processes which in no way add to the authority, or warrant the veracity, of the sentiments from which they derive their own stimulus and borrow whatever glow of conviction they may themselves possess. In short, you suspect that I am planning to defend feeling at the expense of reason, to rehabilitate the primitive and unreflective, and to dissuade you from the hope of any Theology worthy of the name.

To a certain extent I have to admit that you guess rightly. I do believe that feeling is the deeper source of religion, and that philosophic and theological formulas are secondary products, like translations of a text into another tongue. But all such statements are misleading from their brevity, and it will take the whole hour for me to explain to you exactly what I mean.

When I call theological formulas secondary products, I mean that in a world in which no religious feeling had ever existed, I doubt whether any philosophic theology could ever have been framed. I doubt if dispassionate intellectual contemplation of the universe, apart from inner unhappiness and need of deliverance on the one hand and mystical emotion on the other, would ever have resulted in religious philosophies such as we now possess. Men would have begun with animistic explanations of natural fact, and criticized these away into scientific ones, as they actually have done. In the science they would have left a certain amount of 'psychical research,' even as they now will probably have to re-admit a certain amount. But high-flying speculations like those of either dogmatic or idealistic theology, these they would have had no motive to venture on, feeling no need of commerce with such deities. These speculations must, it seems to me, be classed as over-beliefs, buildings-out performed by the intellect into directions of which feeling originally supplied the hint.

But even if religious philosophy had to have its first hint supplied by feeling, may it not have dealt in a superior way with the matter which feeling suggested? Feeling is private and dumb, and unable to give an account of itself. It allows that its results are mysteries and enigmas, declines to justify them rationally, and on occasion is willing that they should even pass for paradoxical and absurd. Philosophy takes just the opposite attitude. Her aspiration is to reclaim from mystery and paradox whatever territory she touches. To find an escape from obscure and wayward personal persuasion to truth objectively valid for all thinking men has ever been the intellect's most cherished ideal. To redeem religion from unwholesome privacy, and to give public status and universal right of way to its deliverances, has been reason's task.

I believe that philosophy will always have opportunity to labor at this task.[1] We are thinking beings, and we cannot exclude the intellect from participating in any of our functions. Even in soliloquizing with ourselves, we construe our feelings intellectually. Both our personal ideals and our religious and mystical experiences must be interpreted congruously with the kind of scenery which our thinking mind inhabits. The philosophic climate of our time inevitably forces its own clothing on us. Moreover, we must exchange our feelings with one another, and in doing so we have to speak, and to use general and abstract verbal formulas. Conceptions and constructions are thus a necessary part of our religion; and as moderator amid the clash of hypotheses, and mediator among the criticisms of one man's constructions by another, philosophy will always have much to do. It would be strange if I disputed this, when these very lectures which I am giving are (as you will see more clearly from now onwards) a laborious attempt to extract from the privacies of religious experience some general facts which can be defined in formulas upon which everybody may agree.

Religious experience, in other words, spontaneously and inevitably engenders myths, superstitions, dogmas, creeds, and metaphysical theologies, and criticisms of one set of these by the adherents of another. Of late, impartial classifications and comparisons have become possible, alongside of the denunciations and anathemas by which the commerce between creeds used exclusively to be carried on. We have the beginnings of a 'Science of Religions,' so-called; and if these lectures could ever be accounted a crumb-like contribution to such a science, I should be made very happy.

But all these intellectual operations, whether they be constructive or comparative and critical, presuppose immediate experiences as their subject-matter. They are interpretative and inductive operations, operations after the fact, consequent upon religious feeling, not coordinate with it, not independent of what it ascertains.

The intellectualism in religion which I wish to discredit pretends to be something altogether different from this. It assumes to construct religious objects out of the resources of logical reason alone, or of logical reason drawing rigorous inference from non-subjective facts. It calls its conclusions dogmatic theology, or philosophy of the absolute, as the case may be; it does not call them science of religions. It reaches them in an a priori way, and warrants their veracity.

Warranted systems have ever been the idols of aspiring souls. All-inclusive, yet simple; noble, clean, luminous, stable, rigorous, true;— what more ideal refuge could there be than such a system would offer to spirits vexed by the muddiness and accidentality of the world of sensible things? Accordingly, we find inculcated in the theological schools of today, almost as much as in those of the fore-time, a disdain for merely possible or probable truth, and of results that only private assurance can grasp. Scholastics and idealists both express this disdain. Principal John Caird, for example, writes as follows in his *Introduction to the Philosophy of Religion*:—

"Religion must, indeed, be a thing of the heart; but in order to elevate it from the region of subjective caprice and waywardness, and to distinguish between that which is true and false in religion, we must appeal to an objective standard. That which enters the heart, must first be discerned by the intelligence to be *true*. It must be seen as having in its own nature a *right* to dominate feeling, and as constituting the principle by which feeling must be judged.[2] In estimating the religious character of individuals, nations, or races, the first question is, not how they feel, but what they think and believe—not whether their religion is one which manifests itself in emotions, more or less vehement and enthusiastic, but what are the *conceptions* of God and divine things by which these emotions are called forth. Feeling is necessary in religion, but it is by the *content* or intelligent basis of a religion, and not by feeling, that its character and worth are to be determined."[3]

Cardinal Newman, in his work, *The Idea of a University*, gives more emphatic expression still to this disdain for sentiment.[4] Theology, he says, is a science in the strictest sense of the word. I will tell you, he says, what it is not—not 'physical evidences' for God, not 'natural religion,' for these are but vague subjective interpretations:—

"If," he continues, "the Supreme Being is powerful or skillful, just so far as the telescope shows power, or the microscope shows skill, if His moral law is to be ascertained simply by the physical processes of the animal frame, or His will gathered from the immediate issues of human affairs, if His Essence is just as high and deep and broad as the universe and no more; if this be the fact, then will I confess that there is no specific science about God, that theology is but a name, and a protest in its behalf an hypocrisy. Then, pious as it is to think of Him, while the pageant of experiment or abstract reasoning passes by, still, such piety is nothing more than a poetry of thought or an ornament of language, a certain view taken of Nature which one man has, and another has not, which gifted minds strike out, which others see to be admirable and ingenious, and which all would be the better for adopting. It is but the theology of Nature, just as we talk of the *philosophy* or the *romance* of history, or the *poetry* of childhood, or the picturesque, or the sentimental, or the humorous, or any other abstract quality, which the genius or the caprice of the individual, or the fashion of the day, or the consent of the world, recognizes in any set of objects which are subjected to its contemplation. I do not see much difference between avowing that there is no God, and implying that nothing definite can be known for certain about Him."

What I mean by Theology, continues Newman, is none of these things: "I simply mean the *Science of God*, or the truths we know about God put into a system; just as we have a science of the stars, and call it astronomy, or of the crust of the earth, and call it geology."

In both these extracts we have the issue clearly set before us: Feeling valid only for the individual is pitted against reason valid universally. The test is a perfectly plain one of fact. Theology based on pure reason must in point of fact convince men universally. If it did not, wherein would its superiority consist? If it only formed sects and schools, even as sentiment and mysticism form them, how would it fulfill its programme of freeing us from personal caprice and waywardness? This perfectly definite practical test of the pretensions of philosophy to found religion on universal reason simplifies my procedure to-day. I need not discredit philosophy by laborious criticism of its arguments. It will suffice if I show that as a matter of history it fails to prove its pretension to be "objectively" convincing. In fact, philosophy does so fail. It does not banish differences; it founds schools and sects just as feeling does. I believe, in fact, that the logical reason of man operates in this field of divinity exactly as it has always operated in love, or in patriotism, or in politics, or in any other of the wider affairs of life, in which our passions or our mystical intuitions fix our beliefs beforehand. It finds arguments for our conviction, for indeed it *has* to find them. It amplifies and defines our faith, and dignifies it and lends it words and plausibility. It hardly ever engenders it; it cannot now secure it.[5]

Lend me your attention while I run through some of the points of the older systematic theology. You find them in both Protestant and Catholic manuals, best of all in the innumerable text-books published since Pope Leo's Encyclical recommending the study of Saint Thomas. I glance first at the arguments by which dogmatic theology establishes God's existence, after that at those by which it establishes his nature.[6]

The arguments for God's existence have stood for hundreds of years with the waves of unbelieving criticism breaking against them, never totally discrediting them in the ears of the faithful, but on the whole slowly and surely washing out the mortar from between their joints. If you have a God already whom you believe in, these arguments confirm you. If you are atheistic, they fail to set you right. The proofs are various. The 'cosmological' one, so-called, reasons from the contingence of the world to a First Cause which must contain whatever perfections the world itself contains. The 'argument from design' reasons, from the fact that Nature's laws are mathematical, and her parts benevolently adapted to each other, that this cause is both intellectual and benevolent. The 'moral argument' is that the moral law presupposes a lawgiver. The 'argument *ex consensu gentium*' is that the belief in God is so widespread as to be grounded in the rational nature of man, and should therefore carry authority with it.

As I just said, I will not discuss these arguments technically. The bare fact that all idealists since Kant have felt entitled either to scout or to neglect them shows that they are not solid enough to serve as religion's all-sufficient foundation. Absolutely impersonal reasons would be in duty bound to show more general convincingness. Causation is indeed too obscure a principle to bear the weight of the whole structure of theology. As for the argument from design, see how Darwinian ideas have revolutionized it. Conceived as we now conceive them, as so many fortunate escapes from almost limitless processes of destruction, the benevolent adaptations which we find in Nature suggest a deity very different from the one who figured in the earlier versions of the argument.[7] The fact is that these arguments do but follow the combined suggestions of the facts and of our feeling. They prove nothing rigorously. They only corroborate our pre-existent partialities.

If philosophy can do so little to establish God's existence, how stands it with her efforts to define his attributes? It is worth while to look at the attempts of systematic theology in this direction.

Since God is First Cause, this science of sciences says, he differs from all his creatures in possessing existence *a se*. From this 'a-se-ity' on God's part, theology deduces by mere logic most of his other perfections. For instance, he must be both *necessary* and *absolute*, cannot not be, and cannot in any way be determined by anything else. This makes Him absolutely unlimited from without, and unlimited also from within; for limitation is non-being; and God is being itself. This unlimitedness makes God infinitely perfect. Moreover, God is *One*, and *Only*, for the infinitely perfect can admit no peer. He is *Spiritual*, for were He composed of physical parts, some other power would have to combine them into the total, and his aseity would thus be contradicted. He is therefore both simple and non-physical in nature. He is *simple metaphysically* also, that is to say, his nature and his existence cannot be distinct, as they are in finite substances which share their formal natures with one another, and are individual only in their material aspect. Since God is one and only, his *essentia* and his *esse* must be given at one stroke. This excludes from his being all those distinctions, so familiar in the world of finite things, between potentiality and actuality, substance and accidents, being and activity, existence and attributes. We can talk, it is true, of God's powers, acts, and attributes, but these discriminations are only 'virtual,' and made from the human point of view. In God all these points of view fall into an absolute identity of being.

This absence of all potentiality in God obliges Him to be *immutable*. He is actuality, through and through. Were there anything potential about Him, He would either lose or gain by its actualization, and either loss or gain would contradict his perfection. He cannot, therefore, change. Furthermore, He is *immense, boundless*; for could He be outlined in space, He would be composite, and this would contradict his indivisibility. He is therefore *omnipresent*, indivisibly there, at every point of space. He is similarly wholly present at every point of time—in other words *eternal*. For if He began in time, He would need a prior cause, and that would contradict his aseity. If He ended, it would contradict his necessity. If He went through any succession, it would contradict his immutability.

He has *intelligence* and *will* and every other creature-perfection, for *we* have them, and *effectus nequit superare causam*. In Him, however, they are absolutely and eternally in act, and their *object*, since God can be bounded by naught that is external, can primarily be nothing else than God himself. He knows himself, then, in one eternal indivisible act, and wills himself with an infinite self-pleasure.[8] Since He must of logical necessity thus love and will himself, He cannot be called 'free' *ad intra*, with the freedom of contrarieties that characterizes finite creatures. *Ad extra*, however, or with respect to his creation, God is free. He cannot *need* to create, being perfect in being and in happiness already. He *wills* to create, then, by an absolute freedom.

Being thus a substance endowed with intellect and will and freedom, God is a *person*; and a *living* person also, for He is both object and subject of his own activity, and to be this distinguishes the living from the lifeless. He is thus absolutely *self-sufficient*: his *self-knowledge* and *self-love* are both of them infinite and adequate, and need no extraneous conditions to perfect them.

He is *omniscient*, for in knowing himself as Cause He knows all creature things and events by implication. His knowledge is *previsive*, for He is present to all time. Even our free acts are known beforehand to Him, for otherwise his wisdom would admit of successive moments of enrichment, and this would contradict his immutability. He is *omnipotent* for everything that does not involve logical contradiction. He can make *being*—in other words his power includes *creation*. If what He creates were made of his own substance, it would have to be infinite in essence, as that substance is; but it is finite; so it must be non-divine in substance. If it were made of a substance, an eternally existing matter, for example, which God found there to his hand, and to which He simply gave its form, that would contradict God's definition as First Cause, and make Him a mere mover of something caused already. The things he creates, then, He creates *ex nihilo*, and gives them absolute being as so many finite substances additional to himself. The forms which he imprints upon them have their prototypes in his ideas. But as in God there is no such thing as multiplicity, and as these ideas for us are manifold, we must distinguish the ideas as they are in God and the way in which our minds externally imitate them. We must attribute them to Him only in a *terminative* sense, as differing aspects, from the finite point of view, of his unique essence.

God of course is holy, good, and just. He can do no evil, for He is positive being's fullness, and evil is negation. It is true that He has created physical evil in places, but only as a means of wider good, for *bonum totius præeminet bonum partis*. Moral evil He cannot will, either as end or means, for that would contradict his holiness. By creating free beings He *permits* it only, neither his justice nor his goodness obliging Him to prevent the recipients of freedom from misusing the gift.

As regards God's purpose in creating, primarily it can only have been to exercise his absolute freedom by the manifestation to others of his glory. From this it follows that the others must be rational beings, capable in the first place of knowledge, love, and honor, and in the second place of happiness, for the knowledge and love of God is the mainspring of felicity. In so far forth one may say that God's secondary purpose in creating is *love*.

I will not weary you by pursuing these metaphysical determinations farther, into the mysteries of God's Trinity, for example. What I have given will serve as a specimen of the orthodox philosophical theology of both Catholics and Protestants. Newman, filled with enthusiasm at God's list of perfections, continues the passage which I began to quote to

you by a couple of pages of a rhetoric so magnificent that I can hardly
refrain from adding them, in spite of the inroad they would make upon
our time.[9] He first enumerates God's attributes sonorously, then cele-
brates his ownership of everything in earth and Heaven, and the dependence of all that happens upon his permissive will. He gives us scholastic
philosophy "touched with emotion," and every philosophy should be
touched with emotion to be rightly understood. Emotionally, then, dogmatic theology is worth something to minds of the type of Newman's. It
will aid us to estimate what it is worth intellectually, if at this point I
make a short digression.

What God hath joined together, let no man put asunder. The Con-
tinental schools of philosophy have too often overlooked the fact that
man's thinking is organically connected with his conduct. It seems to me
to be the chief glory of English and Scottish thinkers to have kept the
organic connection in view. The guiding principle of British philosophy
has in fact been that every difference must *make* a difference, every theoretical difference somewhere issue in a practical difference, and that the
best method of discussing points of theory is to begin by ascertaining
what practical difference would result from one alternative or the other
being true. What is the particular truth in question *known as*? In what
facts does it result? What is its cash-value in terms of particular experience? This is the characteristic English way of taking up a question. In
this way, you remember, Locke takes up the question of personal identity.
What you mean by it is just your chain of particular memories, says he.
That is the only concretely verifiable part of its significance. All further
ideas about it, such as the oneness or manyness of the spiritual substance
on which it is based, are therefore void of intelligible meaning; and
propositions touching such ideas may be indifferently affirmed or
denied. So Berkeley with his 'matter.' The cash-value of matter is our
physical sensations. That is what it is known as, all that we concretely
verify of its conception. That, therefore, is the whole meaning of the
term 'matter'—any other pretended meaning is mere wind of words.
Hume does the same thing with causation. It is known as habitual
antecedence, and as tendency on our part to look for something definite

to come. Apart from this practical meaning it has no significance whatever, and books about it may be committed to the flames, says Hume. Dugald Stewart and Thomas Brown, James Mill, John Mill, and Professor Bain, have followed more or less consistently the same method; and Shadworth Hodgson has used the principle with full explicitness. When all is said and done, it was English and Scotch writers, and not Kant, who introduced 'the critical method' into philosophy, the one method fitted to make philosophy a study worthy of serious men. For what seriousness can possibly remain in debating philosophic propositions that will never make an appreciable difference to us in action? And what could it matter, if all propositions were practically indifferent, which of them we should agree to call true or which false?

An American philosopher of eminent originality, Mr. Charles Sanders Peirce, has rendered thought a service by disentangling from the particulars of its application the principle by which these men were instinctively guided, and by singling it out as fundamental and giving to it a Greek name. He calls it the principle of *pragmatism*, and he defends it somewhat as follows:—[10]

Thought in movement has for its only conceivable motive the attainment of belief, or thought at rest. Only when our thought about a subject has found its rest in belief can our action on the subject firmly and safely begin. Beliefs, in short, are rules for action; and the whole function of thinking is but one step in the production of active habits. If there were any part of a thought that made no difference in the thought's practical consequences, then that part would be no proper element of the thought's significance. To develop a thought's meaning we need therefore only determine what conduct it is fitted to produce; that conduct is for us its sole significance; and the tangible fact at the root of all our thought-distinctions is that there is no one of them so fine as to consist in anything but a possible difference of practice. To attain perfect clearness in our thoughts of an object, we need then only consider what sensations, immediate or remote, we are conceivably to expect from it, and what conduct we must prepare in case the object should be true. Our conception of these practical consequences is for us the whole of our conception of the object, so far as that conception has positive significance at all.

This is the principle of Peirce, the principle of pragmatism. Such a principle will help us on this occasion to decide, among the various attributes set down in the scholastic inventory of God's perfections, whether some be not far less significant than others.

If, namely, we apply the principle of pragmatism to God's metaphysical attributes, strictly so called, as distinguished from his moral attributes, I think that, even were we forced by a coercive logic to believe them, we still should have to confess them to be destitute of all intelligible significance. Take God's aseity, for example; or his necessariness; his immateriality; his 'simplicity' or superiority to the kind of inner variety and succession which we find in finite beings, his indivisibility, and lack of the inner distinctions of being and activity, substance and accident, potentiality and actuality, and the rest; his repudiation of inclusion in a genus; his actualized infinity; his 'personality,' apart from the moral qualities which it may comport; his relations to evil being permissive and not positive; his self-sufficiency, self-love, and absolute felicity in himself:—candidly speaking, how do such qualities as these make any definite connection with our life? And if they severally call for no distinctive adaptations of our conduct, what vital difference can it possibly make to a man's religion whether they be true or false?

For my own part, although I dislike to say aught that may grate upon tender associations, I must frankly confess that even though these attributes were faultlessly deduced, I cannot conceive of its being of the smallest consequence to us religiously that any one of them should be true. Pray, what specific act can I perform in order to adapt myself the better to God's simplicity? Or how does it assist me to plan my behavior, to know that his happiness is anyhow absolutely complete? In the middle of the century just past, Mayne Reid was the great writer of books of out-of-door adventure. He was forever extolling the hunters and field-observers of living animals' habits, and keeping up a fire of invective against the 'closet-naturalists,' as he called them, the collectors and classifiers, and handlers of skeletons and skins. When I was a boy, I used to think that a closet-naturalist must be the vilest type of wretch under the sun. But surely the systematic theologians are the closet-naturalists of the deity, even in Captain Mayne Reid's sense. What is their deduction of metaphysical attributes but a shuffling and matching of pedantic dictionary-adjectives, aloof from morals, aloof from human needs, something that might be worked out from the mere word 'God' by one of those logical machines of wood and brass which recent ingenuity has contrived as well as by a man of flesh and blood. They have the trail of the serpent over them. One feels that in the theologians' hands, they are only a set of titles obtained by a mechanical manipulation of synonyms; verbality has stepped into the place of vision, professionalism into that of life. Instead of bread we have a stone; instead of a fish, a serpent. Did such a con-glomeration of abstract terms give really the gist of our knowledge of the deity, schools of theology might indeed continue to flourish, but religion, vital religion, would have taken its flight from this world. What keeps reli-gion going is something else than abstract definitions and systems of con-catenated adjectives, and something different from faculties of theology and their professors. All these things are after-effects, secondary accre-tions upon those phenomena of vital conversation with the unseen divine, of which I have shown you so many instances, renewing themselves *in sæcula sæculorum* in the lives of humble private men.

So much for the metaphysical attributes of God! From the point of view of practical religion, the metaphysical monster which they offer to our worship is an absolutely worthless invention of the scholarly mind.

What shall we now say of the attributes called moral? Pragmatically, they stand on an entirely different footing. They positively determine fear and hope and expectation, and are foundations for the saintly life. It needs but a glance at them to show how great is their significance.

God's holiness, for example: being holy, God can will nothing but the good. Being omnipotent, he can secure its triumph. Being omniscient, he can see us in the dark. Being just, he can punish us for what he sees. Being loving, he can pardon too. Being unalterable, we can count on him securely. These qualities enter into connection with our life, it is highly important that we should be informed concerning them. That God's purpose in creation should be the manifestation of his glory is also an attribute which has definite relations to our practical life. Among other things it has given a definite character to worship in all Christian countries. If dogmatic theology really does prove beyond dispute that a God with characters like these exists, she may well claim to give a solid basis to religious sentiment. But verily, how stands it with her arguments?

It stands with them as ill as with the arguments for his existence. Not only do post-Kantian idealists reject them root and branch, but it is a plain historic fact that they never have converted any one who has found in the moral complexion of the world, as he experienced it, reasons for doubting that a good God can have framed it. To prove God's goodness by the scholastic argument that there is no non-being in his essence would sound to such a witness simply silly.

No! the book of Job went over this whole matter once for all and definitively. Ratiocination is a relatively superficial and unreal path to the deity: "I will lay mine hand upon my mouth; I have heard of Thee by the hearing of the ear, but now mine eye seeth Thee." An intellect perplexed and baffled, yet a trustful sense of presence—such is the situation of the man who is sincere with himself and with the facts, but who remains religious still.[11]

We must therefore, I think, bid a definitive good-by to dogmatic theology. In all sincerity our faith must do without that warrant. Modern idealism, I repeat, has said good-by to this theology forever. Can modern idealism give faith a better warrant, or must she still rely on her poor self for witness?

The basis of modern idealism is Kant's doctrine of the Transcendental Ego of Apperception. By this formidable term Kant merely meant the fact that the consciousness 'I think them' must (potentially or actually) accompany all our objects. Former skeptics had said as much, but the 'I' in question had remained for them identified with the personal individual. Kant abstracted and depersonalized it, and made it the most universal of all his categories, although for Kant himself the Transcendental Ego had no theological implications.

It was reserved for his successors to convert Kant's notion of

Bewusstsein überhaupt, or abstract consciousness, into an infinite concrete self-consciousness which is the soul of the world, and in which our sundry personal self-consciousnesses have their being. It would lead me into technicalities to show you even briefly how this transformation was in point of fact effected. Suffice it to say that in the Hegelian school, which today so deeply influences both British and American thinking, two principles have borne the brunt of the operation.

The first of these principles is that the old logic of identity never gives us more than a post-mortem dissection of *disjecta membra,* and that the fullness of life can be construed to thought only by recognizing that every object which our thought may propose to itself involves the notion of some other object which seems at first to negate the first one.

The second principle is that to be conscious of a negation is already virtually to be beyond it. The mere asking of a question or expression of a dissatisfaction proves that the answer or the satisfaction is already imminent; the finite, realized as such, is already the infinite *in posse.*

Applying these principles, we seem to get a propulsive force into our logic which the ordinary logic of a bare, stark self-identity in each thing never attains to. The objects of our thought now *act* within our thought, act as objects act when given in experience. They change and develop. They introduce something other than themselves along with them; and this other, at first only ideal or potential, presently proves itself also to be actual. It supersedes the thing at first supposed, and both verifies and corrects it, in developing the fullness of its meaning.

The program is excellent; the universe *is* a place where things are followed by other things that both correct and fulfill them; and a logic which gave us something like this movement of fact would express truth far better than the traditional school-logic, which never gets of its own accord from anything to anything else, and registers only predictions and subsumptions, or static resemblances and differences. Nothing could be more unlike the methods of dogmatic theology than those of this new logic. Let me quote in illustration some passages from the Scottish transcendentalist whom I have already named.

"How are we to conceive," Principal Caird writes, "of the reality in

which all intelligence rests?" He replies: "Two things may without difficulty be proved, viz., that this reality is an Absolute Spirit, and conversely
that it is only in communion with this Absolute Spirit or Intelligence
that the finite spirit can realize itself. It is absolute; for the faintest movement of human intelligence would be arrested, if it did not presuppose
the absolute reality of intelligence, of thought itself. Doubt or denial
themselves presuppose and indirectly affirm it. When I pronounce anything to be true, I pronounce it, indeed, to be relative to thought, but not
to be relative to *my* thought, or to the thought of any other individual
mind. From the existence of all individual minds, as such, I can abstract;
I can think them away. But that which I cannot think away is thought or
self-consciousness itself, in its independence and absoluteness, or, in
other words, an Absolute Thought or Self-Consciousness."

Here, you see, Principal Caird makes the transition which Kant did
not make: he converts the omnipresence of consciousness in general as a
condition of 'truth' being anywhere possible, into an omnipresent universal consciousness, which he identifies with God in his concreteness.
He next proceeds to use the principle that to acknowledge your limits is
in essence to be beyond them; and makes the transition to the religious
experience of individuals in the following words:

"If [Man] were only a creature of transient sensations and impulses,
of an ever coming and going succession of intuitions, fancies, feelings,
then nothing could ever have for him the character of objective truth or
reality. But it is the prerogative of man's spiritual nature that he can yield
himself up to a thought and will that are infinitely larger than his own.
As a thinking self-conscious being, indeed, he may be said, by his very
nature, to live in the atmosphere of the Universal Life. As a thinking
being, it is possible for me to suppress and quell in my consciousness
every movement of self-assertion, every notion and opinion that is
merely mine, every desire that belongs to me as this particular Self, and
to become the pure medium of a thought that is universal—in one word,
to live no more my own life, but let my consciousness be possessed and
suffused by the Infinite and Eternal life of spirit. And yet it is just in this
renunciation of self that I truly gain myself, or realize the highest possi-

bilities of my own nature. For whilst in one sense we give up self to live the universal and absolute life of reason, yet that to which we thus surrender ourselves is in reality our truer self. The life of absolute reason is not a life that is foreign to us."

Nevertheless, Principal Caird goes on to say, so far as we are able outwardly to realize this doctrine, the balm it offers remains incomplete. Whatever we may be *in posse*, the very best of us *in actu* falls very short of being absolutely divine. Social morality, love, and self-sacrifice even, merge our Self only in some other finite self or selves. They do not quite identify it with the Infinite. Man's ideal destiny, infinite in abstract logic, might thus seem in practice forever unrealizable.

"Is there, then," our author continues, "no solution of the contradiction between the ideal and the actual? We answer, There is such a solution, but in order to reach it we are carried beyond the sphere of morality into that of religion. It may be said to be the essential characteristic of religion as contrasted with morality, that it changes aspiration into fruition, anticipation into realization; that instead of leaving man in the interminable pursuit of a vanishing ideal, it makes him the actual partaker of a divine or infinite life. Whether we view religion from the human side or the divine—as the surrender of the soul to God, or as the life of God in the soul—in either aspect, it is of its very essence that the infinite has ceased to be a far-off vision, and has become a present reality. The very first pulsation of the spiritual life, when we rightly apprehend its significance, is the indication that the division between the spirit and its object has vanished, that the ideal has become real, that the finite has reached its goal and become suffused with the presence and life of the Infinite.

"Oneness of mind and will with the Divine mind and will is not the future hope and aim of religion, but its very beginning and birth in the soul. To enter on the religious life is to terminate the struggle. In that act which constitutes the beginning of the religious life—call it faith, or trust, or self-surrender, or by whatever name you will—there is involved the identification of the finite with a life which is eternally realized. It is true, indeed, that the religious life is progressive: but, understood in the light of the foregoing idea, religious progress is not progress *towards*, but *within* the sphere of the infinite. It is not the vain attempt by endless finite additions or increments to become possessed of infinite wealth, but it is the endeavor, by the constant exercise of spiritual activity, to appropriate that infinite inheritance of which we are already in possession. The whole future of the religious life is given in its beginning, but it is given implicitly. The position of the man who has entered on the religious life is that evil, error, imperfection, do not really belong to him: they are excrescences which have no organic relation to his true nature: they are already virtually, as they will be actually, suppressed and annulled, and in the very process of being annulled they become the means of spiritual progress. Though he is not exempt from temptation and conflict, [yet] in that inner sphere in which his true life lies, the struggle is over, the victory already achieved. It is not a finite but an infinite life which the spirit lives. Every pulse-beat of its [existence] is the expression and realization of the life of God."12

You will readily admit that no description of the phenomena of the religious consciousness could be better than these words of your lamented preacher and philosopher. They reproduce the very rapture of those crises of conversion of which we have been hearing; they utter what the mystic felt but was unable to communicate; and the saint, in hearing them, recognizes his own experience. It is indeed gratifying to find the content of religion reported so unanimously. But when all is said and done, has Principal Caird—and I only use him as an example of that whole mode of thinking—transcended the sphere of feeling and of the direct experience of the individual, and laid the foundations of religion in impartial reason? Has he made religion universal by coercive reasoning, transformed it from a private faith into a public certainty? Has he rescued its affirmations from obscurity and mystery?

I believe that he has done nothing of the kind, but that he has simply reaffirmed the individual's experiences in a more generalized vocabulary. And again, I can be excused from proving technically that the transcendentalist reasonings fail to make religion universal, for I can point to the plain fact that a majority of scholars, even religiously disposed ones, stubbornly refuse to treat them as convincing. The whole of Germany, one may say, has positively rejected the Hegelian argumentation. As for Scotland, I need only mention Professor Fraser's and Professor Pringle-Pattison's memorable criticisms, with which so many of you are familiar.[13] Once more, I ask, if transcendental idealism were as objectively and absolutely rational as it pretends to be, could it possibly fail so egregiously to be persuasive?

What religion reports, you must remember, always purports to be a fact of experience: the divine is actually present, religion says, and between it and ourselves relations of give and take are actual. If definite perceptions of fact like this cannot stand upon their own feet, surely abstract reasoning cannot give them the support they are in need of. Conceptual processes can class facts, define them, interpret them; but they do not produce them, nor can they reproduce their individuality. There is always a *plus*, a *thisness*, which feeling alone can answer for. Philosophy in this sphere is thus a secondary function, unable to warrant faith's veracity, and so I revert to the thesis which I announced at the beginning of this lecture.

In all sad sincerity I think we must conclude that the attempt to demonstrate by purely intellectual processes the truth of the deliverances of direct religious experience is absolutely hopeless.

It would be unfair to philosophy, however, to leave her under this negative sentence. Let me close, then, by briefly enumerating what she *can* do for religion. If she will abandon metaphysics and deduction for criticism and induction, and frankly transform herself from theology into science of religions, she can make herself enormously useful.

The spontaneous intellect of man always defines the divine which it feels in ways that harmonize with its temporary intellectual prepossessions. Philosophy can by comparison eliminate the local and the accidental from these definitions. Both from dogma and from worship she can remove historic incrustations. By confronting the spontaneous religious constructions with the results of natural science, philosophy can also eliminate doctrines that are now known to be scientifically absurd or incongruous.

Sifting out in this way unworthy formulations, she can leave a residuum of conceptions that at least are possible. With these she can deal as *hypotheses*, testing them in all the manners, whether negative or positive, by which hypotheses are ever tested. She can reduce their number, as some are found more open to objection. She can perhaps become the champion of one which she picks out as being the most closely verified or verifiable. She can refine upon the definition of this hypothesis, distinguishing between what is innocent over-belief and symbolism in the expression of it, and what is to be literally taken. As a result, she can offer mediation between different believers, and help to bring about consensus of opinion. She can do this the more successfully, the better she discriminates the common and essential from the individual and local elements of the religious beliefs which she compares.

I do not see why a critical Science of Religions of this sort might not eventually command as general a public adhesion as is commanded by a physical science. Even the personally non-religious might accept its conclusions on trust, much as blind persons now accept the facts of optics— it might appear as foolish to refuse them. Yet as the science of optics has to be fed in the first instance, and continually verified later, by facts experienced by seeing persons; so the science of religions would depend for its original material on facts of personal experience, and would have to square itself with personal experience through all its critical reconstructions. It could never get away from concrete life, or work in a conceptual vacuum. It would forever have to confess, as every science confesses, that the subtlety of nature flies beyond it, and that its formulas are but approximations. Philosophy lives in words, but truth and fact well up into our lives in ways that exceed verbal formulation. There is in the living act of perception always something that glimmers and twinkles and will not be caught, and for which reflection comes too late. No one knows this as well as the philosopher. He must fire his volley of new vocables out of his conceptual shotgun, for his profession condemns him to this industry, but he secretly knows the hollowness and irrelevancy. His formulas are like stereoscopic or kinetoscopic photographs seen outside the instrument; they lack the depth, the motion, the vitality. In the religious sphere, in particular, belief that formulas are true can never wholly take the place of personal experience.

In my next lecture I will try to complete my rough description of religious experience; and in the lecture after that, which is the last one, I will try my hand at formulating conceptually the truth to which it is a witness.

17

Conclusions

The material of our study of human nature is now spread before us; and in this parting hour, set free from the duty of description, we can draw our theoretical and practical conclusions. In my first lecture, defending the empirical method, I foretold that whatever conclusions we might come to could be reached by spiritual judgments only, appreciations of the significance for life of religion, taken 'on the whole.' Our conclusions cannot be as sharp as dogmatic conclusions would be, but I will formulate them, when the time comes, as sharply as I can.

Summing up in the broadest possible way the characteristics of the religious life, as we have found them, it includes the following beliefs:—

1. That the visible world is part of a more spiritual universe from which it draws its chief significance;
2. That union or harmonious relation with that higher universe is our true end;
3. That prayer or inner communion with the spirit thereof—be that spirit 'God' or 'law'—is a process wherein work is really done, and spiritual energy flows in and produces effects, psychological or material, within the phenomenal world.

Religion includes also the following psychological characteristics:—

4. A new zest which adds itself like a gift to life, and takes the form either of lyrical enchantment or of appeal to earnestness and heroism.

5. An assurance of safety and a temper of peace, and, in relation to others, a preponderance of loving affections.

In illustrating these characteristics by documents, we have been literally bathed in sentiment. In re-reading my manuscript, I am almost appalled at the amount of emotionality which I find in it. After so much of this, we can afford to be dryer and less sympathetic in the rest of the work that lies before us.

The sentimentality of many of my documents is a consequence of the fact that I sought them among the extravagances of the subject. If any of you are enemies of what our ancestors used to brand as enthusiasm, and are, nevertheless, still listening to me now, you have probably felt my selection to have been sometimes almost perverse, and have wished I might have stuck to soberer examples. I reply that I took these extremer examples as yielding the profounder information. To learn the secrets of any science, we go to expert specialists, even though they may be eccentric persons, and not to commonplace pupils. We combine what they tell us with the rest of our wisdom, and form our final judgment independently. Even so with religion. We who have pursued such radical expressions of it may now be sure that we know its secrets as authentically as anyone can know them who learns them from another; and we have next to answer, each of us for himself, the practical question: what are the dangers in this element of life? and in what proportion may it need to be restrained by other elements, to give the proper balance?

But this question suggests another one which I will answer immediately and get it out of the way, for it has more than once already vexed us.[1] Ought it to be assumed that in all men the mixture of religion with other elements should be identical? Ought it, indeed, to be assumed that the lives of all men should show identical religious elements? In other words, is the existence of so many religious types and sects and creeds regrettable?

To these questions I answer 'No' emphatically. And my reason is that I do not see how it is possible that creatures in such different positions and with such different powers as human individuals are, should have exactly the same functions and the same duties. No two of us have identical difficulties, nor should we be expected to work out identical solutions. Each, from his peculiar angle of observation, takes in a certain sphere of fact and trouble, which each must deal with in a unique manner. One of us must soften himself, another must harden himself; one must yield a point, another must stand firm—in order the better to defend the position assigned him. If an Emerson were forced to be a Wesley, or a Moody forced to be a Whitman, the total human consciousness of the divine would suffer. The divine can mean no single quality, it must mean a group of qualities, by being champions of which in alternation, different men may all find worthy missions. Each attitude being a syllable in human nature's total message, it takes the whole of us to spell the meaning out completely. So a 'god of battles' must be allowed to be the god for one kind of person, a god of peace and heaven and home, the god for another. We must frankly recognize the fact that we live in partial systems, and that parts are not interchangeable in the spiritual life. If we are peevish and jealous, destruction of the self must be an element of our religion; why need it be one if we are good and sympathetic from the outset? If we are sick souls, we require a religion of deliverance; but why think so much of deliverance, if we are healthy-minded?[2] Unquestionably, some men have the completer experience and the higher vocation, here just as in the social world; but for each man to stay in his own experience, whate'er it be, and for others to tolerate him there, is surely best.

But, you may now ask, would not this one-sidedness be cured if we should all espouse the science of religions as our own religion? In answering this question I must open again the general relations of the theoretic to the active life.

Knowledge about a thing is not the thing itself. You remember what Al-Ghazzali told us in the Lecture on Mysticism—that to understand the causes of drunkenness, as a physician understands them, is not to be drunk. A science might come to understand everything about the causes and elements of religion, and might even decide which elements were qualified, by their general harmony with other branches of knowledge, to be considered true; and yet the best man at this science might be the man who found it hardest to be personally devout. *Tout savoir c'est tout pardonner.* The name of Renan would doubtless occur to many persons as an example of the way in which breadth of knowledge may make one only a dilettante in possibilities, and blunt the acuteness of one's living faith.[3] If religion be a function by which either God's cause or man's cause is to be really advanced, then he who lives the life of it, however narrowly, is a better servant than he who merely knows about it, however much. Knowledge about life is one thing; effective occupation of a place in life, with its dynamic currents passing through your being, is another.

For this reason, the science of religions may not be an equivalent for living religion; and if we turn to the inner difficulties of such a science, we see that a point comes when she must drop the purely theoretic attitude, and either let her knots remain uncut, or have them cut by active faith. To see this, suppose that we have our science of religions constituted as a matter of fact. Suppose that she has assimilated all the necessary historical material and distilled out of it as its essence the same conclusions which I myself a few moments ago pronounced. Suppose that she agrees that religion, wherever it is an active thing, involves a belief in ideal presences, and a belief that in our prayerful communion with them,[4] work is done, and something real comes to pass. She has now to exert her critical activity, and to decide how far, in the light of other sciences and in that of general philosophy, such beliefs can be considered *true*.

Dogmatically to decide this is an impossible task. Not only are the other sciences and the philosophy still far from being completed, but in their present state we find them full of conflicts. The sciences of nature know nothing of spiritual presences, and on the whole hold no practical commerce whatever with the idealistic conceptions towards which general philosophy inclines. The scientist, so-called, is, during his scientific hours at least, so materialistic that one may well say that on the whole the influence of science goes against the notion that religion should be recognized at all. And this antipathy to religion finds an echo within the very science of religions itself. The cultivator of this science has to become acquainted with so many groveling and horrible superstitions that a presumption easily arises in his mind that any belief that is religious probably is false. In the 'prayerful communion' of savages with such mumbo-jumbos of deities as they acknowledge, it is hard for us to see what genuine spiritual work—even though it were work relative only to their dark savage obligations—can possibly be done.

The consequence is that the conclusions of the science of religions are as likely to be adverse as they are to be favorable to the claim that the essence of religion is true. There is a notion in the air about us that religion is probably only an anachronism, a case of 'survival,' an atavistic relapse into a mode of thought which humanity in its more enlightened examples has outgrown; and this notion our religious anthropologists at present do little to counteract.

This view is so widespread at the present day that I must consider it with some explicitness before I pass to my own conclusions. Let me call it the 'Survival theory,' for brevity's sake.

The pivot round which the religious life, as we have traced it, revolves, is the interest of the individual in his private personal destiny. Religion, in short, is a monumental chapter in the history of human egotism. The gods believed in—whether by crude savages or by men disciplined intellectually—agree with each other in recognizing personal calls. Religious thought is carried on in terms of personality, this being, in the world of religion, the one fundamental fact. Today, quite as much as at any previous age, the religious individual tells you that the divine meets him on the basis of his personal concerns.

Science, on the other hand, has ended by utterly repudiating the personal point of view. She catalogues her elements and records her laws indifferent as to what purpose may be shown forth by them, and constructs her theories quite careless of their bearing on human anxieties and fates. Though the scientist may individually nourish a religion, and be a theist in his irresponsible hours, the days are over when it could be said that for Science herself the heavens declare the glory of God and the firmament showeth his handiwork. Our solar system, with its harmonies, is seen now as but one passing case of a certain sort of moving equilibrium in the heavens, realized by a local accident in an appalling wilderness of worlds where no life can exist. In a span of time which as a cosmic interval will count but as an hour, it will have ceased to be. The Darwinian notion of chance production, and subsequent destruction, speedy or deferred, applies to the largest as well as to the smallest facts. It is impossible, in the present temper of the scientific imagination, to find in the driftings of the cosmic atoms, whether they work on the universal or on the particular scale, anything but a kind of aimless weather, doing and undoing, achieving no proper history, and leaving no result. Nature has no one distinguishable ultimate tendency with which it is possible to feel a sympathy. In the vast rhythm of her processes, as the scientific mind now follows them, she appears to cancel herself. The books of natural theology which satisfied the intellects of our grandfathers seem to us quite grotesque,[5] representing, as they did, a God who conformed the largest things of nature to the paltriest of our private wants. The God whom science recognizes must be a God of universal laws exclusively, a God who does a wholesale, not a retail business. He cannot accommodate his processes to the convenience of individuals. The bubbles on the foam which coats a stormy sea are floating episodes, made and unmade by the forces of the wind and water. Our private selves are like those bubbles—epiphenomena, as Clifford, I believe, ingeniously called them; their destinies weigh nothing and determine nothing in the world's irremediable currents of events.

You see how natural it is, from this point of view, to treat religion as a mere survival, for religion does in fact perpetuate the traditions of the most primeval thought. To coerce the spiritual powers, or to square them and get them on our side, was, during enormous tracts of time, the one great object in our dealings with the natural world. For our ancestors, dreams, hallucinations, revelations, and cock-and-bull stories were inextricably mixed with facts. Up to a comparatively recent date such distinctions as those between what has been verified and what is only conjectured, between the impersonal and the personal aspects of existence, were hardly suspected or conceived. Whatever you imagined in a lively manner, whatever you thought fit to be true, you affirmed confidently; and whatever you affirmed, your comrades believed. Truth was what had not yet been contradicted, most things were taken into the mind from the point of view of their human suggestiveness, and the attention confined itself exclusively to the aesthetic and dramatic aspects of events.[6]

How indeed could it be otherwise? The extraordinary value, for explanation and prevision, of those mathematical and mechanical modes of conception which science uses, was a result that could not possibly have been expected in advance. Weight, movement, velocity, direction, position, what thin, pallid, uninteresting ideas! How could the richer animistic aspects of Nature, the peculiarities and oddities that make phenomena picturesquely striking or expressive, fail to have been first singled out and followed by philosophy as the more promising avenue to the knowledge of Nature's life? Well, it is still in these richer animistic and dramatic aspects that religion delights to dwell. It is the terror and beauty of phenomena, the 'promise' of the dawn and of the rainbow, the 'voice' of the thunder, the 'gentleness' of the summer rain, the 'sublimity' of the stars, and not the physical laws which these things follow, by which the religious mind still continues to be most impressed; and just as of yore, the devout man tells you that in the solitude of his room or of the fields he still feels the divine presence, that inflowings of help come in reply to his prayers, and that sacrifices to this unseen reality fill him with security and peace.

Pure anachronism! says the survival-theory;—anachronism for which deanthropomorphization of the imagination is the remedy required. The less we mix the private with the cosmic, the more we dwell in universal and impersonal terms, the truer heirs of Science we become.

In spite of the appeal which this impersonality of the scientific attitude makes to a certain magnanimity of temper, I believe it to be shallow, and I can now state my reason in comparatively few words. That reason is that, so long as we deal with the cosmic and the general, we deal only with the symbols of reality, but *as soon as we deal with private and personal phenomena as such, we deal with realities in the completest sense of the term.* I think I can easily make clear what I mean by these words.

The world of our experience consists at all times of two parts, an objective and a subjective part, of which the former may be incalculably more extensive than the latter, and yet the latter can never be omitted or suppressed. The objective part is the sum total of whatsoever at any given time we may be thinking of, the subjective part is the inner 'state' in which the thinking comes to pass. What we think of may be enormous—the cosmic times and spaces, for example—whereas the inner state may be the most fugitive and paltry activity of mind. Yet the cosmic objects, so far as the experience yields them, are but ideal pictures of something whose existence we do not inwardly possess but only point at outwardly, while the inner state is our very experience itself; its reality and that of our experience are one. A conscious field *plus* its object as felt or thought of *plus* an attitude towards the object *plus* the sense of a self to whom the attitude belongs—such a concrete bit of personal experience may be a small bit, but it is a solid bit as long as it lasts; not hollow, not a mere abstract element of experience, such as the 'object' is when taken all alone. It is a *full* fact, even though it be an insignificant fact; it is of the *kind* to which all realities whatsoever must belong; the motor currents of the world run through the like of it; it is on the line connecting real events with real events. That unsharable feeling which each one of us has of the pinch of his individual destiny as he privately feels it rolling out on fortune's wheel may be disparaged for its egotism, may be sneered at as unscientific, but it is the one thing that fills up the measure of our concrete actuality, and any would-be existent that should lack such a feeling, or its analogue, would be a piece of reality only half made up.[7]

If this be true, it is absurd for Science to say that the egotistic elements of experience should be suppressed. The axis of reality runs solely through the egotistic places—they are strung upon it like so many beads. To describe the world with all the various feelings of the individual pinch of destiny, all the various spiritual attitudes, left out from the description—they being as describable as anything else—would be something like offering a printed bill of fare as the equivalent for a solid meal. Religion makes no such blunder. The individual's religion may be egotistic, and those private realities which it keeps in touch with may be narrow enough; but at any rate it always remains infinitely less hollow and abstract, as far as it goes, than a science which prides itself on taking no account of anything private at all.

A bill of fare with one real raisin on it instead of the word 'raisin,' with one real egg instead of the word 'egg,' might be an inadequate meal, but it would at least be a commencement of reality. The contention of the survival-theory that we ought to stick to non-personal elements exclusively seems like saying that we ought to be satisfied forever with reading the naked bill of fare. I think, therefore, that however particular questions connected with our individual destinies may be answered, it is only by acknowledging them as genuine questions, and living in the sphere of thought which they open up, that we become profound. But to live thus is to be religious; so I unhesitatingly repudiate the survival-theory of religion, as being founded on an egregious mistake. It does not follow, because our ancestors made so many errors of fact and mixed them with their religion, that we should therefore leave off being religious at all.[8] By being religious we establish ourselves in possession of ultimate reality at the only points at which reality is given us to guard. Our responsible concern is with our private destiny, after all.

You see now why I have been so individualistic throughout these lectures, and why I have seemed so bent on rehabilitating the element of feeling in religion and subordinating its intellectual part. Individuality is founded in feeling; and the recesses of feeling, the darker, blinder strata of character, are the only places in the world in which we catch real fact in the making, and directly perceive how events happen, and how work is actually done.[9] Compared with this world of living individualized feelings, the world of generalized objects which the intellect contemplates is without solidity or life. As in stereoscopic or kinetoscopic pictures seen outside the instrument, the third dimension, the movement, the vital element, are not there. We get a beautiful picture of an express train supposed to be moving, but where in the picture, as I have heard a friend say, is the energy or the fifty miles an hour?[10]

Let us agree, then, that Religion, occupying herself with personal destinies and keeping thus in contact with the only absolute realities which we know, must necessarily play an eternal part in human history. The next thing to decide is what she reveals about those destinies, or whether indeed she reveals anything distinct enough to be considered a general message to mankind. We have done as you see, with our preliminaries, and our final summing up can now begin.

I am well aware that after all the palpitating documents which I have quoted, and all the perspectives of emotion-inspiring institution and belief that my previous lectures have opened, the dry analysis to which I now advance may appear to many of you like an anti-climax, a tapering-off and flattening out of the subject, instead of a crescendo of interest and result. I said awhile ago that the religious attitude of Protestants appears poverty-stricken to the Catholic imagination. Still more poverty-stricken, I fear, may my final summing up of the subject appear at first to some of you. On which account I pray you now to bear this point in mind, that in the present part of it I am expressly trying to reduce religion to its lowest admissible terms, to that minimum, free from individualistic excrescences, which all religions contain as their nucleus, and on which it may be hoped that all religious persons may agree. That established, we should have a result which might be small, but would at least be solid; and on it and round it the ruddier additional beliefs on which the different individuals make their venture might be grafted, and flourish as richly as you please. I shall add my own over-belief (which will be, I confess, of a somewhat pallid kind, as befits a critical philosopher), and you will, I hope, also add your over-beliefs, and we shall soon be in the varied world of concrete religious constructions once more. For the moment, let me dryly pursue the analytic part of the task.

Both thought and feeling are determinants of conduct, and the same conduct may be determined either by feeling or by thought. When we survey the whole field of religion, we find a great variety in the thoughts that have prevailed there; but the feelings on the one hand and the conduct on the other are almost always the same, for Stoic, Christian, and Buddhist saints are practically indistinguishable in their lives. The theories which Religion generates, being thus variable, are secondary; and if you wish to grasp her essence, you must look to the feelings and the conduct as being the more constant elements. It is between these two elements that the short circuit exists on which she carries on her principal business, while the ideas and symbols and other institutions form loop-lines which may be perfections and improvements, and may even some day all be united into one harmonious system, but which are not to be regarded as organs with an indispensable function, necessary at all times for religious life to go on. This seems to me the first conclusion which we are entitled to draw from the phenomena we have passed in review.

The next step is to characterize the feelings. To what psychological order do they belong?

The resultant outcome of them is in any case what Kant calls a 'sthenic' affection, an excitement of the cheerful, expansive, 'dynamogenic' order which, like any tonic, freshens our vital powers. In almost every lecture, but especially in the lectures on Conversion and on Saintliness, we have seen how this emotion overcomes temperamental melancholy and imparts endurance to the Subject, or a zest, or a meaning, or an enchantment and glory to the common objects of life.[11] The name of 'faith-state,' by which Professor Leuba designates it, is a good one.[12] It is a biological as well as a psychological condition, and Tolstoy is absolutely accurate in classing faith among the forces *by which men live.*[13] The total absence of it, anhedonia,[14] means collapse.

The faith-state may hold a very minimum of intellectual content. We saw examples of this in those sudden raptures of the divine presence, or in such mystical seizures as Dr. Bucke described.[15] It may be a mere vague enthusiasm, half spiritual, half vital, a courage, and a feeling that great and wondrous things are in the air.[16]

When, however, a positive intellectual content is associated with a faith-state, it gets invincibly stamped in upon belief,[17] and this explains the passionate loyalty of religious persons everywhere to the minutest details of their so widely differing creeds. Taking creeds and faith-state together, as forming 'religions,' and treating these as purely subjective phenomena, without regard to the question of their 'truth,' we are obliged, on account of their extraordinary influence upon action and endurance, to class them amongst the most important biological functions of mankind. Their stimulant and anaesthetic effect is so great that Professor Leuba, in a recent article,[18] goes so far as to say that so long as men can *use* their God, they care very little who he is, or even whether he is at all. "The truth of the matter can be put," says Leuba, "in this way: *God is not known, he is not understood; he is used*—sometimes as meat-purveyor, sometimes as moral support, sometimes as friend, sometimes as an object of love. If He proves himself useful, the religious conscious-ness asks for no more than that. Does God really exist? How does He exist? What is He? are so many irrelevant questions. Not God but life, more life, a larger, richer, more satisfying life, is in the last analysis the end of religion. The love of life, at any and every level of development, is the religious impulse."[19]

At this purely subjective rating, therefore, Religion must be consid-ered vindicated in a certain way from the attacks of her critics. It would seem that she cannot be a mere anachronism and survival, but must exert a permanent function, whether she be with or without intellectual con-tent, and whether, if she have any, it be true or false.

We must next pass beyond the point of view of merely subjective utility, and make inquiry into the intellectual content itself.

First, is there, under all the discrepancies of the creeds, a common nucleus to which they bear their testimony unanimously?

And second, ought we to consider the testimony true?

I will take up the first question first, and answer it immediately in the affirmative. The warring gods and formulas of the various religions do indeed cancel each other, but there is a certain uniform deliverance in which religions all appear to meet. It consists of two parts:

1. An uneasiness; and
2. Its solution.

1. The uneasiness, reduced to its simplest terms, is a sense that there is *something wrong about us* as we naturally stand.
2. The solution is a sense that *we are saved from the wrongness* by making proper connection with the higher powers.

In those more developed minds which alone we are studying, the wrongness takes a moral character, and the salvation takes a mystical tinge. I think we shall keep well within the limits of what is common to all such minds if we formulate the essence of their religious experience in terms like these:—

The individual, so far as he suffers from his wrongness and criticizes it, is to that extent consciously beyond it, and in at least possible touch with something higher, if anything higher exist. Along with the wrong part there is thus a better part of him, even though it may be but a most helpless germ. With which part he should identify his real being is by no means obvious at this stage; but when stage 2 (the stage of solution or salvation) arrives,[20] the man identifies his real being with the germinal higher part of himself; and does so in the following way. *He becomes conscious that this higher part is conterminous and continuous with a more of the same quality, which is operative in the universe outside of him, and which he can keep in working touch with, and in a fashion get on board of and save himself when all his lower being has gone to pieces in the wreck.*

It seems to me that all the phenomena are accurately describable in these very simple general terms.[21] They allow for the divided self and the struggle; they involve the change of personal centre and the surrender of the lower self; they express the appearance of exteriority of the helping power and yet account for our sense of union with it;[22] and they fully justify our feelings of security and joy. There is probably no autobiographic document, among all those which I have quoted, to which the description will not well apply. One need only add such specific details as will adapt it to various theologies and various personal temperaments, and one will then have the various experiences reconstructed in their individual forms.

So far, however, as this analysis goes, the experiences are only psychological phenomena. They possess, it is true, enormous biological worth. Spiritual strength really increases in the subject when he has them, a new life opens for him, and they seem to him a place of conflux where the forces of two universes meet; and yet this may be nothing but his subjective way of feeling things, a mood of his own fancy, in spite of the effects produced. I now turn to my second question: What is the objective 'truth' of their content?[23]

The part of the content concerning which the question of truth most pertinently arises is that 'MORE of the same quality' with which our own higher self appears in the experience to come into harmonious working relation. Is such a 'more' merely our own notion, or does it really exist? If so, in what shape does it exist? Does it act, as well as exist? And in what form should we conceive of that 'union' with it of which religious geniuses are so convinced?

It is in answering these questions that the various theologies perform their theoretic work, and that their divergencies most come to light. They all agree that the 'more' really exists; though some of them hold it to exist in the shape of a personal god or gods, while others are satisfied to conceive it as a stream of ideal tendency embedded in the eternal structure of the world. They all agree, moreover, that it acts as well as exists, and that something really is effected for the better when you throw your life into its hands. It is when they treat of the experience of 'union' with it that their speculative differences appear most clearly. Over this point pantheism and theism, nature and second birth, works and grace and karma, immortality and reincarnation, rationalism and mysticism, carry on inveterate disputes.

At the end of my lecture on Philosophy[24] I held out the notion that an impartial science of religions might sift out from the midst of their discrepancies a common body of doctrine which she might also formulate in terms to which physical science need not object. This, I said, she might adopt as her own reconciling hypothesis, and recommend it for general belief. I also said that in my last lecture I should have to try my own hand at framing such an hypothesis.

The time has now come for this attempt. Who says 'hypothesis' renounces the ambition to be coercive in his arguments. The most I can do is, accordingly, to offer something that may fit the facts so easily that your scientific logic will find no plausible pretext for vetoing your impulse to welcome it as true.

The 'more', as we called it, and the meaning of our 'union' with it, form the nucleus of our inquiry. Into what definite description can these words be translated, and for what definite facts do they stand? It would never do for us to place ourselves offhand at the position of a particular theology, the Christian theology, for example, and proceed immediately to define the 'more' as Jehovah, and the 'union' as his imputation to us of the righteousness of Christ. That would be unfair to other religions, and, from our present standpoint at least, would be an over-belief.

We must begin by using less particularized terms; and, since one of the duties of the science of religions is to keep religion in connection with the rest of Science, we shall do well to seek first of all a way of describing the 'more,' which psychologists may also recognize as real. The *subconscious self* is nowadays a well-accredited psychological entity; and I believe that in it we have exactly the mediating term required. Apart from all religious considerations, there is actually and literally more life in our total soul than we are at any time aware of. The exploration of the transmarginal field has hardly yet been seriously undertaken, but what Mr. Myers said in 1892 in his essay on the Subliminal Consciousness[25] is as true as when it was first written: "Each of us is in reality an abiding psychical entity far more extensive than he knows—an individuality which can never express itself completely through any corporeal manifestation. The Self manifests through the organism; but there is always some part of the Self unmanifested; and always, as it seems, some power of organic expression in abeyance or reserve."[26] Much of the content of this larger background against which our conscious being stands out in relief is insignificant. Imperfect memories, silly jingles, inhibitive timidities, 'dissolutive' phenomena of various sorts, as Myers calls them, enters into it for a large part. But in it many of the performances of genius seem also to have their origin; and in our study of conversion, of mystical experiences, and of prayer, we have seen how striking a part invasions from this region play in the religious life.

Let me then propose, as an hypothesis, that whatever it may be on its *farther* side, the 'more' with which in religious experience we feel ourselves connected is on its *hither* side the subconscious continuation of our conscious life. Starting thus with a recognized psychological fact as our basis, we seem to preserve a contact with 'science' which the ordinary theologian lacks. At the same time the theologian's contention that the religious man is moved by an external power is vindicated, for it is one of the peculiarities of invasions from the subconscious region to take on objective appearances, and to suggest to the Subject an external control. In the religious life the control is felt as 'higher'; but since on our hypothesis it is primarily the higher faculties of our own hidden mind which are controlling, the sense of union with the power beyond us is a sense of something, not merely apparently, but literally true.

This doorway into the subject seems to me the best one for a science of religions, for it mediates between a number of different points of view. Yet it is only a doorway, and difficulties present themselves as soon as we step through it, and ask how far our transmarginal consciousness carries us if we follow it on its remoter side. Here the over-beliefs begin: here mysticism and the conversion-rapture and Vedantism and transcendental idealism bring in their monistic interpretations[27] and tell us that the finite self rejoins the absolute self, for it was always one with God and identical with the soul of the world.[28] Here the prophets of all the different religions come with their visions, voices, raptures, and other openings, supposed by each to authenticate his own peculiar faith.

Those of us who are not personally favored with such specific revelations must stand outside of them altogether and, for the present at least, decide that, since they corroborate incompatible theological doctrines, they neutralize one another and leave no fixed results. If we follow any one of them, or if we follow philosophical theory and embrace monistic pantheism on non-mystical grounds, we do so in the exercise of our individual freedom, and build out our religion in the way most congruous with our personal susceptibilities. Among these susceptibilities intellectual ones play a decisive part. Although the religious question is primarily a question of life, of living or not living in the higher union which opens itself to us as a gift, yet the spiritual excitement in which the gift appears a real one will often fail to be aroused in an individual until certain particular intellectual beliefs or ideas which, as we say, come home to him, are touched.[29] These ideas will thus be essential to that individual's religion;—which is as much as to say that over-beliefs in various directions are absolutely indispensable, and that we should treat them with tenderness and tolerance so long as they are not intolerant themselves. As I have elsewhere written, the most interesting and valuable things about a man are usually his over-beliefs.

Disregarding the over-beliefs, and confining ourselves to what is common and generic, we have in *the fact that the conscious person is continuous with a wider self through which saving experiences come*,[30] a positive content of religious experience which, it seems to me, *is literally and objectively true as far as it goes*. If I now proceed to state my own hypothesis about the farther limits of this extension of our personality, I shall be offering my own over-belief—though I know it will appear a sorry under-belief to some of you—for which I can only bespeak the same indulgence which in a converse case I should accord to yours.

The farther limits of our being plunge, it seems to me, into an altogether other dimension of existence from the sensible and merely 'understandable' world. Name it the mystical region, or the supernatural region, whichever you choose. So far as our ideal impulses originate in this region (and most of them do originate in it, for we find them possessing us in a way for which we cannot articulately account), we belong to it in a more intimate sense than that in which we belong to the visible world, for we belong in the most intimate sense wherever our ideals belong. Yet the unseen region in question is not merely ideal, for it produces effects in this world. When we commune with it, work is actually done upon our finite personality, for we are turned into new men, and consequences in the way of conduct follow in the natural world upon our regenerative change.[31] But that which produces effects within another reality must be termed a reality itself, so I feel as if we had no philosophic excuse for calling the unseen or mystical world unreal.

God is the natural appellation, for us Christians at least, for the supreme reality, so I will call this higher part of the universe by the name of God.[32] We and God have business with each other; and in opening ourselves to his influence our deepest destiny is fulfilled. The universe, at those parts of it which our personal being constitutes, takes a turn genuinely for the worse or for the better in proportion as each one of us fulfills or evades God's demands. As far as this goes I probably have you with me, for I only translate into schematic language what I may call the instinctive belief of mankind: God is real since he produces real effects.

The real effects in question, so far as I have as yet admitted them, are exerted on the personal centers of energy of the various subjects, but the spontaneous faith of most of the subjects is that they embrace a wider sphere than this. Most religious men believe (or 'know,' if they be mystical) that not only they themselves, but the whole universe of beings to whom the God is present, are secure in his parental hands. There is a sense, a dimension, they are sure, in which we are *all* saved, in spite of the gates of hell and all adverse terrestrial appearances. God's existence is the guarantee of an ideal order that shall be permanently preserved. This world may indeed, as science assures us, some day burn up or freeze; but if it is part of his order, the old ideals are sure to be brought elsewhere to fruition, so that where God is, tragedy is only provisional and partial, and shipwreck and dissolution are not the absolutely final things. Only when this farther step of faith concerning God is taken, and remote objective consequences are predicted, does religion, as it seems to me, get wholly free from the first immediate subjective experience, and bring a *real hypothesis* into play. A good hypothesis in science must have other properties than those of the phenomenon it is immediately invoked to explain, otherwise it is not prolific enough. God, meaning only what enters into the religious man's experience of union, falls short of being an hypothesis of this more useful order. He needs to enter into wider cosmic relations in order to justify the subject's absolute confidence and peace.

That the God with whom, starting from the hither side of our own extra-marginal self, we come at its remoter margin into commerce should be the absolute world-ruler, is of course a very considerable over-belief. Over-belief as it is, though, it is an article of almost everyone's religion. Most of us pretend in some way to prop it upon our philosophy, but the philosophy itself is really propped upon this faith. What is this but to say that Religion, in her fullest exercise of function, is not a mere illumination of facts already elsewhere given, not a mere passion, like love, which views things in a rosier light. It is indeed that, as we have seen abundantly. But it is something more, namely, a postulator of new *facts* as well.

The world interpreted religiously is not the materialistic world over again, with an altered expression; it must have, over and above the altered expression, *a natural constitution* different at some point from that which a materialistic world would have. It must be such that different events can be expected in it, different conduct must be required.

This thoroughly 'pragmatic' view of religion has usually been taken as a matter of course by common men. They have interpolated divine miracles into the field of nature, they have built a heaven out beyond the grave. It is only transcendentalist metaphysicians who think that, without adding any concrete details to Nature, or subtracting any, but by simply calling it the expression of absolute spirit, you make it more divine just as it stands. I believe the pragmatic way of taking religion to be the deeper way. It gives it body as well as soul, it makes it claim, as everything real must claim, some characteristic realm of fact as its very own. What the more characteristically divine facts are, apart from the actual inflow of energy in the faith-state and the prayer-state, I know not. But the over-belief on which I am ready to make my personal venture is that they exist. The whole drift of my education goes to persuade me that the world of our present consciousness is only one out of many worlds of consciousness that exist, and that those other worlds must contain experiences which have a meaning for our life also; and that although in the main their experiences and those of this world keep discrete, yet the two become continuous at certain points, and higher energies filter in. By being faithful in my poor measure to this over-belief, I seem to myself to keep more sane and true. I *can*, of course, put myself into the sectarian scientist's attitude, and imagine vividly that the world of sensations and of scientific laws and objects may be all. But whenever I do this, I hear that inward monitor of which W. K. Clifford once wrote, whispering the word "bosh!" Humbug is humbug, even though it bear the scientific name, and the total expression of human experience, as I view it objectively, invincibly urges me beyond the narrow 'scientific' bounds. Assuredly, the real world is of a different temperament—more intricately built than physical science allows. So my objective and my subjective conscience both hold me to the over-belief which I express. Who knows whether the faithfulness of individuals here below to their own poor over-beliefs may not actually help God in turn to be more effectively faithful to his own greater tasks?

18

Pragmatism and Religion

At the close of the last lecture I reminded you of the first one, in which I had opposed tough-mindedness to tender-mindedness and recommended pragmatism as their mediator. Tough-mindedness positively rejects tender-mindedness's hypothesis of an eternal perfect edition of the universe coexisting with our finite experience.

On pragmatic principles we cannot reject any hypothesis if consequences useful to life flow from it. Universal conceptions, as things to take account of, may be as real for pragmatism as particular sensations are. They have indeed no meaning and no reality if they have no use. But if they have any use they have that amount of meaning. And the meaning will be true if the use squares well with life's other uses.

Well, the use of the Absolute is proved by the whole course of men's religious history. The eternal arms are then beneath. Remember Vivekananda's use of the Atman: it is indeed not a scientific use, for we can make no particular deductions from it. It is emotional and spiritual altogether.

It is always best to discuss things by the help of concrete examples. Let me read therefore some of those verses entitled "To You" by Walt Whitman—"You" of course meaning the reader or hearer of the poem whosoever he or she may be.

Whoever you are, now I place my hand upon you, that you be my poem;
I whisper with my lips close to your ear,
I have loved many women and men, but I love none better than you.

O I have been dilatory and dumb;
I should have made my way straight to you long ago;
I should have blabb'd nothing but you, I should have chanted
   nothing but you.

I will leave all, and come and make the hymns of you;
None have understood you, but I understand you;
None have done justice to you—you have not done justice to
   yourself;
None but have found you imperfect—I only find no imperfection in
   you.

O I could sing such grandeurs and glories about you!
You have not known what you are—you have slumber'd upon
   yourself all your life;
What you have done returns already in mockeries.

But the mockeries are not you;
Underneath them, and within them, I see you lurk;
I pursue you where none else has pursued you;
Silence, the desk, the flippant expression, the night, the accustom'd
   routine,
if these conceal you from others, or from yourself, they do not conceal you from me;
The shaved face, the unsteady eye, the impure complexion, if these
   balk others, they do not balk me,
The pert apparel, the deform'd attitude, drunkenness, greed,
   premature death,
all these I part aside.

There is no endowment in man or woman that is not tallied in you;
There is no virtue, no beauty, in man or woman, but as good is in you;
No pluck, no endurance in others, but as good is in you;
No pleasure waiting for others, but an equal pleasure waits for you.

Whoever you are! claim your own at any hazard!
These shows of the east and west are tame, compared to you;

These immense meadows—these interminable rivers—you are
    immense and interminable as they;
You are he or she who is master or mistress over them,
Master or mistress in your own right over Nature, elements, pain,
    passion, dissolution.

The hopples fall from your ankles—you find an unfailing sufficiency;
Old or young, male or female, rude, low, rejected by the rest,
    whatever you are promulges itself,
Through birth, life, death, burial, the means are provided,
    nothing is scanted;
Through angers, losses, ambition, ignorance, ennui,
    what you are picks its way.

Verily a fine and moving poem, in any case, but there are two ways of taking it, both useful.

One is the monistic way, the mystical way of pure cosmic emotion. The glories and grandeurs, they are yours absolutely, even in the midst of your defacements. Whatever may happen to you, whatever you may appear to be, inwardly you are safe. Look back, *lie* back, on your true principle of being! This is the famous way of quietism, of indifferentism. Its enemies compare it to a spiritual opium. Yet pragmatism must respect this way, for it has massive historic vindication.

But pragmatism sees another way to be respected also, the pluralistic way of interpreting the poem. The you so glorified, to which the hymn is sung, may mean your better possibilities phenomenally taken, or the specific redemptive effects even of your failures, upon yourself or others. It may mean your loyalty to the possibilities of others whom you admire and love so, that you are willing to accept your own poor life, for it is that glory's partner. You can at least appreciate, applaud, furnish the audience, of so brave a total world. Forget the low in yourself, then, think only of the high. Identify your life therewith; then, through angers, losses, ignorance, ennui, whatever you thus make yourself, whatever you thus most deeply are, picks its way.

In either way of taking the poem, it encourages fidelity to ourselves.

Both ways satisfy; both sanctify the human flux. Both paint the portrait of the *you* on a gold-background. But the background of the first way is the static One, while in the second way it means possibles in the plural, genuine possibles, and it has all the restlessness of that conception.

Noble enough is either way of reading the poem; but plainly the pluralistic way agrees with the pragmatic temper best, for it immediately suggests an infinitely larger number of the details of future experience to our mind. It sets definite activities in us at work. Although this second way seems prosaic and earthborn in comparison with the first way, yet no one can accuse it of tough-mindedness in any brutal sense of the term. Yet if, as pragmatists, you should positively set up the second way *against* the first way, you would very likely be misunderstood. You would be accused of denying nobler conceptions, and of being an ally of tough-mindedness in the worst sense.

You remember the letter from a member of this audience from which I read some extracts at our previous meeting. Let me read you an additional extract now. It shows a vagueness in realizing the alternatives before us which I think is very widespread.

"I believe," writes my friend and correspondent, "in pluralism; I believe that in our search for truth we leap from one floating cake of ice to another, on an infinite sea, and that by each of our acts we make new truths possible and old ones impossible; I believe that each man is responsible for making the universe better, and that if he does not do this it will be in so far left undone.

"Yet at the same time I am willing to endure that my children should be incurably sick and suffering (as they are not) and I myself stupid and yet with brains enough to see my stupidity, only on one condition, namely, that through the construction, in imagination and by reasoning, of *a rational unity of all things,* I can conceive my acts and my thoughts and my troubles as *supplemented by all the other phenomena of the world, and as forming—when thus supplemented—a scheme which I approve and adopt as my own*; and for my part I refuse to be persuaded that we cannot look beyond the obvious pluralism of the naturalist and pragmatist to a logical unity in which they take no interest or stock."

Such a fine expression of personal faith warms the heart of the hearer. But how much does it clear his philosophic head? Does the writer consistently favor the monistic, or the pluralistic, interpretation of the world's poem? His troubles become atoned for *when thus supplemented*, he says, supplemented, that is, by all the remedies that *the other phenomena* may supply. Obviously here the writer faces forward into the particulars of experience, which he interprets in a pluralistic-melioristic way.

But he believes himself to face backward. He speaks of what he calls the rational *unity* of things, when all the while he really means their possible empirical *unification*. He supposes at the same time that the pragmatist, because he criticizes rationalism's abstract One, is cut off from the consolation of believing in the saving possibilities of the concrete many. He fails in short to distinguish between taking the world's perfection as a necessary principle, and taking it only as a possible *terminus ad quem*.

I regard the writer of this letter as a genuine pragmatist, but as a pragmatist *sans le savoir*. He appears to me as one of that numerous class of philosophic amateurs whom I spoke of in my first lecture, as wishing to have all the good things going, without being too careful as to how they agree or disagree. "Rational unity of all things" is so inspiring a formula, that he brandishes it offhand, and abstractly accuses pluralism of conflicting with it (for the bare names do conflict), although concretely he means by it just the pragmatistically unified and ameliorated world. Most of us remain in this essential vagueness, and it is well that we should, but in the interest of clear-headedness it is well that some of us should go farther, so I will try now to focus a little more discriminatingly on this particular religious point.

Is then this you of yous, this absolutely real world, this unity that yields the moral inspiration and has the religious value, to be taken monistically or pluralistically? Is it *ante rem* or *in rebus*? Is it a principle or an end, an absolute or an ultimate, a first or a last? Does it make you look forward or lie back? It is certainly worth while not to clump the two things together, for if discriminated, they have decidedly diverse meanings for life.

Please observe that the whole dilemma revolves pragmatically about the notion of the world's possibilities. Intellectually, rationalism invokes its absolute principle of unity as a ground of possibility for the many facts. Emotionally, it sees it as a container and limiter of possibilities, a guarantee that the upshot shall be good. Taken in this way, the absolute makes all good things certain, and all bad things impossible (in the eternal, namely), and may be said to transmute the entire category of possibility into categories more secure. One sees at this point that the great religious difference lies between the men who insist that the world *must and shall be*, and those who are contented with believing that the world *may be*, saved. The whole clash of rationalistic and empiricist religion is thus over the validity of possibility. It is necessary therefore to begin by focusing upon that word. What may the word 'possible' definitely mean?

To unreflecting men the possible means a sort of third estate of being, less real than existence, more real than non-existence, a twilight realm, a hybrid status, a limbo into which and out of which realities ever and anon are made to pass. Such a conception is of course too vague and nondescript to satisfy us. Here, as elsewhere, the only way to extract a term's meaning is to use the pragmatic method on it. When you say that a thing is possible, what difference does it make?

It makes at least this difference that if anyone calls it impossible you can contradict him, if anyone calls it actual you can contradict *him*, and if anyone calls it necessary you can contradict him too. But these privileges of contradiction don't amount to much. When you say a thing is possible, does not that make some farther difference in terms of actual fact?

It makes at least this negative difference that if the statement be true, it follows that *there is nothing extant capable of preventing* the possible thing. The absence of real grounds of interference may thus be said to make things *not impossible*, possible therefore in the *bare* or *abstract* sense.

But most possibles are not bare, they are concretely grounded, or well-grounded, as we say. What does this mean pragmatically? It means, not only that there are no preventive conditions present, but that some of the conditions of production of the possible thing actually are here. Thus a concretely possible chicken means: (1) that the idea of chicken contains no essential self-contradiction; (2) that no boys, skunks, or other enemies are about; and (3) that at least an actual egg exists. Possible chicken means actual egg—plus actual sitting hen, or incubator, or what not. As the actual conditions approach completeness the chicken becomes a better-and-better-grounded possibility. When the conditions are entirely complete, it ceases to be a possibility, and turns into an actual fact.

Let us apply this notion to the salvation of the world. What does it pragmatically mean to say that this is possible? It means that some of the conditions of the world's deliverance do actually exist. The more of them there are existent, the fewer preventing conditions you can find, the better-grounded is the salvation's possibility, the more *probable* does the fact of the deliverance become.

So much for our preliminary look at possibility.

Now it would contradict the very spirit of life to say that our minds must be indifferent and neutral in questions like that of the world's salvation. Anyone who pretends to be neutral writes himself down here as a fool and a sham. We all do wish to minimize the insecurity of the universe; we are and ought to be unhappy when we regard it as exposed to every enemy and open to every life-destroying draft. Nevertheless there are unhappy men who think the salvation of the world impossible. Theirs is the doctrine known as pessimism.

Optimism in turn would be the doctrine that thinks the world's salvation inevitable.

Midway between the two there stands what may be called the doctrine of meliorism, tho it has hitherto figured less as a doctrine than as an attitude in human affairs. Optimism has always been the regnant *doctrine* in European philosophy. Pessimism was only recently introduced by Schopenhauer and counts few systematic defenders as yet. Meliorism treats salvation as neither inevitable nor impossible. It treats it as a possibility, which becomes more and more of a probability the more numerous the actual conditions of salvation become.

It is clear that pragmatism must incline towards meliorism. Some conditions of the world's salvation are actually extant, and she cannot possibly close her eyes to this fact: and should the residual conditions come, salvation would become an accomplished reality. Naturally the

terms I use here are exceedingly summary. You may interpret the word
'salvation' in any way you like, and make it as diffuse and distributive, or
as climacteric and integral a phenomenon as you please.

Take, for example, any one of us in this room with the ideals which
he cherishes, and is willing to live and work for. Every such ideal realized
will be one moment in the world's salvation. But these particular ideals
are not bare abstract possibilities. They are grounded, they are *live* possibilities, for we are their live champions and pledges, and if the complementary conditions come and add themselves, our ideals will become
actual things. What now are the complementary conditions? They are
first such a mixture of things as will in the fullness of time give us a
chance, a gap that we can spring into, and, finally, *our act*.

Does our act then *create* the world's salvation so far as it makes room
for itself, so far as it leaps into the gap? Does it create, not the whole
world's salvation of course, but just so much of this as itself covers of the
world's extent?

Here I take the bull by the horns, and in spite of the whole crew of
rationalists and monists, of whatever brand they be, I ask *why not*? Our
acts, our turning-places, where we seem to ourselves to make ourselves
and grow, are the parts of the world to which we are closest, the parts of
which our knowledge is the most intimate and complete. Why should
we not take them at their face-value? Why may they not be the actual
turning-places and growing-places which they seem to be, of the world—
why not the workshop of being, where we catch fact in the making, so
that nowhere may the world grow in any other kind of way than this?

Irrational! we are told. How can new being come in local spots and
patches which add themselves or stay away at random, independently of
the rest? There must be a reason for our acts, and where in the last resort
can any reason be looked for save in the material pressure or the logical
compulsion of the total nature of the world? There can be but one real
agent of growth, or seeming growth, anywhere, and that agent is the integral world itself. It may grow all-over, if growth there be, but that single
parts should grow *per se* is irrational.

But if one talks of rationality—and of reasons for things, and insists that they can't just come in spots, what *kind* of a reason can there ultimately be why anything should come at all? Talk of logic and necessity and categories and the absolute and the contents of the whole philosophical machine-shop as you will, the only *real* reason I can think of why anything should ever come is that *someone wishes it to be here*. It is *demanded*, demanded, it may be, to give relief to no matter how small a fraction of the world's mass. This is *living reason*, and compared with it material causes and logical necessities are spectral things.

In short the only fully rational world would be the world of wishing-caps, the world of telepathy, where every desire is fulfilled instanter, without having to consider or placate surrounding or intermediate powers. This is the Absolute's own world. He calls upon the phenomenal world to be, and it *is*, exactly as he calls for it, no other condition being required. In our world, the wishes of the individual are only one condition. Other individuals are there with other wishes and they must be propitiated first. So Being grows under all sorts of resistances in this world of the many, and, from compromise to compromise, only gets organized gradually into what may be called secondarily rational shape. We approach the wishing-cap type of organization only in a few departments of life. We want water and we turn a faucet. We want a kodak-picture and we press a button. We want information and we telephone. We want to travel and we buy a ticket. In these and similar cases, we hardly need to do more than the wishing—the world is rationally organized to do the rest.

But this talk of rationality is a parenthesis and a digression. What we were discussing was the idea of a world growing not integrally but piecemeal by the contributions of its several parts. Take the hypothesis seriously and as a live one. Suppose that the world's author put the case to you before creation, saying: "I am going to make a world not certain to be saved, a world the perfection of which shall be conditional merely, the condition being that each several agent does its own 'level best.' I offer you the chance of taking part in such a world. Its safety, you see, is unwarranted. It is a real adventure, with real danger, yet it may win through. It is a social scheme of co-operative work genuinely to be done. Will you join the procession? Will you trust yourself and trust the other agents enough to face the risk?"

Should you in all seriousness, if participation in such a world were proposed to you, feel bound to reject it as not safe enough? Would you say that, rather than be part and parcel of so fundamentally pluralistic and irrational a universe, you preferred to relapse into the slumber of nonentity from which you had been momentarily aroused by the tempter's voice?

Of course if you are normally constituted, you would do nothing of the sort. There is a healthy-minded buoyancy in most of us which such a universe would exactly fit. We would therefore accept the offer—"Top! und schlag auf schlag!" It would be just like the world we practically live in; and loyalty to our old nurse Nature would forbid us to say no. The world proposed would seem 'rational' to us in the most living way.

Most of us, I say, would therefore welcome the proposition and add our *fiat* to the *fiat* of the creator. Yet perhaps some would not; for there are morbid minds in every human collection, and to them the prospect of a universe with only a fighting chance of safety would probably make no appeal. There are moments of discouragement in us all, when we are sick of self and tired of vainly striving. Our own life breaks down, and we fall into the attitude of the prodigal son. We mistrust the chances of things. We want a universe where we can just give up, fall on our father's neck, and be absorbed into the absolute life as a drop of water melts into the river or the sea.

The peace and rest, the security desiderated at such moments is security against the bewildering accidents of so much finite experience. Nirvana means safety from this everlasting round of adventures of which the world of sense consists. The hindoo and the buddhist, for this is essentially their attitude, are simply afraid, afraid of more experience, afraid of life.

And to men of this complexion, religious monism comes with its consoling words: "All is needed and essential—even you with your sick soul and heart. All are one with God, and with God all is well. The everlasting arms are beneath, whether in the world of finite appearances you seem to fail or to succeed." There can be no doubt that when men are reduced to their last sick extremity absolutism is the only saving scheme. Pluralistic moralism simply makes their teeth chatter, it refrigerates the very heart within their breast.

So we see concretely two types of religion in sharp contrast. Using our old terms of comparison, we may say that the absolutistic scheme appeals to the tender-minded while the pluralistic scheme appeals to the tough. Many persons would refuse to call the pluralistic scheme religious at all. They would call it moralistic, and would apply the word religious to the monistic scheme alone. Religion in the sense of self-surrender, and moralism in the sense of self-sufficingness, have been pitted against each other as incompatibles frequently enough in the history of human thought.

We stand here before the final question of philosophy. I said in my fourth lecture that I believed the monistic-pluralistic alternative to be the deepest and most pregnant question that our minds can frame. Can it be that the disjunction is a final one? that only one side can be true? Are a pluralism and monism genuine incompatibles? So that, if the world were really pluralistically constituted, if it really existed distributively and were made up of a lot of eaches, it could only be saved piecemeal and *de facto* as the result of their behavior, and its epic history in no wise short-circuited by some essential oneness in which the severalness were already 'taken up' beforehand and eternally 'overcome'? If this were so, we should have to choose one philosophy or the other. We could not say 'yes, yes' to both alternatives. There would have to be a 'no' in our relations with the possible. We should confess an ultimate disappointment: we could not remain healthy-minded and sick-minded in one indivisible act.

Of course as human beings we can be healthy minds on one day and sick souls on the next; and as amateur dabblers in philosophy we may perhaps be allowed to call ourselves monistic pluralists, or free-will determinists, or whatever else may occur to us of a reconciling kind. But as philosophers aiming at clearness and consistency, and feeling the pragmatistic need of squaring truth with truth, the question is forced upon us of frankly adopting either the tender or the robustious type of thought. In particular *this* query has always come home to me: May not the claims of tender-mindedness go too far? May not the notion of a world already saved *in toto* anyhow, be too saccharine to stand? May not religious optimism be too idyllic? Must *all* be saved? Is *no* price to be paid in the work of salvation? Is the last word sweet? Is all 'yes, yes' in the universe? Doesn't the fact of 'no' stand at the very core of life? Doesn't the very 'seriousness' that we attribute to life mean that ineluctable noes and losses form a part of it, that there are genuine sacrifices somewhere, and that something permanently drastic and bitter always remains at the bottom of its cup?

I cannot speak officially as a pragmatist here; all I can say is that my own pragmatism offers no objection to my taking sides with this more moralistic view, and giving up the claim of total reconciliation. The possibility of this is involved in the pragmatistic willingness to treat pluralism as a serious hypothesis. In the end it is our faith and not our logic that decides such questions, and I deny the right of any pretended logic to veto my own faith. I find myself willing to take the universe to be really dangerous and adventurous, without therefore backing out and crying 'no play.' I am willing to think that the prodigal-son attitude, open to us as it is in many vicissitudes, is not the right and final attitude towards the whole of life. I am willing that there should be real losses and real losers, and no total preservation of all that is. I can believe in the ideal as an ultimate, not as an origin, and as an extract, not the whole. When the cup is poured off, the dregs are left behind forever, but the possibility of what is poured off is sweet enough to accept.

As a matter of fact countless human imaginations live in this moralistic and epic kind of a universe, and find its disseminated and strung-along successes sufficient for their rational needs. There is a finely translated epigram in the Greek anthology which admirably expresses this state of mind, this acceptance of loss as unatoned for, even though the lost element might be one's self:

> "A shipwrecked sailor, buried on this coast,
> Bids you set sail.
> Full many a gallant bark, when we were lost,
> Weathered the gale."

Those puritans who answered 'yes' to the question: Are you willing to be damned for God's glory? were in this objective and magnanimous condition of mind. The way of escape from evil on this system is *not* by getting it 'aufgehoben,' or preserved in the whole as an element essential but 'overcome.' *It is by dropping it out altogether, throwing it overboard and getting beyond it, helping to make a universe that shall forget its very place and name.*

It is then perfectly possible to accept sincerely a drastic kind of a universe from which the element of 'seriousness' is not to be expelled. Whoso does so is, it seems to me, a genuine pragmatist. He is willing to live on a scheme of uncertified possibilities which he trusts; willing to pay with his own person, if need be, for the realization of the ideals which he frames.

What now actually *are* the other forces which he trusts to co-operate with him, in a universe of such a type? They are at least his fellow men, in the stage of being which our actual universe has reached. But are there not superhuman forces also, such as religious men of the pluralistic type we have been considering have always believed in? Their words may have sounded monistic when they said "there is no God but God"; but the original polytheism of mankind has only imperfectly and vaguely sublimated itself into monotheism, and monotheism itself, so far as it was religious and not a scheme of class-room instruction for the metaphysicians, has always viewed God as but one helper, *primus inter pares*, in the midst of all the shapers of the great world's fate.

I fear that my previous lectures, confined as they have been to human and humanistic aspects, may have left the impression on many of you that pragmatism means methodically to leave the superhuman out. I have shown small respect indeed for the Absolute, and I have until this moment spoken of no other superhuman hypothesis but that. But I trust that you see sufficiently that the Absolute has nothing but its superhumanness in common with the theistic God. On pragmatistic principles, if the hypothesis of God works satisfactorily in the widest sense of the word, it is true. Now whatever its residual difficulties may be, experience shows that it certainly does work, and that the problem is to build it out and determine it, so that it will combine satisfactorily with all the other working truths. I cannot start upon a whole theology at the end of this last lecture; but when I tell you that I have written a book on men's religious experience, which on the whole has been regarded as making for the reality of God, you will perhaps exempt my own pragmatism from the charge of being an atheistic system. I firmly disbelieve, myself, that our human experience is the highest form of experience extant in the universe. I believe rather that we stand in much the same relation to the whole of the universe as our canine and feline pets do to the whole of human life. They inhabit our drawing-rooms and libraries. They take part in scenes of whose significance they have no inkling. They are merely tangent to curves of history the beginnings and ends and forms of which pass wholly beyond their ken. So we are tangents to the wider life of things. But, just as many of the dog's and cat's ideals coincide with our ideals, and the dogs and cats have daily living proof of the fact, so we may well believe, on the proofs that religious experience affords, that higher powers exist and are at work to save the world on ideal lines similar to our own.

You see that pragmatism can be called religious, if you allow that religion can be pluralistic or merely melioristic in type. But whether you will finally put up with that type of religion or not is a question that only you yourself can decide. Pragmatism has to postpone dogmatic answer, for we do not yet know certainly which type of religion is going to work best in the long run. The various overbeliefs of men, their several faith-ventures, are in fact what are needed to bring the evidence in. You will probably make your own ventures severally. If radically tough, the hurly-burly of the sensible facts of nature will be enough for you, and you will need no religion at all. If radically tender, you will take up with the more monistic form of religion: the pluralistic form, with its reliance on possibilities that are not necessities, will not seem to afford you security enough.

But if you are neither tough nor tender in an extreme and radical sense, but mixed as most of us are, it may seem to you that the type of pluralistic and moralistic religion that I have offered is as good a religious synthesis as you are likely to find. Between the two extremes of crude naturalism on the one hand and transcendental absolutism on the other, you may find that what I take the liberty of calling the pragmatistic or melioristic type of theism is exactly what you require.

Notes

CHAPTER 1. WHAT IS AN EMOTION?

1. Of course the physiological question arises, *how* are the changes felt?—*after* they are produced, by the sensory nerves of the organs bringing back to the brain a report of the modifications that have occurred? or *before* they are produced, by our being conscious of the outgoing nerve-currents starting on their way downward towards the parts they are to excite? I believe all the evidence we have to be in favor of the former alternative. The question is too minute for discussion here, but I have said something about it in a paper entitled "The Feeling of Effort," in the *Anniversary Memoirs of the Boston Natural History Society*, 1880 (translated in *La Critique Philosophique* for that year, and summarized in *Mind* XX., 582). See also G. E. Müller's *Grundlegung der Psychophysik*, §110.

2. Let it be noted in passing that this personal self-consciousness seems an altogether bodily affair, largely a consciousness of our attitude, and that, like other emotions, it reacts on its physical condition, and leads to modifications of the attitude,—to a certain rigidity in most men, but in children to a regular twisting and squirming fit, and in women to various gracefully shy poses.

3. This is the opposite of what happens in injuries to the brain, whether from outward violence, inward rupture or tumor, or mere starvation from disease. The cortical permeability seems reduced, so that excitement, instead of propagating itself laterally through the ideational channels as before, tends to take the downward track into the organs of the body. The consequence is that we have tears, laughter, and temper-fits, on the most insignificant provocation, accompanying a proportional feebleness in logical thought and the power of volitional attention and decision.

4. It must be confessed that there are cases of morbid fear in which objec-

tively the heart is not much perturbed. These, however, fail to prove anything against our theory, for it is of course possible that the cortical centers normally percipient of dread as a complex of cardiac and other organic sensations due to real bodily change, should become *primarily* excited in brain-disease, and give rise to an hallucination of the changes being there,—an hallucination of dread, consequently, coexistent with a comparatively calm pulse, &c. I say it is possible, for I am ignorant of observations which might test the fact. Trance, ecstasy, &c., offer analogous examples,—not to speak of ordinary dreaming. Under all these conditions one may have the liveliest subjective feelings, either of eye or ear, or of the more visceral and emotional sort, as a result of pure nerve-central activity, with complete peripheral repose. Whether the subjective strength of the feeling be due in these cases to the actual energy of the central disturbance, or merely to the narrowing of the field of consciousness, need not concern us. In the asylum cases of melancholy, there is usually a narrowing of the field.

5. Quoted by Semal: *De la Sensibilité générale dans les Affections mélancoliques*, Paris, 1876, pp. 130–35.

6. "Ein Fall von allgemeiner Anaesthesie," *Inaugural-Dissertation*. Heidelberg, Winter, 1882.

CHAPTER 4. DOES 'CONSCIOUSNESS' EXIST?

1. Articles by Baldwin, Ward, Bawden, King, Alexander, and others. Dr. Perry is frankly over the border.

2. In my *Psychology* I have tried to show that we need no knower other than the 'passing thought.'

3. G. E. Moore: *Mind*, vol. XII, N. S., p. 450.

4. Paul Natorp: *Einleitung in die Psychologie*, 1888, pp. 14, 112.

5. "Figuratively speaking, consciousness may be said to be the one universal solvent, or menstruum, in which the different concrete kinds of psychic acts and facts are contained, whether in concealed or in obvious form." G. T. Ladd: *Psychology, Descriptive and Explanatory*, 1894, p. 30.

6. Here as elsewhere the relations are of course *experienced* relations, members of the same originally chaotic manifold of non-perceptual experience of which the related terms themselves are parts.

7. Of the representative function of non-perceptual experience as a

whole, I will say a word in a subsequent article: it leads too far into the general theory of knowledge for much to be said about it in a short paper like this.

8. *Grundzüge der Psychologie*, vol. I, p. 48.

9. Cf. A. L. Hodder: *The Adversaries of the Sceptic*, New York, 1899, pp. 94–99.

10. For simplicity's sake I confine my exposition to 'external' reality. But there is also the system of ideal reality in which the room plays its part. Relations of comparison, of classification, serial order, value, also are stubborn, assign a definite place to the room, unlike the incoherence of its places in the mere rhapsody of our successive thoughts.

11. Note the ambiguity of this term, which is taken sometimes objectively and sometimes subjectively.

12. In the *Psychological Review* for July [1904] of this year, Dr. R. B. Perry has published a view of Consciousness which comes nearer to mine than any other with which I am acquainted. At present, Dr. Perry thinks every field of experience is so much 'fact.' It becomes 'opinion' or 'thought' only in retrospection, when a fresh experience, thinking the same object, alters and corrects it. But the corrective experience becomes itself in turn corrected, and thus experience as a whole is a process in which what is objective originally forever turns subjective, turns into our apprehension of the object. I strongly recommend Dr. Perry's admirable article to my readers.

13. I have given it partial account of the matter in *Mind*, vol. X, p. 27, 1885, and in the *Psychological Review*, vol. II, p. 105, 1895. See also C. A. Strong's article in the *Journal of Philosophy, Psychology and Scientific Methods*, vol. I, p. 253, May 19, 1904. I hope myself very soon to recur to the matter in this Journal.

14. Spencer's proof of his 'Transfigured Realism' (his doctrine that there is an absolutely non-mental reality) comes to mind as a splendid instance of the impossibility of establishing radical heterogeneity between thought and thing. All his painfully accumulated points of difference run gradually into their opposites, and are full of exceptions.

15. I speak here of the complete inner life in which the mind plays freely with its materials. Of course the mind's free play is restricted when it seeks to copy real things in real space.

CHAPTER 5. A WORLD OF PURE EXPERIENCE

1. The psychology books have of late described the facts here with approximate adequacy. I may refer to the chapters on 'The Stream of Thought' and on the Self in my own *Principles of Psychology*, as well as to S. H. Hodgson's *Metaphysic of Experience*, vol. I, chap. VII and VIII.

2. For brevity's sake I altogether omit mention of the type constituted by knowledge of the truth of general propositions. This type has been thoroughly and, so far as I can see, satisfactorily, elucidated in Dewey's *Studies in Logical Theory*. Such propositions are reducible to the *S-is-P* form; and the 'terminus' that verifies and fulfils is the *SP* in combination. Of course percepts may be involved in the mediating experiences, or in the 'satisfactoriness' of the P in its new position.

3. These articles and their doctrine, unnoticed apparently by any one else, have lately gained favorable comment from Professor Strong in this Journal, for May 12, 1904. Dr. Dickinson S. Miller has independently thought out the same results, which Strong accordingly dubs the James-Miller theory of cognition.

4. Mr. Bradley, not professing to know his absolute *aliunde*, nevertheless derealizes Experience by alleging it to be everywhere infected with self-contradiction. His arguments seem almost purely verbal, but this is no place for arguing that point out.

5. Of which all that need be said in this essay is that it also can be conceived as functional, and defined in terms of transitions, or of the possibility of such.

6. The notion that our objects are inside of our respective heads is not seriously defensible, so I pass it by.

7. Our minds and these ejective realities would still have space (or pseudo-space, as I believe Professor Strong calls the medium of interaction between 'things-in-themselves') in common. These would exist *where*, and begin to act *where*, we locate the molecules, etc., and *where* we perceive the sensible phenomena explained thereby.

8. I have said something of this latter alliance in an article entitled "Humanism and Truth," in *Mind*, October 1904.

CHAPTER 6. HOW TWO MINDS
CAN KNOW ONE THING

1. Vol. 1, p. 477, September 1, 1904.

2. "A World of Pure Experience," *ibid.*, Vol. I, p. 564, October 13, 1904.

3. "The Thing and Its Relations," in the present volume of this Journal, p. 29.

4. For an explanation of this expression, see above, Vol. I, p. 489.

5. I call them 'passing thoughts' in the book—the passage in point goes from pages 330 to 342 of Vol. I.

6. Shadworth Hodgson has laid great stress on the fact that the minimum of consciousness demands two subfeelings, of which the second retrospects the first. (Cf. the section 'Analysis of Minima' in his *Philosophy of Reflection*, vol. I, p. 248; also the chapter entitled 'The Moment of Experience' in his *Metaphysic of Experience*, vol. I.) 'We live forward, but we understand backward' is a phrase of Kierkegaard's which Höffding quotes.

CHAPTER 7. THE WILL TO BELIEVE

1. Compare the admirable page 310 in S. H. Hodgson's *Time and Space*, London, 1865.

2. Compare Wilfrid Ward's Essay, "The Wish to Believe," in his *Witnesses to the Unseen*, Macmillan & Co., 1893.

3. Since belief is measured by action, he who forbids us to believe religion to be true, necessarily also forbids us to act as we should if we did believe it to be true. The whole defense of religious faith hinges upon action. If the action required or inspired by the religious hypothesis is in no way different from that dictated by the naturalistic hypothesis, then religious faith is a pure superfluity, better pruned away, and controversy about its legitimacy is a piece of idle trifling, unworthy of serious minds. I myself believe, of course, that the religious hypothesis gives to the world an expression which specifically determines our reactions, and makes them in a large part unlike what they might be on a purely naturalistic scheme of belief.

4. *Liberty, Equality, Fraternity*, p. 353, 2d edition. London, 1874.

CHAPTER 8. THE FUNCTION OF COGNITION

1. 'The Relativity of Knowledge,' held in this sense, is, it may be observed in passing, one of the oddest of philosophic superstitions. Whatever facts may be cited in its favor are due to the properties of nerve-tissue, which may be exhausted by too prolonged an excitement. Patients with neuralgias that last unremittingly for days can, however, assure us that the limits of this nerve-law are pretty widely drawn. But if we physically could get a feeling that should last eternally unchanged, what atom of logical or psychological argument is there to prove that it would not be felt as long as it lasted, and felt for just what it is, all that time? The reason for the opposite prejudice seems to be our reluctance to think that so *stupid* a thing as such a feeling would necessarily be, should be allowed to fill eternity with its presence. An interminable acquaintance, leading to no knowledge-*about*,—such would be its condition.

2. See, for example, Green's Introduction to Hume's *Treatise of Human Nature*, 1886, vol. 1, p. 36.

3. If A enters and B exclaims, "Didn't you see my brother on the stairs?" we all hold that A may answer, "I saw him, but didn't know he was your brother"; ignorance of brotherhood not abolishing power to see. But those who, on account of the unrelatedness of the first facts with which we become acquainted, deny them to be 'known' to us, ought in consistency to maintain that if A did not perceive the relationship of the man on the stairs to B, it was impossible he should have noticed him at all.

4. It seems odd to call so important a function accidental, but I do not see how we can mend the matter. Just as, if we start with the reality and ask how it may come to be known, we can only reply by invoking a feeling which shall *reconstruct* it in its own more private fashion; so, if we start with the feeling and ask how it may come to know, we can only reply by invoking a reality which shall *reconstruct* it in its own more public fashion. In either case, however, the datum we start with remains just what it was. One may easily get lost in verbal mysteries about the difference between quality of feeling and feeling of quality, between receiving and reconstructing the knowledge of a reality. But at the end we must confess that the notion of real cognition involves an unmediated dualism of the knower and the known. See Bowne's *Metaphysics*, New York, 1882, pp. 403–12, and various passages in Lotze, e.g., *Logic*, § 308. ["Unmediated" is a bad word to have used.—1909.]

5. The thoroughgoing objector might, it is true, still return to the charge,

and, granting a dream which should completely mirror the real universe, and all the actions dreamed in which should be instantly matched by duplicate actions in this universe, still insist that this is nothing more than harmony, and that it is as far as ever from being made clear whether the dream-world refers to that other world, all of whose details it so closely copies. This objection leads deep into metaphysics. I do not impugn its importance, and justice obliges me to say that but for the teachings of my colleague, Dr. Josiah Royce, I should neither have grasped its full force nor made my own practical and psychological point of view as clear to myself as it is. On this occasion I prefer to stick steadfastly to that point of view; but I hope that Dr. Royce's more fundamental criticism of the function of cognition may ere long see the light. [I referred in this note to Royce's *Religious Aspect of Philosophy*, then about to be published. This powerful book maintained that the notion of *referring* involved that of an inclusive mind that shall own both the real q and the mental q, and use the latter expressly as a representative symbol of the former. At the time I could not refute this transcendentalist opinion. Later, largely through the influence of Professor D. S. Miller (see his essay "The Meaning of Truth and Error," in the *Philosophical Review* for 1893, vol. 2, p. 403) I came to see that any definitely experienceable workings would serve as intermediaries quite as well as the absolute mind's intentions would.]

6. That is, there is no *real* 'Ivanhoe,' not even the one in Sir Walter Scott's mind as he was writing the story. That one is only the *first* one of the Ivanhoe-solipsisms. It is quite true we can make it the real Ivanhoe if we like, and then say that the other Ivanhoes know it or do not know it, according as they refer to and resemble it or no. This is done by bringing in Sir Walter Scott himself as the author of the real Ivanhoe, and so making a complex object of both. This object, however, is not a story pure and simple. It has dynamic relations with the world common to the experience of all the readers. Sir Walter Scott's Ivanhoe got itself printed in volumes which we all can handle, and to any one of which we can refer to see which of our versions be the true one, i.e., the original one of Scott himself. We can see the manuscript; in short we can get back to the Ivanhoe in Scott's mind by many an avenue and channel of this real world of our experience—a thing we can by no means do with either the Ivanhoe or the Rebecca, either the Templar or the Isaac of York, of the story taken simply as such, and detached from the conditions of its production. Everywhere, then, we have the same test: can we pass continuously from two objects in two minds to a third object which seems to be in *both* minds, because each mind feels every

modification imprinted on it by the other? If so, the first two objects named are derivatives, to say the least, from the same third object, and may be held, if they resemble each other, to refer to one and the same reality.

7. Among such errors are those cases in which our feeling operates on a reality which it does partially resemble, and yet does not intend: as for instance, when I take up your umbrella, meaning to take my own. I cannot be said here either to know your umbrella, or my own, which latter my feeling more completely resembles. I am mistaking them both, misrepresenting their context, etc.

We have spoken in the text as if the critic were necessarily one mind, and the feeling criticized another. But the criticized feeling and its critic may be earlier and later feelings of the same mind, and here it might seem that we could dispense with the notion of operating, to prove that critic and criticized are referring to and meaning to represent the *same*. We think we see our past feelings directly, and know what they refer to without appeal. At the worst, we can always fix the intention of our present feeling and *make* it refer to the same reality to which any one of our past feelings may have referred. So we need no 'operating' here, to make sure that the feeling and its critic mean the same real q. Well, all the better if this is so! We have covered the more complex and difficult case in our text, and we may let this easier one go. The main thing at present is to stick to practical psychology, and ignore metaphysical difficulties.

One more remark. Our formula contains, it will be observed, nothing to correspond to the great principle of cognition laid down by Professor Ferrier in his *Institutes of Metaphysic* and apparently adopted by all the followers of Fichte, the principle, namely, that for knowledge to be constituted there must be knowledge of the knowing mind along with whatever else is known: not q, as we have supposed, but q plus myself, must be the least I can know. It is certain that the common sense of mankind never dreams of using any such principle when it tries to discriminate between conscious states that are knowledge and conscious states that are not. So that Ferrier's principle, if it have any relevancy at all, must have relevancy to the metaphysical possibility of consciousness at large, and not to the practically recognized constitution of cognitive consciousness. We may therefore pass it by without further notice here.

8. Is an incomplete 'thought about' that reality, that reality is its 'topic,' etc.

9. Though both might terminate in the same thing and be incomplete thoughts 'about' it.

10. The difference between Idealism and Realism is immaterial here. What is said in the text is consistent with either theory. A law by which my percept shall

change yours directly is no more mysterious than a law by which it shall first change a physical reality, and then the reality change yours. In either case you and I seem knit into a continuous world, and not to form a pair of solipsisms.

11. "There is no distinction of meaning so fine as to consist in anything but a possible difference of practice. . . . It appears, then, that the rule for attaining the [highest] grade of clearness of apprehension is as follows: Consider what effects, which might conceivably have practical bearings, we conceive the object of our conception to have. Then, our conception of these effects is the whole of our conception of the object." Charles S. Peirce: "How to make our Ideas clear," in *Popular Science Monthly*, New York, January, 1878, p. 293.

CHAPTER 9. WHAT PRAGMATISM MEANS

1. Translated in the *Revue Philosophique* for January, 1879 (vol. vii).

2. "Theorie und Praxis," *Zeitsch. des Oesterreichischen Ingenieur u. Architecten-Vereines*, 1905, Nr. 4 u. 6. I find a still more radical pragmatism than Ostwald's in an address by Professor W. S. Franklin: "I think that the sickliest notion of physics, even if a student gets it, is that it is 'the science of masses, molecules and the ether.' And I think that the healthiest notion, even if a student does not wholly get it, is that physics is the science of the ways of taking hold of bodies and pushing them!" (*Science*, January 2, 1903.)

CHAPTER 10. PRAGMATISM'S CONCEPTION OF TRUTH

1. A. E. Taylor, *Philosophical Review*, vol. xiv, p. 288.

2. H. Rickert, *Der Gegenstand der Erkenntniss*, chapter on 'Die Urtheils-nothwendigkeit.'

3. I am not forgetting that Professor Rickert long ago gave up the whole notion of truth being founded on agreement with reality. Reality, according to him, is whatever agrees with truth, and truth is founded solely on our primal duty. This fantastic flight, together with Mr. Joachim's candid confession of failure in his book *The Nature of Truth*, seems to me to mark the bankruptcy of rationalism when dealing with this subject. Rickert deals with part of the prag-

matistic position under the head of what he calls 'Relativismus.' I cannot discuss his text here. Suffice it to say that his argumentation in that chapter is so feeble as to seem almost incredible in so generally able a writer.

CHAPTER 11. THE PRAGMATIST ACCOUNT OF TRUTH AND ITS MISUNDERSTANDERS

1. I see here a chance to forestall a criticism which some one may make on Lecture III of my *Pragmatism*, where, on pp. 96–100, I said that 'God' and 'Matter' might be regarded as synonymous terms, so long as no differing future consequences were deducible from the two conceptions. The passage was transcribed from my address at the California Philosophical Union, reprinted in the *Journal of Philosophy*, vol. 1, p. 673. I had no sooner given the address than I perceived a flaw in that part of it; but I have left the passage unaltered ever since, because the flaw did not spoil its illustrative value. The flaw was evident when, as a case analogous to that of a godless universe, I thought of what I called an 'automatic sweetheart,' meaning a soulless body which should be absolutely indistinguishable from a spiritually animated maiden, laughing, talking, blushing, nursing us, and performing all feminine offices as tactfully and sweetly as if a soul were in her. Would any one regard her as a full equivalent? Certainly not, and why? Because, framed as we are, our egoism craves above all things inward sympathy and recognition, love and admiration. The outward treatment is valued mainly as an expression, as a manifestation of the accompanying consciousness believed in. Pragmatically, then, belief in the automatic sweetheart would not *work*, and in point of fact no one treats it as a serious hypothesis. The godless universe would be exactly similar. Even if matter could do every outward thing that God does, the idea of it would not work as satisfactorily, because the chief call for a God on modern men's part is for a being who will inwardly recognize them and judge them sympathetically. Matter disappoints this craving of our ego, so God remains for most men the truer hypothesis, and indeed remains so for definite pragmatic reasons.

2. I need hardly remind the reader that both sense-percepts and percepts of ideal relation (comparisons, etc.) should be classed among the realities. The bulk of our mental 'stock' consists of truths concerning these terms.

3. The ambiguity of the word 'practical' comes out well in these words of

a recent would-be reporter of our views: "Pragmatism is an Anglo-Saxon reaction against the intellectualism and rationalism of the Latin mind. . . . Man, each individual man is the measure of things. He is able to conceive none but relative truths, that is to say, illusions. What these illusions are worth is revealed to him, not by general theory, but by individual practice. Pragmatism, which consists in experiencing these illusions of the mind and obeying them by acting them out, is a *philosophy without words*, a philosophy of *gestures and of acts*, which abandons what is general and holds only to what is *particular*." (Bourdeau, in *Journal des Débats,* October 29, 1907.)

4. Sensations may, indeed, possess their objects or coalesce with them, as common sense supposes that they do; and intuited differences between concepts may coalesce with the 'eternal' objective differences; but to simplify our discussion here we can afford to abstract from these very special cases of knowing.

5. The transcendental idealist thinks that, in some inexplicable way, the finite states of mind are identical with the transfinite all-knower which he finds himself obliged to postulate in order to supply a *fundamentum* for the relation of knowing, as he apprehends it. Pragmatists can leave the question of identity open; but they cannot do without the wider knower any more than they can do without the reality, if they want to *prove* a case of knowing. They themselves play the part of the absolute knower for the universe of discourse which serves them as material for epistemologizing. They warrant the reality there, and the subject's true knowledge, there, of it. But whether what they themselves say about that whole universe is objectively true, *i.e.,* whether the pragmatic theory of truth is true *really*, they cannot warrant—they can only believe it. To their hearers they can only *propose* it, as I propose it to my readers, as something to be verified *ambulando*, or by the way in which its consequences may confirm it.

CHAPTER 13. THE DILEMMA OF DETERMINISM

1. And I may now say Charles S. Peirce—see the *Monist,* for 1892–93.

2. "The whole history of popular beliefs about Nature refutes the notion that the thought of a universal physical order can possibly have arisen from the purely passive reception and association of particular perceptions. Indubitable as it is that men infer from known cases to unknown, it is equally certain that this procedure, if restricted to the phenomenal materials that spontaneously

offer themselves, would never have led to the belief in a general uniformity, but only to the belief that law and lawlessness rule the world in motley alternation. From the point of view of strict experience, nothing exists but the sum of particular perceptions, with their coincidences on the one hand, their contradictions on the other.

"That there is more order in the world than appears at first sight is not discovered *till the order is looked for.* The first impulse to look for it proceeds from practical needs: where ends must be attained, we must know trustworthy means which infallibly possess a property, or produce a result. But the practical need is only the first occasion for our reflection on the conditions of true knowledge; and even were there no such need, motives would still be present for carrying us beyond the stage of mere association. For not with an equal interest, or rather with an equal lack of interest, does man contemplate those natural processes in which a thing is linked with its former mate, and those in which it is linked to something else. *The former processes harmonize with the conditions of his own thinking*: the latter do not. In the former, his *concepts, general judgments,* and *inferences* apply to reality: in the latter, they have no such application. And thus the intellectual satisfaction which at first comes to him without reflection, at last excites in him the conscious wish to find realized throughout the entire phenomenal world those rational continuities, uniformities, and necessities which are the fundamental element and guiding principle of his own thought." (Sigwart, *Logik*, bd. 2, s. 382.)

3. Speaking technically, it is a word with a positive denotation, but a connotation that is negative. Other things must be silent about *what* it is: it alone can decide that point at the moment in which it reveals itself.

4. A favorite argument against free-will is that if it be true, a man's murderer may as probably be his best friend as his worst enemy, a mother be as likely to strangle as to suckle her first-born, and all of us be as ready to jump from fourth-story windows as to go out of front doors, etc. Users of this argument should properly be excluded from debate till they learn what the real question is. 'Free-will' does not that say that everything that is physically conceivable is also morally possible. It merely says that of alternatives that really *tempt* our will more than one is really possible. Of course, the alternatives that do thus tempt our will are vastly fewer than the physical possibilities we can coldly fancy. Persons really tempted often do murder their best friends, mothers do strangle their first-born, people do jump out of fourth-story windows, etc.

5. To a reader who says he is satisfied with a pessimism, and has no objec-

tion to thinking the whole bad, I have no more to say: he makes fewer demands on the world than I, who, making them, wish to look a little further before I give up all hope of having them satisfied. If, however, all he means is that the badness of some parts does not prevent his acceptance of a universe whose *other* parts give him satisfaction, I welcome him as an ally. He has abandoned the notion of the *Whole*, which is the essence of deterministic monism, and views things as a pluralism, just as I do in this paper.

6. Compare Sir James Stephen's *Essays by a Barrister*, London, 1862, pp. 138, 318.

7. Cet univers est un spectacle que Dieu se donne à lui-même. Servons les intentions du grand chorège en contribuant à rendre le spectacle aussi brillant, aussi varié que possible.—Renan.

8. The burden, for example, of seeing to it that the *end* of all our righteousness be some positive universal gain.

9. This of course leaves the creative mind subject to the law of time. And to any one who insists on the timelessness of that mind I have no reply to make. A mind to whom all time is simultaneously present must see all things under the form of actuality, or under some form to us unknown. If he thinks certain moments as ambiguous in their content while future, he must simultaneously know how the ambiguity will have been decided when they are past. So that none of his mental judgments can possibly be called hypothetical, and his world is one from which chance is excluded. Is not, however, the timeless mind rather a gratuitous fiction? And is not the notion of eternity being given at a stroke to omniscience only just another way of whacking upon us the block-universe, and of denying that possibilities exist?—just the point to be proved. To say that time is an illusory appearance is only a roundabout manner of saying there is no real plurality, and that the frame of things is an absolute unit. Admit plurality, and time may be its form.

10. And this of course means 'miraculous' interposition, but not necessarily of the gross sort our fathers took such delight in representing, and which has so lost its magic for us. Emerson quotes some Eastern sage as saying that if evil were really done under the sun, the sky would incontinently shrivel to a snakeskin and cast it out in spasms. But, says Emerson, the spasms of Nature are years and centuries; and it will tax man's patience to wait so long. We may think of the reserved possibilities God keeps in his own hand, under as invisible and molecular and slowly self-summating a form as we please. We may think of them as counteracting human agencies which he inspires *ad hoc*. In short, signs

and wonders and convulsions of the earth and sky are not the only neutralizers of obstruction to a god's plans of which it is possible to think.

11. As long as languages contain a future perfect tense, determinists, following the bent of laziness or passion, the lines of least resistance, can reply in that tense, saying, "It will have been fated," to the still small voice which urges an opposite course; and thus excuse themselves from effort in a quite unanswerable way.

CHAPTER 14. THE MORAL PHILOSOPHER AND THE MORAL LIFE

1. *The Principles of Psychology*, New York, H. Holt and Co., 1890.

2. All this is set forth with great freshness and force in the work of my colleague, Professor Josiah Royce: *The Religious Aspect of Philosophy*, Boston, 1885.

CHAPTER 15. THE ENERGIES OF MEN

1. Thomas De Quincey.

2. This handbook was published last March [1906].

3. *Tour in England, Ireland and France*, Philadelphia, 1833, p. 435.

CHAPTER 16. PHILOSOPHY

1. Compare Professor W. Wallace's Gifford Lectures, in *Lectures and Essays on Natural Theology and Ethics*, Oxford, 1898, pp. 17 ff.

2. John Caird, *Introduction to the Philosophy of Religion*, London and New York, 1880, p. 174, abridged [and italicized].

3. *Ibid.*, p. 186, abridged and italicized.

4. John Henry Newman, *The Idea of a University*, London, 1899, Discourse II, §7.

5. As regards the secondary character of intellectual constructions, and the primacy of feeling and instinct in founding religious beliefs, see the striking

work of H. Fielding, *The Hearts of Men*, London, 1902, which came into my hands after my text was written. "Creeds," says the author, "are the grammar of religion, they are to religion what grammar is to speech. Words are the expression of our wants; grammar is the theory formed afterwards. Speech never proceeded from grammar, but the reverse. As speech progresses and changes from unknown causes, grammar must follow" (p. 313). The whole book, which keeps unusually close to concrete facts, is little more than an amplification of this text.

6. For convenience's sake, I follow the order of A. Stöckl's *Lehrbuch der Philosophie*, 5te Auflage, Mainz, 1881, Band ii. B. Boedder's *Natural Theology*, London, 1891, is a handy English Catholic Manual; but an almost identical doctrine is given by such Protestant theologians as C. Hodge: *Systematic Theology*, New York, 1873, or A. H. Strong: *Systematic Theology*, 5th edition, New York, 1896.

7. It must not be forgotten that any form of *dis*order in the world might, by the design argument, suggest a God for just that kind of disorder. The truth is that any state of things whatever that can be named is logically susceptible of teleological interpretation. The ruins of the earthquake at Lisbon, for example: the whole of past history had to be planned exactly as it was to bring about in the fullness of time just that particular arrangement of debris of masonry, furniture, and once living bodies. No other train of causes would have been sufficient. And so of any other arrangement, bad or good, which might as a matter of fact be found resulting anywhere from previous conditions. To avoid such pessimistic consequences and save its beneficent designer, the design argument accordingly invokes two other principles, restrictive in their operation. The first is physical: Nature's forces tend of their own accord only to disorder and destruction, to heaps of ruins, not to architecture. This principle, though plausible at first sight, seems, in the light of recent biology, to be more and more improbable. The second principle is one of anthropomorphic interpretation. No arrangement that for *us* is 'disorderly' can possibly have been an object of design at all. This principle is of course a mere assumption in the interests of anthropomorphic Theism.

When one views the world with no definite theological bias one way or the other, one sees that order and disorder, as we now recognize them, are purely human inventions. We are interested in certain types of arrangement, useful, aesthetic, or moral—so interested that whenever we find them realized, the fact emphatically rivets our attention. The result is that we work over the contents of the world selectively. It is overflowing with disorderly arrangements from our point of view, but order is the only thing we care for and look at, and by choosing, one can always find some sort of orderly arrangement in the midst of any chaos. If I should throw down a thousand beans at random upon a table, I could doubtless, by eliminating a sufficient number of them, leave the rest in almost any geometrical pattern you might propose to me, and you might then say that that pattern was the thing prefigured beforehand, and that the other beans were mere irrelevance and packing material. Our dealings with Nature are just like this. She is a vast *plenum* in which our attention draws capricious lines in innumerable directions. We count and name whatever lies upon the special lines we trace, whilst the other things and the untraced lines are neither named nor counted. There are in reality infinitely more things 'unadapted' to each other in this world than there are things 'adapted'; infinitely more things with irregular relations than with regular relations between them. But we look for the regular kind of thing exclusively, and ingeniously discover and preserve it in our memory. It accumulates with other regular kinds, until the collection of them fills our encyclopaedias. Yet all the while between and around them lies an infinite anonymous chaos of objects that no one ever thought of together, of relations that never yet attracted our attention.

The facts of order from which the physico-theological argument starts are thus easily susceptible of interpretation as arbitrary human products. So long as this is the case, although of course no argument against God follows, it follows that the argument for him will fail to constitute a knockdown proof of his existence. It will be convincing only to those who on other grounds believe in him already.

8. For the scholastics the *facultas appetendi* embraces feeling, desire, and will.

9. Newman, *The Idea of a University*, Discourse III, §7.

10. In an article, "How to make our Ideas Clear," in the *Popular Science Monthly* for January, 1878, vol. xii. p. 286.

11. Pragmatically, the most important attribute of God is his punitive justice. But who, in the present state of theological opinion on that point, will dare maintain that hell fire or its equivalent in some shape is rendered certain by pure logic? Theology herself has largely based this doctrine upon revelation, and, in discussing it, has tended more and more to substitute conventional ideas of criminal law for a priori principles of reason. But the very notion that this glorious universe, with planets and winds, and laughing sky and ocean, should have been conceived and had its beams and rafters laid in technicalities of crim-

inality, is incredible to our modern imagination. It weakens a religion to hear it argued upon such a basis.

12. John Caird: *An Introduction to the Philosophy of Religion*, London and New York, 1880, pp. 246–50, and 293–99, much abridged.

13. A. C. Fraser: *Philosophy of Theism*, second edition, Edinburgh and London, 1899, especially part ii, chaps. vii. and viii; A. Seth [Pringle-Pattison]: *Hegelianism and Personality*, Edinburgh and London, 1893, passim.

The most persuasive arguments in favor of a concrete individual Soul of the world, with which I am acquainted, are those of my colleague, Josiah Royce, in his *Religious Aspect of Philosophy*, Boston, 1885; in his *Conception of God*, New York and London, 1897; and lately in his Aberdeen Gifford Lectures, *The World and the Individual*, 2 vols., New York and London, 1900–1901. I doubtless seem to some of my readers to evade the philosophic duty which my thesis in this lecture imposes on me, by not even attempting to meet Professor Royce's arguments articulately. I admit the momentary evasion. In the present lectures, which are cast throughout in a popular mould, there seemed no room for subtle metaphysical discussion, and for tactical purposes it was sufficient, the contention of philosophy being what it is (namely, that religion can be transformed into a universally convincing science), to point to the fact that no religious philosophy has actually convinced the mass of thinkers. Meanwhile let me say that I hope that the present volume may be followed by another, if I am spared to write it, in which not only Professor Royce's arguments, but others for monistic absolutism shall be considered with all the technical fullness which their great importance calls for. At present I resign myself to lying passive under the reproach of superficiality.

CHAPTER 17. CONCLUSIONS

1. For example, on pages 135, 163, 333, above.

2. From this point of view, the contrasts between the healthy and the morbid mind, and between the once-born and the twice-born types, of which I spoke in earlier lectures (see pp. 162–67), cease to be the radical antagonisms which many think them. The twice-born look down upon the rectilinear consciousness of life of the once-born as being 'mere morality,' and not properly religion. "Dr. Channing," an orthodox minister is reported to have said, "is excluded from the highest form of religious life by the extraordinary rectitude

of his character." It is indeed true that the outlook upon life of the twice-born—holding as it does more of the element of evil in solution—is the wider and completer. The 'heroic' or 'solemn' way in which life comes to them is a 'higher synthesis' into which healthy-mindedness and morbidity both enter and combine. Evil is not evaded, but sublated in the higher religious cheer of these persons (see pp. 47–52, 362–65). But the final consciousness which each type reaches of union with the divine has the same practical significance for the individual; and individuals may well be allowed to get to it by the channels which lie most open to their several temperaments. In the cases which were quoted in Lecture IV, of the mind-cure form of healthy-mindedness, we found abundant examples of regenerative process. The severity of the crisis in this process is a matter of degree. How long one shall continue to drink the consciousness of evil, and when one shall begin to short-circuit and get rid of it, are also matters of amount and degree, so that in many instances it is quite arbitrary whether we class the individual as a once-born or a twice-born subject.

3. Compare, e.g., the quotation from Renan on p. 37, above.

4. 'Prayerful' taken in the broader sense explained above on pp. 463 ff.

5. How was it ever conceivable, we ask, that a man like Christian Wolff, in whose dry-as-dust head all the learning of the early eighteenth century was concentrated, should have preserved such a baby-like faith in the personal and human character of Nature as to expound her operations as he did in his work on the uses of natural things? This, for example, is the account he gives of the sun and its utility:

"We see that God has created the sun to keep the changeable conditions on the earth in such an order that living creatures, men and beasts, may inhabit its surface. Since men are the most reasonable of creatures, and able to infer God's invisible being from the contemplation of the world, the sun in so far forth contributes to the primary purpose of creation: without it the race of man could not be preserved or continued. . . . The sun makes daylight, not only on our earth, but also on the other planets; and daylight is of the utmost utility to us; for by its means we can commodiously carry on those occupations which in the night-time would either be quite impossible, or at any rate impossible without our going to the expense of artificial light. The beasts of the field can find food by day which they would not be able to find at night. Moreover we owe it to the sunlight that we are able to see everything that is on the earth's surface, not only near by, but also at a distance, and to recognize both near and far things according to their species, which again is of manifold use to us not only in the business necessary to human life, and when we are traveling, but also for the scientific knowledge of Nature, which knowledge for the most part depends on observations made with the help of sight, and, without the sunshine, would have been impossible. If anyone would rightly impress on his mind the great advantages which he derives from the sun, let him imagine himself living through only one month, and see how it would be with all his undertakings, if it were not day but night. He would then be sufficiently convinced out of his own experience, especially if he had much work to carry on in the street or in the fields. . . . From the sun we learn to recognize when it is midday, and by knowing this point of time exactly, we can set our clocks right, on which account astronomy owes much to the sun. . . . By help of the sun one can find the meridian. . . . But the meridian is the basis of our sun-dials, and generally speaking, we should have no sun-dials if we had no sun." *Vernünfftige Gedanken, von den Absichten der natürlichen Dinge*, 1752, pp. 71–84.

Or read the account of God's beneficence in the institution of "the great variety throughout the World of Men's Faces, Voices, and Hand-writing," given in Derham's *Physico-Theology*, a book that had much vogue in the eighteenth century. "Had Man's Body," says Dr. Derham, "been made according to any of the Atheistical Schemes, or any other Method than that of the infinite Lord of the World, this wise Variety would never have been: But Men's Faces would have been cast in the same, or not a very different Mould, their Organs of Speech would have sounded the same or not so great a Variety of Notes; and the same Structure of Muscles and Nerves would have given the Hand the same Direction in Writing. And in this Case, what Confusion, what Disturbance, what Mischiefs would the world eternally have lain under! No Security could have been to our persons; no Certainty, no Enjoyment of our Possessions; no Justice between Man and Man, no Distinction between Good and Bad, between Friends and Foes, between Father and Child, Husband and Wife, Male or Female; but all would have been turned topsy-turvy by being exposed to the Malice of the Envious and Ill-natur'd, to the Fraud and Violence of Knaves and Robbers, to the Forgeries of the crafty Cheat, to the Lusts of the Effeminate and Debauched, and what not! Our Courts of Justice can abundantly testify the dire Effects of mistaking Men's Faces, of counterfeiting their Hands, and forging Writings. But now as the infinitely wise Creator and Ruler hath ordered the Matter, every Man's Face can distinguish him in the Light, and his Voice in the Dark; his Hand-writing can speak for him though absent, and be his Witness, and secure his Contracts in future Generations. A manifest as

well as admirable Indication of the divine Super-intendence and Management"
[pp. 310–12].

A God so careful as to make provision even for the unmistakable signing of
bank checks and deeds was a deity truly after the heart of eighteenth century
Anglicanism.

I subjoin, omitting the capitals, Derham's vindication of God by the institution of hills and valleys, and Wolff's altogether culinary account of the
institution of Water:

"The uses," says Wolff, "which water serves in human life are plain to see
and need not be described at length. Water is a universal drink of man and
beasts. Even though men have made themselves drinks that are artificial, they
could not do this without water. Beer is brewed of water and malt, and it is the
water in it which quenches thirst. Wine is prepared from grapes, which could
never have grown without the help of water; and the same is true of those
drinks which in England and other places they produce from fruit. . . . Therefore since God so planned the world that men and beasts should live upon it
and find there everything required for their necessity and convenience, he also
made water as one means whereby to make the earth into so excellent a
dwelling. And this is all the more manifest when we consider the advantages
which we obtain from this same water for the cleaning of our household uten-
sils, of our clothing, and of other matters. . . . When one goes into a grinding-
mill one sees that the grindstone must always be kept wet and then one will get
a still greater idea of the use of water" [pp. 354–56].

Of the hills and valleys, Derham, after praising their beauty, discourses as
follows: "Some constitutions are indeed of so happy a strength, and so confirmed an health, as to be indifferent to almost any place or temperature of the
air. But then others are so weakly and feeble, as not to be able to bear one, but
can live comfortably in another place. With some, the more subtile and finer air
of the hills doth best agree, who are languishing and dying in the feculent, and
grosser air of great towns, or even the warmer and vaporous air of the valleys
and waters. But contrariwise, others languish on the hills, and grow lusty and
strong in the warmer air of the valleys.

"So that this opportunity of shifting our abode . . . from the hills to the
vales, is an admirable easement, refreshment, and great benefit to the valetudi-
narian, feeble part of mankind; affording those an easy and comfortable life,
who would otherwise live miserably, languish, and pine away.

"To this salutary conformation of the earth we may add another great convenience of the hills, and that is affording commodious places for habitation, 'serving (as an eminent author wordeth it) as screens to keep off the cold and nipping blasts of the northern and easterly winds, and reflecting the benign and cherishing sunbeams and so rendering our habitations both more comfortable and more cheerly in winter' . . .

"Lastly, it is to the hills that the fountains owe their rise and the rivers their conveyance, . . . and consequently, those vast masses and lofty piles are not as they are charged, such rude and useless excrescences of our ill-formed globe; but the admirable tools of nature, contrived and ordered by the infinite Creator, to do one of its most useful works. . . . For, was the surface of the earth even and level, and the middle parts of its islands and continents, not mountainous and high (as now it is), it is most certain there could be no descent for the rivers, no conveyance for the waters; but, instead of gliding along those gentle declivities which the higher lands now afford them quite down to the sea, they would stagnate, and perhaps stink, and also drown large tracts of land. . . .

"[Thus] the hills and vales, though to a peevish weary traveler, they may seem incommodious and troublesome, yet are a noble work of the great Creator, and wisely appointed by him for the good of our sublunary world" [pp. 72–73, 76–77, 80].

6. Until the seventeenth century this mode of thought prevailed. One need only recall the dramatic treatment even of mechanical questions by Aristotle, as, for example, his explanation of the power of the lever to make a small weight raise a larger one. This is due, according to Aristotle, to the generally miraculous character of the circle and of all circular movement. The circle is both convex and concave; it is made by a fixed point and a moving line, which contradict each other; and whatever moves in a circle moves in opposite directions. Nevertheless, movement in a circle is the most 'natural' movement; and the long arm of the lever, moving, as it does, in the larger circle, has the greater amount of this natural motion, and consequently requires the lesser force. Or recall the explanation by Herodotus of the position of the sun in winter: It moves to the south because of the cold which drives it into the warm parts of the heavens over Libya. Or listen to Saint Augustine's speculations: "Who gave to chaff such power to freeze that it preserves snow buried under it, and such power to warm that it ripens green fruit? Who can explain the strange properties of fire itself, which blackens all that it burns, though itself bright; and which, though of the most beautiful colors, discolors almost all that it touches and feeds upon, and turns blazing fuel into grimy cinders? . . . Then what won-

derful properties do we find in charcoal, which is so brittle that a light tap breaks it and a slight pressure pulverizes it, and yet is so strong that no moisture rots it, nor any time causes it to decay." *City of God*, book xxi, ch. iv.

Such aspects of things as these, their naturalness and unnaturalness the sympathies and antipathies of their superficial qualities, their eccentricities, their brightness and strength and destructiveness, were inevitably the ways in which they originally fastened our attention.

If you open early medical books, you will find sympathetic magic invoked on every page. Take, for example, the famous vulnerary ointment attributed to Paracelsus. For this there were a variety of receipts, including usually human fat, the fat of either a bull, a wild boar, or a bear; powdered earthworms, the *usnia*, or mossy growth on the weathered skull of a hanged criminal, and other materials equally unpleasant—the whole prepared under the planet Venus if possible, but never under Mars or Saturn. Then, if a splinter of wood, dipped in the patient's blood, or the bloodstained weapon that wounded him, be immersed in this ointment, the wound itself being tightly bound up, the latter infallibly gets well—I quote now Van Helmont's account—for the blood on the weapon or splinter, containing in it the spirit of the wounded man, is roused to active excitement by the contact of the ointment, whence there results to it a full commission or power to cure its cousin-german, the blood in the patient's body. This it does by sucking out the dolorous and exotic impression from the wounded part. But to do this it has to implore the aid of the bull's fat, and other portions of the unguent. The reason why bull's fat is so powerful is that the bull at the time of slaughter is full of secret reluctancy and vindictive murmurs, and therefore dies with a higher flame of revenge about him than any other animal. And thus we have made it out, says this author, that the admirable efficacy of the ointment ought to be imputed, not to any auxiliary concurrence of Satan, but simply to the energy of the *posthumous character of Revenge* remaining firmly impressed upon the blood and concreted fat in the unguent. J. B. Van Helmont: *A Ternary of Paradoxes*, translated by Walter Charleton, London, 1650.—I much abridge the original in my citations.

The author goes on to prove by the analogy of many other natural facts that this sympathetic action between things at a distance is the true rationale of the case. "If," he says, "the heart of a horse slain by a witch, taken out of the yet reeking carcase, be impaled upon an arrow, and roasted, immediately the whole witch becomes tormented with the insufferable pains and cruelty of the fire, which could by no means happen, unless there preceded a conjunction of the spirit of the Witch with the spirit of the horse. In the reaking and yet panting heart, the spirit of the Witch is kept captive, and the retreat of it prevented by the arrow transfixed. Similarly hath not many a murdered carcase at the Coroner's inquest suffered a fresh haemorrhage or cruentation at the presence of the assassin?—the blood being, as in a furious fit of anger, enraged and agitated by the impress of revenge conceived against the murderer, at the instant of the soul's compulsive exile from the body. So, if you have dropsy, gout, or jaundice, by including some of your warme blood in the shell and white of an egge, which, exposed to a gentle heat, and mixt with a baite of flesh, you shall give to a hungry dog, or hog, the disease shall instantly pass from you into the animal, and leave you entirely. And similarly again, if you burn some of the milk either of a cow or of a woman, the gland from which it issued will dry up. A gentleman at Brussels in a combat, had his nose mowed off, but the celebrated surgeon Tagliacozzus dig'd a new nose for him out of the skin of the arm of a Porter at Bologna. About thirteen moneths after his returne to his owne countrey, the engrafted nose grew cold, putrefied, and in a few dayes dropt off, and it was then discovered, that the Porter had expired, near about the same punctilio of time. There are still at Brussels eye-witnesses of this occurrence," says Van Helmont; and adds, "I pray what is there in this of superstition or of exalted *Imagination*?" [abridged and slightly altered].

Modern mind-cure literature—the works of Prentice Mulford, for example—is full of sympathetic magic.

7. Compare Lotze's doctrine that the only meaning we can attach to the notion of a thing as it is 'in itself' is by conceiving it as it is *for* itself, i.e., as a piece of full experience with a private sense of 'pinch' or inner activity of some sort going with it.

8. Even the errors of fact may possibly turn out not to be as wholesale as the scientist assumes. We saw in Lecture IV how the religious conception of the universe seems to many mind-curers 'verified' from day to day by their experience of fact. 'Experience of fact' is a field with so many things in it that the sectarian scientist methodically declining, as he does, to recognize such 'facts' as mind-curers and others like them experience, otherwise than by such rude heads of classification as 'bosh,' 'rot,' 'folly,' certainly leaves out a mass of raw fact which, save for the industrious interest of the religious in the more personal aspects of reality, would never have succeeded in getting itself recorded at all. We know this to be true already in certain cases; it may, therefore, be true in others as well. Miraculous healings have always been part of the supernaturalist

stock in trade, and have always been dismissed by the scientist as figments of the imagination. But the scientist's tardy education in the facts of hypnotism has recently given him an apperceiving mass for phenomena of this order, and he consequently now allows that the healings may exist, provided you expressly call them effects of 'suggestion.' Even the stigmata of the cross on Saint Francis's hands and feet may on these terms not be a fable. Similarly, the time-honored phenomenon of diabolical possession is on the point of being admitted by the scientist as a fact, now that he has the name of 'hystero-demonopathy' by which to apperceive it. No one can foresee just how far this legitimation of occultist phenomena under newly found scientist titles may proceed—even 'prophecy,' even 'levitation,' might creep into the pale.

Thus the divorce between scientist facts and religious facts may not necessarily be as eternal as it at first sight seems, nor the personalism and romanticism of the world, as they appeared to primitive thinking, be matters so irrevocably outgrown. The final human opinion may, in short, in some manner now impossible to foresee, revert to the more personal style, just as any path of progress may follow a spiral rather than a straight line. If this were so, the rigorously impersonal view of science might one day appear as having been a temporarily useful eccentricity rather than the definitively triumphant position which the sectarian scientist at present so confidently announces it to be.

9. Hume's criticism has banished causation from the world of physical objects, and 'Science' is absolutely satisfied to define cause in terms of concomitant change—read Mach, Pearson, Ostwald. The 'original' of the notion of causation is in our inner personal experience, and only there can causes in the old-fashioned sense be directly observed and described.

10. When I read in a religious paper words like these: "Perhaps the best thing we can say of God is that he is *the Inevitable Inference*," I recognize the tendency to let religion evaporate in intellectual terms. Would martyrs have sung in the flames for a mere inference, however inevitable it might be? Original religious men, like Saint Francis, Luther, Boehme, have usually been enemies of the intellect's pretension to meddle with religious things. Yet the intellect, everywhere invasive, shows everywhere its shallowing effect. See how the ancient spirit of Methodism evaporates under those wonderfully able rationalistic booklets (which every one should read) of a philosopher like Professor Bowne (*The Christian Revelation, The Christian Life, The Atonement*: Cincinnati and New York, 1898, 1899, 1900). See the positively expulsive purpose of philosophy properly so called:

"Religion," writes M. Vacherot (*La Religion*, Paris, 1869, pp. 313, 436, *et passim*), "answers to a transient state or condition, not to a permanent determination of human nature, being merely an expression of that stage of the human mind which is dominated by the imagination. . . . Christianity has but a single possible final heir to its estate, and that is scientific philosophy."

In a still more radical vein, Professor Ribot (*Psychologie des sentiments*, p. 310) describes the evaporation of religion. He sums it up in a single formula—the ever-growing predominance of the rational intellectual element, with the gradual fading out of the emotional element, this latter tending to enter into the group of purely intellectual sentiments. "Of religious sentiment properly so called, nothing survives at last save a vague respect for the unknowable x which is a last relic of the fear, and a certain attraction towards the ideal, which is a relic of the love, that characterized the earlier periods of religious growth. To state this more simply, *religion tends to turn into religious philosophy.*—These are psychologically entirely different things, the one being a theoretic construction of ratiocination, whereas the other is the living work of a group of persons, or of a great inspired leader, calling into play the entire thinking and feeling organism of man."

I find the same failure to recognize that the stronghold of religion lies in individuality in attempts like those of Professor Baldwin (*Social and Ethical Interpretations in Mental Development*, ch. x) and Mr. H. R. Marshall (*Instinct and Reason*, chaps. viii. to xii.) to make it a purely 'conservative social force.'

11. Compare, for instance, pages 203, 219, 223, 226, 249 to 256, 275 to 278.

12. *American Journal of Psychology*, vii., p. 345.

13. Above, p. 184.

14. Above, p. 145.

15. Above, p. 400.

16. Example: Henri Perreyve writes to Gratry: "I do not know how to deal with the happiness which you aroused in me this morning. It overwhelms me; I want to *do* something, yet I can do nothing and am fit for nothing. . . . I would fain do *great things*." Again, after an inspiring interview, he writes: "I went homewards, intoxicated with joy, hope, and strength. I wanted to feed upon my happiness in solitude far from all men. It was late; but, unheeding that, I took a mountain path and went on like a madman, looking at the heavens, regardless of earth. Suddenly an instinct made me draw hastily back—I was on the very edge of a precipice, one step more, and I must have fallen. I took fright, and

gave up my nocturnal wanderings." A. Gratry: *Henri Perreyve*, London, 1872, pp. 91, 89.

This primacy, in the faith-state, of vague expansive impulse over direction is well expressed in Walt Whitman's lines (*Leaves of Grass*, 1872, p. 190):

> "O to confront night, storms, hunger, ridicule, accidents, rebuffs,
>> as the trees and animals do. . . .
> Dear camerado! I confess I have urged you onward with me,
>> and still urge you, without the
> least idea what is our destination,
> Or whether we shall be victorious, or utterly quell'd and defeated."

This readiness for great things, and this sense that the world by its importance, wonderfulness, etc., is apt for their production, would seem to be the undifferentiated germ of all the higher faiths. Trust in our own dreams of ambition, or in our country's expansive destinies, and faith in the providence of God, all have their source in that onrush of our sanguine impulses, and in that sense of the exceedingness of the possible over the real.

17. Compare Leuba: *American Journal of Psychology*, vii., pp. 346–49.

18. "The Contents of Religious Consciousness," in *The Monist*, xi., p. 536, July 1901.

19. Ibid., pp. 571–72, abridged. See, also, this writer's extraordinarily true criticism of the notion that religion primarily seeks to solve the intellectual mystery of the world. Compare what W. Bender says (in his *Wesen der Religion*, Bonn, 1888, pp. 85, 38): "Not the question about God, and not the inquiry into the origin and purpose of the world is religion, but the question about Man. All religious views of life are anthropocentric." "Religion is that activity of the human impulse towards self-preservation by means of which Man seeks to carry his essential vital purposes through against the adverse pressure of the world by raising himself freely towards the world's ordering and governing powers when the limits of his own strength are reached." The whole book is little more than a development of these words.

20. Remember that for some men it arrives suddenly, for others gradually, whilst others again practically enjoy it all their life.

21. The practical difficulties are: 1, to 'realize the reality' of one's higher part; 2, to identify one's self with it exclusively; and 3, to identify it with all the rest of ideal being.

22. "When mystical activity is at its height, we find consciousness possessed by the sense of a being at once *excessive* and *identical* with the self: great enough to be God; interior enough to be *me*. The 'objectivity' of it ought in that case to be called *excessivity*, rather, or exceedingness." Récéjac: *Essai sur les fondements de la connaissance mystique*, 1897, p. 46.

23. The word 'truth' is here taken to mean something additional to bare value for life, although the natural propensity of man is to believe that whatever has great value for life is thereby certified as true.

24. Above, p. 445 [this volume p. 343].

25. *Proceedings of the Society for Psychical Research*, vol. vii. p. 305. For a full statement of Mr. Myers's views, I may refer to his posthumous work, "Human Personality in the Light of Recent Research," which is already announced by Messrs. Longmans, Green & Co. as being in press. Mr. Myers for the first time proposed as a general psychological problem the exploration of the subliminal region of consciousness throughout its whole extent, and made the first methodical steps in its topography by treating as a natural series a mass of subliminal facts hitherto considered only as curious isolated facts, and subjecting them to a systematized nomenclature. How important this exploration will prove, future work upon the path which Myers has opened can alone show. Compare my paper: "Frederic Myers's Services to Psychology," in the said *Proceedings*, part xlii, May, 1901.

26. Compare the inventory given above on pp. 483–84, and also what is said of the subconscious self on pp. 233–36, 240–42.

27. Compare above, pp. 419 ff.

28. One more expression of this belief, to increase the reader's familiarity with the notion of it:

"If this room is full of darkness for thousands of years, and you come in and begin to weep and wail, 'Oh, the darkness,' will the darkness vanish? Bring the light in, strike a match, and light comes in a moment. So what good will it do you to think all your lives, 'Oh, I have done evil, I have made many mistakes'? It requires no ghost to tell us that. Bring in the light and the evil goes in a moment. Strengthen the real nature, build up yourselves, the effulgent, the resplendent, the ever pure, call that up in everyone whom you see. I wish that everyone of us had come to such a state that even when we see the vilest of human beings we can see the God within, and instead of condemning, say, 'Rise, thou effulgent One, rise thou who art always pure, rise thou birthless and deathless, rise almighty, and manifest your nature.' . . . This is the highest prayer that the Advaita teaches.

This is the one prayer: remembering our nature." . . . "Why does man go out to look for a God? . . . It is your own heart beating, and you did not know, you were mistaking it for something external. He, nearest of the near, my own self, the reality of my own life, my body and my soul.—I am Thee and Thou art Me. That is your own nature. Assert it, manifest it. Not to become pure, you are pure already. You are not to be perfect, you are that already. Every good thought which you think or act upon is simply tearing the veil, as it were, and the purity, the Infinity, the God behind, manifests itself—the eternal Subject of everything, the eternal Witness in this universe, your own Self. Knowledge is, as it were, a lower step, a degradation. We are It already; how to know It?" Swami Vivekananda: *Addresses*, No. XII., "Practical Vedanta," part iv, p. 174, London, 1897; and Lectures, *The Real and the Apparent Man*, 1901, p. 24, abridged.

29. For instance, here is a case where a person exposed from her birth to Christian ideas had to wait till they came to her clad in spiritistic formulas before the saving experience set in:

"For myself I can say that spiritualism has saved me. It was revealed to me at a critical moment of my life, and without it I don't know what I should have done. It has taught me to detach myself from worldly things and to place my hope in things to come. Through it I have learned to see in all men, even in those most criminal, even in those from whom I have most suffered, undeveloped brothers to whom I owed assistance, love, and forgiveness. I have learned that I must lose my temper over nothing, despise no one, and pray for all. Most of all I have learned to pray! And although I have still much to learn in this domain, prayer ever brings me more strength, consolation, and comfort. I feel more than ever that I have only made a few steps on the long road of progress; but I look at its length without dismay, for I have confidence that the day will come when all my efforts shall be rewarded. So Spiritualism has a great place in my life, indeed it holds the first place there." Flournoy Collection.

30. "The influence of the Holy Spirit, exquisitely called the Comforter, is a matter of actual experience, as solid a reality as that of electro-magnetism." W. C. Brownell: *Scribner's Magazine*, vol. xxx, p. 112.

31. That the transaction of opening ourselves, otherwise called prayer, is a perfectly definite one for certain persons, appears abundantly in the preceding lectures. I append another concrete example to reinforce the impression on the reader's mind:

"Man can learn to transcend these limitations [of finite thought] and draw power and wisdom at will. . . . The divine presence is known through experience. The turning to a higher plane is a distinct act of consciousness. It is not a vague, twilight, or semi-conscious experience. It is not an ecstasy. It is not a trance. It is *not* super-consciousness, in the Vedantic sense. It is *not* due to self-hypnotization. It is a perfectly calm, sane, sound, rational, common-sense shifting of consciousness from the phenomena of sense-perception to the phenomena of seership, from the thought of self to a distinctively higher realm. . . . For example, if the lower self be nervous, anxious, tense, one can in a few moments compel it to be calm. This is not done by a word simply. Again I say, it is not hypnotism. It is by the exercise of power. One feels the spirit of peace as definitely as heat is perceived on a hot summer day. The power can be as surely used as the sun's rays can be focussed and made to do work, to set fire to wood." *The Higher Law*, Boston, August, 1901, vol. iv, pp. 4–6.

32. Transcendentalists are fond of the term 'Over-soul,' but as a rule they use it in an intellectualist sense, as meaning only a medium of communion. 'God' is a causal agent as well as a medium of communion, and that is the aspect which I wish to emphasize.

Sources and Editing Methods

This volume's chapters reproduce the text of James's original publications, listed below. These chapters represent the texts as James intended them at the time of his death. Only a small number of corrections to these texts have been made for publication in this volume. These corrections consist of those that James recorded himself, plus spelling corrections taken to be necessary by subsequent editors of James's works, and a small number of stylistic modifications to punctuation to ensure contemporary readability.

PART ONE: EXPERIENCE AND MIND

1. "What Is an Emotion?" *Mind* 9, no. 2 (April 1884): 188–205.
2. "The Stream of Consciousness." Chapter 11 of *Psychology: Briefer Course* (New York: Henry Holt, 1892), pp. 151–75.
3. "The Self." Chapter 12 of *Psychology: Briefer Course* (New York: Henry Holt, 1892), pp. 176–81, 195–205, 215–16.
4. "Does 'Consciousness' Exist?" *Journal of Philosophy, Psychology, and Scientific Methods* 1, no. 18 (September 1, 1904): 477–91.
5. "A World of Pure Experience." *Journal of Philosophy, Psychology and Scientific Methods* 1, no. 20 (September 29, 1904): 533–43 (October 13, 1904): 561–70.
6. "How Two Minds Can Know One Thing." *Journal of Philosophy, Psychology, and Scientific Methods* 2, no. 7 (March 30, 1905): 176–81.

PART TWO: KNOWLEDGE AND ACTION

7. "The Will to Believe." Chapter 1 in *The Will to Believe and Other Essays in Popular Philosophy* (New York: Longmans, Green, 1897), pp. 1–31.
8. "The Function of Cognition." Chapter 1 in *The Meaning of Truth* (New York: Longmans, Green, 1909), pp. 1–42.
9. "What Pragmatism Means." Chapter 2 in *Pragmatism: A New Name for Some Old Ways of Thinking* (New York: Longmans, Green, 1907), pp. 43–81.
10. "Pragmatism's Conception of Truth." Chapter 6 in *Pragmatism: A New Name for Some Old Ways of Thinking* (New York: Longmans, Green, 1907), pp. 197–236.
11. "The Pragmatist Account of Truth and Its Misunderstanders." Chapter 8 in *The Meaning of Truth* (New York: Longmans, Green, 1909), pp. 180–216.
12. "The Meaning of the Word Truth." Chapter 9 in *The Meaning of Truth* (New York: Longmans, Green, 1909), pp. 217–20.

PART THREE: ETHICS AND RELIGION

13. "The Dilemma of Determinism." Chapter 5 in *The Will to Believe and Other Essays in Popular Philosophy* (New York: Longmans, Green, 1897), pp. 145–83.
14. "The Moral Philosopher and the Moral Life." Chapter 6 in *The Will to Believe and Other Essays in Popular Philosophy* (New York: Longmans, Green, 1897), pp. 184–215.
15. "The Energies of Men." *Philosophical Review* 16, no. 1 (January 1907): 1–20.
16. "*The Varieties of Religious Experience*: Philosophy." Chapter 18 in *The Varieties of Religious Experience* (London and New York: Longmans, Green, 1902), pp. 430–57.
17. "*The Varieties of Religious Experience*: Conclusions." Chapter 20 in *The Varieties of Religious Experience* (London and New York: Longmans, Green, 1902), pp. 485–519.
18. "Pragmatism and Religion." Chapter 8 in *Pragmatism: A New Name for Some Old Ways of Thinking* (New York: Longmans, Green, 1907), pp. 273–301.

Index

aesthetic, 47, 54, 61, 85, 87, 351, 395
agnosticism, 158, 234, 248
analysis, 67, 179, 185
a priori, 12, 33, 167, 200, 292, 300
Aristotle, 167, 200, 226–27, 401
atheism, 39, 166, 202, 265, 330, 378, 399
Augustine, 401

Bain, Alexander, 51, 56, 284, 286, 335
Baird-Smith, Richard, 312
Baldwin, James Mark, 405
behavior, 9, 25, 30, 36–37, 320
behaviorism, 12
belief
    over-belief, 326, 344, 354, 360–64, 378
    practical, 26, 39, 113–14, 158, 161–63, 181–82, 198, 203–204, 216–20, 241–42, 252, 320, 335
    truth and, 29, 32–33, 163, 169–70, 205–206, 211–13, 216–17, 220, 227–28, 237–46, 252
    and will, 26, 39–40, 158–77, 211–12, 237, 385

Bell, Charles, 51
Bellamy, Edward, 286
Bender, Wilhelm, 406
Bentham, Jeremy, 284, 286
Berkeley, George, 79, 109, 123, 125, 139–40, 182, 200, 231, 334
Boedder, Bernard, 395
Bowne, Borden Parker, 386, 404
Bradley, Francis Herbert, 255, 384
brain
    function, 12–13, 47–48, 77, 80–81, 179, 381–82, 386
    structure, 9–10, 12–13, 36, 49–50, 54–55, 58, 61, 63, 71
British Society for Psychical Research, 187, 407
Brown, Thomas, 335
Bucke, Richard, 355

Caird, John, 328, 339–42, 394, 397
Calvin, John, 297
Carlyle, Thomas, 274–75
Carpenter, Edward, 309
causation, 125, 143, 256
chance
    freedom and, 37, 160, 264–69, 279–81, 341, 372–74

law and, 37, 257–63, 278, 280, 350, 393

Chesterton, G. K., 309

Chopin, Frederic, 62

Clifford, William Kingdon, 162–63, 166, 169–70, 172, 350, 363

concept
and experience, 24, 40–41, 137–39, 183–84, 199, 335–36, 389
and percept, 19–21, 111, 115, 132–35, 191, 343, 365–66

Condillac, Etienne Bonnot de, 180

consciousness
as epiphenomenal, 13, 35–36, 350
fringes of, 80–82
function of, 9–11, 13, 84–85, 105–21, 151–53, 179–80, 189–92
as personal, 14–16, 55, 72–74, 89–94, 100–103, 107, 150–51, 190, 289–90, 338–40
stream of, 14–24, 67–75, 79–82, 97–98, 102–103, 125–27, 142–49
subconscious and, 80–82, 359–60
See also experience

Dante, 58

Darwin, Charles, 7–8, 50–51, 209, 300, 331, 350

Delboeuf, Joseph, 255

democracy, 214

Democritus, 110

Derham, William, 399–400

Descartes, Rene, 9, 12, 14, 118, 167

determinism
free will and, 13, 35, 36–37, 257–58

morality and, 36–37, 87, 259–81
scientific, 35–37, 257–65

Dewey, John, 7–9, 12, 17, 195, 203–204, 206–207, 211, 215, 231–32, 246, 252, 384

dualism
knower-known, 17–18, 22, 29–31, 107–109, 115–18, 129–34, 251
mind-matter, 9, 12–13, 17–18, 117
percept-object, 18–21, 108

Duhem, Pierre, 203

education, 54, 320
moral, 57, 321

ego, 89, 94–95, 98, 349, 352, 390
transcendental, 14–15, 18, 103, 105, 144, 338

Emerson, Ralph Waldo, 7, 173, 231, 347, 393

emotion
body and, 47–59, 61–66, 310–11, 381–82
religion and, 326, 328, 334, 365
thought and, 54–59, 63–65, 71, 90, 93–94, 100, 110, 120, 320, 405

empiricism
pragmatism and, 8, 10–12, 168–69, 200–204, 252
radical, 8, 17–22, 41, 124–28, 137–40, 144–45, 252
rationalism and, 12–13, 31, 124–26, 165, 202, 208, 210–13, 224–25, 228–29, 234, 369–70, 389

Epicurus, 297

epiphenomenalism, 10, 13, 35–36, 350

epistemology
  metaphysics and, 31–33, 135, 195,
    228, 237–39, 251, 391
  psychology and, 133, 229, 248
ethics, 34–38, 87–88, 283–87,
    293–305, 324
Euclid, 33, 203, 227
evolution, 7, 8, 10–11, 35, 54, 256,
    284
experience
  personal, 15–17, 19–20, 67–70,
    100–101, 150–52, 190,
    289–90, 338–40
  practical, 16–17, 25–28, 86–87,
    201–206, 216–17, 245–48,
    251–54, 286, 377–79
  pure, 20–24, 67–75, 79–82,
    97–98, 102–103, 106, 110–
    11, 116–19, 123–27, 133–35,
    147–49, 152
  reality and, 17–23, 27–32, 107–
    108, 112–16, 120, 130–35,
    188–92, 217–20, 350–52
  relations and, 15–24, 75–77, 80–
    82, 110, 115–17, 124–28, 137–
    40, 143–45, 147–48, 221–25,
    243–44, 252, 382, 396
  religious, 39–41, 327–28, 342–44,
    357–59
  thought and, 9–17, 27–30, 86–87,
    108–114, 118–22, 128–39,
    150–52, 186–93, 195, 201–
    205, 217–20, 230–231,
    242–44
  truth and, 17–18, 22, 29–31, 107–
    109, 115–18, 129–34, 208,
    222–27, 251

faith
  reason and, 157–58, 165–68,
    173–76, 180–81, 260, 330,
    340–43, 362–64
  will and, 163–64, 177–79,
    304–305, 318–20, 355–56,
    376–78, 385, 406
  See also consciousness; perception
Fechner, Gustav, 11, 94, 153, 310
feeling, 48–60, 63, 65, 71, 74–78,
    83, 93–94, 120, 150–51, 179–
    88, 193, 238–39, 326–38, 386
  thought and, 74–78, 93–94,
    179–84, 326–28, 354–55, 381
Ferrier, James Frederick, 47, 388
Fichte, Johann Gottlieb, 388
Fielding, Harold, 395
Fletcher, Horace, 322
Fouillee, Alfred Jules Emile, 255
Fourier, Charles, 286
Fraser, Alexander Campbell, 343, 397
freedom,
  chance and, 37, 160, 259–69, 264–
    69, 279–81, 341, 372–74, 392
  religion and, 18, 168, 321, 332–33
free will, 9, 162
  determinism and, 13, 25, 35–37,
    198, 255, 257–58, 277, 375

Galton, Francis, 79
Garibaldi, Giuseppe, 320
God, 14, 18–19, 180, 191, 310,
    331–51, 390
  ethics of, 270, 292–93, 362–64,
    376–78, 395
  knowledge of, 39–40, 157, 209,
    330–34

pragmatic value of, 160–61,
    167–68, 213–14, 303–304,
    328–30, 345–47, 355–62
Goethe, Johann Wolfgang von, 72
good
    evil and, 267–70, 274, 301, 333
    moral, 38, 172–74, 269–71,
        294–99, 301–303
    psychology of, 284–92
    truth and, 175–76, 210–12,
        219–20, 229
Green, Thomas Hill, 183, 255, 299,
    386
Grote, John, 183

habit
    brain and, 9, 36, 66, 310, 318
    mental, 35–36, 86, 162, 335–36
    moral, 37
    natural, 37
    value of, 226, 318, 335–36
Hegel, Georg Wilhelm Friedrich, 11,
    167, 182, 184, 239, 255, 273,
    339, 342, 397
Heine, Heinrich, 297
Helmholtz, Hermann, 11, 71
Herbart, Johann Friedrich, 61, 72
Hinton, Charles, 167, 255
Hodder, Alfred, 383
Hodge, Charles, 395
Hodgson, Shadworth, 116, 179, 200,
    255, 257, 335, 384–85
Hoffding, Harald, 385
Howison, George Holmes, 199
Hugo, Victor, 304
humanism, 138, 146, 207, 248, 252,
    377

Hume, David, 14, 17, 29, 76, 79,
    124–25, 160, 200, 334–35, 386
Huxley, Thomas, 79, 161, 163
hypnosis, 318, 324
hypothesis
    genuine, 158–61, 175–77, 373
    practical, 25–26, 39, 362, 377
    scientific, 25, 362

idealism, 10–12, 248
    absolute, 8, 18, 19, 126
    personal, 17–19, 139
    transcendental, 15, 123, 128–29,
        135–39, 210, 232, 338, 343,
        360, 393
imagination, 26, 29, 34, 75, 79, 119,
    231–22
immortality, 14, 358
individuality, 14, 32, 95, 124, 186,
    246, 324, 338, 343, 353–54, 359
    society and, 92–93
induction, 202, 327, 343
introspection, 12, 35, 48, 75–76,
    107, 179

James, Henry (brother), 7
James, Henry (father), 7
James, William
    career of, 7–8
Janet, Pierre, 307–308, 313–14
Joachim, Harold Henry, 389

Kant, Immanuel, 11–12, 14–15, 102,
    105, 107, 121, 152, 167, 182,
    234, 248, 297, 330, 335, 338,
    340, 355
Kepler, Johannes, 203

Khayam, Omar, 265
Kierkegaard, Soren, 385
knowledge
  acquaintance, 18, 20, 30–32, 81,
    108, 130, 138, 183–85, 190–
    94, 386
  a priori, 12, 33, 167, 200, 292, 300
  dualism and, 17–18, 29–31,
    107–109, 117, 129, 238, 251
  experience and, 26–31, 73–76, 89,
    94–95, 98–103, 106–107,
    115–17, 120–21, 129–38,
    149–53, 185–91, 217, 238–
    39, 269, 334–35, 386
  perception and, 11, 18, 29–30,
    112, 129–30, 135, 193–99
  practical, 26, 30–31, 33–34, 163,
    169, 173, 177, 182–84, 190–
    91, 195, 210–12, 217, 223–29
  relational, 17–18, 22, 29–31,
    107–109, 115–18, 129–34,
    182–83, 220–25, 228–29, 251
  representational, 10–11, 16, 18,
    26–27, 31, 110, 129, 133, 135,
    139, 151, 232
  verification, 28–29, 165–67, 180–
    91, 195, 210, 212, 217, 223–
    27, 234–35, 238–39, 334–35

Ladd, George Trumbull, 382
language, 49, 75, 77, 183, 203
law
  civil, 170–71
  moral, 288, 291, 294–95, 329–30
  natural, 9, 11, 13, 36–37, 119, 161,
    202–203, 256, 301, 349, 351,
    392

Lessing, Gotthold Ephraim, 225
Leuba, James Henry, 355–56, 406
Lincoln, Abraham, 159
Locke, John, 29, 72, 109, 200, 334
logic
  experience and, 23–24, 26, 61,
    132, 163–64, 221, 244–45,
    327, 339, 373, 376
  inductive, 202, 327, 343
  psychology and, 35, 61, 132, 173,
    227, 229, 330, 384
  reality and, 40, 167, 213, 252
Lotze, Hermann, 11, 88, 132, 139,
    386, 403
Loyola, Ignatius, 315

Mach, Ernst, 203, 225, 404
Marshall, Henry Rutgers, 405
materialism, 8–11, 13, 35, 40–41,
    210, 348, 363
Maxwell, James Clerk, 215, 224
meaning, 11, 27–28, 245, 246, 335,
    370
meliorism, 369–71, 378–79
memory, 107, 396
metaphysics
  dualistic, 9, 12–13, 17–18, 22,
    29–31, 117, 251
  pluralistic, 8, 19, 41, 146, 276–78,
    367–69, 374–78
  pragmatism and, 194, 197–99,
    248, 287–88
  rationalistic, 135–39, 201,
    336–39, 343, 360, 388
Mill, James, 95, 125, 335
Mill, John Stuart, 72, 125, 139, 284,
    335

Miller, Dickinson, 384, 387
mind
  body and, 9–10, 12–13, 17, 18,
    117, 129
  experience and, 8–13, 15–19,
    84–88, 115, 124–26, 131,
    138–44
  other minds, 69, 140–44, 147–52,
    189, 193
  self and, 15–20, 68–78, 103
  See also consciousness; experience
monism, 34, 260, 266, 360, 367–69,
  372–75, 377–78
Moore, G. E., 382
morality
  basis of, 287–93, 295–99, 301–302
  ethical ideals of, 296–302
  freedom and, 36–37, 87, 259–81
  habit and, 57, 321
  intuition, 277–78, 284–85, 301
  meliorism and, 278, 369–71,
    377–79
  moral holiday, 211–13
  moral law and, 288, 291, 294–95,
    329–30
  reason and, 172–74, 285–86, 294
  religion and, 34–41, 174–75,
    293–96, 302–304, 330, 333,
    337–38, 341, 369
  strenuous mood and, 303–306,
    314, 320, 375–78
  subjective, 270–73, 288–90
Morris, William, 286
Muller, Georg, 381
Munk, Georg, 47
Munsterberg, Hugo, 105, 112
Myers, Frederic, 359, 407

Nansen, Fridtjof, 159
Natorp, Paul, 105, 382
naturalism, 9–10, 123–24, 139, 142,
  171, 206, 278, 336, 348, 391–92
  nonreductive, 12
  pluralistic, 14, 116, 188, 351, 363,
    368, 379
nature
  knowability of, 29–32
  laws of, 9, 11, 13, 36–37, 119, 161,
    163, 202–203, 256, 301, 349,
    351, 392
Newman, John Henry, 163, 297,
  328–29, 333–34, 394, 396
Newton, Isaac, 119, 191–93, 227
nominalism, 125, 202
Norton, Charles Eliot, 312

Olivier, Sydney, 311
organicism, 11
Ostwald, Wilhelm, 199, 203, 389,
  404

Paley, William, 191–93, 297
panpsychism, 22, 145
pantheism, 209
Papini, Giovanni, 202, 213, 323–24
Pascal, Blaise, 160–61, 164, 172
Peirce, Charles Sanders, 8, 17, 25–27,
  30, 32, 198–99, 335–36, 389,
  391
perception
  conception and, 16–21, 111, 115,
    132–35, 191, 343, 365–36
  knowledge and, 11, 18–21, 29–32,
    81, 108, 112, 129–30, 135,
    138, 183–85, 193–99, 386

reality and, 10–11, 16, 18–21,
    26–27, 31, 108–110, 129,
    133, 135, 139, 151, 232
    See also experience; sensation
Perry, Ralph Barton, 382–83
pessimism, 266–72, 276–78, 392,
    395
    optimism and, 267–79, 273–75,
        322, 371, 376
phenomenalism, 79, 109, 123, 140,
    182, 225, 234, 334, 373
Plato, 186, 243
pluralism, 8, 19, 41, 146, 276–78,
    367–69, 374–78
Poincare, Henri, 203
positivism, 202, 213, 234–35
pragmatism
    on empiricism, 8, 10–12, 17–22,
        41, 124–28, 137–40, 168–69,
        200–204, 252
    on ethics, 278, 287–93, 295–99,
        301–306, 314, 320, 369–79
    on knowledge, 26, 30–31, 33–34,
        163, 169, 173, 177, 182–84,
        190–91, 195, 210–12, 217,
        223–29
    on meaning, 11, 27–28, 245, 246,
        335, 370
    on metaphysics, 194, 197–99, 248,
        287–88
    on rationalism, 12–13, 31,
        124–26, 165, 202, 208,
        210–13, 224–25, 228–29,
        234, 369–70, 389
    on realism, 17–18, 22, 29–31,
        107–109, 117, 238, 251–54
    on religion, 39–41, 160–61,
        167–68, 213–14, 303–304,
        327–30, 342–47, 355–59
    on truth, 29, 39–40, 158–77,
        180–91, 195, 205–206,
        210–13, 216–17, 223–28,
        234–46, 252, 334–35
Prince, Morton, 145, 313
Pringle-Pattison, Andrew Seth, 343, 397
psychical research, 187, 326, 407
psychologist's fallacy, 17
psychology
    abnormal, 313, 345–46
    associationist, 10, 97–98, 284
    descriptive, 180
    experimental, 7–12, 16, 25, 47
    functional, 8–9, 27, 307

radical empiricism, 8, 17–22, 27, 41,
    124–28, 137–40, 144–45, 252
Ramsay, William, 206
rationalism, 12–13, 31, 124–26, 165,
    202, 208, 210–13, 224–25,
    228–29, 234, 369–70, 389
realism
    epistemological, 17–18, 22, 29–31,
        107–109, 117, 238, 251–54
    natural, 123, 139, 142–43, 383
Recejac, Edouard, 407
reflex, 54, 63, 65
Rehmke, Johannes, 105
Reid, Thomas, 167, 182
Reid, Thomas Mayne, 336–37
relations
    in experience, 15–24, 75–77, 80–
        82, 110, 115–17, 124–28, 137–
        40, 143–45, 147–48, 221–25,
        243–44, 252, 382, 396

in knowledge, 17–18, 22, 29–31,
107–109, 115–18, 129–34,
182–83, 220–25, 228–29, 251
relativism, 33–34, 181, 227, 234, 386
religion
emotion and, 326, 328, 334, 365
experience and, 18, 39–41, 168,
321, 327–28, 332–33, 342–
44, 357–59
healthy-minded, 267–69, 273–74,
322, 371, 376
monistic, 260, 266, 360, 367–69,
372–75, 377–78
morality and, 34–41, 174–75,
293–96, 302–304, 330, 333,
337–38, 341, 369
practical, 39–41, 160–64, 167–68,
175–79, 210–14, 219–20,
229, 303–305, 318–20, 327–
30, 342–47, 355–62, 376–78,
385, 406
reason and, 157–58, 165–68,
173–76, 180–81, 260, 330,
340–43, 362–64
saints and, 271, 325, 337, 342,
354–65, 404
science of, 327–29, 343–44, 347–
49, 359–60, 397
sick-minded, 266–72, 276–78,
375, 392, 395
See also God
Renan, Ernest, 274, 348, 393, 398
Renouvier, Charles, 255
representationalism, 10–11, 16, 18,
26–27, 31, 110, 129, 133, 135,
139, 151, 232
Rickert, Heinrich, 389

Rousseau, Jean-Jacques, 274
Royce, Josiah, 18, 114, 387, 394, 397
Ruskin, John, 62
Ruyssen, Theodore, 203

Sanford, Edmund C., 307
Schelling, Friedrich Wilhelm Joseph
von, 11
Schiller, F. C. S., 17, 195, 203–204,
206–207, 211, 215, 231–32,
235–36, 246, 248–49, 252
Schneider, Georg Heinrich, 50
Schopenhauer, Arthur, 87, 266, 271,
297, 371
Schubert-Soldern, Richard von, 105
Schuppe, Wilhelm, 105
science
determinism and, 35–37, 257–65
laws of, 9, 11, 13, 36–37, 119, 161,
163, 202–203, 256, 301, 349,
351, 392
method of, 26–32, 161–64, 171–
72, 181–82, 194–95, 198–99,
203–204, 223–24, 256–57,
349–53, 358, 363, 389
reality and, 8–11, 13, 35, 38–41,
123–24, 139, 142, 171, 206,
210, 278, 336, 348, 363,
391–92
Scott, Walter, 387
Secretan, Charles, 175
self
as ego, 89, 94–95, 98, 349, 352, 390
individual, 14, 32, 95, 99–103,
124, 186, 246, 324, 338, 343,
353–54, 359
material, 90–91

personal, 15–17, 19–20, 67–70,
    72–78, 89–96, 99, 100–103,
    107, 150–52, 190, 289–90,
    338–40
social, 91–93
spiritual, 93–94
transcendental, 18, 94, 103, 105,
    131, 144, 180, 185
sensation, 10–15, 16–17, 51, 61, 67,
    70–71, 76, 85–86, 184–85, 191,
    194, 334–36, 340, 391
Shaw, George Bernard, 309
Sigwart, Christoph, 203, 392
skepticism, 18, 26, 29
Socrates, 200
solipsism, 19, 31, 140, 181, 188–89,
    193, 247–48
Spencer, Herbert, 171, 271, 297, 383
spiritualism, 322
    mind-cure, 309, 322
Stephen, Fitzjames, 157, 178
Stephen, James, 303, 393
Stephen, Leslie, 157
Stewart, Dugald, 335
Stockl, Albert, 395
stoicism, 354
Stout, George Frederick, 236–37
stream of consciousness, 14–24,
    67–75, 79–82, 97–98, 102–103,
    125–27, 142–49
Strong, Augustus Hopkins, 395
Strong, Charles Augustus, 145
Strumpell, Adolph, 64–66
subconscious, 80–82, 359–60, 407

Taine, Hippolyte, 87, 113, 133
Taylor, Alfred Edward, 389

teleology, 11–12, 61, 123, 395
Titian, 62
Tolstoy, Leo, 286, 355
transcendentalism, 14–15, 18, 102,
    123, 135–39, 232, 338–39, 343,
    360, 391
truth
    a priori, 12, 33, 167, 200, 292, 300
    belief and, 29–33, 163, 169–70,
        205–206, 211–13, 216–17,
        220, 227–28, 237–46, 252
    correspondence, 10–11, 16, 18,
        26–29, 31, 110, 129, 133, 135,
        139, 151, 232
    experience and, 17–18, 22, 28–31,
        107–109, 115–18, 129–34,
        208, 222–27, 251
    practical, 26, 30–31, 33–34, 163,
        169, 173, 177, 182–84, 190–
        91, 195, 210–12, 217, 223–29
    verification and, 28–29, 165–67,
        180–91, 195, 210, 212, 217,
        223–27, 234–35, 238–39,
        334–35

Van Helmont, Joan Baptista,
    402–403
Voltaire, 267
voluntarism, 11–12, 26–27
von Schelling, Friedrich Wilhelm
    Joseph. See Schelling, Friedrich
    Wilhelm Joseph von
von Schubert-Soldern, Richard. See
    Schubert-Soldern, Richard von

Wallace, William, 394
Ward, Wilfrid, 382, 385

Weismann, August, 171
Wells, H. G., 309
Whitehead, Alfred North, 24
Whitman, Walt, 347, 365, 406
will
    faith and, 163–64, 177–79, 304–
        305, 318–20, 355–56, 376–
        78, 385, 406
    to believe, 26, 39–40, 158–77,
        211–12, 237, 385
    See also free will

Winter, Georg, 64
Wolff, Christian, 398, 400
Wundt, Wilhelm, 11

Zeno, 76, 297
Zola, Emile, 274